D1064132

After Black Lives Matter

After Black Lives Matter

Policing and Anti-Capitalist Struggle

Cedric Johnson

VERSO
London • New York

First published by Verso 2023
© Cedric Johnson 2023

All rights reserved

The moral rights of the author have been asserted

1 3 5 7 9 10 8 6 4 2

Verso
UK: 6 Meard Street, London W1F 0EG
US: 388 Atlantic Avenue, Brooklyn, NY 11217
versobooks.com

Verso is the imprint of New Left Books

ISBN-13: 978-1-80429-167-2
ISBN-13: 978-1-80429-169-6 (US EBK)
ISBN-13: 978-1-80429-168-9 (UK EBK)

British Library Cataloguing in Publication Data
A catalogue record for this book is available from the British Library

Library of Congress Cataloging-in-Publication Data

Names: Johnson, Cedric, 1971– author.
Title: After Black Lives Matter : policing and anti-capitalist struggle /
   Cedric Johnson.
Description: London ; New York : Verso, 2023. | Includes bibliographical
   references.
Identifiers: LCCN 2022048814 (print) | LCCN 2022048815 (ebook) | ISBN
   9781804291672 (hardcover) | ISBN 9781804291696 (ebk)
Subjects: LCSH: Black lives matter movement. | Police-community
   relations—United States. | African Americans—Social conditions. |
   Racism—United States. | Equality—United States.
Classification: LCC E185.615 .J5889 2023 (print) | LCC E185.615 (ebook) |
   DDC 323.1196/073—dc23/eng/20221014
LC record available at https://lccn.loc.gov/2022048814
LC ebook record available at https://lccn.loc.gov/2022048815

Typeset in Sabon by MJ & N Gavan, Truro, Cornwall
Printed and bound by CPI Group (UK) Ltd, Croydon, CR0 4YY

Contents

Introduction: The Frayed Thin Blue Line   1

1. Policing Capitalist Society   35

2. Making Consumers and Criminals: The Postwar
   Urban Transformation and the Origins of Policing
   as We Know It   79

3. The Roots of Black Lives Matter: Racial Liberalism
   and the Problem of Surplus Population   124

4. The World of Freddie Gray: Dispossession, Rebellion
   and Containment in Revanchist Baltimore   180

5. Whose Streets? Building the Just City in Rahm
   Emanuel's Chicago and Beyond   215

6. The Labor of Occupation   273

Conclusion: Abolish the Conditions   327

Acknowledgments   351
Notes   353

Introduction

The Frayed Thin Blue Line

The fundamental role of the police service is not crime prevention per se. Rather, policemen consider themselves as a "containing element"—a thin line of blue which stands between the law-abiding members of society and the criminals who prey upon them.

William H. Parker, "Surveillance by Wiretap or Dictograph: Threat or Protection? A Police Chief's Opinion" (1954)

I personally believe that people are feeling black right now. I think our national dialogue is making people feel as though they're black … And so when they hear the term "Black Lives Matter" I think they're actually hearing that their lives matter.

Eric Adams, Brooklyn Borough president and former New York Police Department Captain (June 6, 2020)

George Floyd's Body Politic

Standing atop the rubble of a bombed-out building in Idlib, Syrian artist Aziz Asmar painted a bold fresco on a solitary column. "No to Racism" and "I Can't Breathe" were wrapped like a halo around the visage of George Floyd, a forty-six-year-old African American man who was strangled to death by Minneapolis police in late May 2020. When Asmar watched the viral video of Floyd's death and heard his cries for mercy, he remembered the pleas of dying civilians who Syrian president Bashar al-Assad had attacked with sarin gas three years prior in Eastern Ghouta. Six thousand miles away, protestors in Minneapolis had burned down the Third Police Precinct, home to the four officers who arrested Floyd. They then went on to torch a Target store, an AutoZone and other nearby businesses. All told, some 220 buildings were reported damaged in that city alone. Contrary to the corporate media line pitting peaceful law-abiding citizens against unlawful mobs of looters, anarchists and outside agitators, support for the protests ran deep. When businessman Don Flesch surveyed the smoldering shell of his Central Camera store after a night of arson and looting had engulfed Chicago's downtown, he harbored no ill will towards the protestors. "I'm upset that people didn't stay with Black Lives Matter," he said. "That's why this whole thing started to come about."[1] Millions took to the streets in peaceful marches and vigils, filling parks and public squares in all fifty states, from the nation's largest cities to small towns in every region. The police killing of Floyd was seen as resuscitating a dormant movement, producing what some have argued is the largest wave of mass protests in US history.[2]

In some towns, police chiefs joined the marchers, locking arms, and in some instances "taking a knee," in the fashion of National Football League (NFL) quarterback Colin Kaepernick's protest from years prior. In other cities, peaceful protestors were met with a phalanx of riot police night after night, with clouds of tear gas, hails of rubber bullets, and screams filling the air wherever curfews were strictly enforced. At other times, peaceful assemblies were disrupted by counterprotesters, with flak-jacketed militia brandishing assault rifles stalking city streets and intimidating unarmed protesters. Police power in cities like Chicago and New York was met at times with improvised and intrepid maneuvers, as rebels burned squad cars and built barricades from garbage dumpsters and newspaper boxes, outflanking the police and foiling their attempts to squash demonstrations through "kettling" and other riot tactics. Manuals detailing these strategies for confronting police power circulated through social media and activist networks. In some moments, it seemed the rebels might prevail. Atlanta police stood on the first floor of CNN's headquarters staring down an emboldened crowd who threatened to take the building, in a scene played out across the nation for weeks.[3] The rebellion grabbed the consciousness of the nation and the broader world. Charred wood and pepper spray commingled with optimism, adrenaline and chants of defiance. It seemed that revolution was in the air.

The energy of the protests quickly translated to the world of professional sports. A dozen or so players in the National Football League (NFL) uploaded a short video affirming their support for Black Lives Matter (BLM) and calling on the league bosses to demonstrate their antiracist commitments. A day later, NFL commissioner Roger Goodell did exactly that, in his own short online video. When the National Basketball Association (NBA) resumed its season in mid-summer, after being suspended by the coronavirus pandemic, players donned jerseys emblazoned with Black Lives Matter messaging like "Say Their Names," "Peace," "I Am a Man," "Listen to Us" and "Ally." And after the police shooting of Jacob Blake in Kenosha, Wisconsin in August, NBA players staged a wildcat strike of sorts, delaying playoff games to negotiate with the league a response to recent events.

Mass protests went beyond the immediate problem of police violence, with many demonstrations taking aim at the symbols of white supremacy. In New Orleans, crowds yanked down the bust of slave owner John McDonough and rolled it into the Mississippi River. Across the Atlantic, activists in England gave the same treatment to the bronze likeness of the slave trader Edward Colston, tossing it into Bristol's harbor and erecting a new statue of local black activist Jen Reid with her fist raised in a Black Power salute. On Richmond, Virginia's Monument Avenue, where activists have long demanded the removal of confederate statuary, protestors scrawled "ACAB" and "Fuck the Police" on pedestals, transforming the thoroughfare into a celebration of multiracial America that stood in sharp contrast to the world of racial slavery J. E. B. Stuart and Robert E. Lee fought to preserve. Back in Minnesota's Twin Cities, activists energized by the moment and led by organizers from the American Indian Movement toppled a ten-foot bronze statue of Christopher Columbus outside the state capitol in St. Paul.

For a moment, it seemed a war for the city and nation had begun. In the weeks after Floyd's death, Minneapolis activists barricaded the vicinity of 38th and Chicago Avenue, making the area a no-go zone for police, and later declaring the occupied zone "George Floyd Square." After police relinquished control of Seattle's East Precinct station, activists briefly occupied six city blocks—the Capitol Hill Autonomous Zone (later renamed CHOP, Capitol Hill Occupied Protest, by some activists)—and initiated a social experiment in life beyond policing, a "new protest society" complete with a community garden and "no cop co-op."[4] The Seattle police chief defended the temporary abandonment of the zone as an "exercise in trust" intended to de-escalate the protests. President Donald Trump condemned the actions, charging Seattle leaders with losing control of the city and painting them as political weaklings. Amid heated protests near the White House, however, Trump retreated to an underground bunker, only to reemerge days later to stage a proto-fascist spectacle. He deployed federal law enforcement to expel peaceful protestors from Lafayette Park, clearing a path with chemical weaponry so he could walk to a nearby church for a photo-op. Jumping into the fray, Washington, DC mayor Muriel Bowser commissioned a street mural, where artists painted "Black Lives Matter" in bright yellow lettering on 16th Street and just north of the White House. Guerilla artists later added "Defund the Police" to the mural, revising the official endorsement with playful rebellion.

Throughout the summer and into the fall, demonstrations ran the emotional gamut, from collective mourning and nights of rage, burning and looting, to moments of jouissance and pure exuberance. After looting provoked vigilante actions and racist scapegoating between black and brown neighborhoods in Chicago, with some armed residents attacking motorists and anyone else they suspected were looters, organizers brokered a truce and filled the streets with interracial solidarity marches and gatherings.[5] In September, Adam Hollingsworth, the "Dreadhead Cowboy," rode his pinto mare NuNu for seven miles down the Dan Ryan expressway and across Chicago's South side, flanked by an escort of motorcycles. Hoping to bring attention to violence against black children in his hometown, Hollingsworth slowed rush hour traffic to a standstill and drew cheers from fans and supporters.[6] Police arrested him on misdemeanor counts of reckless conduct and trespassing, and a felony count of animal cruelty. Hollingsworth joined the thousands of protestors who crowded the country's jails throughout the summer months. In just the first week after George Floyd's death, more than 11,000 people were arrested, 2,700 in Los Angeles alone. More than the "long hot summers" of the sixties, which saw ghetto rebellions rip through most major American cities, this was something else —more sprawling, steady burning, intermittently explosive and uncontrollable, more akin to the concurrent raging wildfires that devastated the western United States during summer and fall 2020 as well. Throughout the summer, expressions of solidarity and condemnation of police wilding were ubiquitous, in store windows, pasted on billboards, permeating public consciousness. Millions of Americans finally embraced the basic premise of Black Lives Matter activists, that the US carceral apparatus disproportionately targets black civilians, often with lethal and unjustifiable force.

In life, Floyd was a black working-class everyman who lived in relative obscurity. In death, he became an international symbol of racial violence, but he also became an avatar of the broader social discontent defining America under the reign of Trump. Floyd was a Houston native, beloved by his family, friends and former football and basketball teammates at Jack Yates high school, who called him "Perry" and "Big Floyd." As a child, he dreamed of becoming a police officer or a judge. In eulogies and testimonials, Floyd was recalled as a gentle giant and peacemaker. In one widely circulated video, Floyd is heard making a heartfelt plea to youth to end gun violence.[7] During the nineties he was a rapper and appeared on numerous mixtapes produced by Houston's legendary DJ Screw. In 2014, he migrated to the Twin Cities through a church ministry that provided men struggling with addiction with a fresh start and gainful employment. Floyd found work as a truck driver and security guard. Like millions of Americans, he lost his job when the restaurant where he worked as a bouncer was shuttered by the Covid-19 shelter-in-place order. In April, Floyd tested positive for the virus.

On the fateful day of his encounter with Minneapolis police, he was simply enjoying the Memorial Day weekend with his friends, like millions of other Americans trying to find a moment of respite after months of restricted social activity and the overwhelming uncertainty of the pandemic. Police were called to Cup Foods in the Powderhorn Park section of Minneapolis after a store clerk claimed that someone had used a counterfeit $20 to purchase cigarettes. Four officers questioned Floyd and removed him from his vehicle, with the events recorded by bystander cell phones, police bodycams and nearby store surveillance. The most startling footage, taken by seventeen-year-old Darnella Frazier, captured police officer Derek Chauvin kneeling on Floyd's neck for almost nine minutes, despite the vocal protests of witnesses and offers by an off-duty firefighter to render aid, with Floyd calling for his mother and screaming out repeatedly, "I can't breathe." The last minutes of Floyd's life were eerily reminiscent of those of Eric Garner, who was choked to death by New York police in 2014.

Floyd's death was part of a succession of vigilante and police killings that had stoked public outrage in the preceding months. In February, Ahmad Arbery, a twenty-five-year-old black man, was hunted down while jogging and shotgunned to death by a trio of white self-appointed neighborhood watchmen. In mid-March, Breonna Taylor, a twenty-six-year-old black woman, was shot and killed by Louisville police as they executed a no-knock search warrant at her home. On May 6, Dreasjon "Sean" Reed, a twenty-one-year-old black man and former Air Force serviceman, live-streamed his fatal shooting by Indianapolis police. In the next twenty-four hours, Indianapolis police killed two other civilians. On May 7, McHale Rose, a nineteen-year-old black man, was shot to death, and later that night an Indianapolis police cruiser struck and killed Ashlynn Lisby, a pregnant white woman, the second fatal pedestrian accident by Indianapolis police in less than a month.

The groundswell of outrage over the police killing of Floyd and others was made possible by the ongoing work of antipolicing activists, but it was also a consequence of the conditions created by the coronavirus pandemic. As veteran cop and Brooklyn Borough President Eric Adams poignantly noted, the dire conditions of the pandemic had many Americans "feeling black," in the sense of feeling that their lives did not matter. The illiberal character of the Trump administration, his gross mishandling of the coronavirus crisis, unemployment reaching levels not seen since the Great Depression, and the staggering death rate and mass anxiety of the pandemic, all amplified the social costs of racial disparity and the precarity facing many Americans. This was fertile ground for the rebirth and expansion of Black Lives Matter sentiments.

The pandemic's initial hotspots, such as the Bronx, New Orleans, Chicago's South Side and Detroit, all saw higher rates of infection and death concentrated among black and brown populations. Some like Keeanga-Yamahtta Taylor claimed that the novel coronavirus constituted a "black plague," with dozens of other reports and editorials highlighting the broader problem of racial disparities in health care and health outcomes.[8] While accepting the fact of disparities, such language was hyperbolic and premature, but politically impactful, stirring latent Black Lives Matter sentiments. Black and brown urban populations were disproportionately poor, uninsured or underinsured, and more likely to possess comorbidities, such as obesity, diabetes or heart disease, which undermine the likelihood of surviving the virus. The most comprehensive work, such as that of Les Leopold, suggests that these racial disparities are in fact reflective of class inequality, with income serving as the most significant driver of Covid-19 deaths.[9] The pandemic was as much a senior citizens plague, since age was also a predictor of those who were likely to be hospitalized and felled by the virus, and assisted-living and nursing homes were routinely reported as sites of super-spreader events. Unfortunately, the plight of seniors does not carry the same moral freight as antiracism, nor does it serve as an equally powerful source of mobilization in American life. Moreover, the demography of the pandemic, of course, changed as the disease spread beyond urban centers into smaller towns and rural areas, which lacked the health care infrastructure to handle spiking caseloads. In many ways, Trump helped to organize BLM's second wave.

The Trump administration responded to the pandemic at first with open denial of its potential dangers before undertaking a more sober approach. It pledged support to state and local officials to expand hospital capacity and build MASH-style facilities in convention centers. In conjunction with the Republican-led Congress, the administration delivered a massive recovery bailout to American corporations, but only three rounds of relief payments to some US citizens, despite the fact that 40 million of them were out of work, and millions more had little or no savings, were struggling with missed rents and mortgage payments, and had difficulty meeting basic needs. The administration's woefully inadequate pandemic response would soon sink to new lows as medical experts on the White House task force were effectively muzzled and the public health crisis was turned into a political issue and campaign vehicle by the right. By spring, Trump had joined Republican governors and state-level political leaders in flipping the mandatory shelter-in-place, globally understood as a key strategy in reducing viral spread, into an infringement on personal liberty and a death sentence to the economy. Large-scale rallies in red states and suburbs demanded that the economy be reopened. Trump supporters, though, were not the only ones suffering from cabin fever and desiring a return to some version of normal.

The mandatory shelter-in-place was a social pressure cooker, as many Americans lost the valuable *third space*, that realm of activity beyond our working lives and households where our primary social connections and activities unfold. Coming just as the shelter-in-place orders in many states and cities were relaxed, the protests over Floyd's death brought the return of the social. The mass gatherings across the nation were simultaneously memorials, reunions and fêtes—moments where public life was reclaimed. Most of all, like earlier mass protests, BLM's second wave provided a school of civic engagement, and its impacts at the individual, generational, neighborhood and community levels are not yet fully perceptible. What should be clear, however, is this wave of demonstrations, vigils and marches constituted a different body politic than the one reflected in Trump's White House, as millions of Americans rejected the notion that any citizen could be killed by police with impunity or left to die from the novel coronavirus in the race to restart capital's engines.

In the midst of the rebellion, Trump seized upon the weathered "law and order" campaign script, first articulated by Ronald Reagan in his 1966 California gubernatorial race and aped by George Wallace, Chicago mayor Richard J. Daley and Richard Nixon during the political maelstrom of 1968. Trump defended the actions of armed militia and white nationalist counterprotestors throughout the summer, and when asked to repudiate white supremacy on the presidential debate stage, he refused to do so, telling the self-described western chauvinist group, the Proud Boys, to "stand back and stand by." In the midst of intensifying protests in Kenosha, Wisconsin, Trump sided with seventeen-year-old militia-hopeful Kyle Rittenhouse, who travelled across the Illinois border with an assault rifle and shot three protestors, killing two, saying he acted in self-defense. As *New York Times* columnist Paul Krugman wrote, since the since the late sixties, "wealthy elites weaponized white racism to gain political power, which they used to pursue policies that enriched the already wealthy at workers' expense."[10] Trump's administration has made it impossible to deny the grave consequences of this shopworn and cynical strategy.

Securitization and policing, xenophobia, racist exclusion and repression of dissent were central features of Trump's ascent to the presidency, and of his subsequent approach to governing.[11] He had made his "Blue Lives Matter" allegiances clear many times before. During the summer of 2016, when his election still seemed like a long shot to many, Trump was emphatic in his support for the police. His response to the events of that July 4th week— which included mass protests over the fatal police shootings of Philando Castile in St. Paul and Alton Sterling in Baton Rouge, as well as two separate incidents where black snipers killed cops —foreshadowed the hallmarks of his eventual presidency. Responding to the violence that July, Trump offered only vague passing acknowledgement of the deaths of "two motorists"— although Sterling was not driving at the time of his fatal arrest —ignoring their blackness and the fact that they were killed by police. Trump seized upon the black gunmen's assaults on police, however, saying "We must stand in solidarity with law enforcement, which we must remember is the force between civilization and total chaos," echoing the core ideological justification that has animated US law enforcement since the Cold War.

Like Los Angeles Police Chief William H. Parker, who coined the phrase the "thin blue line" over half a century earlier, Trump viewed the repressive arm of the state as necessary to protect the law-abiding, virtuous citizenry from criminals, non-citizens and all others he viewed as unworthy of protection and rights. When Parker first uttered the phrase, the notion of protecting civilization was seen as politically legitimate among its propertied beneficiaries, but it was morally dubious, a means of protecting an unjust racist order, one that held blacks in legal apartheid in the South and de facto segregation in Northern cities. After decades of documented police abuse, corruption and violence, and a process of carceral expansion that dwarfs all other advanced industrial nations, the view that policing "protects" the civilized from barbarism is untenable. *The thin blue line has grown worn and frayed*, especially when viewed from the vantage point of its millions of victims—families who have lost loved ones in arrest-related incidents, those tortured in black site interrogation rooms, the surveilled, the harassed, the arrested, the deported, the incarcerated and the paroled. That Trump could claim to be on the right side of the dividing line between "civilization and total chaos" was absurd.

Instead of making the nation great again and ending "American carnage," as his campaign had promised, Trump's presidency brought Americans to the brink of chaos with vicious police repression of peaceful demonstrations, armed militia patrolling city streets, looting of marquee commercial districts, masses in open rebellion, and 200,000 deaths due to the coronavirus pandemic in less than a year. Rather than resuscitating the halcyon days of Cold War suburban prosperity, his administration revealed all the failings and contradictions of the postwar consumer capitalism he imagines as the high point of civilization. Trump doubled down on the New Right strategy, but the political, economic and demographic ground has shifted in the half century since the reactionary "silent majority" was first conjured into being. The consumer society remains, but the American dream of middle-class life, which was never available to all, is more fraught than ever. The consumer façade of the good life, if not the security associated with the Cold War American dream, is kept alive through the proliferation of opportunities for gigging and entrepreneurial activity, the flood of easy credit (and debt), low-cost imported goods, and digitized entertainment and streaming services, all made possible by globalized and capital-intensive production, the very forces that have undermined gainful employment and livable wages for millions of Americans.[12] Do the massive protests following the death of George Floyd portend alternative visions of society, where deep inequality is addressed through socially progressive statecraft rather than carceral power? Will such popular forces give momentum to moderate, technocratic reforms, as they did during the Barack Obama administration? Or, in the absence of effective counterpower, will we witness more reactionary changes that legitimate the daily violence of capital, or at least remove the most offensive aspects from plain sight? These are the kinds of alternatives Black Lives Matter has pressed into public consciousness, and that preoccupy and animate the chapters that follow.

The Meanings of Black Lives Matter

Given the sheer scale, magnitude and diversity of 2020's resurgent Black Lives Matter protests, many pundits, scholars and activists celebrated the George Floyd rebellion as an historic watershed, one where the possibility of real reform came into view. For too many, however, the euphoria of the moment suspended any critical analysis of what it all meant. This is a deeper problem on the US left—the tendency to read protests as always prefigurative rather than contingent, and as a manifestation of real power rather than a reflection of potential. Such wish-fulfillment thinking, however, forgets that mass mobilization is not the same as organized power, and that mass mobilization is much easier now with the endless opportunities for expressing discontent provided by social media, online petitions, memes and vlogging. The scale of protests can be misleading, and their actual effectiveness, regardless of their size, is dependent on historical conjunctures, such as the balance of political forces, the organized power and capacity of opposition and the clarity of objectives among activists. Throughout the opening decades of this century, ever larger protests have proved incapable of consolidating in a manner that might effectively oppose ruling-class prerogatives. In recent memory, we have witnessed successive mass protests—turn-of-the-century demonstrations against global capitalism, protests against the Bush administration's so-called War on Terror, Occupy Wall Street encampments, anti-eviction campaigns, the

March for Our Lives following the Parkland High School mass shooting, protests against police violence and ICE deportations, among others—but these have done little to depose capitalist class power and the advancing neoliberal project. If anything, the hegemony of finance capital, the war-making powers of the national security state, the criminalization of immigration, the power of the gun lobby and the unaccountability of police are as entrenched as ever.

Some activists immediately seized on the 2020 protests as evidence of Black Lives Matter's resonance, and it was clear at least from some public opinion polls that a new majority of Americans momentarily accepted the core claims of BLM.[13] While many Americans now opposed the most racist excesses of policing, however, the majority did not accept the demands about defunding and dismantling police that many activists were now pushing.[14] In Minneapolis, after a summer of intense protests, the majority of residents supported repurposing police funds towards social spending, but only 35 percent of black residents and 40 percent of whites wanted to see reductions in police staffing in their neighborhoods.[15] This was true nationally as well, and across all racial and ethnic statistical groups. The George Floyd rebellion not only had the effect of intensifying public opposition to the Trump presidency, but also of bringing the internal contradictions of Black Lives Matter into sharper relief, in particular the tensions between the liberal valence of the slogan and the more progressive and radical left forces who have taken up the mantle.

During the Obama years, Black Lives Matter protests created a seeming crisis of legitimacy for policing as an institution. In one city after another, in social media threads and corporate news coverage, Black Lives Matter shifted the terms of debate, expanding public discussion from the specific demand for trial justice for victims and restitution for their families to demands for deeper systemic reforms and, in its most radical corners, the abolition of policing and prisons altogether. From its inception, however, Black Lives Matter was essentially an

expression of racial liberalism, made more urgent and militant by the context of the early Obama years. During Obama's
campaign and through the opening years of his administration,
the first black president faced a hail of racist attacks from Tea
Party protestors and the Birthers, led by Trump, who questioned
his citizenship and the constitutionality of his presidency. Such
attacks were read by many black citizens against the backdrop
of their own hardships due to the subprime mortgage crisis and
the subsequent Great Recession. For many blacks, the racism
towards Obama was symptomatic of the unresolved problem of
the color line. If the BLM hashtag grew out of the rising political
efficacy engendered by the Obama phenomenon, it was equally a
rejection of the conservative claim that his election signaled the
dawning of a post-racial society. Within the specific context of
policing and vigilante violence, Black Lives Matter insisted that
blacks deserve equal protection before the law, that is, direct and
meaningful enforcement of the US Constitution—an absolutely
worthy and also definitionally liberal goal. In our twenty-first-
century cultural landscape, the problem of unequal protection
has been captured graphically in viral videos of police killings
and abuse of black citizens.

The most immediate impact of the hashtag and the kind of
public monitoring of police activity it facilitated was to make
public what were historically clandestine activities. Police torture
and violence are a longer-standing problem, with generations
of formal complaints, litigation and activist campaigns as evidence. Black Lives Matter sentiments, however, combined with
societal surveillance and the instantaneous information flows
of networked cellular communication, made these incidents
more visible than ever before. In a manner reminiscent of the
televised coverage of civil rights demonstrations, which forced
some white northerners to witness the brutality experienced by
black southerners demanding basic rights, the viral videos of
police killings created a similar dissonance between the much-
vaunted progress symbolized in the election of Barack Obama
and the brutal treatment of black civilians by police. Millions of

Americans became bystanders and witnesses to police violence. The videos, investigations and demonstrations that followed undermined public trust in official reports that routinely justified lethal force. Familiar defenses like "he was reaching into his waistband," "the suspect was the aggressor," "she resisted arrest," etc., were falsified by one viral video after another. The videos most often humanized the victims in ways that carefully worded press briefings and departmental chicanery would never permit, sparking a growing chorus demanding institutional reforms and immediate justice for the victims.

In a few short years, the mass protests, public forums, pressure tactics and community organizing produced some notable reforms aimed at creating greater police accountability and transparency and more public oversight and decision-making capacity. Cities like Baltimore and Chicago saw federal Justice Department investigations in response to well-publicized deaths in police custody. In numerous cities, offending officers were fired and, in some cases, indicted and brought to trial with mixed results. In Baltimore, all four of the officers involved in the 2015 death of Freddie Gray were indicted, but none were convicted of wrongdoing. In Chicago, Jason Van Dyke was convicted on sixteen counts of second-degree murder in the 2014 death of Laquan McDonald—one count for each shot Van Dyke fired into McDonald's body. The Obama Task Force on 21st Century Policing recommended procedural modifications such as implicit bias training, revision of use-of-force policies, and processes that might identify problem officers. The administration also supported a federal program to underwrite the purchase of body cameras for local police departments.

During the Obama years, other state and local measures aimed at reforming the carceral regime came to fruition, many of them aimed at repairing the damage of the War on Drugs and addressing the ways that the poor are punished for survival crimes. Organizations like the Innocence Project worked to overturn scores of wrongful convictions. Decriminalization and legalization of cannabis became a reality in the more urbane and progressive parts of the country, with some states including expungement and exoneration for previous, low-level cannabis offenses as part of the legislation. Organizations like Just Leadership USA advanced a "Bill of Rights for Criminalized Workers" to address the unemployment and discrimination ex-offenders face.[16] Decriminalization of sex work gained momentum in some cities, especially those where such labor is a critical but dishonored and illegal aspect of the tourist economy, and where sex workers face routine arrest and imprisonment as well as violence and precarity in an unregulated labor market. Other counties and states took steps towards ending cash bail, seen as a penalty on the poor and a cause of overcrowding in many jails. And many jurisdictions pushed for e-carceration, or the use of electronic monitoring rather than physical detention, as a way of uniting offenders with their families and communities and scaling back the carceral state.[17]

While such reforms provide the grounds for building an even broader popular opposition to the carceral regime, the public relations maneuvers and investments of corporations and non-profits in the wake of the George Floyd rebellion will likely promote neoliberal public-private partnerships and incremental reforms into the near future, eclipsing the more progressive demands of abolitionist forces. In June 2020 alone, corporations pledged upward of $2 billion in support of various antiracist initiatives and causes. The executives of Warner, Sony Music and Wal-Mart each committed $100 million. Apple pledged the same amount for the creation of a racial equity and justice initiative. Google pledged $175 million largely towards the incubation of black entrepreneurship. YouTube announced a $100 million initiative to amplify black media voices. Hundreds of companies posted pro-Black Lives Matter messages on Blackout Tuesday. In solidarity with protestors demanding justice for Breonna Taylor, media mogul Oprah Winfrey paid for twenty-six billboard portraits of Taylor throughout Louisville, Kentucky. Portraits of Taylor also appeared on the covers of *Vanity Fair* and Winfrey's *O Magazine*. Streaming services like Hulu, Netflix and Amazon Prime showcased black cinema, television series and documentary films in a fashion usually reserved for Black History Month. General Motors, Best Buy, Lyft, Amazon, Mastercard, the National Football League, Nike, Spotify and other companies granted employees a paid holiday for Juneteenth, originally an East Texas holiday commemorating slaves in Galveston receiving belated word of emancipation.

This corporate response is not co-optation as some have claimed. Co-optation is a process whereby entrenched powers concede to popular struggles and embrace their leadership out of necessity because those forces threaten the preservation of the status quo. The massive outpouring of financial support from mainstream institutions was an instance of ideological convergence —between the militant racial liberalism of Black Lives Matter and the operational racial liberalism of the investor class.

This convergence was already present well before the George Floyd protests and the wave of corporate blackwashing that followed. NFL player Colin Kaepernick energized BLM forces when he knelt in silent protest of police violence during the national anthem at the start of every game. His actions provoked backlash from right-wing fans and politicians like Trump, and ultimately led to his being blacklisted by the League's team owners. What happened next? Nike signed the unemployed Kaepernick to a multi-million-dollar deal to produce his own line of athletic apparel and shoes. Billboards with Kaepernick's pensive face soon appeared in urban centers with the caption, "Believe in something, even if it means sacrificing everything." This kind of corporate liberal pablum, which historian Thomas Frank identified as taking shape in Madison Avenue advertising agencies during the sixties, is now indistinguishable from the organic protest itself.[18] If the opportunistic and facile character of Nike's gesture was not clear enough, the company extended its eight-year deal with the NFL at the tune of $1 billion. The line between existential protest and corporate interest was equally blurred during superstar Beyoncé Knowles's much-celebrated 2016 Superbowl half-time show. When the singer and her dancers donned leather jackets and berets and threw up Black Power fist salutes, social media was flooded with celebrations of this homage to the Black Panther Party and of ongoing protests against police brutality. Somehow the celebrations of the performance lost sight of the glaring contradiction that Knowles had chosen to turn a profit and make peace with the very organization that had curtailed players' free speech rights when they protested police brutality. On a certain level, this might seem like stunning hypocrisy, but it is not if we accept that elements of Black Lives Matter and the corporate media-entertainment complex are united in their commitment to a more racially just capitalist order. Moreover, elements of the nonprofit and foundation world have been present in Black Lives Matter organizing from the very beginning.

Although BLM's first wave had a liberal cast, struggles against police violence have long been a part of civil rights, labor, socialist and anarchist left politics in the United States, movements that often confronted police power as a defender of capitalist class interests. Likewise, post-segregation black politics gave birth to some of the earliest intellectual criticism of what would eventually be called mass incarceration. Police violence against black civilians has been the precipitating event of most black urban rebellions since the sixties. Likewise, struggles against police brutality gave rise to the monitoring patrols undertaken by black activists after the 1965 Watts rebellion, as well as the formation of the Black Panther Party for Self-Defense in Oakland in 1967 and its popularity throughout working-class black enclaves across the country.[19] The false imprisonment of Black Power radicals and their legal defense campaigns, Jonathan Jackson's failed attempt to free the Soledad Brothers in 1970, and the Attica uprising the following year where prisoners demanded better conditions, all provoked critical popular and academic analyses of policing and mass imprisonment.[20] Some recent antipolicing forces are descended from these earlier struggles.

Even before the Black Lives Matter hashtag was coined, Occupy Oakland activists, community groups, student organizations and union longshoremen staged massive protests after Oscar Grant was killed by Bay Area Rapid Transit (BART) cops in 2009. Unlike some later BLM tendencies, which were animated by liberal antiracist politics, these more left-wing struggles connected the problem of overpolicing to a broader critique of global capitalism, gentrification, the subprime mortgage crisis and the Great Recession, and the deep wealth inequality in American life. Subsequent Black Lives Matter organizations like the Black Youth Project 100, Assata's Daughters and the Dream Defenders, among other local tendencies, advanced a more progressive-to-radical left politics than that of the hashtag's creators and well-known personalities like DeRay McKesson, Johnetta Elzie and lawyer Ben Crump. This book is inspired and informed by the left-wing of contemporary antipolicing struggles, especially those forces that treat the problem of policing as a dimension of late capitalism and are committed to a redistributional politics focused on public goods.

America after Black Lives Matter

After Black Lives Matter critically engages the thought and politics of contemporary antipolicing struggles, and their meaning for the American left more generally. The book grounds the origins and central dynamics of the contemporary carceral regime within the social contradictions of capitalism. As Sidney L. Harring asserted some time ago, "in a very real sense, class struggle is at the core of police function."[21] Class is understood throughout this book as a social relation and process of capital accumulation, not merely as some demographic metric or spigot variable, like income or education, used for the purpose of statistical analyses. The central class division within capitalist society is between capital and labor, the owners of the means of production and those who must sell their labor power to survive; this fundamental antagonism is generative of a dynamic system of class fractions and intra-class conflict. Class interests are not strictly economically determined, but shaped through historical processes and politics. Hence, classes are not without their own internal social, political, sectoral and other divisions, and the *situated-class experiences* of various historical protagonists—the urban poor, politicians, middle-class gentrifiers, beat cops, union bureaucrats, assembly-line workers, activists, real estate developers, combat veterans, etc.—are foregrounded throughout this book.

Far from being distractions from putatively more important issues, popular struggles against policing and mass incarceration are addressed to core dimensions of consumer capitalism and neoliberalization. Policing continues to exist for the advancement of the interests of capital, but in our times its function has evolved along with the shift away from a Fordist economy, reflecting new technological capacities, social requirements and political motives. As this book details, policing as we know it exists for the defense of property relations, for the protection of retail and touristic spaces of consumption and processes of metropolitan real estate valuation and development, and for the regulation of relative surplus populations who are deemed threats to this accumulation regime. The urban black working class has borne the brunt of carceral power because of its particular structural position, which was produced out of the postwar transformation of American cities and the inadequate liberal antipoverty measures of the Second Reconstruction. That precarious structural position was further compounded by the concomitant processes of deindustrialization, globalized production and austerity, making the black urban poor durable cultural symbols of the society's failures and limits.

Thinking about American inequality primarily through essentialist understandings of race does not help us to see how policing operates beyond the urban theater of Black Lives Matter protests, nor its fundamental class character.[22] Black citizens are more likely to be surveilled, assaulted and killed by police. Of those people, white or black, who are killed by police, black citizens are also more likely to be unarmed. As Adam Rothman and

Barbara Fields caution, however, "white skin does not provide immunity" in matters of policing and police violence.[23] Since the invention of the Black Lives Matter hashtag, whites still account for half of those shot by police annually. Although the data on class is not as extensive as that on race, those who live in working-class and poor neighborhoods are more likely to be killed by police.[24]

Slogans like "the New Jim Crow" and "Black Lives Matter," and the view that the carceral apparatus exists to "control black bodies," appeal to liberal commonsense understandings of American inequality. It should also be noted that thinking of inequality primarily in racial terms came to dominate American culture during the Cold War, at the very same time that left anticapitalist views were being banished from acceptable political debate. Even as it inspires popular mobilizations, racial justice discourse obscures the broader national dynamics of policing and imprisonment, which are widely experienced by the most submerged elements of the working class of all colors. This emphasis on structural racism prompts liberal solutions, such as implicit bias training, body cameras, hiring more black police officers and administrators, and so forth. The singular focus on race also truncates constituencies, erects unnecessary barriers between would-be allies and confuses the central logic of policing—how it is connected to the reproduction of the market economy, processes of real estate development in central cities and the management of surplus populations.

The class character of policing is evacuated by the overwhelming power of the racial justice narrative, and at other times the material realities uniting victims regardless of color are suppressed by activists for progressive reasons. As a preemptive strategy, many antipolicing activists, victims' families and lawyers have often fought attempts to dredge up the criminal records or personal missteps of police victims. Right-wing critics and police unions routinely use any negative aspect of the victim's background to justify police actions and to defuse public criticism. Conservatives looking to demonize victims should be rebuked, but when liberal advocates suppress uncomfortable details, they render the victims' common experiences among the subproletariat invisible. George Floyd was unemployed and allegedly used counterfeit money. Eric Garner was selling "loosies"—single and untaxed cigarettes—to earn a living. Alton Sterling was selling used and pirated compact discs in front of a gas station. At the time of his fatal arrest, Walter Scott was under warrant for delinquent child support payments. Dozens of fatal police encounters result from minor infractions like a broken taillight, an expired registration or an unpaid ticket, which are more symptoms of economic hardship than any genuine threat to public safety.

And then there is the class dimension of successive drug wars and the network of unethical, arbitrary and unjust laws that continue to punish the poor for survival crimes. Freddie Gray had a record of minor drug offenses, as did many other victims of police violence. Rayshard Brooks was shot in the back while running away from police after a scuffle in June 2020, setting off a surge of protests in Atlanta.[25] He too was an ex-offender. Only a few months before his death, Brooks gave a video interview where he talked openly about his experiences after prison, the difficulties of finding employment and outliving the stigma of incarceration. At one point in the interview he says he wished "the system could look at us as individuals ... not just do us as if we're animals."[26] Activists are right to resist official attempts to impugn victims, but the fact that so many resorted to survival crimes or criminalized forms of work to make a living remains critically important for understanding the common class predicament of those Americans who are overpoliced and brutalized.

The class character of policing shows up in other ways as well. Persons who may not be engaged in survival crimes, but who live in zones targeted for police control, can be swept into the dragnet with lethal consequences. The police killing of Breonna Taylor is one such example. The twenty-six-year-old emergency medical worker was slain by police who raided her home with a "no knock" search warrant targeting her ex-boyfriend. In the months of protests after her death, activists emphasized that Taylor lived in a gentrifying zone where police sweeps were part of a broader strategy of clearing the neighborhood for real estate valuation.[27] Technical fixes to these problems—better training, building more effective police–community relations and all the rest— might reduce incidences in some places, but the root causes lie deeper, in the very system of accumulation that produces disposable people and values property and profit-making over the lives and peace of communities.

The George Floyd rebellion reflected an emerging antiracist majority, but not necessarily the local coalitions and governing majorities needed to achieve concrete policy reforms around police misconduct. Both Minneapolis and Seattle city councils had ostensibly achieved veto-proof majorities in favor of dismantling the police department and devising nonviolent, restorative and progressive means of achieving public safety, but the path to actually achieving those reforms collapsed by the end of the summer.[28] Such reforms seem even less likely in cities like Jackson, Mississippi, which was touted by many on the left as a model of radical black political leadership once the late Chokwe Lumumba, a veteran of the Black Power organization the Republic of New Afrika, was elected mayor in 2013, and when his son Chokwe Antar Lumumba won the same position in 2017.[29] Despite its left progressive mayoral leadership and majority-black citizenry, Jackson's city council passed measures in September 2020 to increase police pay and improve health benefits for single officers, as well as approved plans to rent additional jail space to handle misdemeanor arrests. As in Minneapolis and Seattle, when the protesting ends, Jackson is governed by vested interests who see policing as necessary to municipal order and economic development, i.e., the donor class, real estate developers, multinational corporations and investors who live beyond the city limits. Whether the popular protests of 2020 cohere into a force capable of governing will depend on how well activists and supporters can build real constituencies beyond cycles of protests and avoid some of the problems that already threaten sustained cooperation.

After the formative Black Lives Matter demonstrations orchestrated by black activists and organizations in Ferguson, Missouri, Baltimore and Chicago, during the George Floyd rebellion the epicenter shifted to some of the nation's whiter cities, such as Minneapolis (63.8 percent white), Seattle (65.7), Portland (72.2) and Kenosha (67.3). The shifting racial composition of protests in these cities was so dramatic that some black activists were unnerved, adopting their own rendition of the conservative "outside agitator" discourse and complaining loudly that their movement had been highjacked.[30] Whites had always participated in Black Lives Matter demonstrations, but the influx of white support changed the character of many protests, with black bloc tactics more visible and anarchist sensibilities competing with the practices of local BLM organizers. In Portland, the majority-white Wall of Moms, who stood arm-in-arm wearing sunflower yellow shirts to protect protestors from police, and the "Naked Athena," an anonymous performance artist who confronted the federal agents Trump dispatched onto Portland streets, inspired many across the country. Some black activists, however, were outraged, viewing these actions as distracting and arguing that Black Lives Matter needed to remain black-led.[31]

The George Floyd rebellion has revealed how identity politics continues to serve as a powerful source of mobilization, but remains a temperamental, unsound means of movement-building and protracted political work. Compassion for black victims of police violence was crucial to these mobilizations, but by fall 2020 public support for Black Lives Matter, especially among whites, had subsided, returning to the modest white support of the Obama years. In Wisconsin, support for BLM dropped from 61 percent in mid-June 2020 down to 48 percent in late August, after the Kenosha police shot Jacob Blake in front of his children and left him paralyzed.[32] Such slippage likely reflects not only compassion fatigue but also the limits of white privilege and other idioms of antiracist discourse employed as organizing strategies.[33] The prevailing claim that carceral power is animated by structural racism, and the cultural commitments to black vanguardism–white allyship, a vestige of sixties New Left politics, remain formidable impediments to the development of a genuine popular consensus dedicated to a progressive carceral reform agenda.

Our current policing regime is not derived from and maintained through white supremacy, as some activists hold; rather, the carceral expansion of the late twentieth century was propelled by manifold political and economic interests, which are not reducible to the cynical mobilization of racism but include the interests and felt needs of working-class, urban African American and Latino constituencies, whose residents desired peace and an end to the unacceptable levels of drug-related and violent crime that still define urban life for millions of Americans.[34] For the ghettoized black and brown working class, the thin blue line has always been fraught, but the popular mobilizations of the last decade have awakened the wider public to systematic failures, malice and police abuses. Likewise, as the socially disruptive processes of capital intensification and globalized production have proceeded apace, and neoliberalization has hollowed out the benevolent functions of the old welfare state, more and more Americans find themselves on the wrong side of the thin blue line. Eric Adams's point about how so many Americans were "feeling black" amidst the precarity of the pandemic speaks to this reality, but as with so much of Black Lives Matter sentiment, the symbolic language of race fails us. It is at once a powerful means of recalling and naming the limits of America's unfulfilled liberal democratic project, and yet at the same time such rhetoric obscures the power of capital over our lives, and the role of police in maintaining its omnipotence.

Policing is central to maintaining the commercial, real estate and tourist-entertainment sectors we all depend on for our working lives, leisure and daily reproduction. Developing a popular power capable of transforming this system will likely need to advance from a mass rejection of racism, which is worthwhile on its own terms, towards a shared vision of the good society, one that transcends capitalist exploitation, dispossession and violence, and which, through popular democratic means, determines the specific state interventions, personal and collective sacrifices and distributional politics necessary to create and sustain that society. Inasmuch as activists can construct a broadly redistributive left politics centered on public goods—as a means of eliminating deprivation and crime, securing public safety through greater equality and economic security, and improving the quality of life throughout urban society—powerful coalitions built on shared self-interests can emerge. "Reining in murderous police, investing in schools rather than prisons, providing universal health care (including drug treatment and rehabilitation for addicts in the rural heartland), raising taxes on the rich, and ending foolish wars," Rothman and Fields make plain, "are policies that would benefit a solid majority of the American people."[35] The fights to defund, demilitarize and dismantle police departments, which forcefully entered public debate amid the George Floyd rebellion, represent a possible opening towards a more just order, but they also deserve critical analysis and serious debate.[36]

What Is to Be Done?

Although focused on the specific problem of police violence against black civilians, Black Lives Matter has served as a powerful valence and means of mobilization, drawing attention to the limits of the Second Reconstruction. It is a response to the many ways that the promise of the civil rights movement has been undermined by the concomitant collapse of the New Deal coalition and spread of neoliberalization, the hollowing of the welfare state, and the restoration of capitalist class power over living labor, society, governance and planetary resources. The Biden administration's first 100 days saw significant movement in the realm of racial justice. The long-languishing reparations bill, HB40, the passion project of the late Detroit congressman John Conyers, was finally advanced from committee stage for full House consideration. An Anti–Asian American hate crimes bill was passed after a rash of violent incidents. Attorney General Merrick Garland announced full DOJ investigations into the police departments of Louisville and Minneapolis.[37] The power of the Black Lives Matter slogan lies in how well it reasserts racial injustice as a central contradiction, but its popularity among the powerful is also evidence of its limits in terms of forming a genuine opposition to the capitalist social order.

These measures may represent a significant cultural awakening, but the same reform strategies have done little to improve use-of-force practices or reduce the prevalence of fatal police–civilian encounters. George Floyd was murdered in a city that had implemented "best practices," but that did not prevent Chauvin, a decorated officer with seventeen civilian complaints against him, from remaining on the force and acting with impunity.[38] As many other scholars and pundits have made clear, reforming police practices may be necessary and will hopefully reduce harm, but technocratic reform will not resolve the problem at hand.

This book holds that racial liberalism is inadequate to the tasks of addressing the current carceral crisis and protecting the most vulnerable citizens who are managed through police power. That is not to say that liberal reforms cannot have an impact on harm reduction and improve police–community relations, or that a more humane system of criminal justice is not possible. The slate of reforms that have now become part of the public mainstream—such as national use-of-force standards, mandatory and universal body cameras for police units, decriminalization and decarceration, the so-called Camden model of policing, restrictions on qualified immunity for law enforcement officers, and so forth—may well create a more tolerable set of circumstances for police departments and millions of Americans, but none of these reforms transform the fundamental function of police under late capitalism.

On April 20, 2021, Derek Chauvin became the first white officer in Minnesota ever convicted for killing a black civilian. In recent memory, the only other Minneapolis officer to have been convicted for such a crime was Mohamed Noor, found guilty of the 2017 murder of Justine Damond, who had called 911 when she suspected someone was being sexually assaulted nearby, and was shot in her pajamas, unarmed and holding her cell phone. That case was met with different demands for racial justice by local activists, who thought Noor, one of the first Somali immigrants to serve on the Minneapolis force, was being singled out and treated more harshly for killing a white woman.[39] The trial of Chauvin, however, left little room for ambivalence. The brutality of his actions, the unjust and undeserved death of Floyd, and the sense that all of this might have been avoided with just a little more mercy and humanity, made this particular case the flashpoint of BLM's return to public consciousness. Crowds gathered across the country, and in Minneapolis's George Floyd Square, shouted in jubilation as the verdict was handed down, declaring Chauvin guilty on the charges of second-degree unintentional murder, third-degree murder and second-degree manslaughter. The forty-five-year-old former Minneapolis officer's eyes darted nervously as the verdict was read out, and moments later he was escorted out of the court in handcuffs. In the hours and days that followed, liberal pundits and online chatter filled the air with declarations of victory, with some extrapolating from this single case to a larger victory in which court justice for George Floyd's murder spoke to the unfulfilled hopes of generations of African Americans.

As more radical and veteran activists pointed out amid these celebrations, however, court justice did little to address the systemic nature of the problem. Over 100 Americans were killed in police encounters over the three-week duration of the Chauvin trial. On Chicago's southwest side, two Latino youth were killed in separate incidents involving foot chases by police. In the early morning hours of March 29, police responded to shots fired in the Little Village neighborhood and pursued thirteen-year-old Adam Toledo and twenty-one-year-old Ruben Roman, Jr. down an alley behind Farragut Career Academy High School. Bodycam footage recorded Toledo complying with officer commands, tossing a gun through a fence gap and holding his hands in the air before being shot multiple times. Less than forty-eight hours later, a similar police chase in the Portage Park neighborhood ended with the fatal shooting of twenty-two-year-old Anthony Alvarez. Shot in the back by police, Alvarez can be heard on bodycam footage asking "Why are you shooting me?" in the moments before he loses consciousness. Both incidents precipitated street vigils and protests, and heightened demands for a moratorium on foot pursuits by the Chicago Police Department. In the Minneapolis suburb of Brooklyn Center, only ten miles away from the court where Chauvin's trial was unfolding, police officer Kimberley Potter fatally shot Daunte Wright, a twenty-year-old black man, during a traffic stop on April 11, 2021. And although video footage captures Potter shouting "taser, taser, taser" during the arrest, the twenty-six-year veteran fired her service weapon instead. Within an hour of the Chauvin verdict, Columbus police shot and killed sixteen-year-old Ma'Khia Bryant, after calls for emergency assistance during an altercation outside her house. Police body cameras captured the rapidity of officer Nicholas Reardon's actions, who fired four shots almost immediately after exiting his squad car, and the wailing protests of her family and other witnesses as the teenager lay dying in the street. The day after Chauvin was found guilty, police in Elizabeth City, North Carolina fired multiple shots into the back of Andrew Brown, Jr.'s car as he attempted to drive away during an arrest, killing the forty-two-year-old beloved family man. On the same day in Spotsylvania County, Virginia, police killed Isaiah Brown, a thirty-two-year-old black man, after he requested assistance in a domestic dispute with his brother. After a brief confrontation, police fired ten shots, killing Brown, who was holding a cordless house phone, which police allegedly mistook for a weapon.

Each use-of-force incident is different, and some sadly are justifiable; many cases described here and hundreds of others will end in no charges being filed, others in acquittal, and some families may be awarded settlements by municipal governments. The year between Floyd's death and Chauvin's conviction marked a period of unprecedented, broad public acceptance of Black Lives Matter sentiments, but the continued prevalence of so many heartbreaking cases reveals the limitations of popular mobilization and liberalism as means for addressing the problem of overpolicing. In other words, while the mass protests grew out of the years of groundwork by BLM activists, they also reflected the limits of protests as means of building a new consensus around more progressive methods of achieving public safety. Much more organizing beyond the ranks of the most woke citizenry would be necessary to create legislative majorities capable of producing a more just order.

Antipolicing struggles must ultimately transcend the innate liberalism and ethnic politics of Black Lives Matter, which are political dead-ends too easily usurped by the investor class and mainstream party politics, and instead directly address the underlying, capitalist class contradictions that are driving police killings and America's overgrown carceral apparatus. This book situates the evolution of carceral power in our times within the broader dynamics of capital accumulation and class struggle, and the ways our current political economy and policing regime were set in motion by the urban transformation that followed World War II. The disproportionate presence of black victims and the fact that black movements have amplified the problems of mass incarceration and policing do not negate the capitalist origins of these problems. The black urban poor became the symbol of American inequality during the Cold War, but that symbolism distorted the always multiracial character of the subproletariat. Due to this symbolic politics, geography and presence of black civil rights infrastructure, the urban theater of inequality and police abuse has been the primary stage of Black Lives Matter protests, but the same processes of capital-intensive production, manufacturing contraction, labor redundancy, criminalized work and survival crimes, and the replacement of social provision with carceral power, persist beyond the nation's metropolitan centers, and define life for the most vulnerable segments of the working class wherever they live. When, rather than focusing singularly on racial injury, we define the problem of contemporary policing as one of managing surplus populations and securing the property regime and preconditions for "postindustrial" capital accumulation, a different political vista opens up, one that is not trained on technocratic reform and antiracism alone, but on reorganizing society on a more socially just and humanistic basis.

The demands to defund and dismantle police departments, which have gained momentum in some cities since the murder of George Floyd, have cracked the door onto a more helpful public discussion and raised critical questions. What is policing for? Do we need police to address certain kinds of problems, like the mental health crisis? Can we imagine different ways of securing public safety that do not entail further militarization of society and repression of working-class life? Could the public largesse now dedicated to police departments, and equally to the massive settlements paid out to the families of those killed or maimed in police encounters, be better used towards progressive social programs and investment in communities?

While these demands have reoriented public discussion towards social investment and prompted a rethinking of public safety, they miss the mark in two critical regards. First, by targeting police budgets for redistribution towards social spending, such demands leave too much money on the table, so to speak, inasmuch as they neglect other public expenditures that are equally antisocial and too pro-capitalist in orientation. Policing is implicated in the state-financed economic development strategies so many metropolitan areas rely on to attract investment, creative class entrepreneurs, wealthier residents and visitors, but those strategies also include myriad forms of corporate giveaways and incentives paid out of public coffers which dwarf police budgets and should also be scrutinized and re-routed towards public investments that will benefit the common good. Second, policing plays a particular repressive role under capitalism, securing the conditions for accumulation through control and suppression of the working class, but the critical analysis of this historical function too often obscures the role of coercion as a necessary aspect of political life, especially in regard to securing social justice. It is difficult to have this conversation in the age of online trolling, "cancel culture" and social media's assault on attention spans and meaningful public debate, but a longer historical view problematizes any simplistic demand to dismantle police departments. At various moments in this nation's history, *state coercion was necessary to secure racial justice*, a fact that is lost sight of in the time of Black Lives Matter. Union army occupation of the post-bellum South made the short-lived project of Federal Reconstruction and unprecedented black progress possible. After World War II, the deployment of federal marshals and national guardsmen at critical junctures was indispensable to making real the guarantee of equal protection before the constitution and beginning the process of dismantling Jim Crow laws and every-day practices. Left critics and scholars are right to highlight the repressive actions of southern police chiefs like Bull Connor, the Red Squads of the Chicago police department and the obsessions of Federal Bureau of Investigation chief J. Edgar Hoover, but the broader portrait of the role of policing and black progress is more complicated. Finally, while we should right-size and demilitarize police, it seems rather naive to think that a complex, populous urban society can exist without any law enforcement at all, especially in those moments when forces threaten social justice and even the basic democratic rights of citizens.

Against the most millenarian impulses of abolitionist discourse, this book calls for a different kind of abolition, one that focuses more directly on the fundamental problems of working-class exploitation, joblessness and immiseration, and is achievable within the discrete political terrain of early twenty-first-century American society. *We must abolish the class conditions that modern policing has come to manage.* That work might commence with the redistributive demands Black Lives Matter activists championed in the wake of George Floyd's murder, but such proposals might go further still in scale and social-ist aspirations. We can achieve greater public safety through nonviolent, pro-social means and at the same time enhance the quality of everyday life throughout society, and especially in cities, through public works and the decommodification of basic needs, infrastructure and amenities. This book's call to "abolish the conditions" is not exclusive of other ongoing anticarceral political projects, but works in tandem with other demands and struggles, such as the legalization of recreational drugs, the decriminalization of sex work, treating drug addiction and overdoses as a public health crisis, decarceration, an end to money bail, and revising use-of-force policies in law enforcement branches, which together represent the kind of world that Black Lives Matter and longer-running criminal justice reform advocates have sought to conjure into being.

This book embarks on a conjunctural analysis of carceral power and antipolicing struggles in the hope of illuminating how policing functions within late capitalism and generating political insights that might spur debate and move us closer towards a more just society. The chapters that follow traverse different modes of analysis, shifting from historical interpretation to political and cultural criticism and speculative theory. The first two chapters offer an alternative historical interpretation of the emergence of our current mode of policing, which is not rooted in antebellum slave patrols or even the Progressive-era criminalization of newly urbanizing black migrants, but in the postwar expansion of the consumer society and the dramatic spatial and economic transformation of American cities. These processes gave rise to the idyllic suburban middle class and the urban "underclass" —both conservative ideological notions that undermined working-class consciousness and ultimately drove and justified the carceral build-up. Chapters 3 and 4 shift from this opening historical interpretation of the origins of contemporary policing towards a critical analysis of Black Lives Matter's first wave and the ways BLM revises black ethnic politics even as it rehearses its political limitations. A core criticism developed here is that liberal antiracist politics is itself a class politics, emerging from a rightly anxious black professional-managerial stratum but largely oriented towards making the market economy work while failing to discern the real winners and losers of the neoliberal turn within and beyond the African American population. Finally, Chapters 5 and 6 dive directly into debates over defunding and dismantling police departments, to develop an anticapitalist position that amplifies the book's pro-worker and pro-public goods vision of left politics. The return of genuine public works and the decommodification of basic needs might begin the process of achieving public safety through the universal guarantee of economic security.

1

Policing Capitalist Society

The end of the Cold War and emergence of mass protests against capitalist globalization during the late nineties began an intellectual thaw in American academic and popular life and stoked the revival of Marxist and anarchist analyses. In the opening decades of the twenty-first century, American public debate in some corners slowly shed left euphemisms adopted in response to Cold War anticommunism, with the language of the hardworking middle class, the excesses of corporate power, and left progressivism gradually giving way to more open talk of anticapitalism, workers, class solidarity and socialism. During the time of Black Lives Matter, however, anti-Marxist sentiments have resurfaced, most often in reaction to arguments calling for a popular interracialist left politics, or demanding a more sophisticated, critical analysis of black life. The charge of "class reductionism" is readily hurled against anyone who dares claim that, like the American populace at large, the black population is constituted by classes and that class position matters in terms of understanding the different political interests and aspirations constituting black political life in real time and space. Like most epithets, the charge of class reductionism tells us little about the accused but, as Adolph Reed, Jr. has noted, "tells us a great deal about the accusers—the professional-managerial guardians of elite discourse." "Most of all, the class reductionist myth gives powerful expression to the class-bound desire to address the supposed interests of women, racial minorities, and other marginalized populations at the expense of broad, downward economic distribution," Reed adds. "Nothing declares one's own class allegiances more eloquently, after all, than the accusation that one's opponents only care about class."[1]

The so-called race–class debate that has unfolded during the time of Black Lives Matter is a ruse grounded in notions of American exceptionalism, which have long held that, unlike other nations where social classes struggled for power, the United States is an historical case apart where class has little power over individuals but where race exercises a transhistorical force. Moreover, the "race–class debate" counterposes and conflates two distinctive social phenomena as alternatives to one another when they are not. As historian Barbara Fields made plain some time ago, race and class are concepts of a different order. Both are ideological, but race is purely so—a mischievous concept whose historical power always rest on the false assertion of fundamental biological differences dividing humanity into unique subspecies. The idea that there are essential biological differences defining specific races is spurious. As Fields reminds us, "there is only one human species, and the most dramatic differences of appearance can be wiped out in one act of miscegenation."[2] "The very diversity and arbitrariness of the physical rules governing racial classification," Fields writes, "prove that the physical emblems which symbolize race are not the foundation upon which race arises as a category of social thought."[3] "Ideas about color, like ideas about anything else, derive their importance, indeed their very definition, from their context. They can no more be the unmediated reflex of psychic impressions than can any other ideas. It is the ideological context that tells people which details to notice, which to ignore, and which to take for granted in translating the world around them into ideas about the world."[4]

Of course, the specious character of race does not make it any less real in terms of its social power. Like other popular ideologies, race can be powerful and consequential. However, as Fields rightly cautions, "the reality underlying racial ideology cannot be found where the vocabulary of racial ideology might tempt us to look for it." In contrast, "class is a concept that we can locate both at the level of objective reality and at the level of social appearances."[5] For Fields and the present author, "class refers to a material circumstance: the inequality of human beings from the standpoint of social power." And as she makes clear, the class metrics common to the social sciences, like occupation, income and educational attainment, provide only a dim reflection of class, while the Marxist focus on the social relations of production "reflects it directly."[6] In addition to its ideological dimension, "the reality of class can assert itself independently of people's consciousness, and sometimes in direct opposition to it," says Fields, "as when an artisan who considers himself a cut above the working class is relegated to unskilled labor by the mechanization of his craft, or when a salaried technocrat who thinks he is part of the bourgeoisie suddenly finds himself thrown out of work by the retrenchment of his enterprise."[7]

On matters of mass incarceration and policing, racialist thinking has been especially pernicious, and the aversion to critical analysis of capitalist political economy has limited popular understandings of the historical forces responsible for the current carceral regime. This chapter lays the foundation for countering this obfuscation and advancing a more nuanced, historical understanding of these dynamics.

The chapter begins with a critical overview of the New Jim Crow, which first emerged as a political slogan in the aftermath of the crack cocaine crisis. Michelle Alexander's acclaimed 2010 book, *The New Jim Crow*, lifted the activist slogan into the political mainstream and provided what has become the prevailing liberal-to-left understanding of the origins and central motives of the carceral expansion. While the historical Jim Crow subjected blacks to legally codified second-class citizenship, the New Jim Crow and Black Lives Matter narratives insist that all blacks face a similarly universal threat of bodily harm and incarceration regardless of the real progress in black political and social life since the end of Jim Crow apartheid. "What has changed since the collapse of Jim Crow has less to do with the basic structure of our society," Alexander contends, "than with the language we use to justify it."[8] There are numerous interpretive limitations to Alexander's account, but her use of caste theory to think about carceral power and contemporary inequality has been the most influential and problematic. Alexander helped to popularize the antiracist perspective on the carceral expansion, which has grown more popular through Black Lives Matter mobilizations, but the focus on black exceptionalism is flawed as an explanation of why the most submerged elements of the black working class are overpoliced and overrepresented in US prisons, and obscures the broader class character of the criminal justice system.

In turn, this chapter sketches a historical-materialist analysis of carceral expansion which will be developed in greater detail in subsequent chapters. It stands in opposition to the prevailing philosophical idealism that marks so much thinking on race, carcerality and policing. Modern policing evolved historically as a means of securing the conditions for continuous capital accumulation, but the discrete character and modes of policing needed to achieve those ends have evolved in accordance with shifting valorization requirements. The first urban municipal police forces were raised amid the tumultuous processes of transnational and domestic migrations, along with the rapid urbanization associated with industrial development. Although important exceptions are noted here, within this early industrial context police defended the interests of capital against worker rebellion, disciplined any conduct and behavior that threatened labor readiness, and in general helped maintain notions of social order characteristic of the bourgeoisie during the nineteenth and twentieth centuries. The social role of policing, however, would undergo important transformations after World War II amid the relatively stable compound growth of the Fordist-Keynesian compact, which instigated unprecedented prosperity and class recomposition. The expansion of the consumer middle class and concomitant resegregation and alienation of the black and brown urban poor reoriented the scale and role of policing, producing renewed popular consent to police power among those segments of society who came to see their personal economic interests as indistinguishable from those of US corporations and capital accumulation. At the same time, this reorientation unleashed new forms of social control onto those vulnerable populations who were locked out of the broad prosperity promised by postwar economic growth. Policing in our own time is trained on the regulation of surplus populations: the unemployed and unemployable, those who are pressed to commit survival crimes, those involved in criminalized forms of work to earn a living, and people of all races who live in zones that are targeted for police control.

The Even Stranger Career of the New Jim Crow

During his speech at the conclusion of the Selma to Montgomery march in 1965, Martin Luther King, Jr. declared C. Vann Woodward's 1955 book *The Strange Career of Jim Crow* as the bible of the southern civil rights movement.[9] Woodward was an historian and champion of black civil rights, though he would swing rightward politically later in life, a turn precipitated by his opposition to sixties counterculture. His landmark work remains useful, however, as an antidote to ahistorical thinking about race and the era of Jim Crow segregation, and, equally, as a powerful form of antiracist criticism that seems lost in our own times.

Against biological racism and the standing cultural deference to local custom at the time, Woodward insisted that segregation was neither a natural nor an inevitable state of affairs, insisting through a careful retelling of US history since the Civil War that "things have not always been the same in the South."[10] Woodward pushed back against the tendency to naturalize the southern order either through biological racism or through the shelter of custom and tradition, emphasizing instead the relative historical novelty of Jim Crow as an institution, and making clear that segregation was not an inevitable outcome of slavery or of the collapse of Reconstruction. "In a time when the Negroes formed a much larger proportion of the population than they did later, when slavery was a live memory in the minds of both races, and when the memory of the hardships and bitterness of Reconstruction was still fresh," he wrote, "the race policies accepted and pursued in the South were sometimes milder than they became later." "The policies of proscription, segregation, and disenfranchisement that are often described as the immutable 'folkways' of the South, impervious alike to legislative reform and armed intervention, are of a more recent origin," Woodward concluded, "and the belief that they are immutable and unchangeable is not supported by history."[11] As such, his account sharply contrasts with the shared tendency of both the most vehement and violent segregationists and many contemporary commentators to see slavery, Jim Crow segregation and contemporary police violence as all part of a continuous, unbroken narrative of racial oppression.

Antisegregationist and antiracist politics were central to Woodward's account, which treated race, racism and racist institutions as mutable and changeable. For Woodward, race was a myth whose social power could be contested and dethroned, but the New Jim Crow sensibility suggests the contrary—that race is transhistorical, omnipotent and unchanging. Where Woodward, and the civil rights activists who touted his work, saw historical contingency and the possibilities of movement politics, the New Jim Crow sensibility has provoked mass mobilization around the idea that race and racism are endemic and durable features of American life and society, even when such conclusions are not supported by history. Moreover, the New Jim Crow perpetuates a notion of black exceptionalism, popularized by Cold War liberals who saw black poverty as distinctive from white poverty, rooted in cultural dysfunction and therefore impervious to the progressive state interventions that had supported working-class ethnics in other periods. Indeed, it's striking how many underlying assumptions the New Jim Crow shares with both the most diehard segregationists and supposedly well-meaning Cold War liberals. These problems of interpretation and politics stem from how the "New Jim Crow" originated, first as an activist slogan brandished against a process of neoliberal rollback, which besieged the gains of the civil rights movement, and then popularized through the best-selling book by Michelle Alexander, which advances an analysis by analogy of mass incarceration's origins and motives.

A great strength of Alexander's book is how well it illuminated the processes by which mass incarceration creates new conditions of second-class citizenship. The problem often referred to as "felon disenfranchisement" is multilayered, rooted in a labyrinth of state laws that further penalize those convicted of crimes even after they have served out their court-ordered sentence.[12] In some states, once a person has been convicted they may be legally and effectually denied their right to a job (through mandatory self-reporting on job applications and the discrimination that follows), their parental custody and visitation rights, their right to public assistance, their right to serve on a jury trial, and their right to vote, among other rights available to other citizens. They may also be disqualified from receiving education assistance like Pell grants and federal loans. In the decade since Alexander's book appeared, activists have worked feverishly to dismantle the statutes upholding this second-class citizenship, and ensure that formerly incarcerated peoples have a fair chance at regaining their lives and reconnecting fully with their families, communities and public life.[13] Tough-on-crime might characterize the web of mandatory minimums and other policies designed to reduce crime—often in haste and with faulty reasoning—but the process of felon disenfranchisement was a clear excess to the theory of retributivism, and a sharp deviation from older claims about prisoner rehabilitation. Instead of a second chance, social reintegration or Christian redemption, these policies are guided by a desire to banish and debilitate. In the same spirit, sociologist Loïc Wacquant contends that the carceral apparatus "induces the civic death of those it ensnares by extruding them from the social compact."[14] Whereas institutions of higher learning enable students under optimal conditions to obtain marketable skills, upward mobility and economic security, the carceral apparatus operates in reverse, ensuring that most of its "students" will never attain the trappings of middle-class life, while being denied meaningful citizenship in many parts of the country.

Yet there are problems with Alexander's account of the sources of the carceral expansion. Her account focuses on the War on Drugs and the ways stress policing, sentencing laws and mass incarceration penalized blacks disproportionately. The effects of carceral policy were undoubtedly racial, but the causes of the carceral expansion were less straightforwardly so. White moral panic over urban decline and the crack cocaine crisis helped to produce one set of constituencies calling for law-and-order politics, but what should be clear by now is that in many cities majority-black governing coalitions and popular constituencies also pushed for immediate solutions to the problems they faced, such as rising street violence, theft, alcoholism and drug use, and the declining quality of life in many neighborhoods.[15] Additionally, as a number of critics have point out, Alexander's account overstates the place of drug offenses at the expense of violent crime as a principal driver of mass incarceration from the eighties onward. Drug offenses accounted for most of those persons incarcerated in federal prisons, but not those in state penitentiaries and local jails—which of course make up the vast majority of the nation's population behind bars. In the decade before Alexander's book was published, the majority of the nation's 1.3 million state prisoners were not convicted of drug offenses, which constituted only 20 percent of the state prison population in 2006. Fifty percent were serving sentences for violent crimes and 21 percent for property crimes.[16] In local jails, inmates were divided evenly, with roughly 25 percent for each of the main categories of violent, drug, property and public order offenses.[17] During the 2000s, violent crime accounted for 60 percent of the growth in state prison populations.[18]

The central flaw of Alexander's treatment, however, is its tendency to overstate the problem of mass incarceration as universally and primarily a black problem when it is not. There are moments when Alexander strains against the limits of this interpretation, and she even concedes that mass incarceration "directly harms far more whites than Jim Crow ever did." But her analysis, like so much contemporary thinking on policing and prisons, cleaves to the contention that black people feel it worse than any other group—and they feel it *as a singular group*.

This black exceptionalist account is problematic on at least two counts worth noting here. First, despite the well-known disparities, most black people are never arrested or convicted of crimes. Second, pushing the narrative that this is primarily a black problem stifles serious consideration of what connects black victims of overpolicing, black prisoners and black formerly incarcerated persons to the non-blacks who are overpoliced, incarcerated and punished via disenfranchisement laws, keeping in mind that non-blacks make up the majority population in all these categories. The problem here is the retreat into caste, and the aversion to thinking about class implicit in black exceptionalist discourse.

Rather than focus on class, Alexander opts for viewing the problem in terms of caste: "a stigmatized racial group locked into an inferior position by law and custom."[19] For Alexander, this is the connecting thread between the historical Jim Crow and contemporary mass incarceration. Alexander evokes class in her discussion of the racial caste system, and rightly rejects the popular American sentiment that class is no barrier to upward mobility for the diligent, virtuous and hard-working. Her account of class, however, does not venture beyond conventional social science and does not connect in a sustained way to capitalist political economy. In this regard, she follows a signal tendency of caste-based interpretations that overwrite situated-class experiences and interests with racial caste. Caste discourse as applied to the history of African Americans is essentially a culturalist rearticulation of race which stands opposed to biological racism.

But from the writings of anthropologist W. Lloyd Warner to latter-day purveyors like Alexander and Isabel Wilkerson, caste discourse has always been a bourgeois project that separates racial ascriptive status from class exploitation.[20] Furthermore—and deeply in line with the capitalist status quo—it is an idealist project. What matters here is not the concrete material conditions and configurations of meaningful political and social power in a given time and place, but our *thinking* about race/caste and changing our "customs." Caste was inadequate as an explanation for the origins and even the effects of Jim Crow segregation, and it is even more misguided as an explanation of black life after over half a century of black political and social integration in the wake of the defeat of Jim Crow.

Alexander's interpretive choice of racial caste moves us back towards the familiar American liberal ground of black exceptionalism, which has little bearing on the diverse class experiences of the black population or on the ways that mass incarceration functions within capitalism. At times, she acknowledges the class character of policing and mass incarceration and how it affects a particular segment of the black population. Against the pejorative notion of the "underclass," she opts for the "undercaste," defined as "a lower caste of individuals who are permanently barred by law and custom from mainstream society."[21] Elsewhere, she recognizes the broad dragnet the criminal justice system casts over the poor beyond majority-black and brown urban neighborhoods and communities, but over and again she doubles down on racial caste as offering the most powerful and accurate account of carceral inequality. For Alexander, whites who are overpoliced and incarcerated are merely "collateral damage," incidental casualties in a drug war that intentionally and strategically targeted African Americans and Latinos. This is a problem, and not merely in terms of being an interpretation that prevents us from understanding the character of policing historically and in our own times. Alexander's and other's resurrection of racial caste also sets up some political problems—particularly in an ostensible majoritarian democracy where African Americans make up less than

15 percent of the population. In the time of Black Lives Matter, racial caste and black exceptionalism have spawned a revival of ethnic politics that has done little to illuminate the conditions facing working-class Americans throughout the postindustrial cities and hinterlands, or to address the fundamental causes of the carceral build-up.

Class Dismissed

The 2016 July 4th week was bloody and heartbreaking. That week saw the police killings of Alton Sterling, a thirty-seven-year-old black man, in Baton Rouge, and Philando Castile, a thirty-two-year-old black man, in the Falcon Heights suburb of Saint Paul, Minnesota. Both killings were video recorded and immediately sparked mass protests across the nation. Just after midnight on July 5, Baton Rouge police responded to the Triple S Food Mart on North Foster Drive following reports of a man with a gun. Sterling was a frequent presence at the store, known for selling used and pirated compact musical discs. In the process of apprehending Sterling, Baton Rouge police officers Blane Salamoni and Howie Lake tasered him multiple times. As they attempted to handcuff him, Salamoni shouted that he was reaching for a gun, prompting Lake to shoot Sterling six times in the chest at point blank rage. The arrest and shooting were captured from various angles on multiple cell phones, closed circuit surveillance and police body cameras.

The very next day in suburban Saint Paul, Castile, his girlfriend Diamond Reynolds and her four-year-old daughter were stopped by police officers Jeronimo Yanez and Joseph Kauser, who wrongly suspected that Castile and Reynolds had been involved in a robbery.[22] Castile, whose friends and co-workers called him "Phil," was a cafeteria supervisor at J. J. Hill Montessori Magnet School and a fourteen-year member of the Minnesota Teamsters Local 320. Castile had been stopped forty-nine times in the Saint Paul suburbs in the thirteen years preceding his fatal encounter.

His sister said that his car, a 1997 wide-bodied Oldsmobile, was "mostly stereotyped as a drug-dealer's car," and she complained about also being stopped frequently and without cause whenever she borrowed her brother's car.[23] The fatal traffic stop was caught on police dashcam. Castile calmly announced that he was in possession of a registered firearm, but as he reached for his identification, Yanez fired seven shots at Castile at close range. With incredible poise and presence of mind, Reynolds pulled out her phone and immediately began livestreaming the incident on Facebook and narrating what had happened to the public. The video captured her intense mix of shock, sadness and indignation as Castile fought for his life. Reynolds later reported that the officers did not check for Castile's pulse or try to administer emergency medical aid for several minutes after the shooting, and said she was treated "like a criminal," handcuffed and moved with her daughter to a squad car. Coming at the end of a weekend when most people were celebrating America's war for independence from British rule with parades, fireworks and barbecues, the deaths of Sterling and Castile once again provided a horrific reminder of the nation's persistent racial injustice, deep class inequality and obscene levels of state violence. Both men became part of a grim pantheon.

During that 2016 July 4th week when Sterling and Castile were gunned down, there were a total of ten people nationally who were killed by police. That death toll included Delrawn Small in Brooklyn, Dylan Noble in Fresno, Anthony Nuñez in San Jose, Pedro Erik Villanueva in the Canoga Park section of Los Angeles, Raul Saavedra-Vargas in Reno, Melissa Ventura in Yuma County, Arizona, Vinson Ramos in Los Angeles County, and Alva Braziel in Houston. In total, four black men, one white youth and five Latinos were slain in arrest-related incidents. The deaths of five Latinos and one white youth at the hands of police were totally ignored by the mainstream corporate media and some activist networks. The killing of the two other black victims, Small and Braziel, received less attention as well. The myopic framing here was caused in part by the peculiar dynamics of social media information flows—whether the incident was captured on video, and how rapidly it was circulated publicly—but it is also reflective of a deeper problem of ideology. Some have argued that there has been less mobilization around Latino deaths because in many of the communities where these conflicts with police occur, residents fear speaking out due to their immigration status and the prospect of further state harassment.[24] This may be part of the problem, but the dominant framing, which presupposes that blacks are the primary and, for some, exclusive targets of mistreatment and violence by police, has had the effect of distorting social reality.

A core premise of Black Lives Matter and cognate notions like the New Jim Crow is that these problems of policing and imprisonment are essentially black problems, widely felt by blacks regardless of their class position or social status. By extension, there is the perception that unjust arrests and deaths at the hands of police are not experienced by other groups in any substantive way. These assumptions are factually wrong, but they are repeated enough times and by enough influential voices to have achieved an unimpeachable legitimacy in popular thinking. In his 2018 Netflix standup comedy special, *Tamborine*, Chris Rock appealed to this popular common sense when he joked, "You would think the cops would occasionally shoot a white kid, just to make it look good." His comment drew fire from those who did not appreciate his irreverent style of political criticism, and from others who bristled at the suggestion that whites should be treated to an equal proportion of state violence as blacks.

Among the fast-growing body of literary and artistic expressions of BLM sentiment, autobiographical tracts such as Ta-Nehisi Coates's *Between the World and Me* and Imani Perry's *Breathe* have helped to authorize and enlarge the liberal antiracist accounting of modern policing.[25] Both books are written as letters from black writers to their sons, warning of the dangers that lie ahead in an unjust world. As Perry writes, "an aversion to blackness can turn perfectly lovely people grotesque." Perry's book was in part spurred by her own well-publicized brush with law enforcement, after she was arrested and searched for driving with a suspended license and having an outstanding warrant for unpaid parking tickets.[26]

The authors rehearse a Jim Crow literary device, most famously employed in James Baldwin's *The Fire Next Time*: an epistle that instructs a younger generation on the ways of the world, but is simultaneously intended for a broader audience, those whites complicit in maintaining a racially unjust order and in need of awakening.[27] This literary strategy and its implicit trope of black male endangerment is still evocative, and is guaranteed to gain the attention of whites yearning to hear authentic voices from behind the veil. As a means of social analysis, however, this approach is misleading.

Unlike the world that Baldwin inhabited, one where most blacks, regardless of class position, shared the same ascriptive status and daily indignities of legal segregation, both Coates's and Perry's works appear in a radically changed context. Their attempts to speak the voice of some common black experience inevitably flattens the actual situated-class experiences and heterogeneity of some 46 million African Americans in favor of sentimental commonalities and deceptive abstractions. As polemics, these works truncate the varied and diverse worries black parents actually experience, which are not reducible to fears of police violence and racist encounters but contain all manner of other real concerns. Even for those black working-poor parents whose children are more likely to experience police harassment and jail time than Coates's, Perry's or my own children, there are certainly other matters that consume their attention and cause tremendous anxiety on a day-to-day basis, such as securing a quality education, getting adequate medical attention when needed, finding a good job and gaining some measure of financial security. There are also other more pervasive, looming perils in society, such as automobile accidents, debilitating and terminal illnesses, urban violence, the travails of drug and alcohol addiction, mental health crises, domestic violence, and the like that are more common, more statistically probable than deadly police encounters, and likely to be of more central concern to black parents, especially those without adequate means to shield their children from life's turbulence, heartbreak and unexpected turns. Angie Schmitt, for instance, has revealed how the crisis of pedestrian fatalities affects the poor, people of color and immigrants disproportionately, but this issue has not attracted the same outrage and mass action as police killings, even though pedestrian fatalities far outnumber police killings in any given year.[28] The popular autobiographical essays on police violence by Perry, Coates and others may be emotionally resonant for some audiences, but they are not particularly helpful for understanding the problems of policing and mass incarceration. In addition to these popular expressions of Black Lives Matter sentiment, the manner in which most of us have become acquainted with each new case of police violence against black civilians also produces blind spots to actual demographic realities.

What these accounts get right is the persistence of racist assumptions about blacks as predators, cheats, welfare dependents and losers that permeate society, and how certain black bodies and "black" forms of self-presentation are read, evaluated, mistreated, discriminated against, feared and penalized in the company of strangers and familiars. Such racial encounters on both sides of the veil are not uniform, however, but are mediated by dress, mannerisms, speech, complexion, gender, sexuality, context, relative power and the social stakes of specific situations. Others may choose to do so, but there is no need to debate the fact of persistent and pervasive antiblack discrimination in contemporary US society, such as has been documented through test studies of hiring practices, showing that even "black-sounding" names of job applicants can lead to unfair treatment and consideration, or studies of consumer spaces like nightclubs that demonstrate how black men are routinely denied entry, or charged a higher rate than white patrons, even when wearing identical attire.

The carceral expansion and the underlying antiblack racism and antiurban prejudices that drove law-and-order policy have also produced a troubling increase in social policing and vigilante violence. While police may be granted the use of legitimate force, we have witnessed numerous incidents where vigilante violence against black civilians has been legitimated in court cases, often in states that permit liberal gun-ownership and expansive definitions of permissible civilian use of force. The most infamous case is the killing of black teen Trayvon Martin by a self-appointed neighborhood watchman. The racist fears and siege mentality that prompted George Zimmermann to stalk and kill an unarmed black teenager walking home from a convenience store are reflected in a succession of highly publicized incidents in which whites called the police to report and punish mundane activities and behaviors performed by blacks. A rash of social media memes—such as "BBQ Becky," "Permit Patty," "Golf Cart Gail" and "Corner Store Caroline"—arose in response to what many viewed as the unjust, racist surveillance of blacks in public and social settings.[29] In the midst of Black Lives Matter's second wave, the catch-all "Karen" emerged as a popular epithet hurled against white women who might surveil and police black behavior —so popular in fact, that Chicago mayor Lori Lightfoot dismissed White House press secretary Kayleigh McEnany as a "Karen" during a spat.

These instances of whites-policing-blacks, however, while perhaps analogous in some ways, are nevertheless not equivalent to the problem of policing, which is meted out in more targeted class terms while also mobilizing the power of the state. The prevalence of antiblack racism is too imprecise and limited to explain why particular segments of the black population are subject to routine police surveillance, arrest, prosecution and punishment. Nor does racism help us to understand why other groups —including indigenous people and persons with disabilities or mental health diagnoses—are killed at a higher per capita rate than blacks as a group.

Contemporary policing has a class character that is not reflected in viral videos, which only capture some police–civilian conflicts and are circulated through social media networks

governed by the standing assumptions and ideological predis-
positions of users and their social and psychological needs. These
videos often come at the expense of other evidence like national
Justice Department statistics, privately curated and publicly
accessible databases like the *Guardian*'s "The Counted" project,
the hundreds of annual police assaults and killings that are
not documented by cell-phone camera, and those that do not
conform to the New Jim Crow frame. In the age of social media
and viral videos, seeing is believing, but these cultural phenomena
further anti-intellectualism, and an unwillingness (perhaps for
some an incapacity) to see the social world as something that
must be actively, critically and endlessly studied if any understanding of it is to be reached. We can *see* the race of victims in
those videos that make their way into our social media feeds—
but Alton Sterling's situatedness in an underground economy is
essentially invisible. The blackness of the victims is most often
evocative and foregrounded by popular understandings of why
they were targeted. Their common position among the most
submerged elements of the working class is not as readily legible
for some audiences, however, nor is it a meaningful dimension
of the public discourse on these incidents that might render such
clarity. There is clearly a racial dimension to the contemporary
carceral state, but this reflects the composition of the working
class, whose most dispossessed segments are disproportionately
African American and Latino.

Some 70 million Americans have criminal records, roughly
equal to the number of Americans with baccalaureate degrees. As
Loïc Wacquant and others have noted, however, the term mass
incarceration misses the selective character of the carceral regime,
which is not genuinely "mass" in the same sense as mass consumption or mass culture, which are universally felt by the entire
population.[30] Wacquant offers the interrelated and more precise
terms *hyperghetto* and *hyper-incarceration* to make clear the
more class-intensive segregation of the mostly black and brown
urban poor—first abandoned through urban industrial decline
before and during the seventies and dispossessed by subsequent

neoliberalization and revanchist central city renewal—and how these subproletariats are the most heavily targeted by police and the most likely to be incarcerated.[31] In a similar vein, Brett Story critically engages the concept of the "million dollar block," which denotes the spatially concentrated origins of the nation's 2.3 million prisoners in a handful of dense urban neighborhoods that are the target of massive state investments in policing and incarceration.[32] These new historical conditions require a different analysis. While they may be critical to popular mobilization, accounts that approach carceral power as the "New Jim Crow" or police as "enemies of the working class" do not help us to understand the precise character of carceral power and its function within capitalism.

Underclass ideology can be deployed racially, but it would be incorrect to see it, as many have, as a "new cultural racism." Underclass ideology, crafted by liberal policymakers and academics and advanced to pernicious effect by antiwelfare neoconservatives, has created a tremendous amount of irrational fear, resentment and hatred towards the black urban poor, but, depending on how it is deployed and who its intended targets are, it is not solely an antiblack racist modality. Underclass ideology suffuses anti-Latino and anti-immigrant rhetoric. Latinos too are depicted as dishonest, criminal and undeserving—non-citizen moochers and "anchor baby makers" who take American jobs and resources illegally. Liberal condescension towards and moralizing about "white trash" and white working-class people, which has become a gleeful liberal blood sport in some election cycles, is also a species of the same genus. This form of class contempt is often articulated against the black urban poor, but it is also a product of new conjunctures, is deployed more broadly, and cannot be understood strictly in terms of racism.[33]

Paul J. Hirschfield's 2015 article "Lethal Policing: Making Sense of American Exceptionalism" takes us beyond the familiar antiracist framing of the problem to explore other, more complex sources of the United States' exceedingly high rate of police violence against civilians. Hirschfield readily acknowledges the racial dimensions of policing and police violence, noting that blacks and Latinos who are killed by police are more likely than whites to be unarmed. His explanation of why the US rates of police violence against civilians eclipse those of Canada, Australia, the United Kingdom and other nations focuses on cultural particularities of the United States. Relying on a national database of policing killings spanning January 2013 to early May 2015, Hirschfield contends that the "elevated rates of police killings are rooted in American-style individualism that emphasizes self-reliance and such corollary values as decentralized government (i.e., self-rule) and individual moral responsibility."[34] For Hirschfield, American gun culture, the mythologized rugged individualism of the country's western frontier, racialized fears and the relatively autonomous and decentralized character of local police departments create a context ripe for police violence. "In gun culture, police are precariously primed for the possibility that suspects are packing," Hirschfield writes. "Thus, American police have killed people after allegedly mistaking such objects as wallets, phones, candy bars, spray nozzles, and Wii remotes for guns. In the United States, it is legally (and culturally?) deemed 'reasonable' for police to kill people ... because hesitation in the event that the threat is real could prove fatal to the officer."[35] This part of his argument is supported by dozens of other analyses that ground the expansion of policing and mass incarceration in the processes of neoliberalization. Hirschfield concludes that "the American ideals of self-reliance, local governance, and individual moral responsibility and the many echoes of Jim Crow, created a peculiar dialectic whereby certain expansive, violent, and oppressive state-sponsored institutions (slavery, prisons, policing) and policies have compensated for weakened state sponsorship and governance in other domains (e.g., income supports and mental health)."[36] Policing has come to serve the function of a vanished social welfare state; as Hirschfield points out, of those killed by police in 2015, at least 27 percent exhibited some mental health distress and symptoms, according to family, friends and responding officers. Equally disturbing, Hirschfield notes that the way in which modern policing has evolved from a form of political patronage to a professional occupation has had the effect of transferring power from legislators to the police themselves, their unions, think tanks, professional organizations and career administrators. Hence, lawmakers may develop laws governing the use of lethal force, but bureaucratic rulemaking and discretion mean that police departments have an enlarged role in determining how such laws will be implemented.

Hirschfield's arguments are alluring and provide a better alternative to a one-note analysis that reduces the problems of overpolicing and mass incarceration to racism. That said, the cultural traits he discusses are not eternal features of American life, but social phenomena that need to be historicized. Popular fears regarding crime, racist perceptions about black criminality, the prevalence of firearms and the expansion of liberal gun laws, and the Wild West–style individualism that pervades contemporary US society are artifacts of the transformation of American urbanism through decades of suburbanization and fiscal abandonment of central cities, as well as the privatization of public goods, the dismantling of social welfare state and the active promotion of market rule.

Some might view these more complex sources of police violence —gun culture, decentralization and bureaucratic rulemaking, austerity and the rollback of social democracy and so forth—as simply an evasion of making a strong ethical claim against racial injustice as the core problem. They should not. Understanding these actually existing historical processes and social relations should be seen as necessary for building a broader and potentially more powerful coalition capable of producing a different social order, one that is not predicated on containment and repression for the sake of market freedom, but on emancipation and self-determination in a society organized around use value rather than profit-making for the few. We should think through these complex social realities and develop analyses of the root causes of the current crisis that do not limit themselves to the historical realities of Jim Crow segregation.

Although the regime of policing was anchored in the criminalization of the black and brown poor, the discrete force of policing and the demography of incarceration were more widely felt, especially in those small towns and rural areas that were excluded from prevailing media narratives of urban dystopia and the loss of the city to dark hordes. The victims of police killings in rural America closely resemble urban victims in many vital respects. They are predominantly men, often armed, and the majority were struggling with drug addiction or a mental health crisis at the time of the incident.[37] Those optics also obscure the fact that white drug usage and white poverty, in raw numbers, has always exceeded that of blacks and Latinos. The opioid crisis, the latest of successive epidemics in the War on Drugs, highlighted the fact of both poverty and informality among white Americans. There has always been the potential for building a broad movement to roll back the carceral state, but too often the racial justice frame—whether in the mold of the racial profiling techniques introduced to police cadet trainees or that of the antiracist politics animating Black Lives Matter protests—has not provided the unifying language to encompass the broad experiences of those who shoulder the greatest weight of the carceral regime. Adding to this lack of broad rallying slogans, most shootings of working-class whites occur in more isolated places where police bodycams are not mandatory, there is no video evidence of the confrontation, and often the stigma of addiction or mental health prevents families and advocates from contesting local authorities, especially in jurisdictions where social relations are close-knit and intimate.[38] There is growing evidence too that the more intensive policing of the informal trade in prescription medications has led to increased incarceration rates of white men, especially in rural areas and less populous states.[39] Rather than a movement focused singularly on mitigating racial disparities within the criminal justice system, what is needed, as some activists have argued, are broad-based policy campaigns that transgress the geopolitical and mental boundaries produced by the postwar economic boom, a politics that lays bare the class impetus for contemporary policing as the management of surplus populations within the context of high technology capitalism.

The New Jim Crow sensibility neglects recent and well-publicized trends in carceral demography, changes that further erode the claim that the carceral expansion of the last four decades was primarily driven by racial disparity in antidrug policy. As Marie Gottschalk argues, the shifting carceral geography of the American countryside has produced both "potential roadblocks but also potential opportunities to forge successful urban-rural coalitions to raze the carceral state and challenge other widening political and economic inequalities in the United States."[40] In recent years, the risks of going to prison have risen faster for Latinos and white males than for African Americans. Contrary to popular perceptions, this change has been even more pronounced for working-class white men. The risk of imprisonment for black and Latino male high school dropouts born in the late seventies was five times higher than for their counterparts born in the late forties. For white male college dropouts, the same risk was seven times higher than for their predecessors.[41] Between 2000 and 2015, the black male incarceration rate dropped by more than 24 percent, while rates for white men climbed slightly.[42] During the same period, the incarceration rate for black women declined by nearly 50 percent, while the inverse was true for white women, who experienced a 53 percent increase. In a sense, the declines in incarceration rates among blacks might be read as progress on the racial justice front, perhaps a consequence of the sharpening public debate and the growing intensity of local and state-level organizing. At the same time, such changes are a reminder that the carceral state's underlying motives are not fully captured in slogans like the "New Jim Crow" or "Black Lives Matter."

The focus on racial disparities only provides a narrow window on the carceral crisis, and, more crucially, offers an unnecessarily narrow path forward to deep progressive changes. That is a window that we are familiar with, it connects rather easily to liberal interpretations of American society and organizing strategies that survived the Cold War, when other modes of working-class analysis and social action were criminalized and eviscerated. Shifting our attention to the problem of relative surplus population allows us to see the connections between, say, the plight of black teenagers from Chicago's "wild hundreds" arrested for their part in a "flash mob" robbery of a Magnificent Mile clothing store, and that of a white middle-aged mother, her son and his live-in girlfriend who are arrested for selling Oxy-Contin in their small town in Southern Missouri.

Capitalist Class Interests and Policing

The growth, formalization and professionalization of police power in the United States developed in tandem with urban industrialization and the increased power of the mass worker. In more recent times, law enforcement's militarization and capacity for lethality has intensified in the post–welfare state context. Policing is not merely about upholding or enforcing the law, but like other executive bureaucracies has a quasi-legislative function, determining the precise meaning of the law in concrete practice and daily interpretation. Policing plays a deeply ideological role in society, actively drawing the boundaries of permissible social and political behavior through the exercise of legitimate violence. As Mark Neocleous argues, police, "along with equally fetishised sister concepts of 'order,' 'security' and 'law,' is a central category in the self-understanding of bourgeois society." Furthermore, he contends, "policing has been central not just to the repression of the working class and the reproduction of order, but to the *fabrication of order* ... as order became increasingly based on the bourgeois mode of production, so the police mandate was to fabricate an order of wage labour and administration of the class of poverty."[43]

The scale, technological capacity and historical role of policing has evolved according to the process and state of class struggle. As Sidney Harring warns, against instrumentalist Marxist views of the state, capitalist class power is never absolute, nor is its

control over the state apparatus and policing. "This kind of simplistic analysis negates the role of any other class in the process of
class struggle and denies the true nature of that process," Harring
writes; "it is a *struggle*, with continual victories and losses and
with continual adjustments to keep the capitalist system functioning in the face of these changes."[44] What it means to secure the
conditions for capital accumulation is conjunctural, calibrated to
broad social needs, patterns of consumption and opportunities
for profit-making, and shifting across time and space as different
blocs of capital achieve dominance and as the same powerful
forces adjust to that most "peculiar commodity," labor power,
and to the recurring struggles of workers and popular forces to
impose limits on capital's power over their lives. Though taking
on different historical forms, policing is central to the processes
of accumulation by dispossession, enclosure, criminalization and
discipline of the working class, and the repression of worker self-
activity and rebellion.

Police are central to the ongoing process of accumulation by dispossession. Marx referred to the historical processes of enclosure
—the seizure of the commons, e.g., forests, grazing lands and
streams available for fishing, hunting, gathering, firewood, water
sources, etc., and hence the removal of a vital source of subsistence for the peasantry—as a moment of primitive accumulation.
"This primitive accumulation plays approximately the same
role in political economy," Marx argues, "as original sin does
in theology."[45] Capital was made available through this process
of forceful removal and privatization, a history "written in the
annals of mankind in letters of blood and fire." The disruption
of communal practices transformed the commons into property,
nature into raw materials, and peasants and yeoman into wage
laborers. David Harvey has offered the term "accumulation by
dispossession," because what Marx describes in terms of primary
accumulation is not simply the originary stage of capitalist development, but rather a central recurring dimension of capitalism as
an historical process. "The state, with its monopoly of violence
and definitions of legality," Harvey makes clear, "plays a crucial

role in both backing and promoting this process."[46] State violence played a central role, Marx writes, in "the forcible creation of a class of free and rightless proletarians, the bloody discipline that turned them into wage-labourers, the disgraceful proceedings of the state which employed police methods to accelerate the accumulation of capital by increasing the degree of exploitation of labour."[47] The continual destruction of the bases of working-class autonomy—whether in the form of non-commodified means of basic subsistence, public goods and services, mutual aid associations, unions and other institutions of worker self-assertion—has been central to the process of capital accumulation from the earliest expropriation of the commons and the forceful evictions of tenant farmers, to the conquest of indigenous peoples and the obliteration of precolonial systems of land tenure, through to the rounds of mass evictions and assaults on the social wage in our own times.

Contrary to prevailing liberal antiracist sentiments, the enslaved were exploited as workers, and the regulation of black life by slave catchers and later urban police departments has been part of the broader process of regulating labor for the benefit of capitalist class interests, whether of planters or industrialists. One result of the renaissance of strident antiracist politics is the popularization of a *rummage sale approach* to historical interpretation, where the historical record is something to be picked over in search of whatever artifacts and remainders satisfy our contemporary needs, immediate preoccupations and personal fancies. Ahistorical appreciations of historical processes are rife. This approach has been fueled by a broader cultural backlash against science and the virtue of scholarly investigation and expertise, a development that has produced the viral spread of conspiracies and crackpot theories. The belief that American policing has its roots in slavery has become an unquestioned truth in activist and academic circles. In a similar vein, popular culture has done its part in promoting the view that racial disparities and racism have always been at the heart of American policing. Ava Duvernay's popular documentary film *13th* develops the claim that mass incarceration originates in the 13th Amendment's exception clause, which permits slavery and forced servitude as punishment for a crime.[48] Cameos by scholars like Jelani Cobb, Khalil Gibran Muhammad and Angela Davis aid and abet the documentary's ahistorical premise, even as the film's most substantive discussions emphasize the unique social conditions and political forces of the Reagan–Bush years as the context of carceral expansion. In the same vein, Nikhil Pal Singh writes of the "whiteness of police" as an enduring problem woven into the fabric of the American republic. Singh contends that "the ongoing racial differentiation of society over several centuries—which now includes accretive rejections of formal, legal racial ascription beginning in the second half of the twentieth century—has been continuously remade as the quasi-democratic counterpart to publicly sanctioned private accumulation and the social costs, divisions, and crises that it engenders."[49] In asserting the "ongoing racial differentiation of society over several centuries," Singh rehearses a common maneuver in contemporary discussions of race in the United States—the tendency to treat racial hierarchy as a foundational aspect of US society. This is a powerful moral claim, one that evokes and leverages well-known racial injustices, but it is less helpful as social theory, does damage to our understandings of historical processes, and says little about the particular historical conjunctures responsible for the contemporary carceral infrastructure. Such accounts work well as a form of moral denunciation, but not as persuasive analyses of actually existing historical conditions nor as serious attempts to change our world.

Slave patrols were certainly part of the broader landscape of carceral technology in colonial and antebellum America, but we should not overstate their centrality or the racist element in the country's carceral beginnings. Rather, slave patrols were one form of the emerging social control of different laboring classes, part of a broader national context where urban policing was also taking shape, and where vigilante and mob justice were regularly meted out against lumpen whites.[50] Predating the first documented slave patrol, nightwatch patrols had been organized in American colonial cities and towns to address petty crimes, provide fire prevention, and give protection against wild animals. Boston established the first nightwatch patrol in 1636. New York followed in 1658 and Philadelphia in 1700.[51] All of these forerunners of standing police departments originated before the first slave patrol in 1704.

Beginning in the mid-nineteenth century and through World War I, permanent police forces were raised throughout the United States and employed to secure the interests of the ruling classes. Prior to that, municipal governance in the country had been relatively small in terms of power and responsibilities, with many functions like policing undertaken by private militia (by no means necessarily a preferable arrangement). The first modern constabulary was born in London in 1829. In Jacksonian America, however, some publics resisted the importation of this model out of fear a "standing army" might threaten civil liberties; the result was a largely privatized force of paid police, slave patrols, nightwatchmen, and at times mobs who meted out frontier justice. Waves of urban riots, along with escalating gang warfare and mobbing throughout the 1830s and 1840s, shaped the formation of the first US professional police forces. Christian Parenti notes that much of this violence had racial and political overtones, often instigated by partisans and machine functionaries.[52] New Orleans created the first full-time civilian patrol, and Boston and Philadelphia soon followed, but these patrols were unarmed and not uniformed.[53] New York City would create the first regimented, armed, "London-style" police force in 1845.[54] It is also worth noting that securing the power of the police—not abolishing them as a transhistorical institution of white supremacy—was a key goal of the day's leading advocates of racial equality. The Reconstruction-era Metropolitan Police in New Orleans were instrumental in beating back multiple white supremacist insurrections after the Civil War. Similarly, across the South, the most radical of African American Republicans sought and won election to sheriff's offices with the purpose of maintaining interracial equality and black civil rights.

During the tumultuous process of industrial urbanization, Sidney Harring reminds us, the "city emerged as a great reservoir of workers ... American cities became great slums as immigrants crowded into cheaply built apartment houses and tract housing ... Slums radiated outward from the factory districts, forcing workers to commute long distances to work and providing huge profits to private streetcar companies."[55] Consequentially, the advent of police power represented "an enormous extension of the power of the bourgeoisie and one that is absolutely necessary."[56] The industrializing cities of nineteenth-century America were characterized by a very visible and palpable class terrain. As Harring explains: "Whole sections of the city were off limits to members of some classes, either informally through fear, or semi-officially, as police picked up and questioned strangers. Notions about class society that may seem abstract now were concrete and obvious in the late-nineteenth-century industrial city."[57] Waves of urban immigration from foreign shores and domestic hinterlands intensified class distinctions and ethnic conflicts, and the presence of strangers made crimes of anonymity like mugging and theft more prevalent in rapidly expanding cities, all justifying the need for standing police departments to maintain order.

At times police played the role of personal escorts for the wealthy, or guardians protecting wealthy estates and recovering stolen merchandise. In concert with various religious institutions, the Temperance movement and other social reformers, police disciplined working-class behaviors that were at odds with the specific needs of industrial interests as well as the broader mores of bourgeois social ideology. Drunks were rounded up and detained so they might dry out. Various states and local jurisdictions sought to discourage idleness through laws against vagabondage, vagrancy, truancy, tramping and loitering. The task set before the newly formed city police forces was perpetual and impossible: to regulate living labor and maintain the conditions for its exploitation. As the young Friedrich Engels remarked on the role of police power in managing class antagonisms in industrial Manchester during the mid-nineteenth century, police regulations were "as plentiful as blackberries; but they can only hedge the distress of the workers, they cannot remove it."[58]

Throughout the final decades of the nineteenth century and into the twentieth, police in conjunction with private forces like Pinkertons, the American Legion and hired thugs brutally repressed workers whenever they attempted to demand better conditions and wages and more autonomy over their working lives. In addition to the well-known pivotal battles such as the 1886 Haymarket bombing, the 1894 Pullman strike, the 1912 Lawrence Textile strike and the 1913 Paterson silk workers strike, as many as 57,000 strikes were waged across the nation's industrial towns and cities in the mere quarter century between 1889 and 1915. Overall, police clashes with workers at the turn of the twentieth century accounted for some 300 documented deaths and countless more injuries. The violence did not end once the strikes were over; working-class leaders were often arrested, brought to trial, imprisoned and, most infamously following Haymarket, executed.[59]

Contemporary historiographers and antiracist commentators on policing and prisons have tended to view black experiences of these institutions as separate and sociologically distinct from that of the broader laboring classes. Historian Khalil Gibran Muhammad offers a meticulous account of how thinking about race and criminality evolved during the black southern peasantry's formative mass migration and urbanization, exploring "how ideas of racial inferiority and crime became fastened to African Americans by contrast to ideas of class and crime that shaped views of European immigrants and working-class whites." Muhammad declares in the opening pages of his book *The Condemnation of Blackness* that the "link between race and crime is as enduring and influential in the twenty-first century as it had been in the past," drawing an explicit linkage between contemporary carceral power and the longer history of race and punishment. "By the same token," he continues, "white crime statistics are virtually invisible, except when used to dramatize the excessive criminality of African Americans." "White criminality gradually lost its fearsomeness," Muhammad claims, going on to ask "how did European immigrants—the Irish and the Italians and the Polish, for example—gradually shed their criminal identities while blacks did not?"[60]

Muhammad's arguments regarding how racial criminalization took shape during the primary wave of black southern migration seem straightforward enough. His analysis is strongest as an antidote to racist claims that black crime and incarceration are rooted in some racially specific traits, either the biological differences advanced by eugenicists and white supremacists, or the alleged cultural dysfunction and social pathology of the black poor touted by Cold War liberals, the New Right and New Democratic partisans alike. Despite such merits, however, there are problems with Muhammad's analysis. His work evokes class at times, only to diminish its historical importance, settling on what is basically the old ethnic group assimilation account of twentieth-century America, an interpretation that neglects the fact of interracialism in industrial unionism, social life and politics. His thoroughly researched treatment also manages to be both historically nuanced and yet faithful to the prevailing metanarrative of racial oppression favored by the whiteness and critical race studies tendencies he aligns with; as such, his book legitimates contemporary ahistorical and anti-intellectual understandings of the origins and motives of the carceral state today.

Muhammad's arguments overstate how well and by what means ethnic whites were able to shed the cultural stigma of dysfunction and criminality and assimilate into American life. Many white ethnics became middle class and wealthy through the favorable policy context and economic conditions of the postwar era, but such success was not universal and did not result in the wholesale abolition of pejorative stereotypes and ethnic myths. Many carried this stigma with them into suburbia. Recall the protests by various Italian-American organizations after the 1972 film adaptation of Mario Puzo's *The Godfather*.[61] Such widely accepted notions regarding Italian involvement in organized crime persist even into our own times. Moreover, the war against the mafia endured for decades and was the intensive focus of the FBI, local police departments, regional task forces, district attorneys and the federal Justice Department. Muhammad's claims also do not square with the actual demographic composition of American prisons for most of the twentieth century, where whites remained the majority of the incarcerated population during and after the time frame his study addresses. In 1948 and 1949, 70 percent of all prisoners in state and federal prisons in the United States were white.[62] Even when Ronald Reagan made his successful presidential run in 1980, whites still constituted 58 percent of the prison population. Between the 1920s and 1980s, the proportion of black inmates would more than double, from 21 percent to 44 percent, but the sources of that expansion have more to do with the postwar transformation of American cities, characterized by new regimes of capital accumulation and residential segregation made possible through federal policies of suburban expansion and urban renewal.

There is little room for politics in Muhammad's and similar accounts that reduce complex historical motives and interests to the affects and consequences of racial stratification. "The idea of black criminality was crucial to the making of modern urban America," Muhammad writes. "In nearly every sphere of life it impacted how people defined fundamental differences between native whites, immigrants and blacks. It also impacted, by comparison, how people valued black people's presence—the Negro Problem, as it was once called—in the urban North."[63] "Native whites and immigrants," Muhammad concludes, "were much more likely to benefit directly from the most thoughtful and forward-thinking (or progressive) social work and social science during the early twentieth century."[64] In broad outline such claims are of course true, but the conclusions drawn about the power of racist ideology take us only part of the way towards understanding twentieth-century punishment, and, perhaps unintentionally, they lend credence to errant and ahistorical arguments spawned by Black Lives Matter fervor. Racist criminalization of blacks alone does not explain the disproportionate incarceration rates of blacks during the Jim Crow era, and certainly not after. As others have noted, blacks were more likely to be the victims *and* perpetrators of violent crime, in particular homicides, throughout most of the twentieth century and especially during the post-segregation crime spikes that were concentrated in majority-minority cities.[65] During the Jim Crow period, black communities suffered from the particular affliction of urban crimes such as robbery, born out of the material desperation and cloak of anonymity the city provides the assailant. Though they faced high crime rates, those same communities suffered from the neglect and lack of police service, a peculiar fact of black urban life that seems strange in the latter-day context of the overpolicing of black communities. The racial demography of crime and the discrete historical conditions that produced the carceral regime of today need to be explained historically, sociologically and critically. The metanarrative of racial oppression does not accomplish those ends. Instead, such accounts perpetuate the errant practice of using race as a shorthand for class: because black people represent a disproportionate percentage of the working class and poor, race becomes an analytic proxy for processes that can only be effectively understood in terms of class. This interpretative move has its roots in the postwar urban transformation and continues to foster confusion about American life and politics.

Policing Surplus Population

Policing in the United States since World War II has not been trained against the broad population or against organized workers as it was during earlier more intensive episodes of capital-labor conflict; rather, its immense technological capabilities and resources are focused on the regulation of *relative surplus population*.[66] Thinking about contemporary policing and mass incarceration in terms of surplus population helps us to name more precisely those who are regularly surveilled and harassed by police, and who are the most likely to have their lives determined by the long reach of the carceral state. Unlike the New Jim Crow framing, discussing relative surplus population focuses our attention on which portions of the black population are most likely to be subject to intensive surveillance and policing. Recall that many of the most well-known victims of police killings either lived in neighborhoods that are heavily policed or were targeted for engaging in criminalized, informal commerce, e.g., Freddie Gray (petty drug sales), Alton Sterling (sale of used and pirated CDs), Eric Garner (sale of "loosies," or individual cigarettes sold after purchase). Although many blacks experience discriminatory profiling in policing practices and in retail consumer contexts, class is a much more powerful determinant of who is most likely to experience particularly fraught and regular police encounters, and of who is routinely arrested, assigned a public defender, convicted, sentenced and incarcerated.[67]

Marx develops the interchangeable notions of relative surplus population and the reserve army of the unemployed to explain how unemployment and the threat of wagelessness are advantageous to capital. Class relations exist in historical motion, and the reserve army represents a relative, contingent condition of the working class, rather than a durable, ascriptive status. Marx described four fluid layers of the reserve army: a *floating* reserve of the temporarily employed; a *latent* segment made up of those not actively looking for work, but who may be mobilized to meet capital's shifting valorization requirements; a *stagnant* portion of those with "extremely irregular" employment; and lastly, the sphere of *pauperism*, which is the "hospital of the active labour-army and the dead weight of the industrial reserve army."[68] At the very bottom of this reserve is the *lumpenproletariat*, most often translated as the proletariat in rags. In their earlier writings, both Marx and Engels saw this stratum as a danger to working class. The lumpenproletariat lacked class consciousness, and, because of their desperation, were easily mobilized by bosses against other workers. This surplus population is, however, not fixed, its size and composition varying relative to the dictates of capital's need for living labor.

In Marx's typology, the size of the surplus population always exercises downward pressure on the wages of those employed. Likewise, the presence of those who are willing to do more work for less, out of starvation, exacerbates the social divisions within the laboring classes, such as differences of ethnicity or immigration status. And when those working assert themselves against the dictates of bosses and rulers, the ranks of the unemployed and idle provide a reservoir of strikebreakers, saboteurs and hired guns. The incessant technological development of the means of production, in ways that heighten efficiency, secures a greater proportion of surplus value and reduces the need for living labor, further compounding these tensions within the working class to capital's advantage. "In proportion as capital accumulates, the situation of the worker, be his payment high or low, must grow worse," Marx notes; "the law which always holds the relative surplus population or industrial reserve army in equilibrium with the extent and energy of accumulation rivets the worker to capital more firmly than the wedges of Hephaestus held Prometheus to the rock."[69]

Surplus populations, however, and in particular the so-called lumpenproletariat, come to play a different role in the story of mass incarceration and policing as we know it. Whereas in Marx's day these "dangerous classes" were a threat to the working class more broadly, within the context of the post–World War II United States, surplus populations are a real threat to the ideological hegemony of the liberal democratic order, with its promises of unlimited individual freedom and prosperity. Likewise, in an odd historical twist, their fight to survive poses a threat to those segments of the working class who no longer see themselves as working class but as middle-class, entrepreneurial, property-owning and deeply implicated in the maintenance of American empire. Subsequent chapters examine and discuss these emerging class contradictions after World War II, and how policing evolved as a primary solution to the effects of the ongoing dismantlement of New Deal social democracy.

This book situates the emergence of policing as we know it within the New Deal political compromise between labor and capital intended to generate stability and secure the basic conditions for mass consumer capitalism, and the postwar urban revanchist transformation that reoriented the terms of that compromise more forcefully around real estate and infrastructural development, defense contracting and metropolitan spatial expansion. This had the combined effect of transforming class relations, productive forces and class consciousness in ways that entrenched capitalist class power. "The incorporation of the industrial union movement into the national process of political organizing and into a more cooperative relationship via collective bargaining with monopoly capital, the resulting ideological consensus for capitalist rule, and the unchallenged political hegemony of monopoly capital," Rhonda Levine concludes, "all combined to produce the conditions for a new phase of capitalist development."[70] This transformation was not immediate, however; as some historians have noted, the passage of the Wagner Act in 1935 spawned an unprecedented wave of labor organizing across the country.[71] Moreover, strike activity persisted throughout World War II and after. Indeed, in 1952, a higher percentage of the workforce went out on strike than in any year before or since. The more decisive clamping down on labor militancy would take shape during the postwar years, with the active state persecution of trade union militants and communists, the passage of pro-capitalist labor laws and the suburbanization and embourgeoisement of large portions of the industrial working class all combining to secure popular consent for capitalist development. Though still presided over by New Deal Democrats, this postwar growth regime might be more accurately characterized as commercial Keynesian in orientation, in that collective bargaining rights and federally funded and managed public works—the most social democratic manifestations of the Roosevelt years—were respectively weakened and shelved in favor of the state financing and subsidization of corporate economic development. The boom and slow bust of the Fordist-Keynesian economy during the postwar years saw a corresponding transformation in policing, giving rise to the carceral regime we know today.

In terms of periodicity, this work joins others in locating the origins of mass incarceration in the social and political volatility of the sixties. Such works have linked the expansion of policing and mass incarceration to the liberal policy failings of the collapsing New Deal coalition, the racist backlash against civil rights reforms and the "law-and order" panic that followed urban rebellions, and the counterinsurgency that marshalled federal and state police power to destroy black movements.[72] This body of scholarship provides a wealth of insights, but generally these works neglect the implications of the postwar expansion of the consumer society, the interconnected processes of embourgeoisement and suburbanization, the intensification of productive forces and the resulting urban decline and deindustrialization. Rather than anchoring the carceral turn within these changes in productive relations, capitalist culture and class politics, however, these authors (like so much of the literature on policing and mass incarceration) focus on segregation and racism, but too often in a manner that does not take seriously the Second Reconstruction and its consequences for the transformation of black life, particularly in terms of class composition and political integration.

Within the US context, the expansion of the consumer society and of middle-class prosperity, the suburbanization of American cities and the resegregation of urban space, and the merging of popular aspirations and material interests with those of American imperialism, all marked the beginning of profound shifts within the institution of policing. In this context of class recomposition and more expansive mass cultural and public relations apparatuses, policing came to take on both repressive and ideological roles depending on its interface with different segments of the public. Rather than "enemies of the working class," police served as guardians and role models of civic virtue for tens of millions of the middle classes and their aspirants—white and black alike—while existing as an "occupying army" in relation to those segregated from the affluent society. Contemporary policing evolved to achieve several connected economic and social ends simultaneously: securing the conditions for perpetual accumulation; soothing middle-class anxieties regarding property crime, urban violence and perceived threats to their relative class position; and managing surplus population, the ranks of the poor and unemployed who were only nominally integrated into the consumer society.

In the broader literature on the postwar roots of mass incarceration, Jordan Camp's work is most kindred with my own, and shares an affinity for the conjunctural analysis of Stuart Hall, Chas Critcher, Tony Jefferson, John Clarke and Brian Roberts' classic work, *Policing the Crisis*. There are, however, two limitations of Camp's account of the origins of mass incarceration that this book seeks to redress. Both entail moments where his attempt to center racial justice as an interpretative and political commitment undermines the goals of conjunctural analysis. As Hall once wrote, conjunctural analysis requires "facing the things as they exist, not as you'd like them to be, not as you think they were ten years ago, not as they're written about in sacred texts, but as they really are: the contradictory, stony ground of the present conjuncture."[73]

First, Camp sees the brutal repression of black movements during the sixties and seventies as central to the genesis of mass incarceration, but this position flattens the contradictory role that police played for and against civil rights and Black Power struggles, and excludes other contemporary sources of police expansion during the postwar period. "The long civil rights movement against Jim Crow racial regimes represented a crisis of legitimacy for US capital and the state," Camp writes; "capital and the state responded to struggles from below with mass criminalization."[74] The tremendous powers of the FBI and local police were used to surveil, infiltrate, harass, blackmail, arrest, imprison and murder labor leaders, black activists throughout the civil rights and Black Power movements. And yet at the same time, police power was mobilized at critical junctures, often through White House executive orders, to pry open the doors of segregated schools, ballot boxes and public accommodations, and against southern politicians, state and local law enforcement agencies, hooded vigilantes and wild-eyed white mobs. The role of law enforcement during the "long civil rights movement" was decidedly more contradictory than the focus on black repression allows.

In part, Camp is right to situate the roots of modern policing in the broader context of Cold War ideological preoccupations and capitalist interests. Indeed, black intellectuals throughout the sixties offered some of the most damning criticisms of police power and made clear the shifting focus of domestic policing from the working class more broadly to the black urban subproletariat in particular. California was home to "the largest prison system in world," as prison intellectual and martyr George Jackson once put it, and black radical Californians offered pioneering analyses of the role of police in managing urban surplus populations. The Black Panthers were repressed for their attempts to mobilize the urban subproletariat. Their willingness to align with Third World socialist regimes and revolutionary struggles also revealed the more expansive coordination and intelligence-sharing between local and national law enforcement agencies. Whereas Marx and Engels saw the lumpen as "bribed tools of reactionary intrigue," the Panthers valorized the unemployed, underemployed and underpaid blacks they encountered in the pool halls and on street corners across the nation as a revolutionary vanguard. The Panthers saw the lumpenproletariat as potentially revolutionary, because unlike the growing numbers of Americans who could now afford suburban homes and middle-class lifestyles, this most submerged segment of the working class was banished to inner-city ghettos, failing schools, inadequate housing, dead-end jobs or wageless life, and police harassment. Hence, their material conditions made them seem ripe for rebellion.[75] It is not surprising, then, that in their efforts to win an armed stand-off with the Panthers, the LAPD used its pioneering Special Weapons and Tactics Unit (SWAT) for the first time. In ensuing decades SWAT units would become a fixture in metropolitan and even small-town police departments. That all being said, Camp's contention that state repression of black movements catalyzed the carceral expansion truncates too much postwar history and produces a narrative that centers racial conflict at the expense of other conjunctural elements.

During the postwar years, police power was marshalled in other consequential ways beyond the repression of black political struggles, and against other perceived threats to the affluent society. In particular, campaigns against organized crime and the regulation of vice districts were priorities for numerous big city police departments, as part of the broader agenda of remaking the city for investment through federal urban renewal. Likewise, while Camp rightly asserts that "class anxieties produced by capitalist restructuring were transformed into racist consent to security, law and order," his account seems to lose sight of the fact of real crime, its pernicious consequences for minority working-class neighborhoods and urban living more generally during the seventies and eighties, and how this propelled the municipal and state-level criminal justice policies that would drive the prison expansion. Crime was not simply the stuff of white nightmares and racial panic but also a grim fact of daily life for millions of city dwellers during the long winter of urban fiscal abandonment and manufacturing decline.

Second, and perhaps more problematic, even as he rightly rejects the New Jim Crow account of mass incarceration's origins, Camp's commitment to historical-materialist analysis falters in regard to illuminating the complexity of black political life and the dramatic consequences of the Second Reconstruction. His use of phrases like "Black freedom movements," "neoliberal racial and security regimes" and "racialized crisis management," and his preference for historiography constructed around canonical black figures and heroic struggles, undermine keen attention not only to the shifting political positions, material interests and felt needs animating black life in real time and space, but also to the profound impact of major civil rights reforms, which produced unthinkable progress and new unforeseen social contradictions within post-segregation black life. Camp is not alone here, and we can find similar problems of vindicationism and difficulty in reckoning with the full spectrum of black political life and all its contradictions within the broader literatures on the "long civil rights movement" his book channels. Likewise, Camp draws on an often-cited passage from Hall and company's *Policing the Crisis*—"Race is the modality in which class is lived"—that is too often decontextualized, and in a manner that forgets the spirit of the authors' structural analysis of industrial labor in postwar Britain, the historical particularities of the national terrain they sought to understand, and, most importantly, the uniqueness of the United States (not as exceptional but as a distinct national context) during the same period. There are certainly immediate parallels between the rise of law-and-order panics on both sides of the Atlantic, but there are also marked differences that are lost in Camp's account—and, for that matter, in Hall's original analysis—as it pertains to US black life.

Stuart Hall and his students at the Birmingham Centre for Contemporary Cultural Studies argued that ruling elites reached for policing and the cultural politics of moral panic and scape-goating of the black urban poor in order to resolve the organic crisis of capitalism. By the seventies, the postwar boom had run aground, and the ideological promise of perpetual compound growth was met with countercultural rebellion, as different social layers rejected the vapidity of the consumer society. Hall and his collaborators referred to the expansion of the repressive state apparatus, which accompanied the repeated assaults on the social wage, unions and other bases of working-class power, as *authoritarian populism*—a repressive regime distinguished from fascism by the retention of formal representative democratic institutions and the capacity to produce active consent.[76]

The closing chapter of *Policing the Crisis* offered a pioneering analysis of black British labor and the structural contradictions of class recomposition in Britain during the seventies. Hall and his Birmingham colleagues' analysis centered on the peculiar predicament of the "Windrush generation." Those black British communities formed out of the postwar migration from the commonwealth, who constituted "an *ethnically distinct class fraction* —the one *most exposed* to the winds of unemployment," provided an easy scapegoat for popular anxieties about moral decay. Such communities were set apart from the circular migrations of "guest workers"—surplus labor drawn from the Mediterranean rim and Northern Africa to meet the valorization requirements of capitalist Europe. Whereas capital bore little responsibility for the reproduction of these itinerant workers, Britain shouldered the costs of its citizens and permanent residents, including those black migrants who chose to settle, putting down roots in its industrial cities. Formative conflicts between migrant men and local whites, often over sexual and social integration at dancehalls and social gatherings, gave way to more intensive xenophobia as the ranks of black settlements swelled when families immigrated to join male migrant laborers. For Hall, however, this was not merely a problem of discrimination. "What we are dealing with here is a structural feature of modern capital," Hall and his collaborators wrote, "and the pivotal role which black labour now plays in the metropoles of capital in a major phase of its recomposition."[77] Such black immigrant communities were hyper-exploited and ghettoized, and their relative participation in criminal activity for survival was seized upon by the right, who blamed black immigrants for rising crime and urban decline.

For Hall and his collaborators, "the strategic and structural position of race" was critically important for understanding the turn to authoritarian populism during the seventies, and equally for devising a plan for left political revitalization and working-class unity.

> Race enters into the way black labour, male and female, is distributed as economic agents on the level of economic practice—and the class struggles which result from it; into the way the fractions of the black labouring class are constituted as a set of political

forces in the "theatre of politics"—and the political struggle which results; and in the manner in which that class is articulated as the collective and individual "subjects" of emergent ideologies and forms of consciousness—and the struggle over ideology, culture and consciousness which results.[78]

This, Hall and his collaborators asserted, "gives the matter of race and racism a theoretical as well as practical centrality to all the relations and practices which affect black labour. The constitution of this class fraction as a class, and the class relations which inscribe it, function as race relations. The two are inseparable. Race is the modality in which class is lived. It is also the medium in which class relations are experienced."[79] While this "does not immediately heal any breaches or bridge any chasms," they caution, "it has consequences for the whole class, whose relation to their conditions of existence is now systematically transformed by race. It determines some of the modes of struggle. It also provides one of the criteria by which we measure the adequacy of struggle to the structures it aims to transform."[80] This fuller "race is the modality" passage is worth recalling because it reveals the authors' political Marxism, their appreciation of the power that structural forces exert over life, as well as their sense that the formation and articulation of historical interests occurs through more complex political processes which may correspond to, but remain irreducible to, class position.

For some academics and activists in the time of Black Lives Matter fervor and ramped up race–class debates, the "race is the modality ..." assertion provides a ready means of signaling both antiracist commitment and a willingness to take a critical approach to capitalist political economy. *Policing the Crisis* offered a critical analysis of deviance as an ideological construct, and an equally prescient analysis of the roots of Thatcherism, but the book's rather formulaic treatment of the US black predicament, which is largely refracted through the ideas of Black Power radicals, should give pause to those who reach for the "race is the modality" quote as a means of understanding American political development during the last decades of the twentieth century, and in particular the origins of mass incarceration. The authors' sense of the US black population as "a distinct, super-exploited class within the wider (white) working class" was rhetorically powerful but empirically anachronistic by the time *Policing the Crisis* was published, and their characterizations of black political life did not reflect the rapid and substantive political and social changes taking place across the Atlantic. "Black politics has," they wrote, "never been able to function exclusively with the advanced industrial vanguard, or to develop exclusively around the point of production. It has been obliged to adopt a more 'populist' approach to its constituency, and to work from a community base."[81] The patent limitations of black ethnic politics, however, and the widening gulf between the policy commitments of black officialdom and interests of black popular constituencies already being painfully felt in places like Harlem, Detroit and New Orleans during the seventies were left uninterrogated.

Rather than treating the "race is the modality" claim as creed, we should instead undertake the kind of conjunctural analysis that Hall and his collaborators actually suggested, an analysis that takes seriously the substantive historical outcomes of the Second Reconstruction and the transformations within black life of the last half century, the complexities of which cannot be reduced to liberal equations of blackness and poverty that dominated the Cold War. Much larger and more well-established than the black British population during the postwar years, the African American population saw waves of tangible gains through civil rights and Great Society reforms. Although African Americans would remain disproportionately poor and unemployed, federal antidiscrimination legislation, access to higher education institutions, antipoverty programs and the growth of black public sector employment all combined to greatly reduce African American poverty during the late sixties and seventies, essentially cutting the black poverty rate in half. While blackness in the United States, as in Great Britain, was still equated with poverty and criminality in popular discourse, such perceptions were openly contested through the pervasive integration of blacks into positions of authority and leadership in public life and the explosive diversification of black representations in popular culture from the seventies onwards—tectonic changes that are too often minimized in popular antiracist accounts of twentieth-century history.

Conjunctural analysis might illuminate the circuitous routes and unexpected political bedfellows that birthed mass incarceration, and, likewise, enable us to see the potential for building a counterpower capable both of contesting the underclass ideology that supports that apparatus and of dismantling the leviathan of local and state ordinances that comprise the current carceral order. Rather than reading the symbolic referents of the urban–suburban class divide as forms of constituency—in other words, seeing black and white as proxies for relative disadvantage and privilege—this account insists that focusing on the policing of relative surplus population is a more helpful way of understanding how policing has come to function in US society since the postwar years. This frame not only brings the strategic and tactical prerogatives of urban policing into sharper focus, it also connects that context to policing modalities in smaller towns, counties and rural areas, which are not fully captured in popular mobilizations around viral-video killings of civilians and slogans like the New Jim Crow and Black Lives Matter. Grounding the development of policing and mass incarceration more fully within political economy might serve as a proper antidote to the common perception of liberals and conservatives alike that the current mode of policing might be made more civil. The problem before us is not one of racist excesses that might be remedied through better training against implicit bias, hiring more minority officers or firing bad cops. The problem, rather, is that the policing of surplus population is necessary for capital's system preservation, which depends on massive dispossession and exploitation.

2

Making Consumers and Criminals

The Postwar Urban Transformation and the Origins of Policing as We Know It

On the side-walk Sunday morning
Lies a body oozing life;
Someone's sneaking 'round the corner
Is that someone Mack the Knife?

      "The Ballad of Mack the Knife,"
      Kurt Weill and Bertolt Brecht (1929)

Today barbarism has taken over many city streets, or people fear it has, which comes to much the same thing in the end.

      Jane Jacobs, *The Death and Life*
      of Great American Cities (1961)

German playwright and Marxist Bertolt Brecht survived the Red inquisition of postwar America, but not without having to reassure the House Un-American Activities Committee that he had never been a member of the Communist Party. Brecht left for Europe the day after his HUAC testimony and died in Berlin in 1956. Perhaps fortunately for him, he did not live to see "Die Moritat von Mackie Messer" (translated as the "Deadly Deed of Mackie Messer"), the theme song from his and Kurt Weill's *The Threepenny Opera*, transformed from a murder ballad into the soundtrack of American consumer culture. Following the 1956 off-Broadway revival of the musical, the lead song was recorded by numerous jazz musicians and popular entertainers. Lifted out of the narrative context of Brecht and Weill's commentary on capitalism and alienation, the song, like those of other popular musicals of the day, was pulled into the vortex of American mass culture. Its critique of capitalist society was slowly softened and then forgotten. When Louis Armstrong first read the English translation of the lyrics, he went nostalgic, immediately identifying with the character, Macheath. "Oh, I'm going to *love* doing this," Armstrong said, "I *knew* cats like this in New Orleans. Every one of them, they'd stick a knife into you without blinking an eye!"[1] Armstrong was no stranger to trouble and hardship as a youth; he had learned to play the cornet at the Home for Colored Waifs, a reform school, where he was sent after discharging his mother's pistol during a New Year's celebration. Armstrong could identify with the lumpen character come to life in Brecht's lyrics, but the song would take on a life of its own after the postwar success of *The Threepenny Opera*.

"Mack the Knife," as it came to be known in the United States, was intended to portray the depravity and violence of a highway robber, but, in an odd turn, it became a popular American hit, a hi-fi stereo favorite at suburban dinner parties and Saturday night bridge games. The gruesome imagery conjured by Brecht's lyrics are made fanciful and ebullient in Armstrong's 1956 recording, where he even adds Weill's widow, the Viennese singer Lotte Lenya, to the list of Macheath's female prey. The song was made innocuous by Bobby Darin's Grammy Award-winning rendition, a favorite of the bobbysoxer set and the "definitive version" according to Frank Sinatra. In Ella Fitzgerald's memorable 1960 concert recording in Brecht's Berlin, the song transcends the lyrics

altogether. Fitzgerald forgot the words and saved the performance through sheer virtuosity and comedic improvisation. The
words no longer mattered. How does this happen?

For many whites the immediate experience of urban danger
evoked in the song was by that point diminished, having become
the stuff of nostalgia, a greying generation's lore of the old inner-
city neighborhood and hard times. For the baby-boomers who
came of age in suburbia, Macheath must have appeared as an
exotic curiosity, glimpsed only momentarily from the highways
connecting greenfield subdivisions to the old downtown main
streets, or in lurid crime stories detailed by newspaper reporters
and noir fiction. The bitter taste of Depression-era poverty and
the alienation of factory life were fading into memory for the
millions who now enjoyed a standard of living that was enviable
across most of the world, even in the former imperial capitals of
Europe still in the process of rebuilding and recovery after World
War II. Rather than a figure who might stir the consciousness
of the laboring classes to action, Macheath was reincarnated as
just another villain in the cornucopic mass culture industry that
enveloped American life.

Excised from the popular hit recordings of "Mack the Knife"
is a final verse that forcefully underscores the capitalist class
relations Weill and Brecht opposed:

> There are some who are in darkness
> And the others are in light
> And you see the ones in brightness
> Those in darkness drop from sight.

Even if those words had remained their meaning may well have
been lost in translation under new epochal conditions, especially
among audiences who now believed class had lost its power over
them. The song gained popularity in the world of McCarthyism,
primary school A-bomb drills and the bucolic middle-class life
of primetime television, a context in which class consciousness
had been radically transformed by consumer identity, and where

older modes of working-class solidarity and political organization had been banished from the realm of permissible civic life. Anxious middle-class Americans still feared the loss of their possessions and new status at the hands of robbers, but in their embrace of Macheath they perhaps had accepted that the virtues of capitalism outweighed its violence, especially now that the system's most destructive forces were out of sight, its victims cordoned off in inner-city ghettos.

This chapter locates the origins of contemporary carceral logics in these Cold War transformations of American capitalism, class relations and politics. The contemporary problems of aggressive policing and mass incarceration originate in the birth of the mid-twentieth-century consumer republic. The middle-class consumer has long been the ideal subject of bourgeois democratic society, but that figure would take on a potent and outsized role in postwar American life.[2] The new American consumer middle class was born in a unique historical context marked by the growing global strategic-military importance of the United States after the 1949 North Atlantic Treaty, by US corporate access to new commodity markets both in war-torn nations and in the decolonizing world, by the availability of cheap energy, and, most importantly for this discussion, by a domestic project of national infrastructure and real estate development that would fundamentally alter the urban fabric. Massive state investments in housing and urban renewal, defense contracting and interstate highway construction transformed American cities, in the process producing rising standards of living, novel and conservative notions of class, popular acceptance of capitalism's virtues, and new social conflicts within the laboring classes. Just as the postwar transformation produced the middle-class consumer citizen, the same historical processes would also create the affluent society's walking contradiction—an industrial reserve of unemployed, mostly black and brown urban dwellers. Political scientist Paul Passavant contends that the US state has been empowered and governs through a "criminal-consumer double"—conjoined forms of subjectivity that govern citizen behavior in accordance with consumer capitalism and private property.[3] The "good shopper" is a disciplined shopper, Passavant concludes: "From the watchful eyes of store employees that lead one to make only 'normal' movements with one's bags, to the information and taste acquired and required to shop knowledgeably and appropriately, to the consumer's governance by the risk assessment of one's credit card (or lack thereof)." Those who did not, or simply could not, abide these new cultural terms were subjected to increasingly pervasive and repressive forms of state discipline. Policing and the carceral state as we know it is rooted in this postwar political economy and the ways in which it produced new winners and losers, but these underlying social contradictions would not be brought fully out into the open until the black political militancy and mass urban rebellions of the sixties.

This chapter offers an alternative to race-centric interpretations of the origins of policing and mass incarceration that have become popular in the time of Black Lives Matter. Although sympathetic to the political intentions of this tendency, the chapter questions accounts that derive from an ossified Cold War liberal discourse of racial inequality which elides class. Instead of the class language of capital and labor that drove workers movements during the interwar period, many contemporary left-liberal accounts of class remain ideologically mired in the consumer middle class, the "underclass" and racial disparities, notions that mark a retreat from open contestation of capitalism, its widely felt contradictions, and crisis-laden character. These common ways of thinking about social inequality mystify both American class relations and the fundamental motors of the carceral expansion.

The chapter revisits the development of the consumer society as a political and economic antidote to the problems that led to the Depression, and the ascendancy of a postwar economic development strategy predicated on massive federal investment in homeownership. During the middle decades of the twentieth century, millions of Americans were transformed into nominal property-holders through the development trajectories set in motion by the New Deal social democratic policies and the commercial-Keynesian turn of Harry Truman's Fair Deal. These combined efforts created the relative middle class as we know it, but, as many have argued, the benefits of these transformations were not universally felt, remaining incomplete and unequal across populations and national geography. In their efforts to point out the racial limits of the New Deal and postwar prosperity, however, some historians and contemporary activists have diminished the actual advances black publics made through mid-century liberalism. Likewise, most commentators have lost sight of the fact of a complex, internal black class politics, whether during the late Jim Crow era, when roughly half of the black population lived in poverty, or in the last half-century of black political and economic integration, during which black poverty rates dropped precipitously.

In the decades after VJ Day, black and brown residents came to symbolize the world the new suburbanites had left behind, an inner-city urban life defined by poverty, segregation, overcrowding and crime. Popular notions of black criminality pre-dated the end of World War II, and earlier moments of southern black migration to central cities were characterized by all manner of "urban menace" stereotypes. Until the end of the sixties, however, white homicide rates were on par with those of blacks, and whites constituted a solid majority of the prison population.[4] Even if many whites thought blacks were more likely to commit crimes, their actual experiences and the prevalence of organized crime among urban white ethnics told another story. Such prejudicial views of blacks as criminals, however, would gain material weight through the postwar expansion, when the wages and living conditions of many whites were radically improved. The postwar remaking of US cities would produce a new cognitive mapping of American life, where "inner city" became synonymous with dread, crime, social exclusion, danger and despair, and where the suburbs would for a time be associated with middle-class aspiration, individual freedom, patriarchal family values, joyous consumer experiences, the good life, peace and safety.

As others have noted, the carceral build-up of the Reagan–Bush War on Drugs was not merely the handiwork of conservative Republicans.[5] Rather, mass incarceration was the creation of various constituencies—black and white; urban, suburban and rural; liberal and conservative—who supported more punitive laws, increased funding for prisons, and the like. Some would support these policies for staunchly ideological reasons, while others would do so out of desperation, seeing punishment as the only plausible antidote to worsening crime and urban conditions, especially as the tangible benefits of social democracy were no longer part of the lived experiences and popular memory of millions of Americans. The roots of this dilemma lie in the Cold War liberal turn away from public works and redistributive public policy, and towards civil society and cultural solutions to urban poverty.

The chapter concludes with a discussion of two influential liberal urbanists, Jane Jacobs and Daniel Patrick Moynihan, and how each furthered the turn away from left class analysis and politics and authorized solutions to inequality that did not alter capitalist class power. Both were deeply concerned about the spread of crime and poverty in American cities, and both proposed cultural remedies to the mounting urban crisis that was clearly visible to anyone paying attention. Jacobs contested the housing and mega-infrastructure projects that master builder Robert Moses unleashed on postwar New York City, and how these damaged the social fabric and daily rhythms of neighborhood life, while Moynihan turned the nation's attention to the problem of durable unemployment and poverty among urban blacks. Their progressive social commitment is not in question, but here I offer a critique of how each accepts the new postwar social terrain, and how critical analysis of class relations and political economy are either suspended or evacuated altogether in their accounts of the Cold War city. In different ways, both reorient the terms of public debate around urban inequality away from the kinds of progressive state interventions pushed by unions and other left forces during the Depression years, offering instead civil society and market-oriented solutions. Jacobs celebrates community self-policing and surveillance as a means of achieving public safety, while Moynihan advances behavioral modification, rather than jobs, better wages and union protections, as a solution to black poverty. Neither can be blamed for the "law-and-order" politics that would take hold, but both Jacobs and Moynihan conceded to the retreat from social democracy, and in their embrace of privatism set the stage for the neoliberal urbanism to come.

The Consumer Republic and the New Urban Spatial Class Divide

Contemporary accounts of the birth and expansion of the prison state have typically neglected the significance of the post–World War II urban transformation and the class decomposition, new status distinctions and aspirational mythology it produced, which sharpened conflicts within the working class along racial and urban-suburban divides, while cementing the interests of the most secure segments, the *relative middle class*, to the interests of capital. Both popular and academic accounts have focused on racial conflict, the police repression of the black mass riots of the sixties, and the rise of anticrime and pro-policing measures in the War on Drugs, but these accounts too often forget the complex local narratives and unexpected alliances that came together at different moments to advance the prison build-up.[6] The commonly held thesis of black–white racial conflict does not explain why some black publics supported tough-on-crime policies.[7]

Thinking about class was made more complicated in the United States during the postwar years, when established notions of class identity mutated and became politicized in conservative ways. From its origins, the American liberal project has elided class, instead proffering the view that inherited bonds and social restrictions do not bridle the pursuit of individual economic autonomy and personal fulfillment, even though the nation was established as a slave-holding republic which excluded non-propertied whites, women and enslaved Africans from the franchise. However, in response to both the powerful working-class movements of the interwar period and the decisive role of the Soviet Union in World War II, American popular ideology and institutions during the Cold War were forcefully reoriented against notions of class struggle and revolutionary socialism.

The birth of the postwar suburban middle class as a lived social reality *and* an aspirational identity, the increasing availability of consumer goods, and the ways that these became associated with success and, sadly, human worth within popular culture together produced a new social terrain, one marked by renewed commitments to liberal individualism, new anxieties about social status, novel everyday preoccupations and seismic political realignments. On the one hand, class became associated with one's capacity to consume, rather than a collective-social relationship to production as such. On the other hand, the role of policing was expanded to "serve and protect" middle-class lifestyles and consumer spaces.

This era produced two powerful myths of class: the consumer middle class and the "underclass." These were myths to the extent that both obscured actual capitalist class relations at the time, treating those who occupied the same objective experience of dependency and exploitation as dissimilar classes, a cultural development that would have profound implications for American politics in the decades to come. "Middle class" and "underclass" would emerge as popular ways of talking about class that no longer focused on productive relations but instead on consumption. Both the middle class and the underclass were figments of Cold War ideology, and mirrored narratives of American exceptionalism.

During the Cold War, the middle class were viewed as virtuous consumer-citizens, those who earned their keep and contributed to the economic health of the nation through their labor, consumer activity and property taxes. As Michael Zweig has argued, the vast majority of Americans remained working class despite their increased consumer capacity.[8] The millions of Americans who enjoyed the postwar prosperity through new homes, automobiles, home appliances, fashion and leisure might at best be described as a relative middle class because most continued to be wage laborers rather than the managerial supervisors or petit bourgeoisie typically implied in the notion of middle class. The profit-sharing norms born out of interwar labor victories secured higher wages and benefits for millions of workers, but their newfound lifestyles were still dependent upon work. Wages and even suburban homeownership did not make them property owners in the same sense as capital.

The so-called underclass, on the other hand, would come to be reviled from the sixties onwards as a social burden on the middle class. The basic needs and survival of the desperately poor during the sixties and seventies were dependent upon government programs, e.g., public housing units, Section 8 vouchers, WIC vouchers, food assistance, Headstart, public afterschool programs, health clinics, etc., financed through taxation of the affluent. Rather than seeing the poor as some distinct entity, Zweig contends they are merely ruined workers. The vast majority of the American poor work multiple jobs to survive.[9] This is the context of class decomposition and conservative ideology that fostered the growth and racialization of policing and prisons as we know it.

This new Cold War ontology of class expunged the language of workers and the working class from popular and political debate in favor of the middle class, and offered up the underclass as the antithesis of the aspirational middle class. For decades thereafter, most Americans would come to define themselves as middle class even when their earnings and consumer capacity fell short of their dreams. Politicians as well retooled their appeals away from populist overtures to the "working man" and towards the new middle class, or at best "working families," all the while criticizing the excesses of the wealthy and the alleged moral depravity of the desperately poor. Targeting the extremes of the American social order on the campaign trail carried few real consequences for candidates, since the donor class understood the difference between the rhetorical flourishes of campaign stumping and politicians' actual policy commitments within the machinations of day-to-day governing. Likewise, neither the donor class nor the elites of either party saw the "underclass" as a real constituency that might matter electorally. The middle class provided a safe and soft target for the campaign appeals and policy prescriptions of both New Deal Democratic liberalism and Republican neoconservatism. If the middle class came to be understood as white, suburban, law-abiding, virtuous, affluent, property owning, hardworking, autonomous and Republican, then the underclass was black and brown, urban, poor, criminal, dysfunctional, dispossessed, lazy, dependent and apathetic. Demystifying this new symbolic language of class, which has come to dominate American politics, and coming to terms with the landscape of power and uneven development we now inhabit should be a central left intellectual and political task. Moreover, understanding the making of the consumer society, its contradictions and unique historical character, and how it gave rise to the current carceral state should help us to clarify the underlying class relations that are codified in black and white, but not reducible to those identities.

Historians Jefferson Cowie and Nick Salvatore refer to the reign of the New Deal coalition as a long exception in American history, an "historical aberration—a byproduct of the massive crisis of the Great Depression rather than the linear triumph of the liberal state." For them, "there is more continuity in American political culture between [William Graham] Sumner and [Richard] Nixon than between Roosevelt and the rest of American history." Liberalism would endure beyond Franklin D. Roosevelt's tenure, but "the version generated by the trauma of Depression and war proved both distinct and brittle." The historic weakness of labor in the United States, the "burdens of race" and the power of religion are central to Cowie and Salvatore's account of America's cultural and political conservatism. Each of these facets was changed by the power of New Deal reforms, but, they hold, "each also maintained often overlooked continuities with the deeper impulses of American history—not the least of which was the primacy of business in American life."[10] This last allusion to the historical power of capital, however, is not only understated in their historical explanation of the limits of progressive left reform, but somehow remains disconnected from the drama of racial, ethnic and religious conflict that progressive reformers, union organizers, anarchists and communists labored to surmount decades before their popular struggles found partial recognition in New Deal legislation.

Cowie and Salvatore offer a "constraint of race" thesis that has become the dominant liberal account of the New Deal and explanation of the difficulty of achieving social democracy on American soil, i.e., the thesis that any effort to achieve broadbased redistributive reform is always and everywhere hobbled by racism. This now widely embraced narrative, however, often rests on specious accounts of the historical forces that shaped the reach and limits of the New Deal reforms. In particular, when Cowie and Salvatore develop the claim that the New Deal was constrained by the racism of southern Democrats, they repeat the conventional wisdom that legislation such as the Agricultural Adjustment Act, the National Labor Relations Act and the Fair Labor Standards Act, "each exempted from coverage categories with heavy concentrations of black working people." Ira Katznelson, Ta-Nehisi Coates and others offer the same thesis to explain the exclusion of agricultural and domestic workers from the 1935 Social Security Act.[11] Southern Democrats certainly sought to exclude black workers from protections; however, as historian Touré F. Reed argues, "the most obvious problem with the claim is that it ignores the fact that the majority of sharecroppers, tenant farmers, mixed farm laborers and domestic workers in the early 1930s were white."[12] Some 11.4 million whites were employed as agricultural laborers and domestics compared to 3.5 million blacks. As a consequence, Reed reminds us, the Social Security exemptions excluded 27 percent of all white workers nationally. As an historical explanation of the New Deal's limitations, the

Jim-Crowing-of-national-social-policy thesis does not hold up. Rather, the power of particular capitalist blocs prevailed, in this case the landed interests represented by the Farm Bureau, ensuring the vulnerability of the most submerged and dispossessed workers regardless of color.

Ironically, this New Deal mythology also redacts the record of black support for and influence over the subsequent trajectory of Roosevelt-era reforms, as well as those pursued after World War II. There is little mention in "constraint of race" accounts of the massive public works programs that employed hundreds of thousands of black workers, such as the Civilian Conservation Corps (CCC) and the Works Progress Administration (WPA).[13] These projects were publicly funded and publicly managed, employing millions of Americans from all walks of life. The CCC workers built roads and bridges, refurbished portions of the Appalachian Trail and developed numerous public amenities of the US parks service.

There was no doubt discrimination in the CCC program. Black enrollment was capped at ten percent of the total, which mirrored the black proportion of the national population. As Nick Taylor points out, this level of CCC employment did not meet the high demand for relief among African Americans, who were especially hard hit by the Depression.[14] In the Deep South, CCC work camps were segregated, sadly in conformity with the Jim Crow order, but beyond the Mason-Dixon line many camps were integrated. All told, between 1933 and 1941, some 250,000 blacks were enrolled in the Corps. And most black participants recalled their experiences with some fondness because for many it was the first time they'd received three square meals, a warm bed and a regular income and job training.[15]

There is a similar dissonance between black servicemen's actual experience of the GI Bill's implementation and contemporary efforts to impugn the policy as evidence of transhistorical white supremacy. The claim that blacks did not benefit from the GI Bill's provisions runs a close second to the myth about Social Security as a rhetorical move to short-circuit any talk of fighting for universal public policy in our times. Suzanne Mettler offers a healing inoculation against this contagion, which is promoted by academics and autodidacts alike. Contrary to the prevailing narrative, Mettler shows how Veterans Administration records tell another story, one where higher proportions of nonwhites (49 percent) used the GI Bill's education and training benefits than did whites (43 percent).[16] This pattern held true even in the South, where we might expect suppression of black access to GI Bill benefits given the prevalence of Jim Crow institutions and discrimination during the postwar years. "Strikingly, nonwhite southern veterans' usage surpassed that of white veterans in the region, at 56 percent compared to 50 percent," Mettler's study found. And similarly "in the West, 46 percent of nonwhite veterans went to school on the G.I. Bill, compared to 42 percent of white veterans." "Nationwide, black World War II veterans numbered 1,308,000," Mettler makes clear; "already by 1950, 640,920 of them had benefited from the G.I. Bill's education and training provisions."

It should be noted as well that thousands of black workers were unionized in steel mills, automotive plants, packinghouses and ports across the United States during the Depression, World War II, and after because of the right to collective bargaining granted under the Wagner Act.[17] The wages black laborers earned in these industries, and in many cases the financial contributions of some unions, filled the war chest of the postwar civil rights movement. More evidence of the complex relationship between black popular struggles and the Roosevelt administration can be seen in the passage of Executive Order 8802 in 1941. This measure desegregated the defense industries, drawing thousands of blacks into the wartime workforce, and was signed under the threat of a national protest—the original "March on Washington" movement, organized by black trade unionist A. Philip Randolph.[18] Public works projects, black unionism and the desegregation of the defense industries altered public perceptions about race and gender equality, brought Americans from different backgrounds into regular and often unprecedented contact

with one another, and prefigured the expansion and new asser-
tiveness of desegregation campaigns after the war.

Rather than seeing the New Deal reform years as a great
exception, or as yet another episode of American politics being
hemmed in by the "original sin" of race, this chapter offers a
different account, one that situates the period more firmly within
domestic and international class struggle, the historic effort of
the US capitalist class to save the system from its own contradictions amid the Depression, and the countervailing movement of
popular and labor forces to secure a more just order.[19] This was
exceptional in the sense that it marked a period when capital
took responsibility for the costs of the social reproduction of
labor, a function it has since abandoned with far-reaching and
disruptive social consequences under decades of neoliberalization, the dismantling of the welfare state apparatus and the
privatization of formerly public goods and services.

The postwar prosperity was born in part out of a process of
disenclosure, which historian Thomas Jessen Adams describes
as "removing some basic human needs from the risks, vagaries,
and price fluctuations associated with the profit motive and the
market as moral arbiter."[20] The momentary progress achieved
at mid-century was the consequence of the organized power
of the working class, through trade unionism, popular front
communism and the civil rights movement, among other social
forces. Reforms certainly bore the imprint of capitalist interests and were the handiwork of ruling class-led coalitions, but
popular pressures shaped outcomes as well. Through Democratic
Party participation, shopfloor organizing, social reform and local
mobilization, American workers and citizens were able to achieve
a level of influence over labor relations and social policy that has
not been had since, a process that transformed daily life, national
culture and statecraft. As Adams writes:

> They established and cemented various cultural tendencies
> towards solidarity. Through such institutional tendencies they
> accepted and encouraged state regulation and redistribution. They

turned the meaning of patriotism into sacrifice for the common good. They fought and succeeded in revaluing some labor. They favored narrowing the moral boundaries of the market through the establishment of Social Security, price controls during World War II, federally subsidized public housing and later welfare, Medicare and Medicaid. In short, they wielded a broadly construed class politics in their general interest and against those of capitalist accumulation.[21]

Such reforms had the immediate economic effect of stabilization, raising the floor on basic living conditions for millions of Americans and, after World War II, intensifying national investment in a Keynesian growth project that had the longer-term effect of creating an expansive consumer republic, which from its earliest advocacy in the Roosevelt White House was fundamentally a political project.

In his 1933 statement on the National Industrial Recovery Act, Roosevelt was clear and forthcoming about this cornerstone of New Deal legislation. "The aim of this whole effort," he underscored, "is to restore our rich domestic market by raising its vast consuming capacity." He saw the New Deal's massive program of public works as being of universal benefit to unemployed workers, and he considered their welfare to be central to the longer-term health of the capitalist order. Roosevelt said: "No business which depends for existence on paying less than living wages to its workers has any right to continue in this country. By 'business' I mean the whole of commerce as well as the whole of industry; by workers I mean all workers, the white-collar class as well as men in overalls: and by living wages I mean more than a bare subsistence level—I mean the wages of decent living."[22]

The development of a home realty market and attending mortgage market, as well as the rapid expansion of the consumer economy, were introduced as remedies to the surplus-absorption problem that was partially responsible for the crisis of the Great Depression. The Depression devastated the real estate and housing construction industries. The construction of residential properties plummeted by 95 percent between 1928 and 1933, and home repair expenditures fell by 90 percent during the same period.[23] In 1930 alone, 150,000 non-farm households lost property to foreclosure, and by 1932 that figure reached 250,000. The rapid development and expansion of suburban homeownership created a means for the realization of surplus value. The problems of overproduction and value realization were solved through public subsidization of the real estate industry and, consequentially, a complex process of massive urban expansion. This transformation of the American working class into a nominal property-owning middle class had deep political implications, especially since some elites held fast to the promise that debt-encumbered homeowners were less likely to strike.[24] Between 1941 and 1961, annual consumer expenditures on housing and automobiles more than tripled from an average $718 per household to $2,513.[25] In 1944, annual housing starts were 142,000 nationally, but by 1950 such starts peaked at 2 million and remained relatively constant at 1.3 million in the years after.

The notion of security, understood in terms of financial investment and protection from social conflict, was woven into the birth of the homeowner regime. Real estate valuation and investment under the Homeowners Loan Corporation (HLC) practice of residential security maps were predicated as much on calculations of social risk as they were on some strict appraisal of the market value of physical property and built structures. Federal Housing Administration underwriters were given strict and weighted criteria for assessing the quality of residential areas: 1) relative economic stability (40 percent); 2) protection from adverse influences (20 percent); 3) freedom from special hazards (5 percent); 4) adequacy of civic, social and commercial centers (5 percent); 5) adequacy of transportation (10 percent); 6) sufficiency of utilities and conveniences (5 percent); 7) level of taxes and special assessments (5 percent); and 8) appeal (10 percent). As Kenneth Jackson points out, the two most heavily weighted areas of assessment, "relative economic stability" and "protection from adverse influences," were most often applied in ways that were prejudicial against heterogeneous environments.[26] Contrary to popular belief, however, black neighborhoods were not the only ones subjected to devaluation under redlining—the demarcation of high-risk zones by banks to discourage investment.[27] Older working-class, white ethnic neighborhoods were subject to downgrading as well, spurring an exodus to the suburbs by those with financial means. The poorest working-class districts were generally downgraded on residential security maps, but even class-diverse black neighborhoods, often featuring enclaves of black professionals, were almost universally subjected to this practice.[28]

The postwar housing revolution was marked by the pursuit of a more market-oriented approach, with the public incentivization of real estate industry, national infrastructural development and the defense industry, which combined to produce an economic boom. The pro-market regulatory orientation, however, entrenched racial inequality in the construction sector and produced uneven development across metropolitan space. The postwar years also saw the abandonment of the genuine public works that had defined the New Deal years, i.e., federally funded and publicly managed jobs programs. During this period, "public works" took on a different meaning, with large-scale infrastructural and housing developments undertaken by private contractors and building trades, in a market-oriented process that enabled nepotism, petty patronage and private discrimination, which often excluded blacks as workers and contractors.[29] A manifestation of real estate industry power, the 1949 Housing Act set in motion the radical spatial transformation of American cities, earmarking funds for urban renewal and public housing construction, and expanding the program of federally insured mortgages for single-family home purchases, measures that combined to produce the urban–suburban wealth inequality that would define American public life for over half a century.

Postwar suburbanization ushered in modes of residential settlement more intimately differentiated by income and consumer capacity. In his 1959 book *The Status Seekers*, Vance Packard described this phenomenon of more intensive residential segregation by income as "the creation of many hundreds of one-class communities unparalleled in the history of America." "There is no need to rub elbows with fellow Americans who are of a different class," Packard lamented. "The more expensive of these one-layer communities, where homes cost $50,000, import their teachers, policemen, and store clerks from nearby communities in a lower price range."[30] This property-owning regime reoriented working-class consciousness and aspiration, and dampened the prospects for an assertive working class-centered politics. Many of the adults who had come of age as part of the industrial urban working class were remade as suburban middle class after World War II. The spatial fix to capital's surplus absorption problem was also a cultural fix, which had the effect of refashioning class consciousness from the collectivist and social democratic tendencies of the interwar period towards a more individualist and antiredistributional politics rooted in property ownership and consumption.

In his landmark book, *One-Dimensional Man*, German émigré and Frankfurt School theorist Herbert Marcuse emphasized the integration of notions of individual freedom and satisfaction with those of capital under the expanding consumer society of the postwar years. "The people recognize themselves in their commodities," Marcuse wrote, "they find their soul in their automobile, hi-fi set, split-level home, kitchen equipment."[31] Late in that book, Marcuse offered a string of highly personal sketches to underscore these processes, directly implicating himself. The first of these, where he describes riding in his new car, may be the most poignant, conveying as it does an everyday experience of commodity fetishism most Americans can immediately identify with. It is worth quoting here at length:

> I ride in a new automobile. I experience its beauty, shininess, power, convenience—but then I become aware of the fact that in a relatively short time it will deteriorate and need repair; that its beauty and surface are cheap, its power unnecessary, its size idiotic; and that I will not find a parking place. I come to think of

my car as a product of one of the Big Three automobile corporations. The latter determine the appearance of my car and make its
beauty as well as its cheapness, its power as well as its shakiness,
its working as well as its obsolescence. In a way, I feel cheated. I
believe that the car is not what it could be, that better cars could
be made for less money. But the other guy has to live, too. Wages
and taxes are too high; turnover is necessary; we have it much
better than before. The tension between appearance and reality
melts away and both merge in one rather pleasant feeling.[32]

If the relationship between the automotive showroom and
the assembly line was papered over by Madison Avenue ad
campaigns and Cold War triumphalist talk of the "end of ideology," Marcuse reminded his audience of the affluent society's
underlying exploitation and obsolescence. The interrelation
between the new car smell, its aesthetic allure and horsepower,
"if comprehended," Marcuse warned, "shatters the harmonizing
consciousness and its false realism," as well as the feelings of
liberty on the open road and the status that accrues through our
material possessions.

The material comfort of the relative middle class, their inclusion in the property-owning republic that ringed central cities,
their access to better schools, newly constructed public facilities
and exclusive private amenities, and their desire to protect those
benefits from distributive pressures, gave rise to the political
conservatism that has dominated and defined American political
life for over half a century. Older ethnic bonds and industrial
consciousness faded along with the cherished black-and-white
images so many families kept in the cookie tin, all mementos
of simpler but perhaps tougher times. Cold War propaganda
and the active persecution of labor militancy by anticommu-
nist witch hunts and the FBI further banished socialism from
the popular political imagination. A new republican ideology
of self-governance assumed material form in clapboard and
aluminum siding, and took root alongside red fescue and rye-
grass, in a combination of atomistic individualism, antiurbanism,

provincialism and commitment to liberal capitalist progress. As Marcuse argued, the integration of significant portions of the working class into a new nominal property-owning class had the effect of integrating political horizons as well, making notions of freedom and happiness—momentarily contested by popular, Depression-era left movements—now indistinguishable from those of the ruling class. What these different layers of the consumer middle class shared, however, were their relative advantages compared to those left behind in central cities.

American cities have always been defined by class, racial and ethnic inequality, but the postwar urban transformation facilitated an unprecedented resegregation of residential, commercial and recreational activity, not merely across city blocks but over vast metropolitan spaces, with far-reaching consequences for perceptions of crime, criminality and policing. In an especially perceptive chapter of his book *Fantasy City*, John Hannigan details the transformation of the American retail, entertainment and leisure landscape during the process of postwar suburbanization. Commercial investment followed former urbanites into the new suburbs, exurbs and small towns drawn into expanding metropolitan maps. "Once the leading purveyors of popular culture," Hannigan writes, "entertainment zones in city centers fell on hard times, losing their clientele to the new medium of television, to a host of outdoor leisure-time activities and to new suburban and exurban theme parks, movie theaters and shopping malls."[33] There were different contributing factors to the declining popularity and profitability of central business districts during the sixties and seventies. Hannigan focuses on three main explanations: shifting demographic and lifestyle changes; competition within the retail and entertainment sectors that precipitated experimentation and substitution; and proprietors and investors' avoidance of negative aspects of cities that they viewed as detrimental to profit-making, such as regulatory laws, taxation, crime, etc.

Downtown shopping corridors, bustling public markets, bath houses, gilded movie palaces, bowling alleys, small theaters and ballrooms, night clubs and public parks were abandoned as favored destinations, with many suburbanizing Americans turning to suburban strip malls, "ozoners" or drive-in theaters, large theme parks like Six Flags and Disney, or television and entertaining at home, all redefining the meaning of a "fun night (or day) out." Hannigan notes that the new suburban amusement parks adhered to a common formula: "An exurban location beyond the reach of public transport; a single admission price; cleanliness; attention to maintenance and safety; staff recruited from young people of high-school and college age (as against the old-style 'carny' worker); half-a-dozen themed sections or areas each with a specific motif but loosely connected to a unifying idea; non-stop sensual bombardment and state-of-the-art technical virtuosity."[34] Underlying much of the design, content and business model of the new suburban entertainment was a gnawing fear of urban crime. New strip malls, drive-in complexes and the faux main streets of theme parks provided patrons with controlled, safe forms of amusement that stood in sharp contrast to the creeping decay, swelling social protests and unpredictability that had come to define many American cities during the sixties. By the end of that decade, after most US cities had been rocked by inner-city rebellions, only 22 percent of Americans wished to live in a city.[35]

Surveying the epochal changes in the physical and social landscape of urban society during the early sixties, democratic socialist Michael Harrington observed that "the very development of the American city has removed poverty from the living, emotional experience of millions upon millions of middle class Americans." Not only had suburbanization removed poverty from view for many of the new middle class, but the increasing availability of consumer goods further camouflaged the poor: "Clothes make the poor invisible too," Harrington noted, since it is "much easier in the United States to be decently dressed than it is to be decently housed, fed or doctored." Writing during the Kennedy administration, Harrington not only pointed to the emerging suburban–urban class divide, and the difficulty many Americans might have in even seeing the problem, he also alluded to the absence of any effective social policy to address the urban and rural poverty that persisted amid affluence.

What Race Conceals

Viewing the 1954 film *The Secret of Selling the Negro* today is perhaps more of a revelation than when it was first screened in corporate boardrooms and advertising agencies. The film's Kodachrome portraits of black shoppers and families in domestic bliss, and famed radio personality Robert Trout's matter-of-fact delivery about the growing but neglected black consumer market, presents viewers with facts of Jim Crow black life that have been lost amid the more recent revival of liberal and black nationalist narratives of black oppression. Here, the black population is defined by the same class relations and aspirations as the broader public. Moreover, the film's impetus and content should remind us that, far from being superficial or incidental, class differences among blacks have real implications for social life and politics. The timing and production of the film by Johnson Publishing, at the time the most influential black media organization in the country, illustrate the allure of liberal integrationist ideology, and the relative power of the black professional-managerial class. The film converges with the prevailing Cold War ideology that the American free-enterprise model is sacrosanct, that it is a superior system for organizing industrial society, but one that is marred by racial discrimination. John Johnson, the filmmakers and the activists who took to the streets in the aftermath of the *Brown* decision to contest segregated busing, lunch counters and public pools were animated by a militant commitment to the promise of liberal democratic capitalism. We should be leery of any discussion of twentieth-century black life that treats white and black as synonyms for rich and poor, wealthy and dispossessed.

The postwar spatial fix created a landscape of uneven development with an undeniable racial character, producing largely white middle-class consumer-citizens at the urban periphery and a ghettoized and increasingly criminalized black and brown urban working class in the inner-city core and small southern towns. We should be mindful, however, of the finer details of these broader patterns and of the unique local geographies which varied from block to block and one zip code to another. The contemporary fascination with whiteness overpowers critical understandings of the postwar transformation and the hierarchies it produced, too often reducing an amalgam of material interests that were not shared by all whites to a matter of universal white-skin privilege.[36] White poverty endured during the postwar years, standing at 17 percent in 1959, despite the rapid expansion of the consuming middle class. As an analogy of underlying, disparate class positions and interests, however, whiteness does not help us to understand the root causes of the growing conservatism during the years after World War II, nor the segmented character of the consumer society—how different ethnic groups and classes acclimated to property ownership and consumer lifestyles albeit in variegated ways.[37] While race provides a convenient shorthand for summarizing the broad inequalities produced by the postwar urban transformation, race-centric approaches forget African Americans' different class experiences of the consumer society.

When we approach the postwar years through a critical Marxist analysis of race and capitalism, a different world emerges, not one defined so much by black organicism, but a world where blacks are restricted by second-class citizenship and discrimination, and yet they experience those social restrictions in classed ways. The substantive diversity of these class experiences is not reducible to a shared racial plight—a common rhetorical move that unites Jim Crow and New Jim Crow sensibilities. Rather, they are as distinct as the aspirations and sense of possibility of the black shopkeeper and the unemployed youth who hugs the curb outside his door, as different as the quality of life of the doctor who enjoys ball season with his elite circle and that of the seasonally employed janitor who cleans the hotel when their grand party is over, and as dissimilar in terms of their experiences of authority, abuse and power as the unionized steel worker and the off-the-books domestic who works in the well-appointed homes of more affluent blacks and whites. Despite the Jim Crow regime's broadly imposed limits on black citizenship, rival ideological and class prerogatives contended for power within and beyond the black population. The fact of the mid-twentieth-century black ghetto concealed that complex social reality from many Americans on the other side of the veil, who saw black life as dissimilar, unknowable and inferior to their own. The existence of an internal class politics among blacks still remains invisible to those who view the color line as the fundamental problem of the twentieth century—a formative political statement by W. E. B. Du Bois that achieved liberal orthodoxy during the Cold War. Rather than viewing the black condition as exceptional and race as the singular determinant of black life, a closer examination of black experiences of the postwar urban transformation throws into relief different and at times conflicting interests. We see blacks leaving hazardous slum tenements for newly constructed public housing. Well-established black neighborhoods and commercial corridors are bulldozed to clear the ground for highway construction and urban renewal. Blue-collar black couples are met by angry crowds as they attempt to purchase homes in white neighborhoods. Black professionals and artists live in proximity and relative harmony with whites in the more urbane reaches of society. We see black landlords who behave like white landlords, and black developers posing for photos with gilded shovels in hand as they break ground on exclusive subdivisions for black middle-class residents.

The so-called second ghetto was formed out of wartime migration, black population flows from the South in the decades after the war, and the housing market discrimination and established patterns of ethnic enclave settlement newcomers encountered.[38] Postwar urban renewal further cemented this residential apartheid. Federal interstate highways and other massive public projects bisected black neighborhoods, dispersing residents, tearing apart the urban fabric and devaluing adjacent property. Elevated freeways and other public infrastructure often functioned as physical walls dividing black areas from those of other ethnics. Slum clearance and the construction of tower block housing, widely supported by downtown commercial interests and social reformers, momentarily improved the living conditions of those previously relegated to dangerous, unsanitary tenements, but these developments were in effect a form of vertical ghettoization, often containing the black population in ways that maintained residential segregation and protected the established electoral districts and political turf of local party machines. "The result, if not the intent, of the public housing program of the United States," Kenneth Jackson concluded, "was to segregate the races, to concentrate the disadvantaged in inner cities, and to reinforce the image of suburbia as a place of refuge for the problems of race, crime and poverty."[39]

The postwar period saw the beginning of the end of the class-diverse black ghetto, however, and the development of residential segregation and suburbanization among blacks that conformed to the broader pattern of "one-class communities" taking shape across the nation. The process of urban renewal and public housing construction in the central city unfolded alongside the birth of the new black middle class residential subdivisions. In Chicago, such neighborhoods included Chatham and the "Pill Hill" section of Calumet Heights, named so because of its high concentration of black medical professionals. In the New York metropolitan area, such black middle-class enclaves included St. Albans, Queens and Mount Vernon in Westchester County. In Louisiana, both Pontchartrain Park in New Orleans and Southern Heights in Baton Rouge, an enclave of university professors and government workers, were developed in the fifties.[40] Similar housing developments cropped up in cities and towns across the United States. In the wake of major civil rights reforms, some of these neighborhoods would undergo major social and demographic changes and suffer declining fates through the end of the twentieth century, but for a time they served as a powerful antidote to popular racism and remain an exception to liberal discourses that diminish the fact of black class diversity.

While the frothing white crowds who opposed black newcomers are commonly evoked in accounts of postwar history given by antiracist liberals and reparations advocates, a closer look at the period stretching into the seventies finds nominal but substantive integration proceeding across the country. In 1950, the arrival of scientist Percy Julian in the Chicago border-suburb of Oak Park was met with vigilante violence. His house was firebombed before the family moved in, prompting Julian and his son to stand watch over the house with a shotgun through the night. That was only one chapter, however, in Oak Park's story of racial integration, as white citizen-activists like Roberta "Bobby" Raymond organized to discourage panic selling, promote hospitality towards black newcomers, and push landlords and realtors towards concrete support for integration.[41] Oak Park was not alone in this regard, as places like Willingboro, New Jersey, Pasadena, California, Columbia, Maryland, Rochester's 19th Ward, and Evanston, Illinois, among others, embarked on experiments in racial integration that are too often eclipsed in accounts fixated on black experiences of ghettoization and housing discrimination.

In his study of housing policy in Chicago from 1940 to 1960, *Racial Democracy and the Black Metropolis*, political scientist Preston Smith III offers an exceptional analysis of internal black class politics during the New Deal and Fair Deal years, illuminating the different interests of the black professional-managerial class, the working class and the poor. His work is a stiff tonic against those interpretations that emphasize the ways that "government" produced segregation.[42] In highlighting the active role of black civic elites in making and legitimating housing policy in the city, Smith's work offers a nuanced class analysis of black politics and American life as a whole, a feat that too often eludes proponents of the liberal racial justice frame.[43] Attuned to the fine texture of black public life, Smith examines the implications of black elites' retreat from *social democracy*, the fight for the expansion of the social wage that defined black politics during the late New Deal era, to the defense of *racial democracy*, the guarantee of black access to the fruits of the consumer society in a manner comparable to all of equal class standing. "While a racial and class critique constituted most black political formations during the Depression and the Second World War," Smith writes, "the class critique became increasingly muted after the war. As a result, black policy elites pursued racial politics that did not simply have class implications—it also represented a class politics." Such politics, he adds, "sought to establish and solidify the power of black elites in representing the racial group's housing interests," and in the process "black policy elites pursued racial reform that was not up to the task of confronting the housing industry's class stratification." Smith concludes that not only did the black professional-managerial stratum preserve its power within the city's patron–clientelist structure, but also "the black elites' reforms predictably failed to respond adequately to the housing needs of working class and poor blacks."[44] This shifting orientation towards racial democracy is helpful for understanding national black politics during the postwar years as well.

The postwar civil rights movement helped to rationalize and expand the consumer society, removing legal Jim Crow barriers and shattering widely held racist caricatures, norms and behaviors. As struggles at the point of production receded and left working-class politics were openly repressed through HUAC hearings, red-baiting and state repression, the character and address of the postwar civil rights movement more tightly conformed to the pursuit of integration into the consumer society. Many of its most well-known foot soldiers, such as John Lewis, Diane Nash, Stokely Carmichael and countless others, were black college students who were already poised to take advantage of the opportunities long denied by the Jim Crow system. Sites of public consumption, such as department stores and lunch counters, and the use of public bus systems and inter-city transportation, became critical targets of protest activity. During the Wichita sit-in movement of 1958, and the more publicized 1960 Greensboro sit-ins, students protested national chains like Dockum Drugs and Woolworth's, which served as centers of consumer and social life in many cities and towns. African Americans demanded access to the education, jobs, incomes, housing, commodities and leisure that were denied under Jim Crow and de facto segregation in the North. While black demands for desegregation were made in powerful moral terms, state officials often understood and justified racial progress as being good for business. It is worth noting too that in the *Heart of Atlanta Motel v. the US,* and *Katzenbach v. McClung* Supreme Court cases, the Warren court upheld the constitutionality of the 1964 Civil Rights Act by invoking the commerce clause of the constitution rather than the equal protection clause of the 14th Amendment, deeming discrimination an impediment to inter-state commerce.

The writer and jazz critic Albert Murray remarked on the inseparability of the political and economic implications of civil rights upon returning to his hometown of Mobile, Alabama in the wake of major reforms. Visiting Kresses, a five-and-dime store that had been the center of commercial life in downtown Mobile, he found that its soda-fountain counter was no longer restricted to white patrons. A new day had dawned, Murray reflected, one where the "palest of all pale-face girls are now free to smile their whing-ding service with a red-lipped perfume-counter-faced whing-ding smile at you too (in public)."[45] Murray was enchanted and tickled by the waitress who poured on the hospitality, something unthinkable in the city he knew as a youth, but now part of the new context. It was a process, he wrote, that was "democratizing you and howard-johnsoning you at one and the same time."

The success of the civil rights movement in producing major national legislation and contesting local practices through nonviolent resistance created the conditions for the Johnson administration's War on Poverty. Many saw urban ghettos as a northern manifestation of the American race problem and an equally embarrassing exception to the postwar prosperity and nationally rising standards of living. From the beginning, however, the War on Poverty unfolded in a complex relationship with black popular constituencies and movements. On the one hand, the Community Action Program, created out of the 1964

Economic Opportunity Act, delivered an infusion of federal block grants to local communities for the purpose of fighting poverty, a policy initiative that laid the foundation for the process of black political incorporation in many American cities. On the other hand, the bundle of social programs—Job Corps, Headstart, etc. —offered by the Johnson White House were inadequate to the challenges at hand, as many black activists pointed out. For a time, black professionals and working-class residents saw the possibility of transforming the ghetto—the "black colony" in the parlance of the moment—into a base of political power. That perspective, summarized in the Black Power slogan and demands for indigenous control, would bear fruit, producing black governing regimes in dozens of cities beginning in the late sixties. The liberal Democrats' retreat from the "politics of disenclosure" and their concessions to pro-market forces, however, not only created a losing situation for the new black political elite as they sought to create effective, practical solutions to urban problems of unemployment and capital flight, it also left policing and incarceration as one of the few viable means of addressing the social chaos that defined the heroin epidemic of the late sixties and seventies.

Great Society liberals did not give us the carceral state as we know it; it was the product of a long, complex process that involved different and discordant interests, and was primarily enacted at the state and local level. Adaner Usmani offers a pointed critique of the respective histories of mass incarceration offered by Elizabeth Hinton and Naomi Murakawa, which pin responsibility on Great Society liberals. Against their interpretations, he concludes, "Johnson's failure was not that he allocated existing revenues to punitive institutions, but that he failed to raise revenue to expand the welfare state."[46] Great Society liberals did not produce the carceral state as such. However, in failing to address the specific challenges of structural unemployment facing the urban working class, the Great Society set the stage. As discussed in the next section, prominent Cold War liberals like Jane Jacobs and Daniel Patrick Moynihan championed urban thinking and strategies that emphasized private sector choices over progressive state intervention, thereby prefiguring the transition towards neoliberalization. In their respective activism, Jacobs and Moynihan addressed mounting worries over urban crime and learned to stop worrying about social democracy.

Policing Barbarism, Promoting Civic Virtue

Propelled by resurgent capital and new popular allegiances to an accumulation model rooted in mass consumption and real estate development, the affluent society gave rise to a new social antagonism between suburban haves and inner-city have-nots. Rising anxieties over crime, and the existing role of local and national police were expanded to address real and imagined threats to the Cold War order. Like the bipolar working-class consciousness produced by the postwar urban transformation, with the relative middle class on one side and the depraved urban "underclass" on the other, policing took a dual form, adopting an *emulatory strategy* of promoting the civic virtues of deference and middle-class aspiration, and a *punitive strategy* of defending the propertied and virtuous middle class from the outsiders, those segregated in inner-city ghettos and struggling to survive. William H. Parker, World War II veteran and Los Angeles police chief throughout the fifties and early sixties, imagined his department as a "thin blue line," the only defense separating the virtuous middle class from the barbarism of organized crime, Godless communism and ghetto criminality.

As Ronald Schmidt, Jr. argues in his analysis of the Los Angeles Police Department under Parker, the middle class was policed through the softer emulatory model. Schmidt describes Parker's approach as "a vision of an elite corps that would control crime but, more important, provide the citizens of Los Angeles with a model of civic excellence that they could emulate—indeed, that they would have to emulate."[47] As he surveyed a rapidly growing Los Angeles, Parker saw a society under siege, threatened by its own moral decay. "We're disappointing [George] Washington and the other Founders," he lamented. "By disassociating Virtue from our search for prosperity, we threaten to follow the course of Babylon, Rome, etc." The LAPD, he surmised, might serve as a "great moral leader to pull us from the brink."[48] Parker's emulatory approach expressed dominant notions of Cold War patriotism as anticommunism. "He hoped to create a city of virtue and moral strength," Schmidt writes, "one that could prepare Americans for the struggle to achieve historic glory and fame through a Cold War victory over Communism."[49] To achieve those ends, Parker employed radio, television and social conduits such as African American clergy, although his policies were openly criticized by others, including then beat cop and future mayor, Tom Bradley.[50] Parker worked closely with the makers of the television series *Dragnet* to accurately reflect the daily workings of the LAPD, and to broadcast in a fictionalized form the emulatory model of policing he cherished.

When his attention turned to the ghettoized ranks of black Angelenos, however, Parker took a different tack. These residents were "statistically more likely," he held, to engage in criminal activity, and they were to be met with the full force of the LAPD and its innovative tactics, like the use of police cruising to manage the vast sprawling city. In the wake of the 1965 rebellion in the city's black Watts neighborhood, Parker made clear the limits of his emulatory strategy. That softer mode of policing was intended for the middle class and virtuous; the "underclass" deserved stricter social control. "This is the lesson that we refuse to recognize, that you can't convert every person into a law-abiding citizen," he complained after Watts. "If you want any protection in your home and family in the future, you're going to have to stop this abuse, but you're going to have to get in and support a strong police department."[51] Watts marked an abrupt ending to the Parker regime, and signaled the beginnings of a new era where cities would become firmly associated in the popular imagination with majority blackness, crime and danger.

The mass rioting that erupted across the country throughout the late sixties brought the contradictions of the consumer republic into plain sight. The National Advisory Commission on Civil Disorders—commonly named in honor of its director, the Illinois governor Otto Kerner—was charged with exploring the causes of mass urban conflicts. The Kerner Commission's 1968 report, and other similar investigatory reports of the era, pointed to the huge damages suffered by retail stores which had been looted and burned. Urban rebels, however, often spared black businesses, with hastily made "Soul Brother" or "Please don't burn, Black-Owned" signs, and even those non-black merchants with a reputation for kindness and fair dealing.[52] The investigators pointed out that through such selective protests and looting urban dwellers were punishing those merchants who had subjected them to price gouging, inferior products, disrespect and all-around predatory behavior.[53]

Parker, and other urban leaders such as Chicago's mayor Richard J. Daley, were upfront about how they viewed the role of police and its duty to protect social order against ghetto discontent. In April 1968, Daley would issue his infamous "shoot to kill" order to discourage looting and arson after the assassination of Martin Luther King, Jr. He would marshal the full force of his police department again that year in an effort to crush street demonstrations at the Democratic National Convention.[54] Riding the wave of public anxiety over successive long summers of urban rioting, Richard Nixon entered the White House promising to restore "law and order" to the nation. Under Nixon, the FBI and local police forces would coordinate and intensify their efforts to infiltrate and repress popular struggles and organizations like the Black Panther Party for Self-Defense. The pro-policing stances represented by Parker, Daley, Nixon and the FBI's J. Edgar Hoover were an overt manifestation of the pro-carceral mood, but even progressive liberal voices at the time turned away from social democratic remedies when confronted with the looming problems of urban inequality and the specter of crime. Renowned neighborhood activist and urbanist Jane Jacobs and scholar and antipoverty liberal Daniel Patrick Moynihan both represent the Cold War turn towards cultural and civic solutions to inner-city depravity and crime. Neither supported the kind of aggressive policing of Parker, Daley and the rest, but their approaches diminished the place of redistributive public policy—such as genuine public works, the expansion of the social wage and protection of labor rights—in mitigating the hardships endured by the urban black poor. Their intentions were noble, but their shared view that problems of urban violence and ghetto misery were rooted in cultural deficits (for Jacobs the lack of communal surveillance, for Moynihan the absence of patriarchal families) would provide the ideological pretext for replacing welfare with prisonfare.

In her acclaimed book *The Death and Life of Great American Cities*, and in her grassroots activism, Jacobs offered powerful criticisms of the damage that Robert Moses and urban renewal had wrought on New York and other American cities.[55] Her analysis neglects the underlying class politics of the moment, however, choosing instead to focus selectively on metropolitan social relations of the neighborhood and the pedestrian street without much consideration for how those relations are constituted through political economy, production and social reproduction. Hers is an account written by a middle-class urban holdout fighting to retain a way of life during a moment of intense transition. As others have noted, she does not address the implicit racial and ethnic fault lines in the city. Marxist urbanist Marshall Berman reminds us that her portrait of the life of the street, while deeply poetic, forgets all manner of social antagonisms that always define communities, families and everyday life. Berman writes, "there are occlusions in her vision that even readers who love her can't help but see."[56] Berman rightly questions the selective and utopic nature of Jacobs' depiction of Manhattan neighborhood life:

Are there really no personal or social conflicts on this block? No larcenies or adulteries? No husbands beating up their wives, no couples splitting up, kids turning into dope fiends, families defaulting on their mortgages, tenants losing their jobs and failing to make the rent? No people quietly or noisily going crazy? (And other people mad at them because people going crazy don't keep their houses?) Isn't there more than enough class hatred, religious hatred, ethnic hatred to go around? Aren't there plenty of Jacobs' neighbors seething with stupid prejudices against each other? Isn't the block full of people who would love to knock each other's block off? And isn't everybody on the block caught up in the leaps and lurches of a real estate market that can make success more dangerous than failure?

These blind spots seriously limit Jacobs's much-vaunted discussion of how to create public safety.

"Safety on the streets by surveillance and mutual policing of one another sounds grim, but in real life it is not grim," Jacobs writes. "The safety of the street works best, most casually, and with least frequent taint of hostility and suspicion precisely where people are using and enjoying the city streets voluntarily and are least conscious, normally, that they are policing."[57] Jacobs sees such safety as intimately connected to vibrant commercial life, but such wealth was nowhere to be found in places like Harlem's black ghetto at the time of her writing. "The basic requisite for such surveillance is a substantial quantity of stores and other public places sprinkled along sidewalks of a district," she writes; "enterprises and public places that are used by evening and night must be among them especially. Stores, bars and restaurants, as the chief examples, work in several different and complex ways to abet sidewalk safety."[58] But what of the dispossessed in this account, those whose environs are not defined by bustling legal market activity, and who are not welcomed into such legitimate commercial zones as either proprietors, flâneurs or consumers? She celebrates the role of the storekeepers and small businessmen, "strong proponents of peace and order" who "hate broken windows and holdups; they hate having customers made nervous about safety."[59] Jacobs treats the mid-twentieth-century New York residential block as normative, or at least the optimal basis on which a stable, functioning urban life might occur. The broader exploitative class relations that define the city, especially a city like New York at the time of her writing, are not considered in a critical way. This is consequential because New York was undergoing massive industrial contraction with many small workshops being shuttered, victims of either the coercive laws of economic competition, or of the earthmovers and steamrollers that paved the way for Moses's concrete-and-steel vision of progress. The social dislocations were enormous, but they remain out of view in Jacobs's discussions of public safety.

Jacobs cites grim statistics of rape and aggravated assault in major cities at the time, and reminds us that the fifties and sixties were not a golden age of innocence and peace but one of growing property crime, violence, suspicion and policing. Although her descriptions of the delicate ballet of the well-functioning neighborhood are memorable and often-cited, Jacobs also takes her readers on a tour of the bleaker corners of the Cold War American city, a place defined by "horrifying public crimes," "dispirited gray areas" and "darkened theaters." Certain parts of the city have become a "desert where there are no ears to hear."[60] Yet, on the whole, Jacobs turns away from the underlying economic divide set in motion by the Cold War Haussmannization of American cities. There is much to mine from Jacobs's classic book. Clearly, she deplores the conditions people endure in the tower-block public housing that replaced older neighborhood fabrics. But, true to the ideological mood of the period, she suggests that the remedy lies not in the abolition of capitalist class relations but rather in the power of everyday social relations, architecture and the preservation of aesthetic vestiges of Fordist urbanism.

Peer surveillance ("eyes on the street") is offered up as a means of maintaining public safety and civility, but even at the time of Jacobs's writing, the very ethnic and racial nature of most American cities threw the viability of this strategy into question. Among familiars, even nominally so, and among neighbors who pass one another on a regular basis, her premise holds true. What happens, however, when interlopers or strangers of another color wander into these tightly spun webs of neighborhood interaction? Who is considered suspect? How are different and unfamiliar bodies read? Who gets to decide the boundaries of community? I am not suggesting that we read Jacobs against contemporary incidents —like the 2012 killing of Trayvon Martin or the 2020 killing of Ahmaud Arbery, who were both stalked and assaulted by self-appointed neighborhood watchmen—but even during the city she describes in the late fifties and early sixties, ethnic turf, black and brown ghettoization and a nascent policing regime all trouble the kind of nostalgic, intimate keeping of neighborhood order she celebrates.[61]

At various turns, Jacobs gives us the sense that there is in fact a class dimension to all this, but she never speaks of class in explicit terms. She celebrates the vestiges of mutuality that defined working-class ethnic enclaves for much of the twentieth century, a culture that was determined as much by common old-world origins, kinship networks, social organizations, unionism and political bonds as by street design, building setbacks and the flow of pedestrian traffic. Jacobs alludes to class as well when she points out how residents in upper-income buildings do not monitor the streets in the same way, preferring to outsource security to private guards and doormen. Although some reformers have expressed renewed affection for community policing, most Americans, as the last half century has revealed, would rather outsource policing to the professionals whether they are paid by the state or private corporations, rather than take up the burden of policing themselves.

In retrospect, Jacobs endorsed a civic strategy for maintaining public safety that became only one facet of the broader process of securitization and hyperpolicing that would become dominant. "No amount of police can enforce civilization," Jacobs cautions, "where the normal, casual enforcement of it has broken down." What Jacobs is describing is a culture of civility, a context where social bonds, cosmopolitanism and human kindness are over-flowing. These are the qualities of great cities we adore, but the matter of security is connected to economic well-being in ways that Jacobs sadly neglects. Her account naturalizes the capitalist market order and its underlying class relations, and she even views these arrangements as the means of social order rather than the source of misery, alienation and crisis. The out-of-work day laborer, the billiards hustler, streetwalker or heroin junkie are not invited into the intricate street ballet she celebrates, not even as spectators. They are the strangers and "malefactors" who threaten sidewalk safety.

Although Jacobs hopes order might be maintained through social agreement and responsibility, what she does not and perhaps could not anticipate at the time is how a broader political consensus would expand the formal role and reach of police departments, and how the technological and social relations she observed in the higher rent districts of Manhattan, where policing was outsourced to private security companies, would come to dominate the American setting. In passing, she mentions one possible, but for her undesirable, way of approaching crime, namely the creation of securitized zones, a turf system similar to those of gangs. This, of course, has become the norm in terms of residential settlement in most American cities—first as a segregative logic of the suburban–inner city class divide, but more recently as a new patchwork of gentrified central city zones, created through the processes of urban revanchism that gained momentum in the wake of public housing demolitions and the mortgage foreclosure crisis.[62] These shifting residential patterns have also bore an accompanying configuration of public-private policing strategies, with the size of private security forces now equaling that of public police.

Jacobs's prescriptions are propelled by nostalgia for the pre–World War II ethnic enclaves of most US cities, and by the active deterioration of central cities taking shape during the Cold War period. Her account may well forget that even the well-ordered and apparently safe ethnic enclaves that were then being bulldozed to make way for expressways, tower blocks and civic buildings, also played host to organized crime, racist pogroms where blacks were brutalized, and all manner of domestic violence and sexual predation that went underreported. Jacobs hoists up an idyllic portrait of the pre–World War II city, but only obscures the social contradictions of the new city rising all around her, which was not solely the result of errant modernist design, or the hubris of Moses and his ilk, but a spatial fix advanced by a broader set of real estate interests, city politicians and chamber of commerce leaders. Jacobs claims that a "well-used city street is apt to be a safe street. A deserted city is apt to be unsafe."[63] True enough, but let's try this again with the city as a totality in mind: *A city where all residents are guaranteed a modicum of food, clothing and shelter, and where inequality is not vast and considered some natural ordering, is apt to be safe. The deeply unequal and spatially segregated city is apt to be unsafe.* Jacobs sets aside these economic matters too easily. "Deep and complicated social ills must lie behind delinquency and crime, in suburbs and towns as well as in great cities," she concedes early on, only to say that her "book will not go into speculation on the deeper reasons."[64]

While class relations are placed out of view in Jacobs's account of public safety, Daniel Patrick Moynihan finds a way to talk about class without engaging capitalism. The thread that binds both of their arguments is culture—*either the culture of the middle-class neighborhood that civilizes, or the alleged culture of the poor that breeds barbarism*. Where Jacobs decouples public safety from economic inequality, Moynihan makes a similar maneuver, even while focusing explicitly on the most visible manifestation of inequality in sixties American urban life: the condition of the black urban poor. In a manner that parallels Jacobs's turn to the maintenance of community security through peer surveillance, Moynihan explains the plight of the most dispossessed urban blacks through their putative cultural deficiencies. The result is a notion of black exceptionalism, the underclass myth, that would not only shape the New Right and New Democratic assaults on social provision and the concomitant prison build-up, but would also endure as popular ideology even into the post–welfare state age as a means of explaining inequality and scapegoating the black poor for their plight.[65]

At the heart of the underclass mythmaking is the view that "Negro poverty is not white poverty," to quote Lyndon B. Johnson.[66] In defending his influential 1965 report, *The Negro Family: The Case for National Action*, Moynihan, then serving as Assistant Secretary of Labor under Johnson, argued that it was "necessary to depict, and in terms that would be felt as well as understood, the internal weakness of the Negro community and the need for immense federal efforts if that community was to go beyond opportunity 'to equality as a fact and as a result.'"[67] Moynihan was writing in the aftermath of the 1966 midterm elections, which saw substantial Republican gains in Congress, and his arguments about the distinctiveness of black poverty reflected the accommodation of social liberalism to a cynical electoral strategy, an attempt to appease the virulent white reaction to desegregation and white middle-class angst over black political militancy. By focusing on the alleged cultural pathology of the black family—i.e., the prevalence of single-parent, female-headed households—Moynihan hoped to enlist the support of the "more conservative and tradition-oriented centers of power in American life whose enthusiasm for class legislation is limited indeed."[68] Moynihan's Cold War political calculus created an opening for the rise of the New Right, and, despite his best intentions, his and other Great Society liberals' view that black poverty was rooted in culture rather than in economic structures that impact the working class more generally has cast a long shadow over how Americans tend to think about inequality.

Moynihan advanced an analysis that would only grow more powerful and influential as the New Deal coalition fragmented and as the visions of social justice generated by interwar labor militancy, popular front communism and even progressive Keynesianism lost their hold on the popular imagination. Moynihan's thesis evolved within the context of two overlapping social conflicts. The first, the battle to overthrow Jim Crow segregation, was primarily sectional and openly political. The second, black urban poverty and unemployment, was national and had its roots in peacetime industrial demobilization and changes in the forces of production, namely the increasing use of automation and cybernetic command in manufacturing. The culminating saga of civil rights reform provided the impetus for his work, but Moynihan's 1965 report spoke more directly to the festering problem of relative surplus population in Northern cities. He explained this problem, however, not through economics but through the alleged cultural deficits of black families that he argued were matriarchal and pathological. His thesis, and those of his contemporaries like Oscar Lewis and Kenneth Clark, were penned out of a sense of antiracist commitment and sympathy for the poor, in a conscious political attempt to marshal state aid to address urban inequality and immiseration.[69] Their arguments emphasized the alleged cultural pathology as a legacy of racism and called for antidiscrimination policy and targeted services. But, as Touré Reed illustrates, when addressing the plight of urban blacks, Moynihan rejected the kinds of social democratic measures advocated by labor and civil rights progressives at the time.[70]

Moynihan and other Cold War liberals held that blacks had been left behind by the postwar prosperity primarily because of institutional racism (e.g., redlining, the use of restrictive covenants, and other forms of housing and labor market discrimination), which denied access to jobs and housing. This focus on racial barriers shifted the terms of debate on the left from the underlying forces of structural unemployment towards the cultural sphere. The Cold War liberal tenets expressed in Moynihan's 1965 report—that poverty is due primarily to institutional racism and a dysfunctional culture—have only grown more hegemonic with the end of the Cold War and the era of neoliberalization, which has not only marketized public goods and services, but has also eroded the faith of many Americans that public interventionism might address the mounting social and ecological problems of our times.

Building on the foundation laid by Cold War liberals, the New Right explained inequality exclusively in terms of cultural pathology: the black urban poor, or even the out-of-work black professional, were deemed unassimilable not because of the internal tendencies of capitalism, but due to their personal and cultural flaws. Whereas the black urban poor lacked a work ethic, they held, the out-of-work black professional simply could not compete with more qualified whites. Where they departed from Moynihan, who pointed to the need to correct cultural pathos as a justification for federal action, Republicans argued that the welfare state itself helped to reproduce poverty by disincentivizing economic self-reliance, marriage, work ethic and other alleged cultural markers of suburban middle-class life.

The underclass myth attained hegemony during the closing decades of the twentieth century through various modes of transmission—campaign speeches that stoked racist reaction to civil rights reforms; think tank reports and academic books that gave an air of objective truth to ideological claims; popular films, television, music videos, local news broadcasts; and finally urban legends and family lore of the city as dystopia, a paradise lost to the influx of blacks and immigrants who had taken over the old ethnic enclaves of the pre-war years. Perhaps the most powerful and damaging performance of this script was Ronald Reagan's welfare-queen mythmaking, which presented the poor as conniving, undeserving and criminal. Although his claims were loosely based on a real case of welfare fraud in Cook County, Illinois, Reagan exaggerated the extent of the malfeasance.[71] Although reporters attempted to separate the truth from the fiction, the damage was already done; whether Reagan's claims were true or not did not matter to his supporters, who believed that they were being unfairly asked to support freeloaders. Underclass ideology appealed to an anxious white suburban middle class and those of various ethnic backgrounds who faced uncertainty, redundancy, soaring costs of living and stagnant wages. Welfare cheats and criminals provided the perfect scapegoat.

Conclusion

The 1968 Kerner Commission report offered a contradictory set of prescriptions to avert the possibility of future urban rebellions. In addition to counterinsurgency tactics, the Commission called for the revival of the social democracy of the pre–World War II years, more substantial public investment in housing and job creation, and a greater commitment to antidiscrimination and antisegregation policy. Such prescriptions stood in sharp contrast to the underclass claims of Moynihan and others, in that they located the problems of urban black poverty in capitalist political economy rather than the alleged cultural flaws of the black poor. The Commission's prescriptions, however, constituted a plan without the power to make it a reality. The Democrats possessed legislative majorities but lacked the political will. Perhaps more correctly, the Commission's prescriptions were to the left of the embattled Democratic Party of the late sixties. The New Deal coalition had veered away from the social democratic policies that were responsible for its political emergence and broad legitimacy coming out of the Roosevelt years, while broad political conflicts over desegregation, Vietnam and the urban crisis tore away whatever threads of cohesion remained. Johnson's decision to forgo a re-election campaign in 1968, and the rise of Nixon on a wave of law-and-order sentiment, effectively made the Commission's social democratic provisions a dead letter.

In retrospect, Great Society liberalism marked the beginning of the end of the social reproductive state, and in lieu of policies that addressed basic needs and protected citizens and workers from market volatility and the cyclical crises of capitalism, policing would slowly fill the void the welfare state left behind. In the years after the 1965 Watts rebellion, William H. Parker's thin blue line would come to replace the unemployment line as the chief means for addressing inequality under late capitalism. This process was not instantaneous but would unfold in fits and starts, experimentally and unevenly, as city leaders and state and national politicians attempted to address the deepening problems of urban poverty and rising violent crime. Ironically, the insistence of Moynihan and other social liberals on black cultural exceptionalism—i.e., that the black poor suffer from acute behavioral problems dissimilar from the working class more generally—provided the pretext for the expansion and militarization of police departments. If the problem was bad behavior and social dysfunction stemming from weak parenting and broken families, then the repressive arm of the state would provide discipline and behavior modification where the family structure had failed.

The latent social conflict between the relative middle class and the "underclass" would deepen and expand in the decades after Watts, manifesting first as resentment towards the poor as a social burden, but from the eighties onwards in direct conflicts over space and municipal resources as corporations, big developers and the middle class sought to reclaim the city. During the seventies, the inner city would become synonymous with dystopia, ruin and danger, popular perceptions that were evidenced in actual deteriorating conditions and real crime. Recall Howard Cosell's "the Bronx is burning" commentary during game two of the 1977 World Series, when the flames and smoke columns of that borough's arson epidemic could be seen in the vicinity of Yankee Stadium. While "Mack the Knife" may have lost his menacing quality during the postwar boom, the urban predator reappeared in the American imagination in a new guise during the late sixties and seventies, as the antithesis of the safety and affluence enjoyed by the suburban middle class. This new urban terror was black and brown, and his domination of the cityscape was reflected in the graffitied subway cars of the New York transit authority, as well as in the roving bands of denim-garbed, drug-addled gang members, whose names—the Savage Nomads, Majestic Warlocks Tribe, the Mongols, the Savage Skulls, the Young Sinners, etc.—all embraced barbarism as virtue. News media images of columns of black smoke spiraling up from the South Bronx, once a tight-knit collection of stable working-class ethnic enclaves, reinforced the popular sense that the city had become some seventh circle of hell. Although white suburbanites were less likely to be preyed upon than the black and brown residents who lived in Harlem, the South Bronx and other inner-city ghettos, the fact of real urban danger provided the pretext for more punitive approaches to crime, beginning with expanded funding for SWAT teams and, in concert with urban neoliberalization, the institution of tough-on-crime laws, mandatory minimum sentencing rules and zero-tolerance policing strategies. The crack cocaine years gave rise to heartbreaking rates of urban homicide, much of it drug and gang-related, but equally the consequence of the widespread availability of guns, which made smaller personal feuds and domestic conflicts more lethal. The switchblades, zip guns and "Saturday Night Specials" of seventies New York gave way to the Uzi and TEC-9 submachine guns in the gang wars that escalated on the streets of Chicago and Los Angeles during the late Reagan-Bush years. The expansion of the carceral state during the nineties, and the widespread adoption of more militaristic technologies and strategies by police departments, were also correlated with a project of urban revanchism, which saw the return of middle-class residents as well as the finance, real estate, entertainment and retail sectors—the very forces that had been unleashed in the postwar era, and which combined to constitute the dominant regime of accumulation across urban society.

3

The Roots of Black Lives Matter

Racial Liberalism and the Problem of Surplus Population

Black Lives Matter is at once a protest against police and vigilante killings of black civilians and a liberal democratic reassertion of black equality within the context of an eviscerated welfare state and a shrinking and increasingly precarious American middle class. Black Lives Matter was precipitated by public, and often graphic, acts of police and vigilante violence, which were irreconcilable to professed American ideals of universal inalienable rights and the constitutional guarantee of equal protection. As such, Black Lives Matter is a call for renewal of liberal democratic commitments and practices. Renewal is the appropriate term here. Contrary to the prevailing cynicism of so much contemporary "wokeness," which flattens historical conjuncture and sees racial oppression as an unaltered feature of American society, black life over the last century has been characterized by significant social and political progress, though always unevenly felt and never impervious to political pressure and reversal.

This chapter explores the origins and contradictions of Black Lives Matter and contends that these latest struggles against policing stem from the enduring problems of black urban poverty and joblessness, problems which were not resolved by the omnibus civil rights reforms of the sixties and have only intensified under capitalist globalization and the collapse of the New Deal welfare state. Blackness has continued to symbolize inequality and deprivation, despite real social progress and improved circumstances for millions of African Americans and even as conditions of poverty and redundancy are increasingly more widely felt beyond the ghetto landscapes that define cities in much of the popular imagination.[1] While Great Society liberals sought to ameliorate poverty during the sixties, and their ideological descendants hope to address food deserts, reduce child poverty, shelter the "unhoused" and bridge the digital divide, it has never been in the interest of capital to abolish poverty, which is both a precondition and a consequence of exploitation, not an exceptional or incidental circumstance. After all, as Marx once noted, the existence of a relative surplus population is an intractable and central feature of capitalist valorization, "the background against which the law of supply and demand of labour does its work."[2] Contemporary mass protests against police wilding speak implicitly to this problem of surplus population, though racialized thinking has precluded clear-eyed analyses of the broader dilemma.

This chapter provides a critical account of Black Lives Matter's political origins that contrasts sharply with the first wave of intellectual work on the subject. So many of the early analyses of Black Lives Matter uncritically embraced and promoted activists' assumptions about their lineage and about the fundamental motives and character of policing and imprisonment in our times, and shared their faith in a revitalized black ethnic politics as the key to ending the policing crisis and delivering a more just society. Chris Lebron's *The Making of Black Lives Matter*, for example, is emblematic in its treatment of contemporary demands to end police and vigilante violence against black civilians as descending from a longer strain of black political thinking. For Lebron, Black

Lives Matter conveys "a sentiment that was as old as the desire to be free from slavery," and "represents a civic desire for equality and human desire for respect, the intellectual roots of which lie deep in the history of black American thought."[3] Lebron proceeds to examine the thinking of eight historical figures who "recommend a political ethical comportment to America that suggests an endorsement of the ideal of democracy while soundly and roundly rejecting the distortions and corruptions of *American* democracy without compromise—black humanity will be respected or blacks will no longer endorse the centuries old asymmetrical project Audre Lorde famously spelled as 'america' to demote the idea of grandness and properness to an immature and unformed state of the union."[4] In making claims about what "blacks will no longer endorse," a common rhetorical tendency in such popular and academic discourse, Lebron shifts away from the book's promise of providing an interpretation of Black Lives Matter's emergence towards voicing the will of the black mass, with little evidence to support such ventriloquism. These kinds of imputed and hyperbolic claims do not amount to analysis. We know not only that most blacks have continued to support policing during the time of Black Lives Matter, but also that popular black faith in the democratic promise persisted even during the darkest days of Jim Crow's spectacular abuses and oppression.

Lebron provides us with an idealist interpretation which identifies the liberal lineage of Black Lives Matter thinking. But a more historical analysis is needed to account for BLM's immediate social origins, novelty and popularity, an analysis that is not merely focused on the movement of ideas but understands those ideas as constituted by discrete class formations, shifting political alignments and ruling ideology. Although its advocates often analogize Jim Crow, slavery and settler colonialism, the historical context that produced Black Lives Matter is categorically different from that which produced the various historical figures and sentiments Lebron addresses. Strangely, aside from a few references in his preface, Lebron does not connect Black Lives Matter to Black Power, its most immediate forebear and a source of so much inspiration for contemporary activists. Neither does he take up in any sustained manner the half century of black political development since the sixties—including black political control of most major American cities—and just how profoundly that historical process has rendered obsolete the very ideas about the "black experience" and cohesive black political interests that remain at the heart of so much rhetoric and folklore among activists and the broader US population.

This chapter argues that Black Lives Matter as a political sentiment was born out of the limits of the Second Reconstruction—the wave of federal court decisions, executive orders and congressional legislation that restored black citizenship rights, began the process of dismantling Jim Crow and targeted federal investment for poverty relief and community-led urban revitalization through the Community Action Program and Model Cities initiatives. The Second Reconstruction produced unprecedented black social progress, which included the expansion of the black middle class, in part through antidiscrimination regulation in higher education admissions and labor markets and the resulting cultural enlightenment in corporate recruitment strategies. The growth of black public sector employment and unionization also improved the incomes and living conditions of millions of African Americans.

While the Second Reconstruction reduced national black poverty rates by half in the decades following the 1954 *Brown v. Board of Education* decision, it would not resolve the problem of structural unemployment so glaringly evident in the inner cities. In other words, segments of the black population, alongside other racial and ethnic demographics, would become locked out of the US domestic labor market by a combination of technological change and, as the Cold War came to an end, increasingly globalized production. Racial liberalism provided a readymade, but deeply limited, means of understanding the suppressive policing and carceral expansion that occurred in the wake of this dislocation. These realities came to be viewed as a "New Jim Crow," the latest in a succession of controlling institutions dating back to the plantation and deputized "paddy rollers," or slave catchers. In that regard, policing and mass incarceration have become powerful symbols of the limitations or lost ground of the progress of the civil rights movement and the Second Reconstruction. Racism as metanarrative and allegory, however, has never captured the discrete and localized origins of the carceral expansion, its complex motives and social function, and perhaps most importantly, how carceral power shapes the lives of the most dispossessed segments of the working class across metropolitan and rural geographies and ethnic and racial populations.

This chapter begins by excavating black left analysis of automation and black unemployment during the sixties. In the writings of Detroit autoworker James Boggs and the political program of the Black Panther Party and other groups, we find black activists, citizens and intellectuals thinking critically about the challenges posed by the increasing replacement of living labor with robotics and computerization and what these transformations meant for black life and basic survival. Such left tendencies also saw black communities serving as a vanguard in catalyzing a broader struggle that might unite Americans across social layers towards socialist transformation. This left focus on structural unemployment and anticapitalism would be overtaken in black life by the ascendancy of an expanded black political class during the seventies and eighties, and, eventually, by the neoliberal turn, which engulfed those elements and reoriented black approaches to poverty towards market-oriented solutions and conservative moral rehabilitation. Instead of thinking of the most dispossessed segments of the working class in terms of the reserve army or surplus population, liberal and even progressive left tendencies have come to see the same stratum as "underprivileged" and "underserved" by capital.

The chapter then turns to a brief examination of the neoliberal context that produced the carceral fix, before surveying the earliest protests against expanding police power and prisons in the late eighties and nineties. So much of this discussion ranges over cultural politics because of the relative alienation of black youth and the urban working class from both neoliberal black politics as well as organized left politics, and the outsized role mass culture came to occupy amid deteriorating civic life. Finally, the chapter concludes by discussing Black Lives Matter as militant racial liberalism and examining its political limitations. There are important exceptions, but the birth and popularity of BLM sentiment has meant the revitalization of a black ethnic politics which is elite-driven and pro-capitalist, and therefore, by definition, antithetical to the vast needs and interests of blacks as workers and to the development of a popular anticapitalist politics generally.

An old Jim Crow quip, attributed to Langston Hughes, held that any black man with a new suit and $5 in his pocket can lay claim to being a Negro leader, but it seems that the price of entry has been greatly lowered in the era of Black Lives Matter, where Wi-Fi access and a Twitter handle suffice.[5] A key political conundrum of the post–Second Reconstruction period is how state and corporate investment and an activist black professional-managerial class have elevated a liberal antiracist politics that obscures the ways in which black poverty, like all poverty and dispossession, is connected to capitalist political economy.[6] Black Lives Matter activists have offered compelling criticism of the black political elite, from Baltimore mayor Stephanie Rawlings-Blake to Chicago mayor Lori Lightfoot, but popular demonstrations, especially after the murder of George Floyd, have also accelerated the process of leadership recruitment, social entrepreneurship, downright hustling and a doubling down on liberal remedies to the issues of police abuse and incarceration. Moreover, the simultaneous diversification of black leadership—i.e., more LGBTQ voices, fresh faces, youth, etc.—and entrenchment of black ethnic politics as normative have deterred the emergence of popular and governing majorities capable of contesting the current order. Mass mobilization has forced the problem of police violence into public consciousness, but *organizing a new consensus* around left progressive approaches to public safety and inequality has proven more elusive. Mass demonstrations since the murder of George Floyd have further popularized an interpretation that misses the mark, focusing on America's "original sin" of racism, while neglecting the more immediate problem of surplus population that policing is charged with managing in the post–welfare context.

Outsiders, Expendables, Untouchables, Lumpen

The Second Reconstruction dismantled Jim Crow and through targeted programs attempted to patch over the cracks of the postwar growth regime, which resegregated metropolitan space along sharper racial and class lines. The War on Poverty engineered by Daniel Patrick Moynihan and other functionaries of the Lyndon Johnson administration, however, was inadequate to the task at hand. Great Society liberals rejected strengthening labor rights and unionization for blacks as workers—which had been central to the expansion of the postwar middle class and a consistent demand of the civil rights movement—in favor of investments in moral and community rehabilitation. As argued in the previous chapter, Moynihan's underclass theory prefigured the neoliberal turn. By focusing on the alleged cultural and moral deficits of the black poor, instead of the exploitative dynamics and crisis tendencies of capitalism, he and other Great Society liberals rehearsed arguments that would ultimately come to justify the dismantling of the New Deal welfare state. Much of the civil rights movement stood to the left of Moynihan and his ilk. Figures like A. Philip Randolph, Bayard Rustin and E. D. Nixon were steadfastly committed to improving conditions for black laborers. The 1963 March on Washington was a campaign for "jobs and justice" and, following passage of landmark civil rights legislation, Martin Luther King, Jr. and others were increasingly audacious in using their power and resources to press for justice in housing and economic matters.[7] King's last days were spent lending support to striking sanitation workers in Memphis. After his assassination, his devotees took up the mantle of the Poor People's Campaign, staging a national march and encampment known as "Resurrection City" on the National Mall in order to press Congressional Democrats towards more progressive reform.

Some black activists and thinkers during the sixties were especially prescient in identifying the immediate and potential impacts of the technological changes being implemented in the manufacturing and service sectors. It is important to recall their analyses here, not because their arguments and strategies are some model to be replicated in new times, but rather because their efforts demonstrate the contingency of sixties struggles and spoke to the deeper problem of structural unemployment neglected in both War on Poverty initiatives and contemporary discourse. Likewise, their insistence that the black urban poor might have a progressive or even revolutionary role to play in their own emancipation stood in sharp contrast to the conservative view of dysfunctional black wards of the state and remains to the left of many contemporary articulations of black ethnic politics, which mobilize the imagery and votes of the black working class but do not result in tangible empowerment and effective representation of their felt needs and interests. Recalling here the thinking of James Boggs, and the work of the Illinois Panther Party in building a "vanguard of the oppressed," should serve to counter the contemporary slander that equates anticapitalism with whiteness and force us to reckon with why a liberal race-centric formula came to dominate popular thinking through the end of the Cold War.

Detroit autoworker James Boggs provided an important and overlooked analysis of automation and its implications for the American left and African Americans during the sixties. Boggs's short, insightful book, *The American Revolution: Pages from a Negro Worker's Notebook*, examined the revolution in productive technology and its implications for political revolution in the United States. Boggs saw the black predicament not as an exception but as an intense manifestation of the broader contradictions of US capitalism. For Boggs, "automation not only poses the questions of poverty and employment and related economic questions. It brings into sharp focus that element which the Negroes always bring with them when they struggle for their rights. It makes the question social because it poses the relations of man to man."[8]

The first wave of postwar industrial decline resulted in the loss of thousands of entry-level jobs. African Americans and other less-skilled, less-senior workers were especially vulnerable in those industries that contracted during the peacetime demobilization. By 1960, the rate of joblessness for young black men in Detroit was staggering, reaching 41 percent among eighteen-year-olds, and roughly four times that of their white counterparts more generally.[9] At various points in *The American Revolution*, Boggs contemplated what would happen to those youth who increasingly found factory doors shuttered and the path to lower-middle-class stability foreclosed. The welfare state and entry into the US military provided temporary solutions for some, but Boggs cautioned that the "growing army of the permanently unemployed is the ultimate crisis of the American bourgeoisie."[10]

At various turns, Boggs described these black unemployed youth who were being rendered obsolete by new technology as "outsiders," "expendables," "castaways" and "untouchables." He sensed a novel condition for urban African Americans with grave consequences for work, citizenship and survival. Blacks had long endured material poverty and exploitation, first during the stage of antebellum chattel slavery, then after emancipation in the semi-slave conditions of debt peonage throughout the South, and finally as low-skilled, itinerant workers in the manufacturing centers of the North during the first two thirds of the twentieth century. Under automation, however, blacks faced a new challenge of permanent obsolescence rather than exploitation.

Boggs saw these outsiders, the unemployed young people he encountered on the street corners and in the pool halls of Detroit and cities like Cleveland and Buffalo, as a potentially revolutionary social force. They lacked the political allegiances and bourgeois aspirations of those blacks who had experienced some nominal integration under Fordism. At one point, he even described their plight and aspirations in colonial terms: "Being workless, they are also stateless. They have grown up like a colonial people who no longer feel any allegiance to the old imperial power and are each day searching for new means to overthrow it."[11] This younger generation that was increasingly excluded from wage labor through the deployment of high technology in the manufacturing sector faced a new set of basic economic and political challenges. Boggs's view of the new urban poor as revolutionary political agents capable of ushering in a post-capitalist society stood in sharp contrast to the views of his contemporaries and the notions of the black "underclass" that have become dominant within American public life since the 1960s.

Boggs's response to the coming of automation and the postindustrial society was neither Luddite nor welfare statist. "Whereas the old workers used to hope that they could pit their bodies against iron and outlast the iron," he noted, "this new generation of workless people knows that even their brains are being outwitted by the iron brains of automation and cybernation." Instead of trying to outwit the machines, Boggs argued, this new generation, the outsiders, should focus on "the organization and reorganization of society and of human relations inside society." Their revolution would be "a revolution of their minds and hearts, directed not towards increasing production but towards the management and distribution of things towards the control of relations among people, tasks which up to now have been left to chance or in the hands of the elite."[12]

Boggs eschewed liberal calls for job training and tutelage in bourgeois citizenship as viable antidotes to the unfolding urban crisis. In response to the continual talk of "new training programs," he said emphatically that training was not the answer. "In the very period when individuals are being trained," he concluded, "new machinery is being introduced which eliminates the need for such training."[13] These dynamics have only intensified since the time of Boggs's writing, when the era of computerization was only embryonic, having eliminated entire occupations, such as typesetters in newspaper offices, pattern cutters in industrial garment factories and spot welders in automotive assembly plants, and transformed the nature of white-collar work, subjecting office workers to forms of surveillance and managerial discipline that were previously confined to the shop floor. Even among the skilled sectors of the service economy, new technologies such as automated bank machines and online banking, digital audio synthesizers, word processing and accounting software, self-checkout counters and online shopping and the like have rendered some jobs more precarious and increasingly obsolete. Although job training may enable some workers to achieve a measure of security and self-preservation, capital-intensive production, as Boggs noted again and again, entails a quantitative reduction in socially necessary labor. These new conditions required equally novel notions of revolution. For Boggs, the technological changes in US capitalism demanded a revolution in values and an abandonment of the dogma of work which informed left thinking as much as that of conservatives in the United States. Under high technology capitalism, Boggs argued, "productivity can no longer be the measure of an individual's right to life."[14] What is needed is "a new Declaration of Human Rights to fit the new Age of Abundance."[15] For Boggs, no amount of countercyclical interventions would halt the general dynamic already set in motion: "America is headed towards full unemployment, not full employment." Despite these revolutionary changes in production, Boggs asserted that too many Americans still clung to the assumptions of mass society: "Many people still think in the same terms. They still assume that the majority of the population will be needed to produce material goods and that the production of such goods will still remain the heart of society. They have not been able to face the fact that even if the workers took over the plants they would also be faced with the problem of what to do with themselves now that work is becoming socially unnecessary."[16] Unlike the underclass rhetoric of the War on Poverty initiative that emphasized the putative cultural dysfunction of the poor, Boggs's arguments called for broader societal change rather than the remaking of the most marginalized and dispossessed into better capitalist subjects.

Although he did not anticipate the carceral expansion, in an especially prophetic passage Boggs foresaw how structural unemployment would precipitate a popular reactionary backlash and the rise of the New Right. "As automation spreads, it will intensify the crises of capitalism and sharpen the conflicts among various sections of the population," Boggs wrote, "particularly between those working and those not working, those paying taxes and those not paying taxes." "Out of this conflict will grow a counter-revolutionary movement made up of those from all social layers who resent the continued cost to them of maintaining these expendables but who are determined to maintain the system that creates and multiplies the number of expendables," he continued. "This in turn will mobilize those who begin by recognizing the right of these displaced persons to live and from there are forced to struggle for a society in which there are no displaced persons."[17] This latter political project capable of countering the New Right has yet to materialize, but during the late sixties the most radical left tendencies of Black Power sought to center the experiences and interests of the outsiders Boggs identified, and openly contest police power and brutality.

We get a sense of the emergent nexus of unemployment and incarceration in the writings of George Jackson, the co-founder of the Black Guerilla Family who was killed in an attempted escape from San Quentin prison in August 1971. "This is my eleventh year of being shoveled into every major prison in the most populous state in the nation—and the largest prison system in the world," Jackson wrote. "At each institution I've been in, 30 to sometimes 40 percent of those held are black, and every one of the many thousands I've encountered was from the working or lumpenproletariat class."[18] So while Jackson is clear that blacks are overrepresented, he insisted that there is an underlying unity in that the vast majority of the prison population is drawn from the "proletariat in rags," the most dispossessed segments of the working class.

The most iconic organization of the Black Power period, the Black Panther Party for Self-Defense (BPP), formed in Oakland, California in 1966, set out to make revolution in the heart of urban America. Rather than seeking assimilation into mainstream America, the Panthers condemned the crass materialism and military adventurism that sustained the affluent society. They famously contested carceral power through propaganda, monitoring of police activities, and armed conflicts with law enforcement. The Panthers provided pioneering, lucid criticisms of police power that illuminated the continuities between state repression of the "black colony" and the broader project of American empire and war-making abroad, views that both enthralled and frightened middle-class America. And while the Panthers were deeply committed to black liberation, they also understood that the working class was not restricted to black and brown inner-city ghettos.

Chicago provided the setting for the Panthers' most ambitious attempt to build a multiracial "vanguard of the dispossessed," with magnetic Panther leaders Bob Lee and Fred Hampton leading the way. The Rainbow Coalition forged by the Panthers momentarily united them with the Young Lords, a street gang of mainland Puerto Ricans who had turned to radical left politics, and the Young Patriots, a group of mostly "dislocated hillbillies" living in Chicago's Uptown neighborhood. Founded by Junebug Boykin and Doug Youngblood, the Patriots organization was a descendant of the Students for a Democratic Society, growing out of its JOIN Community Union's antipolice-brutality committee.[19] For a time, the coalition also included another JOIN spin-off organization, Rising Up Angry, comprised mainly of disaffected white working-class youth, so-called greasers. One issue that united these different groups of working people was their vile treatment by the Chicago Police Department.

Much of the grunt work of knitting together the coalition, especially among the white poor on Chicago's northside, was carried out by Bob Lee.[20] A Houston native who first arrived in the city as part of the War on Poverty's Volunteers in Service to

America (VISTA) program, Lee was met with skepticism when he first attempted to garner support from the white southern migrants in Uptown. By 1970, some 40,000 white working-class migrants from the middle South states had come to populate a section of the city's northside that was sometimes called "Hillbilly Harlem." During one of his earliest attempts to organize that community, Lee left a meeting in frustration after it became clear that many of the residents did not seem to trust him or see the virtues of aligning with the Panthers. Shortly after he left, Lee was accosted by police, but within minutes the residents from the meeting poured out of the church and surrounded the squad car, pounding on the hood and demanding his release. Lee recalled, "I'll never forget looking at all those brave white motherfuckers standing in the light of the police car staring in the face of death." The officers relented, and a deeply touched Lee threw himself into organizing the community, living among the residents, sleeping on their couches, breaking bread at their tables and gaining a keen sense of their lives, felt needs and desires.

Federal and local law enforcement waged war against the radical organizations that made up Chicago's Rainbow Coalition.[21] The Chicago Board of Health imposed tighter regulations on the free clinics created by the Panthers, Lords and Patriots in different wards, under the pretext that the clinics provided cover for all manner of illegal activity. One city official summed up their position: "How do we know the Young Patriots aren't using their medical service at 4411 N. Sheridan to treat gunshot wounds, hand out drugs irresponsibly, perform abortions or give shots with unsterile needles?" Rainbow Coalition activists organized a march of 3,000 to a precinct station after the police killings of Young Lords Manuel Ramos and Ralph Rivera in May 1969. Seven months later, Fred Hampton and Peoria Black Panther leader Mark Clark were killed in a pre-dawn police raid in which four other panthers, Blair Anderson, Verlina Brewer, Brenda Harris and Ronald "Doc" Satchel were wounded and arrested. Although initial police and news reports described a firefight between Panthers and police, ballistics tests proved otherwise.

Of the eighty bullets that were fired into the apartment, all but one were from police weapons. Mark Clark was only able to get off a lone, errant shot before he was slain. Hampton was shot at point blank rage, twice in the head. Of course, the story of police repression of left radicals in Chicago was part of a national battlefront, and within a few years the FBI and their allied state and local police departments had succeeded in "neutralizing" grassroots left militancy, leaving mayhem, death and injury in their wake, destroying community initiatives that were a positive force in many peoples' lives and forestalling the possibility of a homegrown socialist politics. It would be wrong, however, to assert that the end of the Rainbow Coalition was strictly due to police repression. That argument begs other questions and should encourage us to consider whether broad popular power connected to other constituencies beyond Chicago's most ghettoized zones might have helped these efforts to endure, despite the police surveillance and harassment.

For a time, the Rainbow Coalition organized city residents who endured ghettoized conditions and strong-arm policing, but their work was sadly short-lived and never transcended the ethnic assumptions about constituency that dominated the infamously segregated landscape of Richard J. Daley's Chicago, nor the burgeoning identity politics of the New Left. The Patriots never used the word "white" to describe their platform, choosing instead to talk in explicitly class terms, but they relied for a time on the Confederate battle flag as a symbol of southern pride, a choice that many Panthers and other coalition partners disapproved of but tolerated. In effect, the Rainbow Coalition represented a potential left politics that still labored under the weight of prevailing ideology and lived segregation and remained isolated from the mainstream of American civic culture and politics. Moreover, the view that the lumpenproletariat might somehow constitute the vanguard capitulated to the prevailing sense that a broad working-class politics was passé. When Panthers and Patriots attempted to engage the citizens of Lakeview and other adjacent neighborhoods on Chicago's North side, they ran into a brick wall of defensiveness, class contempt, Cold War patriotism and reaction that would only deepen in every corner of the nation in the years following the sixties.

Boggs saw the redundant black youth in Detroit and other cities as outsiders, harbingers of the disastrous effects of capital-intensification in industry, but he also saw them as co-creators of a potential revolution that might push the nation towards emancipation from compulsory wage labor and a freer existence. For their part, the Panthers in places like Chicago sought to operationalize that perspective, extolling a view of the black ghetto as an internal colony that might be liberated in the mold of liberation struggles being waged across the colonized world. Like Boggs, they also knew that black political agency alone would not be enough to transform the United States and called for a broader revolutionary politics. The repression of the Panthers, and in particular the war against Hampton and the Illinois chapter, are well known, both subjects having been depicted in Hollywood films, but their repression could only unfold as it did because of their relative isolation from institutional power and the broad complicity of millions of Americans in the preservation of the Cold War order. That conservatism would intensify, as cities further emptied out due to suburbanization, the New Deal coalition showed signs of wear and unraveling, and white Democratic voters in the formerly Solid South shifted their allegiance to the Republican party.

Black Urban Regimes and the Punitive Turn

Many academics as well as activists contend that the turn to mass incarceration was largely driven by white fears about crime and the hubris of white electoral constituencies and legislators, but this widely-accepted narrative does not square with the finer grain of the historical record.[22] Antiurbanism, racism and right-wing rebellion against the New Deal state are all important threads of the story, but equally important were the legislative actions of black-led and diverse city governments and state legislators who scrambled to find solutions to the emerging problems facing their core constituencies in the face of urban deindustrialization and fiscal constraint. The demand for Black Power achieved concrete expression in the election of scores of black officials in cities across the United States, which bore real progressive consequences for black urban life. By the eighties, most American cities with black majorities or pluralities had elected black mayors, and some of these cities were governed by *black urban regimes*, that is, by black mayors and black city council majorities.[23] These newly seated governing regimes faced the daunting task of reversing the dire crime trends that had been mounting during the sixties with the disappearance of urban manufacturing and that would only intensify with urban fiscal decline. Between 1960 and 1990, violent crime increased fivefold, with the homicide rate doubling and property crime tripling nationally.[24] Black political control of cities and conservative control of national Congressional and presidential politics set the stage for carceral expansion as local and state leaders attempted to deal with crime in an environment of reduced fiscal support for cities and a mounting assault on social provision. In that context, policing and imprisonment emerged as a cheap solution to the negative consequences of deep urban inequality.

In hindsight, one signal accomplishment of the first generation of black urban regimes was its tearing asunder of the racist assumption that blacks could not govern, but another was its securing of grassroots consent for pro-growth politics among the very constituencies who had the most to lose in the neoliberal turn. Contrary to another popular left line, such choices were not the consequence of these officials being "sell-outs," which is overly simplistic, uninformed and not helpful in terms of either interpretation or politics. The charge not only reveals an empirically thin understanding of black political development since Jim Crow, but is especially unfair to black politicians during the seventies because it mischaracterizes their origins and prerogatives. The first generation of post–Jim Crow black elected officials most

often cut their political teeth in civil rights struggles and unionism, stood to the left of their white counterparts and remained
committed to the expansion of New Deal social goods even as
white politicians retreated. We should recall their predicament as
urban managers with a mix of scrutiny and a sense of nuance and
tragedy, because governing through the compounded fiscal and
social crises of the seventies and eighties meant making difficult
choices with unforeseen and often regrettable consequences.

Within the urban context of the seventies and early eighties,
the carceral turn was shaped by the complicated motives of
those who pressed for punitive policy, such as black nationalists
who despised criminals as race traitors, committed local activists who sincerely wanted to reverse the cycle of violence at the
level of everyday neighborhood life, and social reformers who
believed, perhaps naively, that prisons might perform the role of
rehabilitation in society. Both Michael Javen Fortner and James
Forman, Jr. have examined the largely neglected prevalence of
law-and-order politics among black urban constituencies in New
York City and Washington, DC in their respective works. Such
arguments have been criticized and in some cases dismissed by
those who treat white backlash as the singular motive of mass
incarceration's genesis.[25] Yet their work, and the critical writings
of John Clegg and Adaner Usmani, among others, are important for pushing past the kind of sideline cheerleading that has
overtaken some academic writing on policing and for providing
empirically grounded work that examines the late twentieth-
century phenomenon of mass incarceration in the United States
and movements that contest its power from a critical left standpoint. This emerging body of work goes a long way towards
divesting us of simplistic understandings of black life and of
equally dangerous assumptions about politics that flow from
identitarian thinking.

Black urban politicians sought to address the problems of crime
and policing in a variety of ways. For starters, many mayors and
city councilors attempted to end the longer-standing problem
of underpolicing and poor emergency service in black urban

neighborhoods and improve responsiveness from city hall and the local precincts to black needs and complaints. For decades, in cities like Atlanta, Chicago, Washington, DC and Los Angeles, black civic leaders and residents demanded the hiring of more black police officers, on the assumption that they would be more responsive and accountable to the communities they served and, unlike racist white beat cops, would be able to discern between law-abiding, upstanding citizens and criminal suspects. Such efforts to diversify police departments during the postwar era may seem strange and even reactionary when read against contemporary abolitionist sentiments, but such struggles represented an important front in the civil rights movement. Hiring more black police officers, firefighters and public workers accelerated after blacks attained majority control of central city governments, conforming to a longer pattern of ethnic succession and political incorporation in American urban history. There is some evidence that, for a time, these hires had some progressive impact, improving relations between black communities and police and reducing the frequency and volume of citizen complaints in cities where there was black political control. Such advances, however, were rather short-lived for a variety of reasons.

As Forman points out, those who were hired to local police departments were not always as civil rights and community minded as the actors who pressed for more black hiring in the first place. Such diversification strategies also pre-dated the instability and violence that would accompany the introduction of the crack cocaine trade, which provided a ready justification for more militarization and strong-arm policing. Yet even before the crack-fueled violence of the eighties, some black constituencies had pushed for more punitive policies in ways that were consonant with white voters, even if their rationale and motivations were miles apart. While many black communities could get behind hiring more black officers during the sixties and seventies, the worsening conditions, rampant crime and daily social disruptions associated with deepening unemployment—e.g., car break-ins, overdoses, litter and vandalism, home invasions, beatings, armed robberies, shootings and murders—forced communities to weigh various solutions for bringing peace to their neighborhoods. Their options, however, were limited. Municipal jobs provided stability and a path to middle-class life for thousands of blacks across the United States, but job creation for lower-skilled and less-educated workers proved more difficult for local leadership, who were increasingly compelled to incentivize and lure corporate investment during an era of heightening capital mobility. Local leaders might muster resources for summer jobs programs targeting youth, or perhaps training programs for a small number of qualified applicants seeking entry-level government work, but such programs would not address the creeping unemployment that came in the wake of the manufacturing capital's abandonment of central cities and the attendant deterioration of ghetto life. The outsiders remained on the outside, and became increasingly dependent on dwindling public assistance, family and social networks and criminalized forms of work to survive. Punitive measures quickly became an expedient and, in hindsight, ill-conceived approach to addressing the compounded problems of youth alienation, violence, robbery and theft, gang culture, prostitution, drug markets and cycles of addiction, recovery and relapse.

Forman's examination of Washington, DC during the heroin epidemic of the sixties and seventies is especially helpful for understanding how well-intentioned solutions can go so wrong, and why historicity is important; that is, working carefully towards understanding the unique perspectives and subject positions animating actors in a given time and location. What we gain from Forman's account of campaigns to ban the handgun, pass mandatory minimum-sentencing rules, hire more black officers, and other measures advanced at different junctures as possible remedies to crime, is a sense of the shifting constituencies and coalitions of supporters who desired the same policy outcome but were often driven by widely different thought processes and interests. Some black support for law-and-order policies was fueled by a "politics of respectability," the desire to remold the black poor in line with propertied interests and bourgeois culture, but according to Forman, the "politics of responsibility" was an even more powerful impetus shaping black perspectives on crime and punishment in places like the District of Columbia during the seventies. In other words, politicians and residents approached the heroin epidemic with a sense of responsibility to the black community, a sense of duty to take whatever steps were necessary to end the scourge that was claiming people as addicts and as victims of violent crime. Many also held puritan views on drug usage, and, against the hippie counterculture that touted the mind-altering effects of psychotropics, many black nationalists saw drug use as a cop out, a destructive and mind-numbing behavior that undermined the project of black liberation.

These actors, like pro-gun advocate and city councilman Douglass Moore, were guided by sincere and long-proven political commitments to black communities. Many accepted the idea prevalent at the time that marijuana was a gateway drug, so they lobbied for harsher penalties for possession and sale of the drug. Their actions, though well intentioned—they hoped to curb addiction and discourage drug selling as a means of income— had unintended consequences, as a generation of black poor were routinely harassed, arrested, convicted and incarcerated for cannabis possession. Such convictions and prison time for petty drug possession and sales, of course, had compounding effects, resulting in alienation from one's family and community, the loss of citizenship rights even after serving time, and longer term, negative drag on employment and earning potential, not to mention a higher likelihood of further incarceration for parole violations.

Detroit, during the reign of longtime mayor Coleman Young, provides an even more stark, heartbreaking and complicated illustration of expanded carceral power under black governance. In their critical history of Detroit, Mark Jay and Phil Conklin dispel the popular conservative narrative that black control ruined the city, noting that its spiral of manufacturing decline and capital flight began nearly three decades before Young was sworn in as the city's first black mayor. They argue, however, that Young, like so many other black mayors, responded to the problems of poverty and crime with a law-and-order posture that galvanized some black constituencies who saw criminality as a betrayal of black progress, and more policing as a necessary choice in a context of receding federal support for cities. As Jay and Conklin note, Young was clear about the economic roots of crime and violence, and equally critical of the national abandonment of progressive antipoverty and pro-urban policies.

Nonetheless, in response to troubling violence, embarrassing publicity and mounting demands from residents to literally staunch the bleeding, Young's administration turned to policing. In the aftermath of street protests and unrest following the arrest of the Livernois Five in 1975, Young responded by reinstating 450 laid-off police officers, establishing a citywide curfew and creating a police gang squad, declaring an "all-out war on juveniles responsible for the increase in crime."[26] The city council followed Young's lead, retooling the city's stop-and-frisk policy, expanding police power and pioneering the kind of stress policing that would become common in American cities through the eighties. The anticrime strategies touted by Young and the city council were embraced by many black Detroiters, who organized a March Against Crime and eventually formed a Coalition to Resist Crime, which sought to "mobilize civil rights tactics against the perceived crime wave gripping the city."[27] As in the District of Columbia, such genuine desires to end crime through law enforcement contributed to a racially unjust carceral expansion, with Michigan's prison population nearly doubling during Young's first decade as Detroit mayor, rising from 8,630 state prisoners to 14,658.

The relationship between black urban regimes, their popular constituencies and the carceral turn is significant for a few reasons. First, we need more historical and social analysis of black life during Jim Crow and after that strives to render this subject matter in all of its complexity and contradictions. That quality of historical thinking about the black population has deteriorated in a period when race-reductionist accounts have become dominant. Second, an accounting of mass incarceration's genesis that takes seriously the experiences and meaningful roles and will of black and brown publics should put the brakes on Black Lives Matter nostalgia for some renewed version of black empowerment as the way forward and foster a more sober and mature approach to thinking about liberal democratic processes. The contemporary revival of race unity, black wealth creation and self-help tropes all accelerate brokerage dynamics, distract from the root causes of mass incarceration and its real victims, and ultimately restabilize the current order, albeit with more diverse representation and patron–client relations, in a reactivation of the same system responses pioneered against Black Power demands during the sixties. Finally, coming to terms with the ways that black urban governors, city councils and activist constituencies grappled with the conundrum of high crime and low resources should remind us of the unique local geography of carceral legislation, and of how local and state-level politics continue to be important arenas for transforming the status quo. Black and brown actors were necessary to secure consent and majority support for punitive measures from the seventies onwards; in the time of Black Lives Matter, building equally powerful electoral and legislative majorities continues to be essential to any efforts aimed at reversing mass incarceration.

From "Fuck tha Police" to Endangered Species

Although during the seventies some black publics coalesced around harsher sentencing laws and other punitive measures, the Reagan-Bush austerity of the following decade sharpened the social and economic contradictions being felt in cities. During the postwar years, Chicago writer Nelson Algren once referred to his beloved city as an "October kind of city even in spring," capturing the mood of a coming deindustrialization already evident in the real hardship felt by the poorest urban communities across the country and in the very characters who populated his fiction.[28] Almost a decade before Reagan announced the start of his presidency as "morning in America," and then worked stridently to win the Cold War and secure US geopolitical hegemony, Gil Scott-Heron and Brian Jackson had declared it was "winter in America." In their 1974 album and a separate, subsequently released single track with the same title, the duo provided a critical, vivid, melancholic and lyrical suite dedicated to the plight of black inner cities facing unrelenting crime, addiction, violence and uncertainty despite the significant achievements of the sixties and the realization of formal black political representation.

Neoliberalization would intensify this urban predicament. During the reign of the New Deal coalition, the city was the locus of massive federal and corporate investment, so it would feel the full effects of the sea changes to come with the emancipation of US-based capital from the constraints of collective bargaining and labor rights, wage compression, progressive taxation, anti-discrimination policies, occupational safety and environmental laws, and nationalization projects throughout the formerly colonized world. Neoliberalization as a process of public divestment and privatization was not cut from whole cloth, but, as historian Andrew Diamond has argued, was already immanent within the postwar growth machinery. Long before Reagan came to symbolize the neoliberal transformation, Democratic and Republican lawmakers were already deeply committed to an extensive process of national urban development, which combined central city urban renewal and public housing construction as well as suburban expansion that was largely privatized in its management execution and financial benefits, albeit paid for mostly out of federal coffers. This shift away from the New Deal model of public investment and public management of massive jobs programs towards expanded patron–client relations between the federal government, Congress and metropolitan governments, and local real estate holders, construction trades and developers is one of the most important but least discussed fractures in the social democratic project. The privatization of public works after World War II was as consequential as the Taft-Hartley Act in weakening the relative power of labor and sealing the fate of any further left progressive intervention from the sixties onwards.

This postwar process of state–capital partnering also spurred the *entrepreneurial city*, intensifying standing patterns of competition between cities and towns for federal support and private investment, processes that would become more pronounced with capital mobility and the withdrawal of national government support during the seventies and eighties. As Diamond details in his work on Chicago, this process was well underway in the city during the fifties and sixties, as Mayor Richard J. Daley "took the city council out of the game and turned over the task of planning the city's future development to an alliance of downtown business interests and technocrats." Consequentially, in Daley's Chicago, "a federally funded urban renewal program intended to uplift the poor ended up subsidizing downtown development projects that reinforced the walls around the black ghetto."[29] The loss of democratic public input, the freeing up of public funds for corporate subsidization, and the inordinate power of capital in shaping metropolitan life became the hallmarks of neoliberal urbanism throughout the United States and around the globe.

Neoliberalization would produce waves of dispossession and displacement among the poorest urban denizens. Cuts to welfare assistance and Medicaid, and the eventual weakening of federal entitlements in favor of time-limited and state-funded mandates, would cause mass misery as politicians chose to bank their re-election campaigns on their opposition to social provision as morally corrupting and an unfair tax burden on the middle class and the rich. Ultimately, neoliberalization would spell the end of the majority-black city born out of postwar black migration, white exodus and black political empowerment, and the process of neoliberal revanchism would literally attack the very basis of black working-class inclusion in the city. Most dramatically, public housing was gutted in favor of voucher programs and mixed-income developments, policy changes that would "clear the ground" of the poor, as sociologist John Arena has argued, especially in places where public housing occupied prime real estate near central business districts and other economic corridors.[30] We should not see revanchism as an episodic moment that has come and gone; rather, like its constitutive processes of neoliberalization and accumulation by dispossession, this forceful seizure of the city by the more powerful and mobile classes is still unfolding in American cities in distinctive localized forms and temporalities. Paradoxically, while it entails a return of affluent residents and investment to the central city, this process is a deeply antiurban phenomenon, bearing all the prejudices, aversions, fears and anxieties that propelled the epochal transformation of American cities during the postwar years. Writing more broadly about the capitalist urban transformation in various global cities, Elizabeth Wilson offered a useful assessment. The combination of growing ecological consciousness, market-centric redevelopment, more intensive ghettoization of the "underclass," and endless suburban sprawl combined to produce the "worst of all worlds," Wilson argued, and an urban life defined by "danger without pleasure, safety without stimulation, consumerism without choice, monumentality without diversity."[31]

Black and brown urban communities responded to neoliberalism's first wave with a broad rejection of conservative policies, especially on policing, and loud criticism of the hollow promise of racial liberalism and of the old-guard civil rights leadership. This urban popular response condemned the right but also, in equal measure, the hobbled and retreating New Deal coalition, and provided experiential accounts of urban implosion and police wilding. Yet, with urban political regimes firmly entrenched in regressive pro-growth orthodoxy and federal urban divestment in full force, the route to progressive left political remedies increasingly appeared cut off. In this context, formative black opposition to neoliberalization and repressive policing ranged from existential protests to calls for community revitalization through black nationalist self-help, gang truces and black unity, entrepreneurship, moral rehabilitation and religious conversion. Perhaps in response to the crisis these popular and youthful criticisms created, many civil rights groups would eventually reinvent themselves in the face of the emerging problems of policing and prison expansion, taking the lead on this emerging policy front by commissioning studies of discrimination in police practices, arrests and convictions, mounting death penalty appeals and legal cases against wrongfully convicted persons, and sponsoring a steady stream of legislation addressed to visible racial disparities in the criminal justice system.

During the Reagan-Bush years, Los Angeles became a crucial national stage for an emerging popular cultural criticism of carceral power. Part of the city's unique role in this regard was derived from its status as the global capital of music, television and film production. At a deeper level, Los Angeles had served for some time as an active laboratory for modern policing strategies, and like other American cities it faced an unfathomable wave of crime and gang violence that precipitated even more intense police militarization. By 1984, even as the city hosted its second Olympic Games to worldwide acclaim, social conditions in the city's ghettos and barrios had worsened dramatically, with residents facing rising unemployment and declining real wages.[32] Mayor Tom Bradley, who had been a trailblazing black member of the Los Angeles Police Department and a vocal opponent of Chief William H. Parker, now found himself increasingly at odds with Darryl Gates, the new LAPD chief who had once served as Parker's personal driver. Long-smoldering tensions between black and Latino communities and the LAPD intensified throughout the eighties and exploded in the 1992 Rodney King rebellion. Public pressure had been mounting for some time over the use of the Monadnock PR-24, a two-foot-long baton—ironically inspired by the Okinawan tonfa, a peasant weapon improvised from a millstone handle—that police often employed in a carotid chokehold to subdue suspects. When confronted with public criticism over the 1982 police killing of James Mincey, Jr., Gates had reached for biological racism: "We may be finding that in some blacks when [the chokehold] is applied," he claimed, "the veins or arteries do not open up as fast as they do in normal people."[33] The video-recorded beating of Rodney King and subsequent acquittal of the four officers directly involved set off nearly a week of protests and looting in the city. Mike Davis later described the Rodney King rebellion was a "hybrid social revolt." "It was a revolutionary democratic protest characteristic of African American history when demands for equal rights have been thwarted by the majority institutions," Davis wrote. "It was also a post-modern bread riot—an uprising of not just poor people but in particular those strata of poor in southern California who've been most savagely affected by recession."[34]

Criticisms of stress policing were articulated and popularized through rap music, rap-rock hybrids, punk, youth subcultures and the resurgence of nationalist politics within black life more broadly. The social power of rap music during the late Reagan-Bush years resided in its still relative outsider status within the music industry, its experimental and competitive subculture and its lyrical content born out of the artists' direct experiences of stress policing and urban life in the age of crack cocaine. Rap music was conceived within the "postindustrial" conditions of black and brown communities in the South Bronx, and within the space of a decade it became a chosen medium of urban black youth across the nation. Rather than a direct reflection of the diverse interests and aspirations of urban youth, however, rap music was always more of a fun-house mirror, reflecting some social conditions and experiences faithfully, while exaggerating and truncating others, and always for the primary purpose of amusement and entertainment. Far from being born as a form of protest, rap music, graffiti, breakdancing and deejaying—the four foundational elements of hip-hop culture—were working-class art forms that reflected a contradictory class consciousness. From its earliest manifestations, hip-hop playfully engaged, criticized and embraced bourgeois norms, high fashion, and consumer culture. Moreover, the subculture was as much about achieving respite and communion amid de-industrial urban hardship, even if city rulers, law enforcement and the anxious middle class viewed the presence of B-boy crews, boomboxes and graffiti as inherently rebellious and undesirable. During the mid-to-late eighties, rap would shift away from the dance-floor orientation of its disco and Jamaican sound-system roots towards more explicit social commentary and political protest. The resonance of race-conscious rap was buoyed by the legitimation of the genre as a distinct, increasingly lucrative market within the corporate recording industry. However, while "Fuck tha police" became a popular rallying cry against police wilding, such sentiments never congealed into a substantial political force, receding instead into black self-help and community-building, overtures that fit neatly within the nascent neoliberal urban milieu.

During the eighties and early nineties, rap music provided some of the most widely circulated criticisms of police violence and captured the ways that black and brown urban communities experienced police as an invading army. Amid the first wave of neoliberal central city revanchism during the Reagan-Bush years, rap music was moving from niche within the broader R&B/Soul market into a full-fledged genre of its own. The expansion of rap labels at the major recording companies, and the advent of commercially viable national tours, such as the New York City Fresh Festival in the mid-eighties, created a powerful platform for younger black artists who were experiencing the drug war first-hand and feeling the crushing force of ramped up policing in inner-city neighborhoods.[35] The result was a flowering of radical, black nationalist inflected rap music, which often took aim at police power and nascent mass incarceration. Indeed, some of these rappers and DJs sparked national dialogue about these problems earlier and more effectively than national civil rights organizations did.

What emerges from rap music's golden age is a broad and internally diverse discourse on police power and the hellish impact of crack cocaine on inner-city life. Its criticisms ranged from one-off lines and random verses against police aggression to dedicated protest anthems, such as MC Shan's "Time for Us to Defend Ourselves," LL Cool J's "Illegal Search," the Geto Boy's "Crooked Officer," Main Source's "Just a Friendly Game of Base-ball" ("Aw shit, another young brother hit, I better go over my man's crib and get the pump, cuz to the cops shooting brothers is like playing baseball and they're never in a slump"), Cypress Hill's "Pigs" and KRS-One's "Sound of da Police" and "Black Cop," as well as full LPs of social commentary documenting run-ins with police and the hellish conditions in America's cities.

Imagining themselves as a cross between rap royalty Run DMC and the legendary British punk band The Clash, Public Enemy crafted a sonic style of black nationalist protest that achieved commercial success and critical acclaim during the late eighties. In their "Black Steel in the Hour of Chaos," rapper and band-leader Chuck D spun a tale of an emancipatory prison riot—"I caught a CO falling asleep on death row. I grabbed his gun and he did what I said so." For his turn as lead emcee, Public Enemy hype man Flava Flav's "911 Is a Joke" captured the disparity in emergency services experienced in black urban neighborhoods. Public Enemy's music, which combined layered and sonically dis-cordant tracks with overt social criticism, reflected the growing unease and protests in New York City following the 1984 police killing of a sixty-six-year-old black woman, Eleanor Bumpurs, during a court-ordered eviction, the shooting that same year of four black men by subway vigilante Bernhard Goetz, and the 1989 murder of Yusef Hawkins, who was shot by vigilantes in the majority-Italian Bensonhurst section of Brooklyn. Together, these and other tracks by Public Enemy offered perceptive com-mentary on the emerging landscape of neoliberalization, a world where policing was quickly replacing social welfare provision as the primary means of managing the black urban laboring classes. Their music and that of many other artists at the time called attention to this ongoing, pernicious political-economic trans-formation, which left social dislocation, misery and morbidity in its wake. Their work spoke to a problem that had not been adequately named as yet, and was only partially glimpsed in the language of "neoconservatism," "fiscal conservatism," "welfare reform," "zero-tolerance" and "tough-on-crime" policy.

Yet, while New York rappers had long defined the genre and established the music's role as social commentary, it was in Los

Angeles, with its large gang population, soaring homicide rates and longstanding history of police brutality, that the antipolicing protest music of the time reached its zenith. N.W.A. (Niggaz Wit Attitudes) provided the most assertive and incendiary condemnation of policing during the Reagan-Bush years—"street knowledge" gained through their direct experiences of the LAPD. Originating in Compton, N.W.A. provoked a warning from the FBI and widespread derision from police departments with their 1988 song, "Fuck tha Police," with Detroit police moving in to shut down their concert when the group defied local orders and performed the song on stage. Two years after N.W.A.'s signature song, the rap-rock group Body Count, featuring rapper Ice-T, released "Cop Killer," which he dedicated to the LAPD. The song was condemned widely by law enforcement and then president George Bush, but millions of Americans could identify with these and other criticisms of police violence and abuse.

Golden age rap music provided the soundtrack of the crack cocaine years and the formative carceral expansion, and in many ways the commentaries of rappers and deejays identified the socially combustible elements—overpolicing, urban decay, crime, racial injustice, and growing inequality—that would explode in South Central Los Angeles in 1992 following the acquittal of the four police tried for the beating of black motorist Rodney King. "Endangered Species (Tales from the Darkside)," a duet between former N.W.A. member Ice Cube and Public Enemy front man Chuck D, sampled the eponymous song by Parliament and riffed on black male endangerment. Capturing the sense of black communities under siege, Ice Cube sums up the perspective on police held by many black youths at the time: "Since I'm young, they consider me the enemy/ They kill ten of me to get the job correct/ To serve, protect, and break a niggas neck." The popular social criticism of late Reagan-Bush era rap music was not without its contradictions and limits, however.

Public Enemy, N.W.A., Ice Cube and others provided powerful protest anthems, capable of expressing the discontent of rap's foundational black urban audience and pricking the conscience of its growing suburban and white consumer base at the time. But most often, the solutions they provided in the recording booth and in interviews were rather conservative. Their accounts were relatable, authentic and impactful, a sharp antidote to the official press conferences and dissemblance, media whiteouts and lack of accountability that trailed every suspicious death of a black civilian during an arrest, each gruesome photo of a brutalized detainee or eyewitness account of police abuse. Like many auto-biographical accounts, however, some of these analyses lacked a sociological imagination. Partially at fault is the medium itself, musical recordings which can reflect and convey political ideas, but are a form of profit-driven entertainment that is only additive in the broader and more complex process of political life. Like much public understanding at the time, many of these rap protests tended to treat police violence as the result of racist cops.

Without connecting the personal experiences or highly publicized incidents of police violence to the ongoing processes of capitalist urban planning, the popular criticism of police brutality and racial inequality in late eighties and early nineties rap music most often turned to self-help and community uplift rather than public policy. This was clearly reflected in the Stop the Violence Movement's 1989 track, "Self-Destruction" and the West Coast Rap All-Star's "We're All in the Same Gang," released the following year. Both were highly successful ensemble records, featuring New York and Los Angeles rappers respectively, and both called for black unity, self-restraint and "knowledge of self" as remedies for the violence that too often marred rap concerts and had become a feature of everyday life for millions of black urban dwellers. This focus on unity and self-help reflected the revival of black nationalist politics, which gained renewed devotion during a period of Republican rule, Democratic retreat from the New Deal welfare state, and the triumphal "end of history" mood that accompanied the end of the Cold War—developments that all sullied liberalism and left interventionism as legitimate approaches to the problems faced by millions of blacks. The black nationalist politics of the resurrected Nation of Islam and the Five Percent Nation (the Nation of the Gods and Earths); the Afrocentric intellectual culture that flourished in some Black Studies departments, independent black-owned bookstores and study group circles; and the renascent black entrepreneurship which flourished amid Reaganism were all central in shaping popular responses to the problems of poverty, drugs and violence throughout this period. Both the Nation of Islam and its Five Percent Nation offshoot maintained a peculiar relationship with the carceral order, with jails and prisons serving as a recruiting ground for members, and the very space where the Five Percent Nation was born. How could organizations who since the postwar years had seen their function as that of essentially unpaid contractors undertaking the rehabilitative function of incarceration mount an effective movement against the carceral expansion of the nineties?

Concerns about black male endangerment were at the heart of so much black nationalist and popular black debate about crime, gang violence and mass incarceration during these years. This emergent discourse completely shifted the terms of debate from policymaking back towards a conservative politics of patriarchal order and personal rehabilitation.[36] Whether reflected in the narrative arc of John Singleton's 1991 film *Boyz n the Hood*, or the Nation of Islam's 1995 Million Man March, such politics were a throwback to the Moynihan report, only now made respectable and normative within black public discourse. In each case, the message was simple: black males as a cohort faced high levels of unemployment, violence and incarceration, and diminished life chances, because of cultural and behavioral pathologies. Black men needed to atone for their personal transgressions and retake their naturally ordained, rightful place in the home and the neighborhood as firm-handed leaders, and then personal and community rebirth would follow. Far from serving as some radical alternative, such thinking was a ringing endorsement of the ongoing bipartisan political assault on the welfare state. The Million Man March was not a protest but a consecration of the emerging logics of workfare and prisonfare.

This episode of pop cultural protest ended by the mid-nineties, and police order was restored in places like Los Angeles and New York, often through ramped-up gang sweeps and pretext stops. Conservative protestors worried over obscenity and the corrupting influence of so-called gangsta rap demanded censorship, successfully securing mandatory parental advisory labels on records containing obscenities. Record company executives and some audiences lost interest in race-conscious rap music. As a result, politically conscious rap music went underground, while the major labels invested in dance-heavy, crossover-friendly artists who would dominate the airwaves and avoid riling white publics with the kind of searing criticisms of hyperpolicing from only a few years prior. The term "hip-hop" was resurrected to describe the culture, as veteran artists and core audiences sought to reconnect rap music to the artforms of turntablism, break dancing and aerosol writing. Corporate purveyors and major media conglomerates seemed to embrace the term as a preferred marketing category in an effort to distance the now increasingly profitable genre from the earlier controversies over "gangsta rap," obscenity, copyright lawsuits and concert violence.

The most critical rap music emerging after the Rodney King rebellion might be characterized as socialist realism *without the socialism*. Artists like Mobb Deep, Wu Tang Clan, Notorious B.I.G. and Nas continued to offer deeply poetic and hyper-realistic depictions of an urban landscape decimated by crack cocaine and street violence, but seldom ventured into the kind of sustained, LP-length commentary on corporate and police power that had defined the music of the preceding years. And while the earlier race-conscious rap music prescribed self-help of the collectivist black nationalist variety, this latest wave offered little more than renditions of American exceptionalism, or a faith in the path to riches for all those willing to hustle, grind and sacrifice. To be sure, politically conscious rap music would endure despite the entrepreneurial turn exemplified in the reign of Sean Combs's Bad Boy Records, Suge Knight's Death Row Records and Master P's No Limit Records. Artists like the Coup, Digable Planets,

Goodie MOB, OutKast, the Fugees and related solo projects of Lauryn Hill and Wyclef Jean, the Soulquarians collective, which included the Roots, Mos Def, Common, Bilal and Erykah Badu, underground institutions like Lyricist Lounge in New York and the Elements in Los Angeles, among many others, carried the mantle of socially engaged music forward, but what was once the mainstream of rap music would now become an underground niche in an industry targeting a popular audience comprised of majority-white middle-class consumers. It is noteworthy as well that, as the twentieth century ended, the very meaning of "the struggle" was transformed, losing its overt political connotation in black parlance during the reign of trap music and related subgenres like Chicago's drill music, which surveyed the dismal landscape the crack cocaine crisis left in its wake. The "struggle" morphed from the late Jim Crow sense of political struggle, the conscious participation in organized opposition to apartheid and oppression, into a euphemism for survival under the new terms of urban life produced by workfare, carceral expansion and joblessness. Such conditions most often were grist for new Horatio Alger myths of ascension from the ghetto to conspicuous consumption and haute bourgeois life. Within this context, "hustling," which once referred to male prostitution, and "pimping" were valorized in hip-hop culture during the crack cocaine crisis, no longer viewed as unfortunate forays into survival crimes or a sign of immorality, but instead as a necessary posture in a world of limited horizons and opportunities.

Curiously, some of the very rappers who openly protested police abuse found a second career playing police officers in television and movies. Ice-T played an undercover cop in the film *New Jack City* and an NYPD detective on the long-running television series *Law and Order: Special Victims Unit*. Ice Cube built a long string of successful films, including the buddy cop comedies *Ride Along* and *21 Jump Street*, and LL Cool J has starred in the successful series *NCIS: Los Angeles*. This is not hypocrisy for those who started from the view that the policing problem was fundamentally to do with racist cops rather than the core function of policing in securing the conditions for capital accumulation. Flowing from that liberal antiracist line of criticism, bad cops just need to be replaced with those who represent the broader communities they serve, and racist attitudes need to be extinguished from police practice through more effective training. This formative soundtrack of the carceral expansion was powerful in illuminating the human toll of policing, and the hubris that defined police interactions with black and brown working-class youth, but it fell short, failing to provide either a full-bodied analysis of policing as an institution or a path towards a more socially just order.

The time of Black Lives Matter has seen the revival of politically engaged music, with songs like Kendrick Lamar's "Alright" becoming new protest anthems and phrases like "Fuck 12," a denunciation of law enforcement popularized by rappers like Gucci Mane, providing a common lexicon and popular slogan for BLM activism. Likewise, the power of popular mobilizations has politicized some artists, shifting the subject matter of their work, and forcing others to take on a larger political role. Rapper Jay-Z, whose string of acclaimed and multi-platinum albums documented his own origins and survival in the drug trade, stepped forward to co-author and narrate an editorial video, published by the *New York Times*, that provided a concise and helpful critical summary of the consequences of the War on Drugs and the problem of mass incarceration.[37] More extensive treatments of the cultural impact of Black Lives Matter, not just on popular culture but on the perceptions of race and social justice held by broader publics, will certainly be written. In the decade of protests that has transpired, it is possible to take stock of some of the ways in which Black Lives Matter as a political tendency has surpassed some of the limitations of the earlier movements and protests discussed here, even as it has run up against familiar political dead ends and new social contradictions.

Black Lives Matter as Militant Liberalism

In early January 2009, some 500 people staged a peaceful protest at Fruitvale Station, a Bay Area Rapid Transit (BART) hub in Oakland, California. The crowd marched across the city and were met with increasingly hostile police units, who fired tear gas and eventually rubber bullets to disperse the marchers. Protestors clashed with police throughout the night, hurling bottles, bricks and whatever they could get their hands on at the police lines. As the conflicts with police escalated, some protestors improvised barricades, setting fire to trash dumpsters, newspaper boxes and cars.[38] Others smashed storefront windows and damaged the façade of the newly renovated Fox Theatre. This night of protests erupted over the police killing of Oscar Grant, a twenty-two-year-old black Hayward native and food service worker, a week earlier. Grant was traveling back to Oakland on BART after attending New Year's Eve celebrations at San Francisco's Embarcadero. He was arrested along with other friends after BART police responded to calls of a large fight on an incoming train. Hundreds on a waiting train and on the platform witnessed the arrests of Grant and others, with many jeering the police and recording the events on cell-phone cameras. As a result, officer Johannes Mehserle's actions were captured from multiple angles. Mehserle and other arresting officers held Grant face down on the platform; during the struggle to cuff him, Mehserle stood upright, unholstered his gun and shot Grant in the back. Grant can be heard yelling "you shot me" on some video recordings, and Mehserle also seems surprised by his actions, exclaiming "Oh my God!" after firing the fatal shot. Grant died the next morning at an Oakland hospital. Mehserle was arrested and charged with second-degree murder as well as involuntary manslaughter. Mehserle's legal defense would later claim "taser confusion," even though tasers are lighter, brightly colored and holstered in a way to prevent confusion with heavier lethal firearms. He was ultimately acquitted of murder but found guilty of the lesser charge, and with the judge's lenient sentencing served less than a year for killing Grant.

Other police killings had provoked riots during the aughts. In 2001, black Cincinnatians rioted after the police killing of an unarmed black teen, Timothy Thomas. The small Lake Michigan coastal town of Benton Harbor saw two days of rioting and looting after a black motorcyclist, Terrance Shurn, was killed while being chased by police. Some 300 Michigan state troopers and local police were mobilized to quell the protests. Such events proved to be episodic and rather isolated, with public attention quickly shifting to other matters along with the temperamental forty-eight-hour news cycle. What was different about the protests over Oscar Grant's killing however, was the broader context of Bay Area radical left organizations, already embroiled in struggles against rent intensification and mass evictions, homelessness and the low-wage economy, and how they connected policing and Grant's death to these broader local transformations.[39] George Ciccariello-Maher contends that those protests were central to a burgeoning anticapitalism in the region. "I'm going to insist as stubbornly as possible," Ciccariello-Maher wrote, "that if there was a fundamental source, not for the *presence* of Occupy Oakland, but for its peculiar *radicalism* and the mantle of national leadership it assumed, this source was to be found in the Oscar Grant rebellions and the political lessons these rebellions contained."[40] Predating the occupation of New York's Zuccotti Park, the Oscar Grant rebellion imparted "lessons in mass strength gleaned from the streets."[41]

Ciccariello-Maher is right to assert the neglected role of these protests in galvanizing disparate social forces into the anticapitalist opposition that would become Occupy, but in retrospect his account reads like all-too-familiar left thinking on black protests as always serving a vanguard role. Moreover, the passage of time should give way to a more sober reckoning with the presumption of mass protests as fulcrums of social change—especially during the year of Grant's death, which did not end in substantial justice for Grant's family or in significant police reform. In fact, the decade that has elapsed since Grant's killing has seen the rise of Black Lives Matter and ever-expanding mass protests, but that has not necessarily translated into mass strength or even progressive left-majority governing coalitions in most large cities. What accounts for this conundrum of ever more spectacular protests and relatively little movement towards majoritarian left power capable of imposing a new order?

Black Lives Matter is an essentially liberal sentiment, one that hinges on a notion of black exceptionalism that has provided dynamism to the capitalist order since the Cold War, rather than genuine opposition, that is, a force capable of replacing the central logics of private property and surplus-value creation.[42] "Black Lives Matter is an ideological and political intervention in a world where Black lives are systematically and intentionally targeted for demise," wrote Black Lives Matter co-creator Alicia Garza, perfectly summarizing this notion of black exception. "It is an affirmation of Black folks' humanity, our contributions to this society, and our resilience in the face of deadly oppression."[43] From this liberal perspective, the problem with the American project is its racism, and the solution is not necessarily the abolition of race and racialist thinking, but the elimination of disparities in wealth, homeownership, criminal justice—in other words, the full enjoyment of American liberal democratic capitalism for all, regardless of color, creed or origin. This is the mainline contention not only of Black Lives Matter, but also of cognate projects such as reparations and the Third Reconstruction, which call for a new round of black integration rather than a deep alteration of the market economy.

In relation to policing, the dominance of this black exceptionalist discourse has been politically counterproductive. BLM discourse truncates the policing problem as one of endemic antiblackness, and cuts off potential constituencies, treating other communities who have suffered police abuse and citizens who are deeply committed to achieving social justice as merely allies, junior partners rather than political equals and comrades. Moreover, characterizing the problem in terms of antiblackness further undermines the possibility of developing the kind of counterpower that is needed, since it promotes brokerage dynamics via the state-corporate/nonprofit complex set in motion by neoliberalism, converting what should be public concerns into new market opportunities, and revitalizing the black professional-managerial class with new blood and fresh faces. The Oscar Grant protests represented what would become the most progressive edge of Black Lives Matter—those local mobilizations that made explicit the connections between state violence against black civilians and the broader urban growth regime predicated on overdevelopment of central business districts, middle-class housing and enhanced spaces of leisure and consumption, and, simultaneously, massive dispossession, low-wage work and unemployment, more policing and shrinking public goods and services. The demand to defund police and instead invest in working-class neighborhoods and livelihoods represents the promise of Black Lives Matter as a political force, but that tendency has been crowded out by a mainline and popular contention that sees "race" and racism as the principal motive of police actions, in ways that neglect the very workings of capitalist political economy and its specific consequences for the working poor across urban and rural geographies.

The strength and centrality of liberal antiracism within contemporary antipolicing protests and black public debate is inseparable from the cultural and ideological consequences of the Obama presidency. Black Lives Matter entered public consciousness at a moment that was radically different from the days of protests following the killing of Oscar Grant, with the essential difference being the completion of Obama's first term and the ways his presidency had already reoriented political expectations and civic debate within the black population and beyond. Less than two months before Grant's death, Obama's unexpected and historic 2008 election victory had lifted black electoral participation and political efficacy on the heels of a devastating housing crisis and ensuing economic recession that hit black homeowners and workers particularly hard. In many ways, Obama's presidency represented the possibility of Democratic Party renewal after the two-term political disaster of George W. Bush, but the

Obama presidency carried its own dangerous freight. His rhetorical skill and ability to evoke the symbolic language of the old New Deal coalition too often camouflaged his actual political commitments, which were unwaveringly neoliberal. The widely accepted historic nature of the Obama presidency, the optics of a black nuclear family in the White House and the mobilization of various black pundits and liberals to provide constant narration and support, all combined to repackage and restore the legitimacy of Third Way centrism as somehow more left than it was.

If Obama was a representative of liberal political renewal, his election had huge consequences for black public life. The rabid right-wing protests against Obama's candidacy and character staged by the Tea Party and Birther movements only cemented popular black faith in Obama as a redemptive liberal figure. Wealthy real estate developer Donald Trump and others who challenged Obama's legal right to the presidency, demanding he make his birth certificate public, only elevated Obama's profile as an avatar of black oppression and achievement against long odds. His election and larger-than-life persona helped to shift public debate away from the grounded reality of the subprime mortgage crisis and Occupy Wall Street's intensifying protests against the 1 percent, and back towards the usual politics of corporate bailouts, a jobless recovery, the expansion of private insurance rather than single-payer health care and the continued Democratic Party retreat from social provision and public goods. Black Lives Matter surfaced in this context of hyperbolic racialism. Even as some Americans declared the dawn of a post-racial America following Obama's historic victory, proto-fascist forces threatened democratic government and openly courted racist conspiracy, while the killings of black civilians by vigilantes and police served as evidence of stalled racial progress and as the flashpoints of new antiracist protests.

The 2012 killing of Trayvon Martin and the birth of Black Lives Matter transpired during Obama's re-election campaign. The phrase "Black Lives Matter" was born as a Twitter hashtag coined by three black feminist activists, Alicia Garza, Patrisse

Khan-Cullors and Opal Tometi, who were responding to the acquittal of George Zimmerman, the self-appointed neighborhood watchman who stalked and killed the unarmed black teenager. Martin was staying at the home of his father's fiancée in Sanford, Florida, and walked to a nearby 7–Eleven convenience store for snacks. Zimmerman called 911 to report a "suspicious" person and disobeyed the emergency dispatcher who told him not to pursue the person. Zimmerman confronted Martin, and after provoking a conflict, shot and killed the teen at close range. In another 911 call made by a neighbor, Martin can be heard wailing and pleading for mercy before the fatal shot. Public outcry erupted when it was revealed that, following the incident, local police did not arrest Zimmerman, who claimed he had acted in self-defense, permissible under Florida's "stand-your-ground" laws.

Public pressure mounted and would produce an arrest, but not the court justice millions demanded. A massive Change.org petition drive led by Kevin Cunningham, which gathered over 2 million signatures, civil rights attorney Benjamin Crump's constant vigilance for Martin's family, and the growing attention to the case brought by cable news networks ultimately led to Zimmerman's arrest. Vying for reelection, Obama weighed in as well, saying "If I had a son, he would look like Travyon and I think they [Travyon's parents] are right to expect that all of us as Americans are going to take this with the seriousness it deserves."[44] His Republican opponent Mitt Romney also called for due process, saying that justice needed to be "carried out with impartiality and integrity."[45] Romney, of course, didn't reflect the general mood of his party, with many Republicans and the pro-gun lobby they serve openly defending Zimmerman's actions and the alleged efficacy of stand-your-ground laws. Ultimately, Zimmerman was acquitted, a decision that sharpened the political fault line separating black communities, criminal justice advocates and renascent antiracist struggles on one side, and the pro-gun lobby, vigilantes, right-wing militia and law-and-order forces on the other, setting the stage for the expansion of Black Lives Matter sentiments.

Cell-phone technology had played a pivotal role in mobilizing against the police killing of Oscar Grant, but Black Lives Matter as a phenomenon was from its inception a creature of social media, and carried with it all the advantages and limitations of that form. Online petitions and the circulation of viral videos have been critical tools in spurring and voicing popular opposition, and the racial justice frame is particularly well suited to this form of media and the kind of public discourse it reproduces. Such online activism has come to entail its own political form, at once laborious, validating for its adherents in certain moments, impactful, intoxicating, illusory and destructive. As Kenneth Warren notes, this "milieu of social media and 24 hour television—the world of tweeting/retweeting, posting/reposting, tagging, texting, and sharing—has become implicated in the aesthetics of memorialization, creating a sensation of living repeatedly through incidents, seemingly infinite in number, constituting a barrage that can leave one at once depleted and on the verge of striking out."[46] Such acts of political support—signing a petition, sharing a video or news article, or posting one's opinion on the latest outrage—are all relatively low-risk activities. All might provoke trolling or fleeting debates, but they are too far removed from the grounded context of real political fights to incur many risks or require sustained political commitment. Certainly, all these forms of online political activity can augment in-real-life political work, but these online practices can also exist completely disconnected from the more laborious process of attending routine face-to-face meetings, undertaking assignments, maintaining relationships, building solidarity, learning to take risks together, and all the other things that make up the process of on-the-ground political organizing and civic life. Once Black Lives Matter hit the streets and became increasingly engaged in political fights against entrenched local power, some of the limitations of online mobilization began to show. The prevalence of social media blogging platforms has not only eroded disciplined scholarly analysis and factually grounded political engagement but has also intensified race-relations dynamics.[47]

The lack of constituency and irresponsible brokering have renewed legitimacy in an era of online political life, the advent of social entrepreneurship, and foundation seeding of do-gooder service delivery projects in lieu of the welfare state.

The vigilante murder of Trayvon Martin birthed Black Lives Matter, but the 2014 police killing of unarmed black eighteen-year-old Michael Brown in Ferguson, Missouri saw the hashtag evolve into a fully-fledged political slogan. The days of street protests and police repression that ensued provided the first real test of the renewed popular struggle against police violence. Both incidents involved the murder of unarmed black teens, but the context of Ferguson—a suburban enclave with a black majority but governed and policed primarily by whites at the time of Brown's death—seemed tailor-made for the New Jim Crow sentiment. Brown and a friend, Dorian Johnson, were walking on Canfield Drive when they were confronted by Ferguson police officer Darren Wilson, who was responding to an alleged theft at a nearby Qwik Trip convenience store. Wilson demanded that Brown and Johnson move out of the street, and, after a scuffle, Wilson exited his squad car and pursued Brown, firing six shots at the unarmed teen. Brown died in the street and his body remained there for hours in plain sight as a growing crowd of residents demanded emergency medical attention and basic respect and decency in handling Brown's body.

Protests erupted the next day as word spread that Brown was shot while surrendering with his hands outstretched. The phrase "hands up, don't shoot" quickly became a new rallying cry at the vigils and demonstrations that spread from Ferguson throughout the country. Police responses to the protesters were egregious and disrespectful, as local officials and police commanders unleashed a brutal crackdown. Eventually, the Oath Keepers, a right-wing militia, joined police, Missouri highway patrol units and national guardsmen to surveil, intimidate and repress Ferguson protestors and residents. The US Justice Department conducted a grand jury investigation into the incident and concluded that Wilson's use of force was justifiable, and no charges were brought against him. The grand jury's announcement was met with disbelief and outrage, reigniting another round of protests and police repression. The protests over Brown's death saw the emergence of new leadership, improvised street tactics and the convergence of new social forces that would come to define Black Lives Matter's first wave. In the years after Ferguson, local BLM chapters, kindred organizations and campaigns served as active laboratories, training grounds where many people entered political life for the first time, where others deepened their acumen as leaders and organizers, and where many more experimented together, discovering new means of collective self-assertion and political devotion.[48]

Among the virtues of Black Lives Matter protests is that activists have generally rejected underclass moralizing, offering sharp dismissals of the respectability politics of some black elites, and chiding police union leadership and anyone else who would justify violence by impugning the victims of state repression. A week after Wilson killed Brown, the Ferguson police department released convenience store surveillance camera footage of Brown and Johnson which appeared to show Brown in an altercation with a store employee. The video was circulated and judged by some to corroborate the line that Brown was a robbery suspect; for the right-wing punditry and pro-police forces, Wilson's attempted arrest and the shooting of Brown were justified. In his documentary about Brown's death, *Stranger Fruit*, filmmaker Jason Pollock complicates this prevailing narrative. Pollock provided store camera footage from the previous night in which Brown appears to barter with a store worker, exchanging a small amount cannabis for a box of cigarillos. Before he leaves, Brown appears to return to the counter and ask the store worker to hold the cigarillos till he returns later. The video released by the Ferguson police only captures the altercation, which likely erupted when Brown returned but was denied the goods that had been promised to him the day before.

Some Black Lives Matter activists have pointed out the undemocratic character of the old-guard black political leadership and criticized the "politics of respectability," opening the door to a more popular democratic manifestation of black political life. Likewise, during Black Lives Matter's first wave, before the election of Donald Trump, mass protests in Ferguson, Baltimore, Chicago and elsewhere were often led by black women, and featured a more explicit intersectional feminist and LGBTQ politics than any popular black struggles of the last century. Amid the Ferguson protests, St. Louis rapper and activist Tef Poe declared, "This ain't your father's civil rights movement," and he was right. Instead of a movement led by clergy and college students, and broadcast via radio and television, Black Lives Matter birthed a new, more diverse cast of leaders, many of whom rejected party politics and nonviolence, and who used cell phones and social media as tools of political organizing. Queer, women and youth leaders were prominent in the new formations in Ferguson and beyond, and they brought to antipolicing protests a commitment to horizontalism and democratic deliberation, an irreverence for institutional politics and an impatience with established black political leadership. This is all to be welcomed and constitutes a progressive advance, but at times this diversification amounted to a renovated politics of recognition. Moreover, the dominant frames of Black Lives Matter mobilizations, such as the New Jim Crow, not only mischaracterize the problem of policing as a universal problem afflicting blacks regardless of class position, but also set up a politics of elite representation and brokerage that allows anyone from Gayle King to LeBron James to just as easily speak the voice of the black collective as the grassroots activists who have labored to fill the streets and demand local government action and police accountability.

The queering of contemporary black movements has not prevented some activists from engaging in the same old politics of black authenticity as a means of establishing leadership claims, one of the features of Jim Crow–era black politics many of these activists claim to be leaving behind. "Ostensibly indicating a concern with those most victimized, those whose voices and needs have been ignored," Kenneth Warren writes, blackness "substitutes claims of shared experience for structures and practices of democratic governance and accountability." "Personal feelings confer authority on anyone who can attest to certain experiences to speak on behalf of a collectivity presumed to feel exactly the same way," Warren continues, "and those who speak the loudest are those for whom commentary on matters of race is part of their job description."[49]

Diversification is an important democratic value on its own terms, but claims that diversification will produce more responsive leadership within organizations and social struggles, or better governance through political integration, are misguided and unfounded. Such claims are most effective in establishing the claims to leadership for those who are part of the diversification, as they promise to do better than predecessors who were deemed too white, too old, too male, too straight and too entrenched. Such claims, however, fail to learn from over half a century of black political integration, which was often pitched on the same grounds, sometimes made significant progress, but at other times was constrained by countervailing forces in metropolitan politics and the national arena. The blackness of the candidates was less important than the power of their electoral and governing constituencies in determining what kind of regime emerged, and how democratic and progressive it would become in historical motion. As Black Power activists quickly found out, a soul brother could just as easily represent corporate class power as the interests of those who elected him.

The new politics of recognition suffers from the same illusions of the old, in particular with its difficulty in maintaining a clear sense that interests, not corporeal identity, are the fundamental basis of political life. Black Lives Matter activists have offered searing criticisms of entrenched neoliberal black leaders, but they have been divided over extending the same criticism to women and queer leaders in their ranks, even in those instances when their commitments to privatization and marketization are indistinguishable from those of sitting politicians. Johnetta Elzie, Brittany Packnett and DeRay McKesson—activists who found the national spotlight amid the Ferguson protests and co-founded the police reform organization Campaign Zero—were later criticized by some activists for their commitments to Teach for America.[50] Activists fighting for public education and unionized teachers felt this association ran counter to the social justice aims of Black Lives Matter because Teach for America gives college graduates an opportunity to teach in distressed school districts, but this non-union labor furthers school privatization. The organization has been rightly criticized for undermining teachers unions and devaluing the craft of K-12 education by promoting the falsehood that anyone can step into a classroom and teach effectively.

In a similar vein, whenever the corporate connections or appearance of impropriety of Black Lives Matter activists has been questioned, the defense almost always amplifies universally felt racial injustice at the expense of any left-critical analysis of actually existing black life. Second-generation black activist Tamika Mallory was criticized for appearing in a Cadillac car commercial. The advertisement was commissioned for Women's History Month and produced by Spike Lee. Cadillac also pledged $10 million towards social justice causes, with some of the initial funding awarded to the NAACP. In the commercial, Mallory talked about coming from a "long line of strong women," expressed her faith that black women will lead the nation to a better place and closed by saying, "We're taking control and we're shaping our stories." Social media threads filled up with condemnations of Mallory for selling out to the automaker. Her podcast co-host, rapper and activist Mysonne Linen, came to her defense, noting that Mallory leveraged her position to secure SAG actors and top wage rates for the black women who appeared in the commercial.[51] Linen claimed that so much of the reaction to Mallory's commercial was based on misinformation and jealousy, and he clearly sees the corporate enthusiasm for Black Lives Matter as progressive. Even before the Cadillac commercial, Samaria Rice, the mother of Tamir Rice, a black twelve-year-old killed by Cleveland police in 2014 while holding a toy gun, condemned Mallory as a "clout chaser" after she performed with rapper Lil Baby at the Grammy Awards. Lisa Simpson, the mother of Richard Risher, an eighteen-year-old who was killed by the LAPD, echoed Rice's criticisms of Mallory and other popular figures as opportunistic and profiting from the deaths of black civilians. "People like Tamika Mallory are making money from this, while I'm homeless living in a hotel," Simpson said. "If they don't give us justice, we're taking it by any means necessary. That goes for the Tamika Mallorys, the Shaun Kings, the NAACP, ACLU, Al Sharpton or anyone trying to get in our way."[52]

In May 2021, Black Lives Matter co-founder Patrisse Khan-Cullors resigned from her post as executive director of the Black Lives Matter foundation after numerous news outlets reported she owned a real estate portfolio worth over $3 million. Both the right-wing press and some Black Lives Matter activists raised suspicion of impropriety, but others like Adrienne Maree Brown defended Khan-Cullors. Brown read the criticism as part of a broader attack on black movements, lamenting that she could not think of "one Black woman leader who I haven't seen gossiped on, mistreated, disrespected, lied on, and violated at the level of reputation or privacy—all while being overworked and underpaid, or unpaid."[53] Brown rightly criticizes the right-wing doxxing of black activists, and misinformation and gossip in movement circles, but she then settles on an indefensible line that reduces all criticism of Khan-Cullors to being motivated by jealousy, and employs anticapitalism in defense of black wealth creation. Such resentment, she claims, is born out of capitalism, which breeds competitiveness without irony or sense of contradiction. "From a hungry, mission-drifted, competitive space, we envy each other's success and abundance, rather than celebrating it with pure hearts," Brown argues, "because we get bought [sic] into the narrative that we are all fighting for the same scraps. I say scraps because the amounts of money for which we turn on each other are chump change to those with real wealth; charitable detritus."[54] This expressed commitment to anticapitalism falls flat, however, as Brown at once demands that we criticize the political-economic system that produces vast inequality and alienation, but simultaneously swats away any criticism of black wealth as mean-spirited and misdirected or, worse, as supported by enemies of "black success and freedom."

The defenses of Mallory and Khan-Cullors are instances of *antiracism as class politics*. In each of these scenarios, any criticism of capital in motion, and of the character of actual relationships between activist figures and nonprofits, transnational corporations and real estate markets are all shunted aside, as if these same forces are not complicit in the reproduction of the very class relations that modern policing manages. If these activists benefit from their complicity in education privatization, corporate public relations strategies or rent-intensifying development, their defenders simply recast these processes as progress or, worse, as the only alternative, despite a mountain of evidence and criticism that shows just how pernicious these same forces have been in producing deep inequality. The postwar commitment to racial democracy, rather than a true left redistributive politics, remains and is unequivocal: racism in policing, housing, employment and education needs to be swept aside so blacks can enjoy the fullness of the American market economy like all others.

It is easy to see how the focus on surplus population and structural unemployment is lost here. This is how liberal antiracism comes to function as a petit-bourgeois class politics, which elides the social power of class even as it authorizes middle-class and corporate brokers as the primary voices in solving the policing crisis. If the problem of police violence is understood as a racial affront and confronting racism is the cure, then any and every perceived slight against blacks, regardless of relative class privilege and power, is viewed as part of the same battlefront. Harvard professor Henry Louis Gates's quarrel with a Cambridge police officer, an unwarranted police call made against a black birdwatcher in Central Park, the surveillance and arrest of unemployed black men on a regular basis, or the execution of an unarmed black teen are all deemed equal cause for outrage, are all viewed as a consequence of endemic white supremacy even when keen analysis reveals they are not. The consequences of policing are much more disastrous and lethal for the most exploited, dispossessed and alienated segments of the black population. Liberal antiracism disappears any left politics that might prioritize the experiences of the laboring classes, especially those toiling away in criminalized zones. Black Lives Matter revises civil rights liberalism and Black Power sentiments in important ways, but it also inherits the contradictions of institutionalized black ethnic politics as a practical, useful but ultimately conservative means of thinking, articulating and advancing black political interests. When police violence is framed as an explicitly and universally black problem, the issue, despite being more widely felt by other Americans, is confined to the terrain of civil rights violations, antiracism remediation and black representational politics.

Since the 1960s, antiracist mobilizations have most often prompted renewed cycles of liberal redemption. Mass protests facilitate and enhance elite brokerage, often generating a new cast of leaders ready to lay claim to offering more authentic black voices than their predecessors. The condemnation of America's history yields more services, increasingly through the private sector and nonprofits in the time of neoliberalism, and more symbolic representation, but not necessarily more responsiveness from government for the most dispossessed and most policed. Ultimately, such protests result in some nominal expansion of capitalism's players through BIPOC business incubators, start-up loans, set asides and minority contracting, etc., but these are all reforms that fall short of addressing the problem of structural unemployment and poverty, which are not exceptions to capitalist economy as liberals like to believe, but outcomes of the exploitation that are always at the heart of profit-making.

Policing and Anticapitalist Struggle

In the aftermath of the Michael Brown rebellion, Marxist geographer David Harvey was criticized when he said, "Frankly, I don't see the current struggles in Ferguson as dealing very much in anticapitalism."[55] "There is a long history in the United States," Harvey continued, "of making sure that the antiracist struggle does not turn anticapitalist and there is immense and paranoid fear within the ruling classes that it might do so."[56] His comments came in response to Alex Dubilet's claim that the "intense forms of resistance and proliferation of disruptive tactics ... and the attempt to disrupt the regular flows of everyday capitalist life [have] made it abundantly clear that ... race is at the very heart of leftist political mobilization."[57] Harvey was correct in pointing out how few popular antipolicing protests took on an overt anticapitalist character, but devotees of these struggles would quickly point out the various socialists and other left organizations in their ranks, and the specific measures some have called for that are socialist in character, demanding demilitarization of police and the rerouting of public funds towards social needs. Moreover, as Dubilet notes, even though such protests may not be overtly and broadly anticapitalist in word, they are in deed, especially in those moments when protestors have hurled their outrage at the feeble infrastructure of black ghettos, e.g., convenience stores and check-cashing centers, and, at other moments, the posh storefronts and big box stores that line the main arteries of the consumer economy. Dubilet overreaches here, nonetheless, and like so many well-meaning activists and academics he imputes a progressive, if not revolutionary, spirit to Black Lives Matter that is only half true and ascribes a unitary character to mass protests and riots that diminishes their complexity and ideological diversity as historical phenomena.[58] Dubilet is not unique in this regard, but he repeats the common practice of too many on the left who approach black political struggles with little sense of their internal ideological conflicts and political interests in motion. The Harvey–Dubilet exchange is relevant to this discussion because it is yet another manifestation of the so-called race–class debate that has paralyzed some corners of the academic-activist left.

This book builds on a truth of Harvey's criticism, which Dubilet misses, namely that some elements of Black Lives Matter are not only pro-capitalist but are also in fact antisocialist, and it is this aspect that undermines addressing the historical motives and social function of modern policing in the United States. The Ferguson uprising revealed the gulf between an antiracist politics with an institutional and discursive tradition in postwar civil rights organizing, and the kind of anticapitalist politics that have defined American leftism since the antiglobalization protests of the Clinton years. Ferguson activist and rapper Tef Poe famously rebuked any discussion of Marxism during the "Generations of Struggle: St. Louis from Civil Rights to Black Lives Matter" panel discussion convened at Harvard in early December 2015. The panel was moderated by historian Elizabeth Hinton, and featured Poe, Jamala Rogers of the Organization of Black Struggle, Percy Green of CORE (Congress of Racial Equality), as well as historians Robin Kelley and George Lipsitz. According to Poe, Marxism was inapplicable to the unfolding struggles in Ferguson because it was "invented by a white man," and he raised the suspicion that Marxism might be "an oppressive force against Black People."[59] Tellingly, neither Kelley nor Lipsitz contested Poe's claims, even as he dismissed the longer rich history of black communist and left politics that these historians have built their careers studying.

Poe's arguments are a replay of black unity, self-help and entrepreneurialism sprouting from the ash and rubble of the Rodney King rebellion. True to the form, Poe's condemnations of Marxism were even more strident on Twitter, where he shrugged off anticapitalism, defended black enterprise and claimed that capital was merely a means to an end. "Not one Marxist or Communist has ever bailed me out of jail or paid my legal fees," Poe wrote. "Get money. It's simply a tool. No different than a pistol. They're both tools. Use correctly."[60] He hurled other unsubstantiated claims about billionaire Marxists and communists funding movements, but the overall effect of his diatribes at Harvard and online were to steer black political thought and action back towards some truce with capitalism and to suffocate the possibility of any popular left politics that is simultaneously antidiscrimination in practice and anticapitalist in horizon. His comments reflect some of the palpable frustrations in Ferguson, where black locals found themselves thrust into the national spotlight after the killing of Michael Brown, which attracted hundreds of embedded journalists, lawyers, civil rights leaders, celebrities and all manner of activists black and white who wanted to express their outrage and solidarity. In the discord, and at times, the crowding out of local voices, Poe's comments read like an attempt to reassert authority based on an authentic connection to the communities of black metropolitan St. Louis, and, as such, his is a legitimate political impulse. These tensions between local interests, touring activists and national political players have persisted and compounded as Black Lives Matter has scaled upward from places like Ferguson to larger stages, and from the fight against police violence to the broader anti-racist campaigns and initiatives we witnessed after the death of George Floyd.

Poe's pro-entrepreneurship is little more than a repeat of earlier responses to black poverty and crime, which have never lived up to the hype. The formative protests against stress policing, refracted through golden age rap music and the mass rebellion after the police beating of Rodney King, illuminated the racial dimensions of the carceral expansion and shattered popular consensus regarding the War on Drugs. Unfortunately, such antipolicing protests and rhetoric from the late Reagan-Bush period too often conflated race and class and did not always explicitly connect policing to the processes of urban revanchism already unfolding from the Tomkins Square Park riots to the archetypal police regimes of Daryl Gates and Bill Bratton. Rather than confronting the powerful forces responsible for worsening conditions through some sustained political movement seeking to change public policy and redistribute wealth, the most common responses simply doubled down on black capitalism and race uplift. The problem of surplus population and structural unemployment so acutely felt by urban black working-class men and youth was understood as the unique problem of the "black community" and the custodianship of race leaders. The result was a range of political responses that led back to black ethnic politics, with many activists arguing that race unity, self-help, entrepreneurship, black male atonement and cultural rehabilitation were the only legitimate solutions to the interconnected problems of urban crime, violence and hyperpolicing.

What those who view anticapitalist politics as "white" miss is how anticapitalism reconnects the problems of estrangement and structural unemployment embodied in the carceral crisis. During the Cold War, race evolved as the chief means of thinking and talking about inequality in America, especially as class politics were discredited and banished from the realm of permissible civic discourse. The Cold War liberal view of poverty as a consequence of some combination of racial discrimination, cultural pathology and personal failing continues to dominate popular thinking. One legacy of the Great Society and Black Power years has been the tendency to think of black urban poverty in terms of cultural alienation, or the relative estrangement from mainstream American institutions and middle-class values. In contesting the relationship between police and urban black communities, Black Lives Matter has amplified this experience of alienation and its many facets—the regular contact with and harassment by police; supervision by courts, welfare bureaucrats, probation officers and predatory enterprises; and the experience of being set adrift in the sea of capitalist volatility and crisis as the raft of social provision has been taken away.

This problem of alienation, however, is too often seen as a racially exclusive experience, a position that too easily disconnects from the broader experience of estrangement under capitalism, albeit in many manifestations—the alienation of workers from the surplus value they produce, estrangement from nature, competition and social conflict among workers, and so forth. More problematically, by focusing on alienation and the need for integration into American institutions, either as beneficiaries of renewed state benevolence or as proto-entrepreneurs, liberal responses to poverty and policing ignore the fact that underneath this alienation is the problem of structural unemployment, which is not an exceptional feature of "postindustrial" capitalism and urban growth politics, but a central animating force. There can be no real solution to the policing crisis without addressing this underlying and fundamental problem of surplus population. And there can be no real resolution of the surplus population problem within the parameters of capitalist political economy.

Our current carceral regime is a fundamental dimension of contemporary capitalism, and, as such, an anticapitalist politics must be at the heart of any attempt to rid society of the problems of policing and mass incarceration that Black Lives Matter protests have forced into public consciousness. Black people are disproportionately targeted by police because blacks are over-represented among the most vulnerable layers of the working class residing in cities, where the heaviest fiscal and technological investments in stress policing have been made. When we make a closer examination of the specific local contexts where some of the earliest and most substantial BLM demonstrations took place, we find that the lives of the victims, and the modes of policing they were regularly subjected to, were intimately connected to the pro-growth regimes of cities like St. Louis, Baltimore and Chicago. Policing secures the entire accumulation process in the urban tourism-entertainment zones, real estate developments and other key sectors of the economy. As such, solutions to the policing crisis that focus on technological upgrades (e.g., more body cams, implicit bias training, non-lethal weapons and the rest) but fail to address the impetus for policing (i.e., to secure property relations and manage the "dangerous classes") will merely further stabilize the problem for the sake of maintaining the status quo that millions of Americans depend on, even if they revile police violence.

4

The World of Freddie Gray

Dispossession, Rebellion, and
Containment in Revanchist Baltimore

*Herein lies the match that will continue to ignite the dynamite
in the ghettos: the ineptness of decision makers, the anachronistic institutions, the inability to think boldly, and above all the
unwillingness to innovate. The makeshift plans put together every
summer by city administrations to avoid rebellions in the ghettos
are merely buying time.*

Stokely Carmichael and Charles V. Hamilton, *Black Power:
The Politics of Liberation in America* (1967)

Throughout the late 1960s, black ghettos in many American
cities were engulfed in annual summer riots, often touched off by
incidences of police harassment and abuse. Against this backdrop
of seasonal rioting, Stokely Carmichael and Charles V. Hamilton
penned their best-selling 1967 book, *Black Power: The Politics of
Liberation in America*. "White America can continue to appropriate millions of dollars to take ghetto teenagers off the streets
and onto nice, green farms during the hot summer months. They
can continue to provide mobile swimming pools and hastily built

play areas," but, Carmichael and Hamilton warned, "there is a point beyond which the steaming ghettos will not be cooled off."[1] The book was read and debated amid the 1967 Newark rebellion, which provoked President Lyndon B. Johnson to convene the National Advisory Commission on Civil Disorders to study its root causes and develop suggestions for preventing future unrest. The official report issued by the Kerner Commission, as it came to be named after its chair, Illinois governor Otto Kerner, famously concluded that "our nation is moving toward two societies, one black, one white—separate and unequal."[2]

Carmichael and Hamilton's writing reflected the deep skepticism many Black Power militants held towards the liberal policies undertaken by local and national leaders. Johnson's War on Poverty had not gone far enough, many argued, in addressing the deplorable housing conditions, chronic unemployment and crowded underfunded schools separating black inner-city life from white suburban prosperity. "It is ludicrous," Carmichael and Hamilton wrote, "for the society to believe that these temporary measures can long contain the tempers of oppressed people."[3] Like many of their contemporaries, Carmichael and Hamilton saw black urban life as being hemmed in by institutional racism; that is, not merely by overt forms of interpersonal prejudice and discrimination, but by more subtle and systemic practices like redlining, restrictive covenants and predatory lending. Liberal strategies might placate the simmering discontent among black ghetto dwellers, but unless systemic changes were made, the alchemy of racism, underdevelopment and desperation would inevitably give way to rebellion. "And when the dynamite does go off," Carmichael and Hamilton wrote, "pious pronouncements of patience should not go forth. Blame should not be placed on 'outside agitators' or on 'Communist influence' or on advocates of Black Power. That dynamite was placed there by white racism and it was ignited by white racist indifference and unwillingness to act justly."[4]

Carmichael and Hamilton's words echo across the decades, and for some they may appear as relevant to our own times, with the ascendency of Black Lives Matter, as they did during the late 1960s. In the face of routine police violence against unarmed black citizens, many activists embrace a similar view of the contemporary United States, not as the post-racial meritocracy touted by some on the right, but as an endemically racist and highly unequal society. Like an acoustic echo that resounds into a void, however, we should be careful not to mistake Carmichael and Hamilton's interpretation of their own historical context as speaking directly to our own times. Ghettos, riots and pervasive inequality defined the late 1960s as they do the contemporary moment, but during the intervening years that separate our respective epochs, the political and social terrain has shifted in critical ways.

Carmichael was the charismatic leader of the Student Nonviolent Coordinating Committee who announced the slogan "Black Power" to the world during the 1966 Meredith March Against Fear, which had been taken over by prominent civil rights leaders after James Meredith was shot by a white vigilante and hospitalized. Hamilton was an Oklahoma native who participated in the 1955 Montgomery Bus Boycott, before earning a PhD in political science from the University of Chicago. Together they set out to operationalize the notion of Black Power, moving it from a pithy slogan to a practical approach for realizing black progress. At certain turns, they draw on the language of internal colonialism to describe the conditions of black oppression; on other pages, their text drifts back towards a view of black political empowerment rooted in well-established notions of ethnic machine politics, which they saw as the *realpolitik* of American city life, and the most effective path for blacks to take as white suburban exodus gave way to majority-black voting publics in many cities.[5] Black Power militants called for revolution, aligning themselves with Third World liberation movements; their sharp criticisms of American society and heady rhetoric of armed struggle incited fear in reactionary whites, who equated black self-assertion with black domination. In practice, however, Black Power would increasingly come to mean black control of political and

economic institutions; what started as an antidote to racial integration—the "thalidomide drug of integration" for Carmichael
—became its elixir.[6] More black representation in civic life,
business and popular culture has not abolished the conditions
of structural unemployment, uneven development and racial
injustice that Carmichael and Hamilton confronted, but it has
provided a means of more effectively managing these social contradictions under late capitalism.

In a pointed analysis of African American politics in the aftermath of the 2015 Baltimore riots and mounting protests against
police brutality, Keeanga-Yamahtta Taylor contended that the
"uprising in Baltimore has crystalized the deepening political
and class divide in black America ... a new development in the
black freedom struggle that historically has been united across
class lines to fight racism."[7] I agree with the spirit of her criticism,
but question the assertion of novelty, the emergence of a discrete
class politics within black life where it was less pronounced, if
not nonexistent, before. While it is true that by the mid-1950s
a broad consensus had developed within the black population,
North and South, around dismantling the legal edifice of Jim
Crow segregation, the very use of the term the "black freedom
struggle," a neologism adopted by many contemporary academics, papers over the range of ideological positions and material
interests animating black public life at every historical juncture.

Even the mid-century moment of broad support for desegregation was characterized by the presence of strong criticisms of
liberal integration and the strategy of nonviolent resistance articulated by black nationalists who favored political and economic
independence, and by a veteran cohort of black unionists and
former communists who insisted that black advancement and
the fight for social democracy were inextricable.[8] Throughout
the Jim Crow era, different African American political tendencies and constituencies have disagreed over how to advance
the race, and fight racism for that matter, cleavages that would
sharpen after the passage of landmark civil rights legislation and
the rise of Black Power militancy. Although there is a tendency

within both academic treatments and popular reminiscence of the Black Power movement to emphasize its most revolutionary aspirations, hindsight should encourage a more sobering account. Black Power meant different things to different people, and in retrospect the period saw the defeat of black political radicalism —both ideologically and by force—and the triumph and consolidation of a mode of black political life amenable to liberal democracy.

The class contradictions that Taylor identifies were woven into the genesis of post-segregation black politics, with its unique prerogatives and institutional constraints, and are a function of how black elite commitments to their core electoral constituencies have been modified amid the shifting electoral calculus and ideological direction of the Democratic Party since the late 1980s. Urban population shifts within most American cities after World War II, historic civil rights reform, and Great Society liberal statecraft combined to produce a post-segregation black political elite. This turn to black ethnic politics, reflected in the writings of Carmichael and Hamilton and many of their contemporaries, was encouraged and shaped by Johnson-era social policy, in particular the Community Action Programs of the 1964 Economic Opportunity Act and later the Model Cities legislation, which extended technical expertise, political access and resources to the most well-positioned and articulate segments of inner-city black populations.[9] Limited but significant political integration has changed the face of public leadership in most American cities, with some having elected successive black-led governing regimes. The crucial development revealed in the rubble and smoke of Baltimore worth noting here is the ascendant power of a bloc of neoliberal black political elites. Unlike their predecessors who operated in the waning days of the New Deal Democratic coalition, this newest cohort of black politicos is more integrated institutionally and ideologically into the New Democratic politics, which sought to play catch-up with Reaganism, and is not beholden to the movement pressures that defined black political life during the 1960s and 1970s.

The election of Barack Obama to the presidency in 2008 represented both a Jackie Robinson–like political milestone and, perhaps more consequentially, the triumph of a refined New Democratic politics, liberal in terms of multicultural representation and inclusiveness, but strongly committed to neoliberalism —the ideological rejection of social democracy and left egalitarian interventionism in favor of the active promotion of forms of regulation that enhance capital flows and profit-making.[10] Carmichael and Hamilton thought that black political control would yield more effective empowerment, sweeping aside the half-hearted reforms of white liberals to deliver real change in the lives of black urban dwellers. Almost five decades after their clarion call, actually existing Black Power has come to serve as a means of legitimating and advancing urban neoliberalization, the rollback of public goods and services and the maintenance of a pro-market order that relegates the unemployed, the undereducated and the undocumented to a life of subsistence in the low-wage economy and often in the informal sector. The role that black political elites play in promoting nonprofit, privatized solutions to unemployment, poverty, failing schools and socioeconomic inequality more generally, and the effect that identitarian assumptions about political affinity have on public debate, are the most formidable barriers to developing a popular movement capable of confronting capitalist class power, contesting the hegemony of carceral logics and resolving the ongoing policing crisis.

Freddie Gray's Baltimore

In April 2015, the death of twenty-five-year-old Freddie Gray brought the policing crisis onto the national stage and into President Barack Obama's backyard, making Baltimore the latest epicenter of national protests over police and vigilante violence against blacks, and the carceral build-up. Gray suffered a severe spinal cord injury while being transported by Baltimore police, and lay in a coma for seven days before succumbing to his injuries on April 19. A cell-phone video taken during Gray's initial arrest records him wailing in agony. At least one bystander reported that Gray's body was bent "like a pretzel" by police who ignored his requests for medical assistance. In the amateur footage, at least one of his legs appears to have gone limp. The officers drag him a short distance before standing Gray on his feet and then lifting him into the awaiting police van. A second cell-phone video, taken by bystanders near the corner of Mount and Baker Streets, shows the arresting officers removing Gray from the van and placing leg shackles on him. When the wagon arrived at the Western District police station, Gray was unresponsive and not breathing. As the news of his death spread, marches and peaceful demonstrations were met by a heavier police presence, with skirmishes and full-scale riots spreading across the city's West Side. Officials estimated some $9 million in property damages. There were 150 reported vehicle fires and sixty structures were burned. According to official reports 250 people were arrested, but activists placed the figure at over 400. About half of those arrested were released without being charged.

In comparison to other urban rebellions in recent memory, such as those in the Mount Pleasant section of the District of Columbia in 1991, South Central Los Angeles in 1992, Cincinnati in 2001, and even Ferguson in 2014, the Baltimore conflict was rather small in scale and duration. The April 2015 events seem especially tame when compared to the 1968 Holy Week riots that rocked the city after the assassination of Martin Luther King, Jr. In 1968, order was restored through the deployment of nearly 11,000 National Guard and federal troops, and in the end 6 people lay dead, 700 were injured and 5,800 were arrested.[11] A thousand businesses reported property damages totaling $12 million in insured losses.[12] The core underlying problem uniting the urban context that Carmichael and Hamilton confronted and that of our own times is the presence of a large black subproletariat struggling to meet basic needs due to structural unemployment in a context of industrial contraction, fiscal abandonment and carceral discipline.

Freddie Gray's life was in many ways typical of many young, black working-class men struggling to survive in a context of violence, few jobs and constant police surveillance. Gray lived in the Gilmor Homes, a public housing development in the Sandtown-Winchester neighborhood. During his early years, Gray's family lived in such squalid conditions that he and his sisters tested positive for toxic lead levels in their blood. Such poisoning from peeling paint was so common in their social world that many referred to the settlement payments Gray and others received as "lead checks."[13] Gray and his siblings struggled with education and health issues. Not surprisingly, Gray was asthmatic and asked for an albuterol inhaler during his fateful arrest. In an attempt to impugn the victim and justify police actions, conservative pundits harped on Gray's multiple arrests—the twenty court cases against him, most of which were for drug-related and nonviolent offenses—but neighbors recalled a gregarious personality who loved football and possessed an infectious smile and playful sense of humor. The picture that emerges from the testimonies of those who knew him best is of a young man who loved his family and friends, and did his best to take care of them financially and emotionally despite the losing hand that American society had dealt him.

Geographer and longtime Baltimore resident David Harvey once remarked that while he had an "immense fund of affection" for the city, Baltimore was "for the most part, a mess. Not the kind of enchanting mess that makes cities such interesting places to explore, but an awful mess."[14] Of course, Baltimore was not always in such a dismal state, not even for its black residents. Like many American industrial cities, it has followed what is by now a familiar arch of development, from a Fordist city with a densely populated streetscape of ethnic enclaves through an age of suburban residential expansion and prosperity after World War II, and then into an epoch of shuttered factories and shifting investment to the financial, tourism and media sectors.[15] Industrial contraction in Baltimore hit the city's black population especially hard because so many black workers had formerly secured gainful employment in the city's steel mills, shipyards and docks. In 1970, Bethlehem Steel employed 30,000 workers, but by the turn of the twenty-first century fewer than 5,000 were needed to maintain the same levels of productivity.[16] In a similar manner, containerization and the increased use of automated ship-loading have greatly reduced the need for living labor in the docks of Baltimore and other cities worldwide.[17] The twentieth-century era of the mass worker has been replaced by an hourglass economy with promising careers, material comfort, security, entertainment and leisure for the majority-white, educated professional classes on the uppermost end, a shrinking core of unionized, well-paid and relatively secure wage labor in the center, and, on the bottom, deteriorating infrastructure, failing schools and contingent, low-wage service-sector employment or precarious informal work for the reserve army.[18]

By the time Gray entered this world, Baltimore had become a showcase of post-Fordist urban redevelopment, having begun the process in the 1970s of renovating its derelict wharfs, warehouses and port infrastructure into a picturesque and coveted ensemble of tourist attractions. By the early 1990s, the Inner Harbor featured an aquarium, science center, chartered boat rides, a festival plaza, multiple restaurants, shopping arcades, numerous hotels and condo buildings and, within a short walk, Orioles Park at Camden Yards, the home field of the city's American League baseball franchise. In the mid-1980s, local elites began the conversion of Baltimore Gas and Electric Company's defunct Pratt Street power plant into an entertainment destination, a process that has involved revolving tenancy and numerous cycles of boom and bust, all heavily subsidized by the public coffers.[19] The Inner Harbor provided Baltimore with a popular face of success, but, as in so many cities, beyond the boundaries of its refurbished downtown lay an altogether different reality.

The efforts to transform Baltimore's Inner Harbor into a tourist destination coincided with the crack cocaine scourge, and birthed Baltimore's equivalent of New York mayor Rudy Giuliani's policing regime. Martin O'Malley was elected mayor in

1999 as an anticrime crusader and immediately initiated the same zero-tolerance policing strategies widely touted with "cleaning up" drug markets in other cities. O'Malley's strategy had the effect of reducing crime rates, but only through the ramped-up arrest and incarceration of young black men in the city's most desperate neighborhoods.[20] Like New York City's much-vaunted transformation, in Baltimore mass incarceration became a vital dimension of post-manufacturing capital accumulation, where removing the poor and securing the gentrifying zones are requisites for real estate–driven development.

The reorganization of Baltimore's economy, the subsidization of the city's downtown tourism and financial sectors, and the national shift towards workfare and prisonfare have produced a landscape of spectacular wealth and leisure amenities for the urban bon vivant on the one hand, and residential apartheid and precarity for the city's mostly black poor on the other. Beginning after World War II, the exodus of more affluent whites and later blacks from the central city to the suburbs of Baltimore County and beyond created new patterns of segregation. Loïc Wacquant has characterized these contemporary spatial configurations in terms of hyper-ghettoization, as a way of distinguishing the black ghetto of the twentieth century, with its internal class diversity, from the conditions we find in places like Gray's Sandtown-Winchester neighborhood today, which are class-exclusive zones where the black poor are relegated and policed.[21] In 2012, the unemployment rate for Baltimore City was 13.9 percent, but in Sandtown-Winchester it was 24.2 percent.[22] When the riots erupted after Gray's death, the city's unemployment stood at 8.4 percent, even though the national rate was falling. Gray's neighborhood was 97 percent black, and 35.4 percent of its households lived in poverty. Writing in the wake of the rebellion, political scientist and Baltimore resident Lester Spence pointed out how the city's spending priorities, and the elite preference for incentivizing pro-corporate growth over neighborhood development and public goods and services, contributed to the 2015 crisis. The city heavily subsidized local corporations like Under

Armour, supporting the construction of their downtown head-quarters with $35 million in tax increment financing.[23] Spence noted that funding for public parks and recreation in Baltimore had stagnated, while spending on policing had surged. The city spent around $165 million on policing in 1991, but by 2015 it was spending $445 million.

True to the neoliberal model, Under Armour has taken up the role of social service delivery, albeit not in any way matching the scale of the problems facing Baltimore. Alongside other NGOs and foundations working the city, such as the Aspen Institute, the Carnegie Foundation and the Rockefeller Brothers Fund, among others, Under Armour sponsored initiatives like Project Rampart, established in 2017, which upgraded sports facilities and outfitted players and coaches in the city's public schools, and advanced various leadership programs for Baltimore youth. Such projects simultaneously fulfilled the mantra of pro-market reformers that private institutions are more effective and efficient service-delivery mechanisms than the old welfare state, and simultaneously camouflaged the vast transfers of public wealth Under Armour's growth has depended on. Baltimore's budgetary and policy priorities are not unique, but are reflective of a general tendency that has come to define American political life over the past four decades. In the face of growing inequality rooted in technological obsolescence and the elimination of the need for large quantities of living labor, American political elites and publics have come to support the extensive use of policing and incarceration to manage relative surplus population, and abandoned public works and the use of progressive state intervention to ensure some modicum of material necessity and equality for all citizens. Justifications for the neoliberal turn, and its punitive impacts on the most vulnerable citizens, have most often involved underclass moralizing—blaming the poor and their alleged cultural deficits for the inequalities that persist. Such underclass narratives were quickly mobilized by ruling elites and corporate media in the wake of the Baltimore rebellion.

Obama's Underclass Moralizing and Neoliberal Crisis Management

In the ruins of West Baltimore, the contradictions of the Obama administration's neoliberal approach to contemporary inequality were forced out into the open; at the same time, the way the conflict was so effectively managed and quelled reveals the social power of black political integration. Even before his election, Obama engaged in a form of underclass mythmaking, one that gestured towards systemic racism and economic structures, before trumpeting the behavioral roots of contemporary inequality and calling for greater parental responsibility, patriarchal authority and bourgeois aspiration as curatives to urban inequality. The notion of the underclass is essentially the view that black poverty results from peculiar cultural deficits: lack of a work ethic, the prevalence of female-headed households, the lack of delayed gratification and so forth. This ideology has its origins in the Cold War liberalism of Daniel Patrick Moynihan, who served as Assistant Secretary of Labor in the Johnson administration, but over the past few decades it has been adopted by generations of conservative Republicans, black nationalists, liberal academics, New Urbanists and New Democrats.[24] Despite the perception by many of Obama's legions of supporters, and as many right-wing critics, who saw him as politically on the left—either a New Deal Democrat or a closeted socialist—on matters of contemporary racial and urban inequality, his public statements have been consistently conservative, emphasizing the dysfunctional behavior of the poor and proffering market-oriented solutions. In Obama's hands, underclass moralizing achieved renewed hegemony. Obama's blackness, the powerful optics of his patriarchal, heteronormative family life, and his skill at emoting with black audiences allowed him to restore the legitimacy of conservative ideas that had been threatened during the 2000s, as a growing chorus of social forces publicly criticized the power of global capital and the military adventurism and domestic disaster that defined the administration of George W. Bush.

At the 2004 Democratic National Convention, Obama offered a full-throated celebration of American exceptionalism. He acknowledged the difficulties faced by contemporary American workers in passing, but overall his speech elided class as a significant determinant in American life. According to Obama, "In a generous America you don't have to be rich to achieve your potential."[25] He diminished the role of the state as a guarantor of equality of opportunity, and instead elevated popular conservative themes of individual responsibility and self-governance in a manner that swept aside the historical and contemporary demands of working-class and popular struggles for protection from volatile market forces. "The people I meet in small towns and big cities, in diners and office parks," Obama claimed, "they don't expect government to solve all their problems. They know they have to work hard to get ahead and they want to. Go into the collar counties around Chicago, and people will tell you they don't want their tax money wasted by a welfare agency or the Pentagon." He then recited now familiar conservative platitudes regarding contemporary racial achievement gaps in education, suggesting that an anti-intellectual culture and the lack of parental involvement are to blame. "Go into any inner-city neighborhood, and folks will tell you that government alone can't teach kids to learn. They know that parents have to parent, that children can't achieve unless we raise their expectations and turn off the television sets and eradicate the slander that says a black youth with a book is acting white." Where his predecessors might have been dismissed for their social meanness—recall Reagan's welfare-queen mythmaking—Obama was able to convey the same ideas about the black poor as distinct and uniquely depraved, but with a sense of sincerity and persuasiveness that resonated with some black audiences, while comforting broader publics who do not want to share their wealth through tax-financed social assistance and public goods.

In his numerous Father's Day speeches, often delivered from the pulpits of black churches, Obama called on black men to be more responsible parents and role models. His delivery had the

appeal of a closed-door chat with his core racial constituency—
"his people"—but like the speeches of any other modern president, such words are circulated widely within the American
public. Obama's uncanny ability to speak in multiple registers
and to different audiences was simultaneously a crucial ingredient in his national electoral success and critical in maintaining
the hegemony of the underclass myth during uncertain economic
times. Time and again, whenever the problems of chronic inner-
city poverty and violence confronted him, Obama resorted to
skillful and charismatic deployment of the underclass ideology.

Not long after his national political debut at the 2004 DNC,
Obama provided a glimpse of things to come when he endorsed
comedian Bill Cosby's controversial remarks about the black
poor. Cosby's comments were made on the occasion of the fiftieth
anniversary of the Supreme Court's landmark 1954 decision in
Brown v. the Board of Education, Topeka, Kansas, which overturned the "separate but equal" precedent that had served as
the cornerstone of Jim Crow segregation. While celebrating the
progress of the black middle class since *Brown*, Cosby lamented
that "the lower economic people are not holding up their part in
this deal," and then proceeded to riff on the alleged behavioral
dysfunction of the black urban poor. In one of his most outland-
ish claims, Cosby questioned the wisdom of anti–police brutality
protests, insinuating that the bad behavior of the poor should be
scrutinized more than the police: "These people are going around
stealing Coca-Cola. People getting shot in the back of the head
over a piece of pound cake and then we run out and we are outraged [saying] 'The cops shouldn't have shot him.' What the hell
was he doing with the pound cake in his hand?"[26]

History has proven Cosby to be an utter hypocrite, as dozens
of women came forward despite public ridicule and character assassination to give sworn testimony that he had drugged
and raped them. In the summer of 2021, Cosby was released
from prison after the Pennsylvania Supreme Court found his
due process rights had been violated, overturning his previous
conviction of aggravated indecent assault of Andrea Constand.

However, at the time of his 2004 "Pound Cake" speech, as it has come to be known, Cosby remained a highly respected public figure who was for decades the seemingly unimpeachable portrait of the successful black patriarch, wise, generous, loving and gregarious. Through both his fictional family, the Huxtables on the long-running *Cosby Show* sitcom, and his real-life family with his longtime wife Camille, Cosby projected the perfect model of black middle-class aspiration for the Reagan-Bush years. He shattered racist assertions about black men and black fathers, becoming for a time America's dad, beloved by millions regardless of their color or national origin. It is not surprising that Obama found consonance in Cosby's words. Obama asserted in an interview with Oprah Winfrey: "Bill Cosby got into trouble when he said some of these things, and he has a right to say things in ways that I'm not going to because he's an older man. But I completely agree with his underlying premise: We have to change attitudes. There's a strain of anti-intellectualism running in our community that we have to eliminate."[27] Obama would expound on this core belief that the fundamental barrier facing the black working poor was their own cultural dysfunction.

Obama's response to mass shooting incidents provides an insightful comparison to his deeply problematic approach to black urban violence. Obama gave more speeches in the aftermath of mass shootings than any other president before him. He delivered his most impassioned call for gun regulation in response to the October 2015 Umqua College massacre in Oregon, where Chris Harper-Mercer, a twenty-six-year-old student, killed a professor and eight students and injured eight others before taking his own life. Obama sounded angrier and more resolute than in his fourteen previous addresses in the wake of mass gun violence. In that moment, he treated mass shootings as matters of national concern. Absent such political pressure, however, he was less likely to address routinized urban gun violence and, when he did, more apt to frame the problem as one of the cultural failings of a specific stratum of US society. In the face of both forms of gun violence, he made a plea for reform of gun laws—more stringent background checks on gun purchases—often pointing out the powerful role of the gun lobby and an obstinate Congress in maintaining the status quo, before calling for the latter's support in reforming the current system to improve public safety. A consistent theme in his speeches on gun violence was sickness. A key difference, however, was that in the case of mass shootings he emphasized the fragile mental state of the lone gunman and called on parents, teachers and community members to watch out for early warning signs, and find help for those who were depressed and in need of mental health services. When he turned to address the problem of urban violence, however, his emphasis was on cultural sickness, the alleged pathologies of the black urban poor as a whole.

More than once during Obama's tenure, the problem of urban violence hit close to home as his adopted hometown of Chicago faced recurrent waves of street violence. In 2009, less than a year into Obama's first term, Derrion Albert, a sixteen-year-old student, was killed in a melee between two rival gangs near Fenger High School in Chicago's Roseland neighborhood. The incident was captured on cell-phone video and the gruesome images of the innocent bystander being bludgeoned to death with a rail tie stood in stark contrast to national news coverage that same week of the Obamas arriving in Copenhagen to make a case for Chicago's Olympic bid.[28] At the start of his second term, Obama was faced once again with another highly publicized murder of an innocent black teen. This time, fifteen-year-old Hadiya Pendleton was gunned down while sitting with her friends in a park less than a mile from the Obamas' Hyde Park home. Pendleton had performed at the president's second inauguration only a week earlier as a majorette in her high school marching band. First Lady Michelle Obama represented the White House at Pendleton's funeral and delivered the eulogy. After the Black Youth Project 100 circulated a petition urging the president to come to Chicago to give an address on gun violence, he conceded, delivering a speech at the Hyde Park Career Academy in February 2013.

His speech alluded to the role of negative economic conditions and called for a modest increase in the national minimum wage, before turning to his familiar combination of remedies: more effective parenting, school privatization and behavior modification. In a fashion that one would have expected from Reagan Republicans a few decades prior, Obama minimized the potential impact of public intervention and valorized the role of civil society and the market. "When a child opens fire on another child," he said, "there's a hole in that child's heart that government can't fill—only community and parents and teachers and clergy can fill that hole." "There's no more important ingredient for success," Obama continued, "nothing that would be more important for us reducing violence than strong, stable families—which means we should do more to promote marriage and encourage fatherhood."[29] In the realm of education, he lauded his former chief of staff and Chicago mayor Rahm Emanuel's program for rewarding high-performance preschools; without explicitly endorsing charterization, he celebrated the work of some Chicago high schools and urged "redesigning" schools for success, clearly a euphemism for the charter school experimentation.

His public remarks in the wake of Freddie Gray's death and the ensuing protests extended these same interpretations and policy themes, despite pressure from anti–police brutality forces who wanted him to give a sterner rebuke. During a White House Rose Garden press conference with visiting Japanese prime minister Shinzo Abe, a reporter asked Obama whether the unfolding events in Baltimore constituted a national crisis. In an extended response, he praised the peaceful protestors for engaging in "the kind of organizing that needs to take place if we're going to tackle this problem," and condemned looters, calling for the restoration of order and arrests and punishment for "the handful of criminals and thugs who tore up the place."[30] Obama then lauded the work of his taskforce on policing, a grant program to assist local departments in purchasing body cameras, and other measures, but he emphasized the limits of his authority— "I can't federalize every police department in the country and force them to retrain." He also resorted, as he had in the past, to the "few bad apples" explanation of police brutality, arguing that it is the fault of a small minority of disturbed or poorly trained individuals, not a problem endemic to the institution of policing itself. He then concluded on the familiar ground of underclass ideology, describing the environment of substance abuse, absentee fathers, desperation and joblessness, where we "send police in to do the dirty work of containing the problems that arise there." Acknowledging again the difficulty of securing support from Congress for the kinds of reforms he would like, in this case more investment in urban communities, Obama pivoted towards the neoliberal model—"we can make a difference around school reform and around job training, and around some investments in infrastructure in these communities trying to attract new businesses in." He was, of course, not alone in these sentiments. His words authorized the dominant mode of thinking about poverty, a view that thrives at the grassroots as well.

Further evidence of the underclass ideology's hegemony could be found in the overnight rise of Toya Graham from an unemployed single mother into a national cause célèbre during the Baltimore riots. Graham became a media sensation when she publicly slapped her son multiple times after finding him among a group of masked protestors outside Mondawmin Mall in West Baltimore. Within days, Graham received invitations for numerous cable news and talk show appearances, a GoFundMe campaign was started to raise money for her and her children, and job offers from Black Entertainment Television, Under Armour and other companies soon followed. Although her son Michael said he joined the protests because he and many of his friends had been mistreated by police, his political views were drowned out in celebrations of his mother's heavy-handed parenting. For some, Graham represented the kind of parent that was missing in the lives of too many young black men—the strong disciplinarian who is willing to embarrass her progeny in order to keep him out of harm's way. The focus on disciplinary parenting, and the charitable responses from foundations and corporations, are longstanding approaches to addressing inequality that have gained an outsized role within the context of the neoliberal dismantling of public goods and services. As Carmichael and Hamilton made clear when faced with similar efforts to placate rebellion, these strategies do not alter the economic practices and fundamental conditions that produce obsolescence and inequality.

In retrospect, the historic significance of the 2015 Baltimore riot lay not in its scale, nor in the ways it galvanized national protests against police brutality, but in how well the Baltimore events were mobilized by conservative reformist political tendencies, perhaps best represented in the Obama administration's My Brother's Keeper Alliance and the local One Baltimore initiative launched by the city's black governing regime. Obama responded to the Baltimore crisis by christening his My Brother's Keeper Alliance, a nonprofit expansion of the initiative he had created the year before. The program would draw on $80 million in private investments from corporate donors—including Sam's Club, Pepsi Co. and Sprint, among a long list of others—and focus on improving the lives of boys and young men of color by targeting literacy education, graduation rates, workforce preparation and programs designed to keep them out of the criminal justice system.[31] Obama named pop singer and school privatization advocate John Legend as the honorary chairman of the Alliance. Unveiling the new project at Lehman College in the Bronx, Obama co-opted the language of Black Lives Matter, repeatedly asserting "you matter" to the group of young men gathered for the press conference.[32] This was yet another manifestation of the approach that was the hallmark of his administration: soft overtures to left social criticism and a heavy dose of underclass moralizing combined with pro-market solutions. Local responses in Baltimore mirrored those of the White House in their neoliberal form and political effects.

Even before Maryland State's Attorney Marilyn Mosby issued indictments against the six officers involved in Freddie Gray's arrest, a broad alliance of national and local elites, celebrity philanthropists, Baltimore Ravens football players, old-guard race men, small business owners, corporate and foundation board members, civic boosters and activists rallied around peaceful demonstrations and acts of volunteerism as the most legitimate means for addressing the poverty and violence in the city's toughest neighborhoods. In the days after Gray's death, as images of burning buildings and youth overturning cars flooded social media and television coverage, the nonprofit organization Big Brothers Big Sisters saw a 3,000 percent increase in inquiries from potential volunteer mentors.[33] Baltimore officials also launched the One Baltimore initiative to coordinate charitable work. Ironically, this official campaign usurped the name of the One Baltimore coalition, a group of grassroots organizations, unions and churches who had rallied a year prior to protest the efforts of Veolia North America, a water privatization corporation, to secure a consulting contract with the city.[34] This latest One Baltimore initiative formed by elites amid the riots, however, was decidedly pro-privatization, created as a means of coordinating nonprofit and philanthropic resources and relief efforts in the riot-torn city.[35] City officials also set up the Baltimore Business Recovery fund, to connect local businesses and firms affected by the riots to various sources of local, state and federal aid for reconstruction.

If the experience of New Orleans after the 2005 Hurricane Katrina disaster provides any indication of trajectory, these initiatives will most likely absorb elements of the potential opposition and further erode support for genuinely public solutions to poverty and urban violence. Even more than New Orleans, Baltimore has long been a hub of national black political activity, due to its large and longstanding black middle class and proximity to the nation's capital. In New Orleans, city elites embarked on a reconstruction centered on property owners that drew heavily on an extensive network of NGOs to carry out renovation and new builds of single family homes. Equally consequential, various nonprofit think tanks, education entrepreneurs, for-profit schools and temporary staffing organizations like Teach for America united to overhaul the city's school system, turning it into the nation's first all-charter school district.[36] The weakening of both public housing and public schools in the city over the course of decades, along with the lore of local corruption, provided traction for the post-disaster privatization efforts. Furthermore, the fact that the neoliberal model was able to produce tangible results for some constituencies, in a context of diminished public goods and services, helped to cement support from a broad, multiracial swath of the city's weary natives, disgruntled activists, newcomers and enterprising investors around an agenda of educational experimentation, volunteerism and entrepreneurship. What emerged in the post-Katrina context was an integrated, pro-growth coalition in which the numbers of black politicos were momentarily diminished due to the loss of black population in the city. As in other places, however, black political and business elites continued to play a crucial role in legitimating the processes of neoliberalization, softening the potential opposition among black neighborhood and activist constituencies by their presence alone, and at other times actively reframing corporate class prerogatives as essential to black advancement. An illustrative case in point is the fate of public housing in post-Katrina New Orleans.

With public housing residents displaced by the flooding, a diverse coalition of wealthy developers, architects, local politicians, housing officials, as well as some former residents, nonprofits and grassroots organizations, coalesced around the demolition of last remaining public housing complexes in the city—the Big Four (the St. Bernard Development, the Lafitte, the B.W. Cooper and the C.J. Peete) and the Iberville—and their replacement with mixed-income developments.[37] As a consequence of these changes, by the time the city commemorated the tenth anniversary of the disaster, New Orleans renters faced a housing crisis as monthly rent costs soared past the national median and some 16,000 families remained on the waitlist for public housing units.[38] The fight to preserve public housing and neighborhood public schools were central axes of conflict on the ground in the city, battlefronts that did not fall neatly along the black–white lines so many academics and pundits abide. The political conflicts over these public goods, and the saturation of New Orleans with charitable and voluntarist activity, also revealed the ways that the advance of nonprofit organizations has had the effect of transforming and conflating the meaning of left political activism in some corners. Rather than policy-oriented activity aimed at contesting investor class interests and achieving popular democratic power, some have come to view nonprofit work that furthers privatization as compatible with left activism.[39] Although the forces aligned against police brutality have framed the problem largely in terms of institutional racism, the power of the humanitarian-corporate complexes in New Orleans and now Baltimore requires a critical analysis of the last half century of black political history and of contemporary conditions where constituted power is often held by multiethnic, and in some cases majority-black, political regimes. It also demands political strategies reoriented towards progressive public interventions that reverse the processes of privatization and instead guarantee vital public goods to all citizens.

The Sale of Two Cities

Since the death of Freddie Gray, Baltimore has seen moments of incremental policy change and small victories in the struggle to address overpolicing, but overall the city has witnessed the restored power of the same neoliberal development regime that has produced such a highly unequal city. Police commissioner Anthony Batts was fired. The six officers who arrested Gray were all charged and tried, but none were convicted. Their respective cases ended either in not-guilty verdicts or dropped charges. The City of Baltimore awarded a $6.4 million settlement to Gray's mother, Gloria Darden, and other family members in September 2015. The financial windfall, however, did little for the grieving mother, who attempted to take her own life less than a month later. The Maryland Assembly voted to approve a reform bill that earmarked funds for community policing as well as incentives for officers to live where they worked. The bill faced opposition from both police union leadership and antipolicing activists, albeit for different reasons. While police opposed the bill as a violation of their union contract, activists expressed concerns over the lack of investigatory power in the proposed civilian review board.

Aside from surface reforms, in the months and years following the rioting, Baltimore plunged deeper into crisis. The bourgeois calls for unity and healing that flooded the ether and corporate network news during the rebellion, as well as all manner of reforms, have provided little respite from the crime, unemployment, misery and inequality that defined Freddie Gray's world. Violent crime spiked. In 2017, there were 342 homicides, making Baltimore one of the most violent cities in America. Some have explained this pattern of worsening public safety as the result of a "quiet riot" by police, idling on the job as a backlash against the increased public scrutiny of policing practices.[40]

If the recent history of Ferguson, Baltimore, Minneapolis and other cities are any evidence, the "point beyond which the steaming ghettos will not be cooled off" has yet to be reached. Carmichael and Hamilton offered a stinging criticism of the shallow patronage doled out to black neighborhoods in the aftermath of the sixties rebellions. When they penned *Black Power*, they anticipated a democratic transformation of American cities, the realization of real black self-determination along the lines of the ethnic incorporation model pursued by Irish, Polish, Italians and other groups in earlier periods. What they did not anticipate was how that process would ultimately have the effect of stabilizing the inequality and desperation of ghetto life in coming decades, and providing a means of managing social discontent through ensuing periods of crises and the worsening conditions produced by neoliberalization. The combination of descriptive racial representation, the substantive and consequential integration of black workers into public sector jobs, and an expansive carceral apparatus all combined to allow black prosperity and progress and black immiseration and alienation to exist side by side—certainly not without conflict, but in a manner that facilitated perpetual capital flows and profit-making in places like Baltimore. We need to be clear about the historical evolution and consequences of these endogenous black politics, especially their implications for building working-class and popular power, and resist the lure of the "old wine, new bottles" racial politics of Black Lives Matter, which blinds us to historical class interests in motion and the actual battle lines that define our world. The route to real self-determination for working-class Baltimoreans should not follow the logic of racial authenticity, which, as history has shown, can easily be assimilated to the neoliberal project through policies that seek to achieve social justice ends through pro-market means, e.g., minority contracting set-asides, black excellence charter schools, urban entrepreneurship incubators, micro-credit lending schemes and so forth. Instead, popular alliances organized against investor class power and for a project of decommodifying social needs, strengthening worker rights and rolling back the carceral apparatus are the only viable path towards the socially just city at this juncture.

Popular forces in Baltimore have unmasked the limits of black officialdom but at the same time remain hampered by black nationalist notions of racial communion and politics. In the aftermath of the Baltimore rebellion, a viral video captured PFK Boom (a.k.a. Davon Neverdon) and Shy Lady Heroin, both local activists and rappers, confronting black mega-church pastor, Jamal Bryant.[41] The conflict began when Bryant showed up at West Wednesdays, a weekly gathering of activists and community members that began in the aftermath of the 2013 police killing of Tyrone West in North Baltimore. Bryant was a former NAACP national youth director and at the time was leader of Empowerment Temple African Methodist Episcopal Church, with some 11,000 parishioners. Boom, wearing shades and draped in a Palestinian keffiyeh, questioned Bryant on why he had taken so long to join their fight, calling him out for his lack of leadership: "You say you for the people, you got our people all up in your church." Bryant was clearly caught off guard and his visible discomfort was met by escalating rhetoric from Boom, who first tells Bryant to stay away from the West Wednesdays gathering: "Don't come! We don't want you nowhere in our city ... The Streets don't want you here." "You ain't even fighting the war with us," Boom continued, "and then you fucking with our oppressors!" "How?" Bryant murmured in response. "What do you mean 'how'?" Boom replied, agitated, "You fucking with [Mayor Stephanie] Rawlings-Blake and all them, man. You trying to kill us, man!" Boom then showers Bryant with a final round of invective, "Get the fuck out of the whole city!!" Clearly bewildered, Bryant chooses to de-escalate and walks away, while Boom mocks the empowerment message emblazoned on the back of Bryant's t-shirt.

As the camera followed Bryant down the street, Shy Lady Heroin steps into the frame to punctuate the video's core point, that black officialdom in Baltimore does not represent the masses of black Baltimoreans. She runs down an inventory of the black elites' failings: "Jamal Bryant, you should be ashamed of yourself, for selling out your people for your fame and your wealth. SRB [Stephanie Rawlings-Blake], we know where them perks went. Fuck twelve. Leave the city that's your first step. Take Davis and the war room and your cousin Brandon Scott, 300 Men and they payments, they love a photo-op. We taking back our city one step at a time. Walk in solidarity. This is the front line. Now the Mosbys gotta go. Billy Murphy, you can leave. Got my right fist high saying 'Fuck the police!'" Perhaps more than Boom's confrontation with Bryant, Shy Lady Heroin's closing rhyme offers the most damning criticism of local black elites like political operative Lester Davis and city councilman Brandon Scott, and their complicity in maintaining the ghettoization of Baltimore's black poor. Instead of the community caretakers and race men who governed segregated black communities of the twentieth century through institution-building and racial uplift, Shy Lady Heroin paints a portrait of leaders driven by avarice, publicity and selfish motives.

The video conveys some of the sharpest criticisms of how the Baltimore rebellion was corralled by local elites, and presents the alternative posed by organizations like 300 Gangstas, which emerged from the grassroots. This organization was formed by Boom and other local activists and inspired by *300*, the comic and Frank Miller feature film that fictionalized the Battle of Thermopylae, when a band of 300 Spartan soldiers attempted to fend off a massive invading Persian army. Boom and the organization's devotees, many former and current gang members, saw themselves as latter-day Spartans, outnumbered and outgunned, defending their communities against the "invading army" of Baltimore police. The organization also arose as a more radical alternative to the voluntaristic antiviolence group, the 300 Men March Movement. In contrast, 300 Gangstas was openly critical of the nonprofit-industrial complex and its political maneuvers after the rebellion.

While this viral video excels as protest, it falls short as politics. The editing, timing of the confrontation, and Shy Lady Heroin's pitch-perfect rap for the occasion all suggest that the conflict was orchestrated, a public relations maneuver suited to the world of social media and the contemporary tendency to measure political importance by "likes" and "hits." Bryant was also easy prey for this kind of grandstanding—a confrontation with a "man of the cloth" and well-known leader was not likely to escalate and backfire in the face of the activists. Setting aside those problems, as propaganda the video is a scathing indictment, and effectively expresses the discontent smoldering beyond the camera frames of corporate news celebrations of volunteers and nonprofits rising to address the city's deep inequalities. And yet at the same time, the criticisms it levels at the black elite are all too familiar, not having advanced much in substance since the publication of Carmichael and Hamilton's *Black Power*, and operate from a flawed logic of black organicism that plagues the broader Black Lives Matter moment. When Boom claims to speak for "the streets," and when Shy Lady Heroin names the various gangs and activist groups aligned with her SWORD (Strong Women of Real

Destiny) Nation, both are claiming to speak the authentic voice of the black masses. The fact that Boom and Bryant reconciled within weeks of that video also gives it all the appearance of a publicity stunt. Black unity and leadership accountability are not the answer to the problems of policing; what is needed is horizontal power built within and beyond Baltimore's most depressed neighborhoods, and advancing a clearly enunciated left political agenda that contests the demands capital makes on labor, urban living and the environment.

The Boom–Bryant YouTube confrontation is powerful in calling into question the legitimacy of figures like Bryant and how poorly they represent the interests of the most dispossessed and precarious segments of the black population, but it trades on the same notion of authentic black leadership it criticizes. Boom claims to speak for the streets, but this is perhaps even more dangerous than thinking of Bryant as a black leader in the traditional sense. It should be noted that Bryant actually has led identifiable constituencies, the NAACP as a young man and, in more recent years, large and well-financed mega-church congregations. Boom's claim to be an authentic voice of the voiceless is descendant from Black Power rhetoric, which was a progressive attempt to disrupt the wrangling and machinations of Negro leaders, and reassert the voices of those black constituencies whose interests were not reflected in the amicus briefs and closed-door conversations in the Oval Office during the Kennedy and Johnson years. Boom's words carry an air of militancy in neoliberal Baltimore, where there is very real dispossession and disempowerment of large swaths of the black working class, but we know that neither he nor anyone else can claim to speak for the hundreds of people living in Gilmor Homes, nor the thousands more in West Baltimore, who may share his outrage at the fact of their shared predicament, but may not embrace his confrontational style or black nationalist politics. Even if they did—and they don't—such posturing has done little to alter the political forces that govern Baltimore: transnational corporations, wealthy developers, the consumer middle class within and beyond the city's corporate limits, the local black professional-managerial class—in other words, embodied capitalist class power—whose strategic choices reproduce their own position and the broader systemic hegemony.

Within a few weeks, Bryant and Boom appeared again in a YouTube video, seeming to make amends. Instead of a face-to-face confrontation on a Baltimore sidewalk, the video catches them seated shoulder-to-shoulder in a slim vertical camera frame, flanked by various activists such as Carlos Muhammad of the Nation of Islam and Big Wolfe (Robert Wolfe) of 300 Gangstas. What did this moment of reconciliation produce? Symbolic unity, or political common cause? Bryant appears in the video wearing 300 Gangstas apparel, but it is not clear that his views have changed much. There is the performance of unity and talk of healing, but it is not clear towards what end. These videos reflect two mirrored dimensions of black nationalist assumptions about race and leadership—on the one hand, the belief that black leaders are unaccountable and need to be confronted and brought in line with the black masses, and on the other hand the view that black unity is a requisite for political advancement. Both notions are flawed. Both assume black organicism, and though the criticism of black leadership is often pitched in sharp tones, such arguments falsely assume that dissimilar black interests, class positions and constituencies can be united under one accord. This kind of facile unity, reflected in the second YouTube video, has little to do with the forces shaping contemporary Baltimore. If we extend Boom's democratic claims about representing the streets, left politics in the city should be about building power among various working-class and popular sectors in Baltimore, and contesting the entrenched power of the city's pro-growth regime, which is driven largely by real estate and tourism-entertainment interests. The underlying revanchist processes of gentrification and displacement, and the hollowing out of the benevolent and reproductive functions of the state, have proceeded apace. While the black nationalist rhetoric illuminates the failings of elected black leaders, the way forward lies not merely in more responsive black leadership but in developing a counterpower capable of contesting capitalist urban planning and the carceral regime that secures real estate and tourism-centered economic revitalization strategies.

When we view Baltimore at a metropolitan scale, the interdependent processes of development and underdevelopment come into clearer focus, not as incidental occurrences, but as embroidered consequences of a discrete historical-territorial accumulation regime. The radical transformation and rebirth of American cities that paralleled Freddie Gray's short life were the outcome of a neoliberal political project that has centered on real estate valuation, and as David Madden and Peter Marcuse have noted, the state has played a crucial role in setting the rules of the game. "It enforces the sanctity of contracts, establishes and defends regimes of property rights," they write, "and plays a central role in connecting the financial system to the bricks and mortar in which people dwell."[42] Far from treating these processes of devaluation, speculation, upscaling and displacement as a "natural" functioning of the free market, Madden and Marcuse insist that we understand them as deeply political. They hold that "housing markets are political all the way down. The balance of power between tenants and landlords, or between real estate owners and communities, cannot be determined in a neutral, apolitical way ... The commodification of housing is a political project that refuses to acknowledge itself as such."[43] Rather than merely demanding accountability from black leaders on the basis of assumed racial communion, activists must build coalitions capable of contesting this political project of urban economic development, which is responsible for vast wealth transfers, impoverishment and dislocation, and the withering of the public good.

Although urban residents have long experienced the city from the vantage points of the neighborhood, the block, religious institutions, kinship networks and ethnic segregation, giving rise to a sense of disconnectedness and turf conflict, in the neoliberal city fashioned by elites for the purposes of accumulation, such differences are secondary, treated as barriers and problems to be managed and transcended. Again, the former longtime Baltimorean David Harvey's work is instructive for understanding the capitalist city as a "city of speculative gain" where "occupancy becomes unstable and ephemeral, social solidarities and neighborhood commonalities disintegrate, and the real estate folk brand upscale, often-gated neighborhoods with fictitious qualities of superior living."[44] Harvey refers us to Glyn Robbins to illuminate how the processes of speculation and real estate development bear grim consequences for the social life of the urban laboring classes. Writing within the context of a crime wave in London, Robbins concludes: "Neoliberal and profit-driven urban policies have produced cities in which many young people literally feel they have no place. They find it almost impossible to find a home they can afford in the communities where they were born, thwarting their ability to develop independent lives. Their social networks, sense of belonging, and feeling of respect from the adult world have been stretched to the breaking point. Nothing could be more perfectly calculated to create a situation in which young people don't care, either about the lives of others, or their own."[45] Robbins's description of the social upheaval, precarity and alienation provoked by neoliberal urbanism could just as easily be derived from Baltimore as London.

In April 2019, more than 120 families in a section of Gilmor Homes, the public housing complex where Freddie Gray was arrested, began moving out. Six buildings, some 132 apartments, were set to be torn down under the city's plan to privatize public housing. This process of public housing demolition and privatization was not unique to Baltimore, but part of the broader model of central city redevelopment set in motion by the federal housing voucher program decades earlier, and intensified under the Clinton-era housing policy. HOPE VI legislation provided federal funding for the demolition of public housing complexes to make way for privatized developments. In the late 1990s, Baltimore began razing its high-rise public housing stock, with Lafayette Courts, Lexington Terrace, Murphy Homes and Flag

House Courts falling in succession. Even with those demolitions, Baltimore continued to rank fifth nationally in terms of public housing volume, with over 11,000 units, even though the city is only the twenty-sixth largest in the country. In cooperation with state and federal government, the city planned to sell 40 percent of its public housing stock to private developers.

Housing officials and city leaders claimed that the move was an anticrime measure. Rawlings-Blake's successor Catherine Pugh described Gilmor Homes as "a really high-crime area," adding "the line of sight is terrible. The residents have complained about the violence ... People complained about not feeling safe."[46] Pugh's mayoral administration would not last long enough to see the Gilmor site renovation. She resigned amid a corruption scandal less than a month after families moved out of the complex. Maryland state delegate Nick J. Mosby, who represents the Sandtown-Winchester area and is husband of State's Attorney Marilyn Mosby, called for the full demolition of the complex, as have other Baltimore political figures like civil rights activist Marvin "Doc" Cheatham. The complex has been afflicted with all manner of problems, including physical deterioration, drugs, crime, rat-infestation, sexual predation and abuse of tenants. In a 2015 lawsuit, the city awarded an $8 million settlement to women residents who were coerced by maintenance workers to perform sexual acts in exchange for basic repairs and pest extermination. As in so many other American cities, these real problems have been used as a pretext for large-scale demolition and redevelopment that does not benefit residents over the long haul, but instead hastens the processes of rent intensification and the affordable-housing crisis. Moreover, the desire of city officials to break up crime zones and improve sight lines for policing the area is a ruse, an undemocratic and profit-oriented approach to housing that has proven disastrous for the working poor in one city after another. The poor themselves do not matter, nor do their friendships, familial and community bonds, connection to place, and certainly not their vision of what their neighborhoods should be. Instead, the process of housing demolition and privatization reflect the soul of the revanchist city, which is fundamentally about reaping surplus value, not creating a city where basic needs are addressed and all residents share in the socially produced material and cultural wealth of the urban process.

As low-income residents left in advance of the wrecking ball, about five miles south of Gilmor Homes work had already begun on Port Covington, a $5.5 billion mega-development project. The brain child of Under Armour CEO Kevin Plank, and facilitated by his Sagamore Development company, Port Covington will redevelop 260 acres of old industrial waterfront in South Baltimore. The project's boosters claim it will create 14.1 million square feet of mixed-used development, some forty-five city blocks of offices, housing, retail and entertainment, forty-plus acres of new parks, and additional light rail transit.[47] Early architectural renderings of the project depicted a row of seven blue glass towers along the Interstate 95 highway, evoking sail boats lining a marina, with smaller and differently scaled buildings fanning out southward over the peninsula. From the new imperial vistas of Port Covington, the daily dramas and hardships that unfold in Sandtown-Winchester will be worlds away, but these two cities are interdependent and co-produced in the capitalist urbanization processes of forceful enclosure, land valuation and uneven development.

To put it bluntly, this project replays all the false promises, corporate giveaways and prioritization of capitalist class interests over those of workers and city residents that defined the Inner Harbor development decades prior. As Harvey concluded in a formative assessment of the Inner Harbor's evolution, the public is bound to lose in these mega-developments. "The private-public partnership," Harvey quips, "means that the public takes the risks and the private takes the profits."[48] The needs of workers and older residential neighborhoods are sacrificed to feed the "downtown monster." Plank and Port Covington's supporters requested some $1.1 billion in local, state and federal subsidies to support infrastructure development for the project, with the city of Baltimore already consenting to its largest ever tax increment financing agreement of $660 million.[49] Port Covington also benefited from the Trump administration's "opportunity zones," which provided tax breaks ostensibly intended to funnel investment to poor areas.[50] This is not new, but rather conforms to the capitalist appropriation of similar programs like the Clinton-era "Empowerment Zones" or New York State's Empire Zones, which also strayed from their expressed purpose of developing distressed areas in favor of tax relief for rent-intensifying and job-killing projects. The official propaganda for such public-private agreements and corporate welfare schemes is always the same. The public capital outlays, so the argument goes, are justified because the property taxes such massive projects allegedly generate will allow the city to better address public concerns over school funding, affordable housing and other conditions that define the "other" Baltimore. Moreover, boosters of the project held that Port Covington will generate thousands of jobs in construction, and others in the various corporate offices, start-ups and tourism-entertainment venues that will spring up on the site.

Even if we accept the internal logic of this development strategy on its stated terms, one immediate problem in a city that should have learned from the previous cycles of boom and bust that defined the Inner Harbor saga is whether this latest megaproject will have an additive effect on the local economy or a subtractive one. In other words, with the ageing Inner Harbor having lost its luster, novelty and perception of safety, whether Port Covington will simply become the latest destination for tourists and "creative class" transplants—not so much an expansion of the local economy as the relocation of hot real estate from the Inner Harbor to the south of Federal Hill and the Interstate 95 flyover. Without government regulation, it is doubtful that private contractors will employ local laborers in the quantities that justify the massive public outlays for this project, let alone target the chronically unemployed young black men who lived in the forgotten city blocks that Freddie Gray inhabited. Underneath the promises of job creation and trickle-down effects, of STEM camps and tech-incubators targeting low-income residents and all the rest, is the truth of such mega-development projects—that their central motive is the profit to be made in the financing, planning and design, demolition and construction, and elevated ground rents that will trail each news story and every real estate industry puff piece about "Baltimore's comeback"—its latest one no less. Anything else flowing from such mega-projects that might benefit working-class Baltimoreans is a sideshow, not the main attraction or motive for the investor class. This is all unconscionable given Baltimore's deep and longstanding inequalities, and the timing of the project, where critical approval by the city council and other governing authorities was granted in the months after the 2015 rebellion. Like New Orleans in the aftermath of Katrina, the new Baltimore that has risen from the ashes of the 2015 riots looks very much like the old one—a neoliberal city that prioritizes the interests of capital over those of the working class, plain and simple. Liberal antiracism provides little traction here. A multi-racial governing coalition is responsible for this state of affairs in Charm City, as in most American cities. True to the neoliberal model, the state responds to the poor with disinvestment, moralizing, overpolicing and punishment, and to middle-class consumers, cognitive workers and the investor class with generous public subsidies, upgraded infrastructure and police protection. Against the old Cold War liberal notion of black poverty as an exception to the affluent society, we should see contemporary unemployment and immiseration as fundamental dimensions of capitalist urban planning.

Obama's approach to urban violence and the elite response to the Baltimore riots both indicate interracial support for neoliberal policies, which are a root cause of worsening conditions for black and brown inner-city residents, and segments of the black middle class whose livelihoods have been negatively affected by the roll-back of public employment. If the various localized campaigns against police brutality are to coalesce into a more powerful movement, activists need to devise a new language, one capable of connecting the policing crisis to the underlying problems of structural unemployment and the commodification of public goods, and of uniting people across different social layers in protracted campaigns with the capacity to make concrete policy reforms that reconstitute the social wage and decommodify housing, health care, education and other vital needs. Otherwise, more mentoring programs, police–community basketball leagues, ribbon-cuttings for mixed-income housing developments, and urban entrepreneurship incubators will serve the same function as the "mobile swimming pools" and "hastily built playgrounds" of the late 1960s, "merely buying time" for those who benefit from the status quo and forestalling the advancement of a real progressive urban agenda capable of achieving social justice for the greatest number.

5

Whose Streets?

Building the Just City in Rahm Emanuel's Chicago and Beyond

Over two days in late October 2018, hundreds of Chicagoans filed into the Dirksen Courthouse to offer input on a draft consent decree that would guide reform of the Chicago Police Department (CPD). Coming in the wake of an Obama Department of Justice (DOJ) investigation that found patterns of systemic abuse and racial discrimination by Chicago police, the decree was the result of several months of negotiations between the CPD, Illinois attorney general Lisa Madigan, Chicago mayor Rahm Emanuel and policing experts. In advance of the public hearings, now former Trump administration attorney general Jeff Sessions condemned the consent decree as "undemocratic," an insult to police and "a colossal mistake."[1] Some police officers and police union representatives who participated in the hearing echoed his sentiment. The vast majority of those Chicagoans who testified, however, spoke about their experiences of police abuse, and the deaths of loved ones, with many recalling harrowing confrontations and life-altering events as they fought back tears.[2]

As an enforceable plan of reform, the decree was designed to improve use-of-force practices and reporting procedures, increase required crisis intervention training, destigmatize officer-wellness programs, expand the suicide prevention initiative, ensure greater transparency regarding complaints against officers, encourage community policing and improve diversity in hiring practices, among other things. With regard to use of force, the decree called for enhanced de-escalation tactics, prohibited the use of tasers on fleeing suspects and discouraged their use in schools, prohibited officers from firing on moving cars and required that police administer life-saving aid to wounded suspects. To improve transparency, the decree would allow the public to track civilian complaints online by 2020. The formal DOJ investigation and the talks that produced the consent decree were the result of years of litigation, organizing and protests by aggrieved families, civil liberties advocates and criminal justice reformers—from the 2000 moratorium on capital punishment enacted by Illinois governor George Ryan; the landmark settlements won by the victims of Jon Burge, the police commander who presided over the serial torture of black suspects; the public outrage over the CPD's Homan Square black site; to the more recent killings of black civilians such as Rekia Boyd, Quintonio LeGrier and Bettie Jones, and Laquan McDonald, among too many others. After activists secured the release of the suppressed dashcam footage of McDonald's killing, mass demonstrations shut down the Magnificent Mile, the city's premier downtown shopping corridor, provoked the firing of police superintendent Garry McCarthy, and set the stage for the indictment and conviction of CPD officer Jason Van Dyke on second-degree murder and sixteen counts of aggravated battery with a firearm, one count for each bullet he fired into McDonald. The fact that Chicago produced a consent decree was a clear reflection of the growing power of local anti-policing and criminal justice reform forces, but it also revealed the limits of executive-managerial remedy.

As a means of reform, a consent decree does not rectify the deeper root causes of police–civilian conflicts in Chicago, or for that matter anywhere else in the United States. The decree is yet another iteration of the familiar liberal strategies for addressing the nested problems of policing and mass incarceration. Such strategies hinge on seeking justice either through the courts or through appeals to executive power to enforce existing laws in a racially unbiased and more socially just manner. Both approaches entail appealing to authority within existing power arrangements rather than building popular power and a broad consensus for a new order. In Chicago, pursuing either approach would seem especially perilous. In order for it to be successful, the decree requires good faith and compliance from the CPD as well as city hall, and both have a stake and interests in the perpetuation of the status quo. For the police, and their union representatives, the decree is in excess of their current union contract—as many have stated, the decree is illegal because it prescribes new work rules outside of collective bargaining. For the mayor and the aldermen who represent the wealthier neighborhoods, those rapidly gentrifying and others plagued with high levels of crime, crime reduction is vital to the success of their re-election campaigns. An effective police presence is seen by many residents of diverse ethnic backgrounds and class positions as necessary for securing public safety. Moreover, the CPD, mayor and city council constitute only the formal face of a broader governing coalition comprised of large developers, financiers, transnational corporations, hoteliers, restaurateurs, transportation companies and "creative class" entrepreneurs who are all united in their commitment to a mode of accumulation rooted in the financial, insurance and real estate (FIRE) sectors, as well as downtown tourism-entertainment.[3] Aggressive policing of the surplus population is a critical component of this growth model.

The consent decree is a step in the right direction, but if they are to have some longevity, concrete forms of social justice must be achieved legislatively. Executive orders and court decisions can provide momentary forms of justice, but such measures are vulnerable to temperamental, shifting governing regimes and lack the broader legitimacy that progressive legislation can achieve. In other words, genuine reforms must produce a new juridical order, one that does not foreground the protection of private property and policing of the poor as normative, but that instead enshrines universal economic security as the basis of public safety, and collective ownership and the abolition of the struggle to meet basic needs as the society's core ideals. If the history of the postwar civil rights movement is any guide, court decisions and executive actions may provide momentary respite, but progressive law-making alters the terms of daily life more substantially, especially when backed by effective enforcement. Executive Order 8802 during World War II and the landmark *Brown* decision of 1954 produced immediate but in many ways limited actions, while the omnibus civil rights reforms passed later by Congress had more durable, if not immediate, effects, outlawing discrimination in job, education and housing markets, as well as the conduct of elections, and spurring a sea change in societal perceptions about discrimination.

The key conundrum facing progressive social forces in Chicago and elsewhere is that this legislative process requires a majoritarian or left popular politics. During the Emanuel years and since, the most left-progressive antipolicing elements in Chicago have fought on multiple fronts; in addition to various lawsuits, they have pushed actively for legislative changes and have begun to achieve significant victories in building popular alliances and securing the votes of do-nothing politicians. The Chicago Alliance Against Racist and Political Repression (CAARP) pushed for the passage of a Chicago Police Accountability Council ordinance, which would create a democratically elected council to oversee the CPD. In summer 2021, the efforts of CAARP and the Grassroots Alliance for Police Accountability achieved victory when the city council voted 36–13 to create such a democratically elected board.[4] Other campaigns included the #NoCop campaign's efforts to halt plans to build a new police academy, as well as the #EraseTheDatabase campaign—a collaboration between Organized Communities Against Deportation, Black Youth Project 100 (BYP100), Mijente, Blocks Together, the Brighton Park Neighborhood Council and the Latino Union— whose goal has been to eliminate the CPD's gang database, which activists argue is racially discriminatory and unconstitutional.[5] Like scores of other campaigns across the country, such as Stop LAPD Spying, these efforts are promising, and stand out against more NGO-oriented and anarchist tendencies within the US left that are skeptical of formal political processes and antagonistic to the basic modes of political activism—voting, lobbying, issue-based and electoral campaigns, union organizing, etc.—needed to win concrete reforms, let alone the dismantling of the carceral state that many activists yearn for.

The 2015 mass protests after the belated release of the Laquan McDonald video were a high watermark of Black Lives Matter protests in the city, a moment where the promise and limits of contemporary antipolicing struggles were on full display. The Black Friday protests discussed below succeeded in buckling Emanuel's administration, prompting a wave of firings, a successful electoral challenge to the sitting Cook County State's Attorney Anita Alvarez, and the conviction of Jason Van Dyke, the first of a Chicago police officer in almost four decades. The consent decree served as a powerful coda to the Emanuel administration, but those who claimed victory when he decided not to seek re-election in 2019 were misguided. Emanuel and the neoliberal regime he presided over were resilient despite successive progressive challenges. He responded to the 2012 Chicago Teachers' Union (CTU) strike with the largest wave of neighborhood school closures in US history. He defeated challenger Jesús "Chuy" Garcia to win re-election in 2015. He weathered the torrent of criticism and calls for his resignation that followed the release of the McDonald video, and, rejecting sundry demands by Black Lives Matter protestors, forged ahead with plans to expand the size of the CPD and make substantial investments in a new police training facility. Emanuel more than earned the "Mayor 1%" title that journalist Kari Lydersen bestowed on him. His resiliency was not merely a personal character trait but a reflection of the powerful capitalist blocs he effectively represented in city hall throughout his tenure as Chicago's mayor. Lydersen perfectly sums up the smug New Democratic brand of neoliberalism and roiling class contradictions that defined Emanuel's reign: "To the extent that Emanuel genuinely wants to make the world a better place for working people, he thinks market forces and business models are the way to do it," she writes, "and he clearly (and perhaps rightly) thinks he understands these institutions far better than any teacher or crossing guard or nurse."[6]

In Emanuel's administration we saw the central contradictions of neoliberal governance displayed in full, with its fulsome public subsidization of corporate profit-making and, at the same time, forceful opposition to working-class demands and withdrawal from the social reproductive functions of the old welfare state. During his tenure, Chicago ranked seventh among the world's largest metropolitan economies, roughly equal to Paris and Beijing in terms of gross domestic product. Emanuel, of course, did not invent the neoliberal project in Chicago, but he inherited the city that Richard M. Daley had made, one defined by a massive wave of public housing demolition, the development of the city's marquee downtown tourist sites, Millennium Park and Navy Pier, and the privatization of the city's parking meters on an unbelievable seventy-five-year contract. Despite early challenges to his residency and eligibility to run, Emanuel rode into office largely thanks to his connection with the Obama administration, having served as the White House Chief of Staff. Unlike Obama, however, who was able to sell the neoliberal model to black constituencies and broader publics through charisma and historical presence, Emanuel's shrewd manner, his whiteness and legendary reputation for meanness, spelled disaster as the full effects of his neoliberal regime were felt by the city's black, brown and working-class neighborhoods. Perhaps the surest evidence of his inability to govern like Obama came during his December 2015 visit to the celebrated Urban Prep Academy, an all-black-male charter school on the city's south side, renowned for having a 100 percent success rate in college admissions for its graduates. Emanuel was there to make a push for Obama's My Brother's Keeper initiative, but the students drowned him out, chanting "16 Shots!" in reference to the number of bullets Van

Dyke fired into McDonald, and voicing solidarity with the anti–police brutality protestors.

Emanuel found himself having to address unique challenges regarding crime and policing, which America's two larger coastal cities have been praised for solving. In 2016, a year after the protests erupted over McDonald's death, Chicago recorded more homicides than New York City and Los Angeles combined. Part of this violent-crime surge was seen as a consequence of protest *by* police, work slowdown and laxed enforcement in response to increased public scrutiny. Chicago's homicide problem cannot be limited to that single year of the Emanuel regime, however. Unlike New York and Los Angeles, where rent intensification has expelled the poorest residents beyond the city limits—pushed out to the high desert and Inland Empire in Southern California, for instance—Chicago has retained large poor and unemployed populations, who have experienced major dislocation due to the public housing demolitions of previous years, a process that has transformed gang culture in the city. In 2017, the newly elected president Donald Trump exploited Chicago's homicide woes, portraying the city as another example of the "American carnage" his administration would address. "If Chicago doesn't fix the horrible 'carnage' going on, 228 shootings in 2017 with 42 killings (up 24% from 2016)," he tweeted in January 2017, "I will send in the Feds!" He was actually referring to 2016 homicide figures, which had increased by 14 percent from the previous year. The facts, as in so much of Trump's rhetoric, did not matter. What mattered most was implicating alleged Democratic incompetence, and urban problems that Trump and other Republicans saw as the result of a bankrupted and overly permissive social liberalism. Despite all his bluster, however, Trump's demands for more aggressive policing were in line with Emanuel's approach.

The response from Emanuel to these conditions was more policing and surveillance, rather than benevolent forms of social policy and aid, often recasting the increase in policing as the will of the people. "When I talk to Chicagoans who live in our most violence-prone neighborhoods, they do not hate the police,"

Emanuel said in a September 2016 address on gun violence at Malcolm X College. "In fact, they tell me they want more cops and fewer gangs. They do not want more officers in cars just driving through their communities. They want officers on the beat in their neighborhoods."[7] There is a germ of truth in Emanuel's words, since many black Chicagoans, not surprisingly, do want safer neighborhoods and better police and emergency services. The falsehood of Emanuel's claims lies in their omission of other strategies that might also shore up security and improve the lives of Chicago's most dispossessed residents. His words suggest that there is no alternative to policing, but this is more an expression of his regime's political commitment to the neoliberal model's duality of corporate benevolence and police violence.

This chapter examines the powerful convergence of progressive and antipolicing forces in response to McDonald's premature, unjust and undeserved death, and celebrates the civil disobedience many of us engaged in to compel the Emanuel administration to action. Unlike previous demonstrations in Ferguson, Missouri and Baltimore, which erupted in black residential quarters and commercial strips, the Chicago protests took place in the city's premier downtown tourist zone, and the most powerful of these demonstrations unfolded on what is typically the most lucrative shopping day of the year, Black Friday. The 2015 Chicago protests brought the contradictions of the neoliberal city out into the open, pitting the interests of capital and consumers against those who desire a different kind of city, one where public safety, freedom and economic security are universally enjoyed and not achieved through repressive and punitive means. Although the 2015 Black Friday demonstration was remarkable, we need to reflect on the limits of this protest action as a strategy for building opposition, how well or poorly it served to capture the attention of the greatest number of Chicagoans beyond the forty-eight-hour news cycle or latest social media outrage. The protests were made possible by the left-wing of Black Lives Matter, led by Black Youth Project 100, Assata's Daughters, Southsiders Organizing for Unity and Liberation, the Workers Center for Racial

Justice, Action Now, CAARP, as well as longer standing organizations like the Rainbow PUSH coalition, among many other formations.

The Chicago protests suggest that contemporary struggles must do more to build popular support for a different and more just order. Ethnic politics, no matter how militant its articulation, simply cannot produce this kind of popular consent, since its essentialist logics of race representation and constituency run counter to building broad social power. The potential for such a new consensus is there if we think about the city as a totality and begin with the question of how we might build a life in common, one where felt needs and quotidian interests, rather than liberal sympathy, become the basis for building solidarity. This chapter engages critical urban theory, and in particular "right to the city" discourse, to make the case that antipolicing protests provide an opening for reclaiming the city from capital. In their symbolic occupation of the city, defense of the most dispossessed and demands for redistributive policy, contemporary antipolicing struggles encourage us to take back the city from the carceral apparatus and neoliberal governance, and reclaim it for democratic purposes and popular needs and desires.

In an extensive and highly generative treatment of mass incarceration and American politics, political scientist Marie Gottschalk cautions that "we need to resist the belief that the only way to raze the carceral state is to tackle the 'root causes' of crime—massive unemployment, massive poverty, and unconscionable levels of social and economic inequality stratified by race, ethnicity and gender." While tackling such inequality is an "admirable goal," Gottschalk notes, "if the aim is to slash the country's incarceration rate and undo its harmful collateral consequences over the next few years, not the next few decades, the root causes approach to progressive penal reform, however well-intentioned, is shortsighted."[8] Surely no one should languish in jail because they cannot afford bail, or be condemned to sit in prison when drug rehabilitation, diversion programs or restorative justice would be more appropriate to the crime and meaningful for their lives and that of their communities. Are the choices before us, however, so stark as that of the abolition of inequality versus immediate criminal justice reform? It is plausible that deep and long overdue reforms like an end to money bail, legalization of marijuana with exoneration and expungement of prior marijuana-related convictions, electronic monitoring rather than prison for nonviolent offenses, legalization of sex work, and drug courts for addiction-related offenses, if all instituted nationally, would go a long way towards scaling back the carceral apparatus. But none of these reforms would eliminate the social and historical rationale for our current modes of policing, which is the containment and regulation of surplus population.

Although I agree full-stop with Gottschalk's demand for immediate reforms, such should be pursued alongside creative strategies for abolishing the conditions the carceral apparatus has evolved to manage. To that end, this chapter sketches the possibility of large-scale public works that could be piloted in cities like Chicago, with its major crime problems, outsized police department and anemic social safety net alongside a resplendent capitalist growth coalition—in short, all the trappings of neoliberal urbanism. Public works might take aim at the problem of structural unemployment and begin the reappropriation of the city's collective wealth for the purposes of meeting popular needs for improved transportation, universal access to child and elder care, improved physical and mental health care, as well as green technologies and sustainable energy. Chicago is a neoliberal city, but one that has produced a vibrant culture of pro-immigrant, antipolicing, pro-union, environmentalist and antiprivatization forces that might unite around city or county-wide public works as a means of achieving public safety through the guarantee of economic security to all citizens, and, ultimately, of reorganizing the city around use value rather than profit-making.

Sixteen Shots Heard Round the World

Black Friday, the day after Thanksgiving and the official start of the Christmas shopping season, is supposed to be a day when retailers expect to see wide profit margins. This particular Black Friday, November 27, 2015, in Chicago would be different, as mass demonstrations paralyzed the Magnificent Mile, the city's premier shopping district and one of the most profitable retail corridors in the nation. The very name, Black Friday, when retailers expect to end the day with their revenue ledgers "in the black," took on a different and more deeply political meaning. Most of us emerging from the Chicago Avenue Redline stop that day were heading to the protest. Walking towards Michigan Avenue, we found the area near Water Tower Place eerily deserted. Gone were the usual throngs of tourists. Car traffic was light. Scattered shoppers seemed disoriented, most of them clutching their coats and not looking especially jolly. The Yuletide was replaced by protest chants, the sweet funk of cannabis and the cadence of an improvised drum core, which echoed along the avenue's curtain walls. Intermittent gusts, cold and drizzle did not dissuade the growing throng of protestors. I hurried to catch up with the marchers, making my way down the center of the empty street and past rows of police who exchanged idle banter within their ranks, pausing now and again to study the scene. Most were in plain dress uniforms, a few flak jacketed. No full riot gear in sight yet. Their official charge was to balance the demonstrators' right to free speech and peaceable assembly with the property rights of the holiday shoppers and the nearly 500 corporate retailers that lined the Magnificent Mile and adjacent side streets. The police themselves were the target of the protest, however, and official concern about escalation had produced an uneasy truce, where protestors were able to engage in civil disobedience without the typical threat of arrest. Only four arrests that day were reported, and compared to the repressive tactics police employed in Ferguson—imposing a curfew and using various munitions against demonstrators—the relative restraint of the CPD on Black Friday enabled direct action protests of global retail giants to continue into the night.

The thousands who protested the police killing of seventeen-year-old Laquan McDonald achieved the unthinkable. We shut down the Magnificent Mile, forcing many stores to close early on the busiest shopping day of the year. Protestors locked arms and barricaded the entrances to the stores of Timberland, Apple, Disney, Wet Seal, Hugo Boss, Ann Taylor, Gap, Nike and dozens of others. A few store managers improvised tactics to keep consumer traffic flowing, ushering shoppers away from picket lines to freight entrances, then through stock rooms and into the main showroom. These adjustments did not numb the effect of mass pressure, with some Mag Mile stores later reporting between 25 and 50 percent sales losses.[9] An Aldo shoe store representative reported that while they anticipated $37,000 in Black Friday sales, they only took in $19,000. Similarly, store associates for Stuart Weitzman shoe store reported coming up $20,000 shy of their $50,000 sales projections.

Chicago officer Jason Van Dyke killed McDonald in October 2014 along a stretch of Pulaski Road on the city's southwest side. Police went to the area after reports of someone breaking into parked tractor trailers. Before Van Dyke arrived in his squad car, some nine other officers were already on the scene, but none of them fired on McDonald. Monitoring his erratic behavior and suspecting that he was intoxicated, they stood down and ordered a taser, as a non-lethal option to be used if necessary. Van Dyke fired his weapon within six seconds of exiting his squad car. The taser arrived about a minute later. Van Dyke was not a CPD rookie, but a ten-year veteran. In that time, some twenty citizen complaints had been filed against him, half of them for use of excessive force and two for the use of a racial slur. Van Dyke was never disciplined in any of these preceding cases.

McDonald's life was short and turbulent.[10] Some media coverage wrongly referred to McDonald as a man, but although he stood six foot two inches tall, he had only recently turned seventeen. His mother Tina Hunter was a ward of the state when McDonald was born. She lost custody of her two children in 2000, and McDonald was shuffled between eight different homes, mostly those of relatives. He was abused by foster parents outside his family and by his mother's boyfriend, and was later diagnosed as suffering from post-traumatic stress disorder. Refusing medical prescriptions for PTSD and other diagnoses, McDonald confided to state authorities that he used marijuana to self-medicate since he did not have the skills to cope with his life's stressors. He had been sentenced to juvenile detention some seventeen times, and had received ten school suspensions. His great grandmother said he would "normally get arrested 2–3 times a week," most often for possessing small amounts of drugs. McDonald's childhood was managed by child protective services and the foster care system, and his adolescence was spent in multiple schools, juvenile detention, drug rehabilitation, probation supervision and electronic monitoring, individual and family counseling and psychiatric hospitalization. Court records referred to him as "resilient," however, and, like most, his life was more than his troubles.

Former teachers and social workers remarked on his joyous side and use of humor to defuse tense situations. Family members, such as Grace Memorial Baptist Church pastor Marvin Hunter and others who knew McDonald well, unanimously described him as charming, funny and "a jokester." He was fiercely protective of his younger sister. The WBEZ audio documentary *16 Shots*, about McDonald's murder and the subsequent trial of Van Dyke, provided a powerful, touching portrait of him. Perhaps the best part of the documentary comes when his close friends, Christian Poole and Aaron Wilson, give their perspective on "Corndog," as they called him, a variation of his nickname "Quan-dog." His friends reminisced on mundane blissful details, the kind of episodes we all cherish from our youth—endless summer days, riding bikes, ribbing each other as only good friends can, and competitive dance offs—McDonald's go-to move was the Bobby Shmurda dance. Poole recalled the moment he first saw the video of McDonald taking his last steps along the centerline of Pulaski Road, saying he knew it was his friend immediately because of that "fast little walk ... like he was on a mission," swaggering and hurried.[11]

McDonald's death was underreported during the 2015 mayoral election season. His family was only apprised of the inconsistencies in the official CPD reporting after they were approached by personnel at Garfield Waters Funeral Home, who were shocked by the sheer volume of bullet entry and exit wounds as they prepared the body for burial. The shooting was captured on police dashcam video that was not released for more than a year after McDonald's death, and only after activist William Calloway and freelance journalist Brandon Smith filed a FOIA request and were granted access by a judge against the city's objections. Incidentally, eighty-six minutes' worth of footage from cameras at a nearby Burger King restaurant, which likely captured the shooting, was seized by police without a warrant and disappeared. As the police dashcam video finally went public, Van Dyke was indicted on charges of murder, aggravated battery and official misconduct. The timing of it all raised suspicion of a larger cover-up by the city's governing regime, a mayoral administration more concerned with avoiding Ferguson-like protests than with the pursuit of justice for a black teen. The video contradicted official police reports of the incident and confirmed what many activists and citizens already suspected—that McDonald was not the aggressor and that a non-lethal arrest could have been made.

The video shows McDonald striding across the center median of Pulaski Road as officers emerge from their squad cars to his left. He continues walking to the right and away from police and is a full traffic lane's distance away when Van Dyke opens fire, the force of the shots spinning the teenager around before he falls. In total Van Dyke fired sixteen shots into McDonald, most of them after the teen was already lying prone and incapacitated. The fact that McDonald's death, the suppression of the incriminating video, witness suppression, inconsistent police testimony and the $5 million out-of-court settlement with McDonald's family all coincided with the hard-fought re-election campaign of Mayor Rahm Emanuel only fueled public suspicion and outrage, with many demanding that police superintendent Garry McCarthy, State's Attorney Anita Alvarez and even Emanuel himself resign over their role in the apparent cover-up. "Sixteen shots and a cover-up!" became the rallying cry during the days of protests that ensued.

The Black Friday protests began that morning with a formal permit march organized by Jesse Jackson's Rainbow PUSH organization, which drew together black clergy, the Cook County Board president Toni Preckwinkle, Congressmen Danny Davis and Bobby Rush, as well as a growing chorus of Chicago aldermen calling for the resignation of McCarthy. The protests that week, however, marked a broader convergence of forces, including BYP100 and other M4BL activists, local student groups, neighborhood peace activists, black nationalists, the Chicago Teachers Union, lawyers, prison abolitionists, the Amalgamated Transit Union Local 308, the International Socialist Organization, local activists who had been working to secure reparations for the Jon Burge torture victims, the families of others killed by police violence, and other concerned citizens. Contrary to the "angry black youth" trope peddled by corporate news media, and the "black youth vanguard" embraced by some activists themselves, the protestors were a multiracial, intergenerational mass. Handwritten protest signs were thrust skywards alongside placards with the words "I Am a Man" in bold block print, resurrecting the slogan used by Memphis sanitation workers during their historic 1968 strike. As the day wore on, the protests swelled and surged, alternating between spontaneous marches up and down Michigan Avenue and semi-spontaneous acts of civil disobedience. In the short run, we won. The mass public pressure that week no doubt prompted the firing of McCarthy. Less than forty-eight hours after his exit, Scott Ando, head of the city's mayor-appointed Police Board, also handed in his resignation, only to be replaced by Chicago political insider and Obama family friend, Sharon Fairley. Although he initially rejected the idea, Emanuel conceded to a federal Justice Department probe of Chicago's police department.

The 2015 Black Friday demonstrations in Chicago brought the central contradictions of the policing crisis and of American society more generally out into the open. The verbal clashes and person-to-person negotiations between protestors and consumers represent the next frontier for left struggles in the United States if they are to become truly popular in the sense of achieving broad societal consent. Achieving such consent requires engaging segments of the population who are not yet persuaded to support progressive reforms, as well as those who may be skeptical, and perhaps some who may be antagonistic. Black Lives Matter demonstrations mobilized supporters, but in Chicago the mobilizations came face-to-face with Americans who were apathetic, uneducated about the problem at hand and in some cases pro-police. The experience of contesting and conversing with Christmas shoppers revealed a set of social and political contradictions that pose a real challenge to building opposition.

That afternoon, I stood arm-in-arm with a dozen other Chicagoans, blocking the doors of one Mag Mile store. We turned away one group of shoppers after another. Most were tourists, a mix of international visitors and suburbanites. A handful of them were black. A few visitors pled their case with us. "Friend, we've come such a long way, why can't we enter?" "We understand your protest, but why can't we go into this store?" "Come on, it's Christmas!" They were met with a barrage of improvised, spirited retorts, such as "Is shopping more important to you than black lives?" As with most acts of civil disobedience, the experience was filled with camaraderie, tension, humor and exhilaration. When one suburban white woman, hoping to enter the store with her son, became visibly irritated by the fact that we stood between her pocketbook and some deep discounts, she blurted out to her son, "Well, this is a real pain in the butt!" To my right was a soft-spoken, greying senior with smiling eyes who had taken a few moments to video chat with her grandson telling him why she was protesting. She started an impromptu call and response that went down the line: "A pain is being shot sixteen times by the police." Others followed: "A pain is living in a city where your neighborhood school has been shut down." "A pain is not having health care." Needless to say, the irritated shopper got the picture, jerking her son's arm as she walked away in disgust.

The shoppers we turned away expressed a variety of emotions and positions regarding the protests. A few seemed somewhat amused by the frenetic energy of the protests. Some were genuinely engaged, expressing their outrage over McDonald's death and sympathy with the protests, albeit with caveats about their disappointment over the inconvenience. Some were indignant and opposed to the action. Others were indifferent. And some were outright malevolent. At one point late in the afternoon, an elderly white woman, the vulgar embodiment of the Gold Coast patrician in her full-length mink coat, sashayed past our line; unable to conceal her contempt, she turned and snarled, "What you people need is to go get a job!" We met her words with laughter, with a few comrades telling her their occupations and calling out her racism. She could not see past her prejudice, faced with this all-black line, which was in fact filled with teachers, pensioners, office workers and artists. How else could she explain our willingness to disrupt this most sacred of holiday spending rituals?

Building the kind of broad counterpower necessary to roll back the carceral apparatus in Chicago will require more than the most deeply committed "woke" activists; it certainly cannot be limited to African Americans and young people, but of necessity must engage different social layers. It is possible to reduce the most detestable manifestations of policing through more accountability mechanisms, better training and public oversight, but as the most radical voices within Black Lives Matter struggles have made clear, what is needed is a bolder redistributive politics. As in Baltimore, policing in Chicago manages a deeply divided urban landscape of wealth and power, ensuring that capital flows and profit-making continue unabated. But such processes are even more dramatic, and the stakes much higher, in Rahm Emanuel's Chicago.

Touring Emanuel's Chicago

The Chicago demonstrations against police brutality and corruption were simultaneously a rejection of the Emanuel administration's failed policies of neoliberal privatization. His New Democratic mayoral regime united a powerful investor class to further enhance the tourist amenities and real estate development imperatives of the so-called Super Loop—a new moniker for the central business district that underscores its rapid growth and expanding geography, bursting past the circular elevated track of the CTA trains, stretching from the city's muscular lakefront skyline westward towards Ashland Avenue, with Roosevelt Road and North Avenue serving respectively as its new southern and northern boundaries. There was a moment during Emanuel's 2015 re-election campaign when his Republican backers echoed the sentiments of Senator Mark Kirk, who had said that Emanuel's re-election was absolutely necessary, otherwise Chicago would become another Detroit. Of course, this familiar slight against Detroit, long the poster child for urban catastrophe, is a barely veiled racist trope and a gross oversimplification of that city's fate, which diminishes the indomitable spirit and vibrancy of its working-class neighborhoods even during the depths of federal urban neglect and global capital flight. Moreover, such comments reflected the smugness of the ruling class within and beyond the city limits, who appeared oblivious to the fact that Chicago was already like Detroit for those many thousands living outside of the Loop and the city's gentrified and upscale zones, in areas that are effectively condemned to underdevelopment. Keeping with their crude analogy, Chicago in the opening decades of the twenty-first century is essentially Detroit and Manhattan sitting side-by-side on the western shore of Lake Michigan—the deindustrialized, working-class city of the South and West sides abutting the global, post-Fordist center of finance, entertainment and wealth, the Loop, and the generally affluent, densely populated and majority-white North side. At the same time, we should be leery of the "most segregated city" and "city of neighborhoods" lore, which keeps too many wedded to the ethnic paradigm as a basis for analysis and mode of political engagement, thereby clouding understanding of the new political alignments and class relations shaping neoliberal Chicago.

The city's Roosevelt Road long served as a racial dividing line separating Chicago's majority-black South side from the Loop and its whiter northern reaches. Today the street provides a tour of another, neoliberal geography, revealing not the residential racial segregation of the mid-twentieth century but a cityscape defined by rent-intensifying development, middle-class return, displacement and dispossession, hyperghettoization and reg-ulation of the poor. If you start out along Roosevelt Road at its easternmost terminus, where Grant Park and the museum campus converge, and travel towards the outer western edge of the city, vastly differently worlds rise, slump and recede. Ghet-toization and gentrification form the broad outlines of Roosevelt Road's contemporary cartography, but the artery also reveals modes of regulation and mobility that are not strictly terrestrial or bound by old cognitive maps. Roosevelt originates at the foot of Grant Park in the shadow of condo towers and the skyscrap-ers that line Michigan Avenue, made up of numerous historic buildings like the Chicago Hilton, a key site of protests at the 1968 Democratic National Convention, and the headquarters of *Ebony* magazine and black-owned Johnson Publications. At the nearby Red Line CTA stop, suburban commuters, yuppies and black Southsiders flow in and out of the elevated terminal. Roosevelt carries you through the gentrifying South Loop, where a hulking Super Target store and the Roosevelt Collection—a complex of retail, housing and cineplex—symbolize the area's rebirth. The area between the southern branch of the Chicago River, which runs underneath Roosevelt, and the I-94 highway is lined with suburban big box stores retrofitted to work in central city space. Partly hidden from view, just north of Roo-sevelt and wedged along the Dan Ryan highway embankment, stands a large tent city of homeless denizens. As you pass the Interstate on-ramps and continue west, you enter the University of Illinois Chicago campus, an urban renewal project advanced by Richard J. Daley during the sixties that leveled Greek, Italian, Mexican and African American neighborhoods, and eventually consumed the old Maxwell Street public market—once referred to as "Jew Town" by working-class blacks who patronized its merchants and hawkers, and the spiritual home of Chicago's electric blues music. Bronze statues of a busker, a hawker, and a shopper resting on a bench are the only reminders of Maxwell's historical importance to the city and to American culture. Further along Roosevelt, there are no memorial markers for the dozen or so blues clubs that lined the road and adjacent blocks, forgotten places like Congo Lounge, Rock Bottom, Tay May and Club Zanzibar. The Illinois Medical District, with its mammoth complex of hospitals, clinics and research centers— the largest urban medical complex in the nation—stretches from Ashland towards Ogden Avenue, a vestige of the old Route 66 highway, and past the Cook County juvenile detention center where Laquan McDonald was once confined.

After you pass Western Avenue, Roosevelt traverses the North Lawndale neighborhood, whose poverty and racial segregation have made it the subject of numerous liberal exposés, not least from Jonathon Kozol and Ta-Nehisi Coates. North Lawndale is in many ways the archetypal hypersegregated ghetto, in which a mostly black reserve army is relegated and policed. The neighborhood became the subject of public outrage after journalists uncovered a police black site in Homan Square, where CPD unlawfully detained and interrogated 7,185 people over the course of a decade, 82 percent of whom were African Americans.[12] When Martin Luther King, Jr. came to Chicago in 1966 to campaign against housing discrimination, he chose North Lawndale as his base, taking up residence in a dilapidated Hamlin Avenue apartment building with a dirt floor vestibule. Once home to numerous industries, in the decades since King's Chicago campaign, North Lawndale has experienced what are by now familiar patterns of labor force contraction, divestiture, population loss, economic informalization and criminalization.

In 1972, the westernmost portion of Roosevelt Road was a spinal column of manufacturing employing some 59,000, but by 2006 that workforce had shrunk to 10,600.

In recent years, North Lawndale has been home to the highest concentration of black men who are formerly incarcerated or under court supervision. Over the past two decades, around 70 percent of the male population between the ages of eighteen and forty-five have had a criminal record, while the official unemployment rate for African American males has typically exceeded 30 percent. The adjacent West side neighborhoods of Garfield Park and Austin share similar problems of poverty and crime, and together are representative of the mutually reinforcing institutions of the carceral state and hyperghettoization. "It is by no means an exaggeration," as Jamie Peck and Nik Theodore note, "to conceive of a criminalized class as a structurally salient, racialized labor market category in cities like Chicago."[13] In 2014, Illinois passed "ban the box" legislation, which no longer requires ex-offenders to self-report their conviction history on job applications. Given limited education and skill, however, the economic prospects for those seeking legal, gainful employment are bleak, and limited to a narrow range of low-wage, unregulated and contingent work in construction, building and grounds maintenance, food service, auto services like car detailing, warehouse and moving services, etc.—all industries that can draw on other pools of low-wage laborers, such as undocumented immigrants, teenagers, students and retirees. Not only do these labor market dynamics reproduce misery and negative social costs for ex-offenders and their families, they also have the effect of further degrading contingent labor jobs across the local urban economy, driving down wage floors and sustaining the informal economy and cycles of incarceration and recidivism.

On the westernmost stretches of Roosevelt, plummeting real estate values and the grim daily existence of residents are everywhere visible. The glass and steel towers and spindly construction cranes on the downtown skyline recede from view, replaced by boarded up buildings, dollar stores, check cashing centers, weed-choked lots, steel curtained storefronts, gas stations, liquor marts and trash-strewn sidewalks. As Roosevelt approaches the intersection at Austin boulevard, the border between Chicago and Oak Park, commercial activity along the route thickens for a few miles as you coast through some of the most diverse and integrated suburbs in Chicagoland, before reaching the whiter and more affluent reaches beyond Cook County. North Lawndale—and the adjacent Garfield Park and Austin—are geographically close, and yet worlds apart from the downtown revival and the suburban dream in either direction.

These western stretches of Roosevelt Road intersect "Chiraq," a portmanteau of Chicago and Iraq used by local rappers and youth to make the conditions they experience on a daily basis legible to audiences beyond their neighborhoods. Rahm Emanuel threatened to pull public subsidies for Spike Lee's 2015 musical dramedy film *Chiraq* if Lee did not change the film's title.[14] Emanuel's response was clearly motivated more by bad publicity, but this stunt was rather hypocritical given that an entire television franchise found success chronicling the experiences of first responders wrestling with the most dreadful parts of Chicago life. NBC's *Chicago PD*, *Chicago Fire*, *Chicago Med* and *Chicago Justice* are all shot locally and incentivized with city and state tax credits. The moniker "Chiraq," with its allusions to the lawlessness and death of a war-torn region is appropriate, demarcating a pervasive landscape of fear, "no-go" zones, and places to be bypassed and escaped. Moreover, the evocative name captures palpable grassroots experiences of police violence, of the "occupying army" as an omnipresent and omnipotent institution defining the lives of thousands in Chicago's poorest neighborhoods. All American cities share this mental geography of race, class, loathing and horror. Since arriving in Chicago, I cannot say how many times locals have looked on in worry when I share with them the places I've been around town. In disbelief, they have listened and offered stern words—"Don't take the Blue Line after dark." These cautionary lectures have come from blacks as well as whites and are often delivered with a special authority by those who have lived in the city their entire lives. When I tell them that I've lived in cities all of my adult days and traveled solo on public transit on six continents, that is not enough to calm their concerns. Such fears, of course, are kept alive by real crime, such as the December 2016 murder of undefeated welterweight boxer Ed Brown, shot along with his sister as they sat in a car in the Garfield Park neighborhood.[15] Stories like this are too common in places like Chicago, and in some ways they are too powerful, crowding out reason, facts, documented trends, statistical probabilities and, most of all, obscuring the policy choices and structural forces responsible for the city's vast inequality which are rarely summarized in the first few minutes of the nightly news or in sensational social media feeds.

This landscape of fear and real violent crime has been a powerful motive in the making of the carceral regime, as cultural anxieties and racist fears grew in proportion to the expansion of the postwar metropolis, providing justification for the expansion of the penal state, harsher sentencing and the federal abandonment of national urban policy, as well as a lucrative home security industry, the proliferation of private and public networks of video surveillance, and all manner of personal defense technologies. Such racist anxieties have been mobilized in the national electoral arena with sinister acumen, from Lee Atwater's "Willie Horton" campaign television commercials, which helped George H.W. Bush defeat Michael Dukakis in the 1988 presidential election, to Donald Trump's claim that illegal immigration flows were allowing "rapist and murderers" to enter the United States from Mexico. As others have argued in response to those who focus on the racial disparities of the drug war and zero-tolerance policing strategies, violent crime has long been and continues to be a pressing problem in cities like Chicago, a major cause of the carceral expansion, and a problem that black and brown communities have suffered from disproportionately, especially during the crack cocaine years.[16] Any attempt to roll back the carceral state should be equally attuned to how we might reduce violence. For generations of big city mayors, neoliberalization has posed the difficult conundrum of how to address the real concerns about public safety of their electoral constituencies in a context where Congressional support for welfare and social spending has not been forthcoming. And yet, assuring public safety is fundamental to attracting new investment and new residents to add to the municipal tax base. This tension is especially acute in Chicago, where violence occasionally spills out beyond the heavily policed neighborhoods.

Throughout the course of Emanuel's administration, the cherished landmarks of Chicago's downtown became sites of youth wilding, threatening the safe passage and tranquility middle-class consumers and tourists expect. Among the more disruptive of these incidents was the December 2014 brawl that erupted at Navy Pier, causing authorities to shut down the annual Winter Wonderfest, and an equally raucous incident near Water Tower Place on the Mag Mile in May 2018.[17] Smaller melees have broken out at Millennium Park, and on State Street, which has long served as the city's "main street," a traditional route for the city's many parades. Most of those engaged in the fights, flash mob robberies, attacks on tourists and general rascality have been African American adolescents, but the majority of black teens traversing downtown are not engaged in this unruly behavior. Dozens of arrests have been made in most of these incidents, and have provided the pretext for stepped up surveillance and repression of black youth, their right to enjoy the city being restricted whenever it might threaten the mobility and leisure of favored classes. Such incidents and the city's high homicide rate in various years were an embarrassment to Emanuel's administration. In 2013, French officials issued an advisory for its citizens traveling to Chicago, dissuading them from visiting the South and West sides of the city because of high crime.[18] Those moments when black teenagers have gathered en masse in the Loop, the Mag Mile and Navy Pier, however, have also thrown into doubt the general assumption of safety, which must be maintained if tourist traffic, convention contracts, new condo towers and corporate headquarters construction are to proceed unabated.

When violence is confined to the netherworlds of the South and West sides, many Chicagoans undoubtedly lament over the problem, but most also see it as beyond their immediate control. When such violence drifts into the more well-heeled quarters, however, it is an abomination, unnerving commuters, drawing sharp rebukes from the local corporate news media and calls for action from politicians. Chicago's durable class and racial inequality may well explain its relative difficulty in reducing crime in comparison to New York City and Los Angeles. Whereas those cities expelled the poor more rapidly through rent pressure and reduced crime through stress policing and displacement, Chicago's revanchist project has been defined by massive housing demolitions, internal displacement and class-intensive segregation of the black poor, dynamics that have produced greater precarity and volatility in the city's working-class neighborhoods.

The specter of gang violence in Chicago may be a drag on luring investors and some tourists, but the neoliberal model's execution in the city is responsible for much of the social disruption and violence that has endured. Robert Aspholm's *Views from the Streets* offers a compelling explanation of Chicago's contemporary gang problem. Aspholm contends that contemporary black gangs in the city are highly fragmented, non-hierarchical and defined by shifting and unpredictable allegiances, unlike the large black gangs of a generation prior, which were hierarchically organized with well-defined leadership and chain of command. This transformation in the basic character of gang affiliation and order is a consequence of a few decades of public housing demolition and residential displacement, which broke up zones of poverty in the fashion many liberal policy advocates desired, but also had the effect of disrupting social bonds and kinship networks, and dissolving old turf boundaries as Chicago Housing Authority high rises were replaced with vacant lots and residents were dispersed across the city and beyond in search of affordable housing.[19] The result has been a volatile and unpredictable context, which is impervious to strategies of conflict mediation that were previously effective under the old gang hierarchies. Indeed, as Aspholm details, celebrated violence intervention programs piloted in the city such as Cure Violence and Operation Ceasefire (the focus of the acclaimed 2011 documentary film, *The Interrupters*)—which rely on interventions by OG's (original gangsters), senior gang members with street credibility, connections and influence—have not been as successful as advertised in reducing violent crime. Despite the stature some long-term gang members might possess in certain circles, it has been difficult for this particular model of conflict reduction to work, Aspholm explains, because contemporary conflicts are "spontaneous, arising from the expressive impulses of young gang members as opposed to the strategic orders of gang leaders."[20] "Increasing numbers of gang shootings occur in the absence of a specific provocation, acute precipitating factor, or even an instrumental end that might pattern violence in a discernable fashion," Aspholm writes. "Identifying, predicting, or, in Cure Violence parlance, detecting potentially violent events under such circumstances can be extremely difficult, if not impossible, even for outreach workers with eyes and ears on the streets."[21]

In cities like Chicago, we have witnessed the potential of urban social movements to contest neoliberalization and its carceral apparatus. Even in an era of declining union membership in many sectors, the Chicago Teacher's Union strike in the fall of 2012, and subsequent waves of faculty and graduate worker strikes and walkouts at the University of Illinois Chicago, Columbia College, Northeastern Illinois University, the City Colleges and the University of Chicago, have demonstrated the power of labor solidarity not only to advance the interests of teachers in primary, secondary and higher education, but also to challenge the encroachment of think tank and foundation-led market reforms that commodify education, reducing classroom learning to corporate performance evaluation and devaluing teachers as workers and leaders in public education. In addition to this renewal of education unionism, Chicago was the site of the 2008 Republic Windows and Doors factory takeover, which began as a response to plant closure and ultimately produced a worker-run cooperative factory, New Era Windows. The city has also been at the epicenter of the Fight for $15, a national campaign to raise the minimum wage to $15 an hour, led by unions representing service industry workers and by community groups that staged demonstrations in some 150 cities in September 2014. Emanuel's declaration of Chicago as a sanctuary city—one that would not comply with the Trump administration's plans for the mass deportation of undocumented immigrants—sparked an even more progressive, citizen-led response. Among other ongoing pro-immigration struggles in the city, the Campaign to Defy, Defend and Expand Sanctuary, founded by Organized Communities Against Deportations (OCAD), BYP100 and Mijente, united various formations in direct action tactics to push for a more expansive notion of sanctuary as freedom from police violence for all Chicagoans. Organizers countered the mayor's focus on sanctuary in relation to repressive federal immigration policy in ways that connected antideportation and antipolicing struggles. In Chicago, we also find a growing chorus of voices against Tax Increment Financing (TIFs), a method of publicly financing private development used throughout the United States, and one that serves as a key patronage mechanism in Emanuel's downtown growth regime.[22] Such struggles sketched a rough draft of a different, more genuinely democratic, socially just Chicago.

The call and response chant, "Whose streets? Our streets!" was heard throughout the 2015 Black Friday protests along Chicago's Mag Mile, and in most Black Lives Matter protests across the United States. The apparent origins of this common protest chant lie in the first wave of urban revanchism in the eighties, when New York City police stormed Tompkins Square Park in Alphabet City as part of the broader attempt of politicians and investors to "clean up" the city by getting rid of homeless people, punks, activists, panhandlers, sex workers and youth, preparing the way for new capital infusions and middle-class return.[23] From those early protests against gentrification and the mass demonstrations against corporate globalization in the late nineties and early aughts, through the Occupy encampments and Black Lives Matter marches, the cry "Whose streets?" has captured the radical democratic hope of these popular struggles, the dream that the city and public space might be returned to the people. In a sense, this aspect of contemporary protest culture shares common ground with the best intuitions and insights of Jane Jacobs. Jacobs, of course, feared the degradation of the pedestrian-oriented street, which was transformed from a human-scaled, center stage of public life into a passageway for automobiles. Since Jacobs's powerful criticisms of automobile-centric urban planning, the street has been subject to multiple unfortunate fates. Since the urban crisis of the sixties, throughout disinvested and abandoned inner cities, the notion of the "street" itself has come to be synonymous with danger and trouble. Far from being a cherished space of in-gathering and civic life, it is most often the subject of cautionary tales of "street life" and "mean streets," a zone of social exclusion and fear, the street as dystopia and the antithesis of liberal democratic life and comfort. The street has also too often been the setting where police lethality has been on full display, with many of the most infamous incidents of police violence—e.g., the killings of Oscar Grant, Eric Garner, Rekia Boyd, Michael Brown, Walter Scott, Freddie Gray, Laquan McDonald, Alton Sterling and Philando Castile—taking place in open urban thoroughfares and public spaces. It is the very public nature of these violent acts against civilians, in contrast to clandestine killings and black site torture, that has made them such a ready touchstone for popular organizing. In the age of gentrification, urban streets beyond the hyperghettoized zones have been reinvented in ways that neither Jacobs nor her arch-nemesis Robert Moses could have fully anticipated, and in a sense that merges Jacobs's concern for civic life with Moses's preoccupation with commercial flows. During the process of revanchist urbanization, we have witnessed the reemergence of the city street as the multimodal passageway of the neoliberal citizen (taking in Uber, livery cabs, rental scooters, bike lanes and Teslas, food and grocery delivery services, e-commerce, etc.); as a zone of revenue extraction through parking tickets, red light cameras and moving violations; and as a space of pervasive surveillance via Police Observation Devices (PODs), private security cameras, Google cars photographing street views, and ubiquitous cell-phone cameras. The street still connects, but not always in ways that nourish democratic public life. Contemporary antipolicing protests—like the antiglobalization and Occupy protests before them—have sought to reclaim and reposition the street as a space of democratic convergence and vibrant public life.

The Right to the Just City

From Ferguson and Chicago to the 2020 George Floyd protests, antipolicing protests and Black Lives Matter activist formations have reclaimed urban space symbolically and momentarily through demonstrations—forming human blockades on highways, disrupting sporting events, staging pickets and "die-ins," filling city streets with marchers and launching direct actions in commercial and financial districts. They have also sought to reclaim the city in terms of pursuing greater democratic power over policing and the urban process. Equally, these same forces have proposed an array of policy alternatives to the existing carceral infrastructure, demanding the downsizing of police department budgets, new means of public oversight and accountability, and greater social spending rather than incarceration. In this regard, antipolicing struggles implicitly connect to a broader set of urban movements and tendencies confronting the neoliberal capitalist city. Although mass incarceration and police violence are broad societal problems that also affect small towns and hinterlands across the nation, the urban context is the place where antipolicing forces have the most plausible chance of achieving broad progressive reform.

The "right to the city" slogan was first coined by the French Marxist Henri Lefebvre amid the May 1968 rebellion, when students, workers and popular sectors momentarily contested the French ruling classes through university and factory takeovers and street demonstrations.[24] In *Le Droit à la Ville*, Lefebvre referred to the right to the city as a "cry and a demand," one that "cannot be conceived as a simple visiting right or a return to traditional cities. It can only be formulated as a transformed and renewed *right to urban life*."[25] In recent years, anti-eviction campaigns and various popular struggles around the world have evoked Lefebvre's slogan, but so have bourgeois and reactionary forces, with some adopting the slogan for poverty reduction and slum-upgrading projects. Such reformist appropriations of the right to the city run the risk of assimilating demands for redistribution and social justice to market logics, contrary to the socialist left politics implicit in Lefebvre's original formulation and that of contemporary writers such as David Harvey, Peter Marcuse and others. The incomplete, suggestive character of Lefebvre's formulation and the liberal rights framing are perhaps partially to blame, but even the corporate and nonprofit appropriations of the slogan speak to the power of contemporary urban struggles to shift the terms of public debate, and, equally, to the gravity of the urban crises wrought by capitalist globalization, where millions struggle to find adequate housing, food and basic services. In recent decades, the right to the city slogan has been embraced by urban housing struggles around the world battling gentrification and mass evictions, but the right to the city as advanced by Lefebvre and others is not limited to the housing question. It is a socialist concept concerned with a deeper contestation of capitalist class power.

Lefebvre characterizes the city as an oeuvre—a work in progress —that is dependent upon broad-based social labor for the city's continual remaking. The process is simultaneously *collective*— as workers, citizens, consumers and visitors we all contribute to the constant remaking of the urban form, its immense cultural and material wealth, its technological and social complexity— and deeply *antisocial*—as the ruling class and capital shape the future in ways that reproduce their power and the conditions of social precarity and exploitation that are essential for perpetuating the accumulation process. Although the right to the city is presented in the liberal language of rights, for socialists the slogan is a call for working-class, popular power, the right of the great majority to determine the course of urban processes through genuinely democratic control. As Harvey notes, the right to the city is not merely the individual right to access urban resources, but rather "a right to change ourselves by changing the city," and it is by definition "a common rather than an individual right since this transformation inevitably depends upon the exercise of collective power to reshape the processes of urbanization." The "freedom to make and remake our cities and ourselves is," Harvey adds, "one of the most precious yet most neglected of our human rights."[26]

The problems of policing and mass incarceration are not limited to inner cities as popular lore might have it, but are problems of urban society. Lefebvre anticipated some time ago that the old town and country divide would be swept away through the complete urbanization of society.[27] In the spirit of Lefebvre, Andrew Merrifield contends that the "urban isn't out there, necessarily observable and measurable, but is immanent in our lives, an ontology not an epistemology, not a transitive attribute of our society but an immanent substance of our society."[28] The urban is where powerful social forces converge, the power of capitalist blocs and of working-class and popular opposition. During the processes of neoliberalization, cities have been the focus of massive public disinvestment, social disruption and capitalist renewal. Throughout the opening decade of the twenty-first century, global anticapitalist popular forces clashed with police guarding the exclusionary meetings of various transnational financial institutions and alliances, including the World Trade Organization, the World Bank and the Free Trade Agreement of the Americas. The urban has long been the arena of politics, the *agora*, where decisions and law-making take place.

Taking up Jean-Jacques Rousseau's *The Social Contract*, Merrifield contemplates the difficulty of translating the meaning of the citizen. He refers us to one of the most often quoted lines from Rousseau's corpus: "Houses make a town, but citizens make a city."[29] Merrifield generates a new hypothesis that salvages Rousseau's radical intentions: "The majority [of people] take a city for the *cité*, and a bourgeois for a citizen. They don't know that houses make a city, but citizens make the urban [*la cité*]." "The urban, in other words, might be better suited for Rousseau's notion of *cité*," Merrifield writes,

> it satisfies more accurately, and maybe more radically, a politically charged concept of citizenship that goes beyond nationality and flag waving (*Cité*, we might equally note, raises the "popular" specter in bourgeois circles, pejoratively evoking *quartiers des sans-culottes*, the no-go *zones sensibles* and global *banlieues*, neighborhoods dreaded by the ruling classes.) For the physical and social manifestation of our landscape, for its bricks and mortar, we have what most people would deem "city." But as a political ideal, as a new social contract around which citizenship might cohere, we have something we might call "the urban": a more expansive realm for which no passports are required and around which people the world over might bond. Citizenship might here be conceived as something urban, as something territorial, yet one in which territoriality is both narrower and broader than both "city" and "nationality"; a territory and citizenship without borders.[30]

"There's a consequent need to redefine not a public realm that's collectively owned and managed by the state," writes Merrifield, "but a public realm of the *cité* that is somehow expressive of the people, expressive of the general will—a will, maybe, that incorporates an affinity of *common notions*, notions that Spinoza always insisted were not universal notions, but universal rights."[31] "So rights, including the right to the city, have no catch-all universal meaning in politics, nor any foundational basis in institutions, neither are they responsive to any moral or legal argument: questions of rights are, first and foremost, questions of *social power*, about who *wins*."[32] Indeed, despite whatever limits or contradictions we might debate regarding Black Lives Matter protests, at the center of these and other latter-day urban social struggles, the demand for greater and real democratic power has been a central thread. Such struggles have pushed for more democratic control over policing in the form of civilian review boards and other accountability mechanisms; more power over municipal budgeting, especially in terms of funding programs for youth and the dispossessed; and, ultimately, the spread of direct democracy, modeled in the open assembly format and human microphones of Occupy and BLM protests, but as yet not constituted in an institutional form of power. Such struggles are popular in form, reflecting radical democratic and anticapitalist values that have gained more support since the Obama years, but these struggles have yet to achieve durable majority acceptance from American mass publics.

Revitalizing an anticapitalist politics in the United States has been stymied by the cultural prevalence of what Don Mitchell has termed *social agoraphobia*. While agoraphobia as a mental health condition refers to an individual's debilitating fear of being in public, for Mitchell, social agoraphobia refers to a generalized social condition, a fear of public spaces and the social heterogeneity and unpredictability of urban life. Mitchell's terminology is useful in summing up the connections between racism, antiurbanism and the cultural consequences of the neoliberal project, which has diminished popular expectations about the state and public life. "We are taught fear of public space," Mitchell contends; anything public "is suspect at best, and more likely dysfunctional while everything private is efficient, clean and to be wondered at."[33] In contrast, "public spaces are the realm of criminal violence, homeless people, drugs, anarchy, terrorists; public hospitals are where one goes to find long lines and waiting lists; public schools 'fail our children' (as American politicians like to put it); and public goods are, by definition, simply inefficient."[34] The antiurban sentiments, disdain for public goods and outright fear of public spaces Mitchell describes have been decades in the making, the outcome of the historic defeat of social democracy generations prior, the criminalization of radical left politics, and the hollowing out of the social reproductive functions of the state through neoliberalization.[35] Likewise, such cultural sentiments are the consequence of the antiurban national development policy that took root during the postwar years, when the federal government made massive investments in suburban housing development and produced generations of Americans who grew up afraid of urban spaces. The result was a noxious mix of racism and antiurbanism, a population that only knew blacks as the criminals and welfare cheats they encountered on screen, and who came to believe that the broad and deep inequalities across the urban landscape were a natural ordering, a consequence of other peoples' failings, whether of culture or breeding did not matter.

Mitchell contends that this widespread fear of public space is "enormously productive for capitalism—and for the state formations that safeguard it." If clinical agoraphobia keeps some Americans cloistered indoors, "social agoraphobia delivers us into the waiting arms of merchants in safe and secure malls, developers of securely gated neighborhoods, and newly redeveloped urban spaces like Times Square so carefully watched over by its army of private security guards and privately operated CCTV cameras."[36] When this performance of control and security breaks down, and these same sites—movie theaters, concerts on the festival mall, office complexes, nightclubs and other private spaces—become the sites of mass homicide, more fortressing, gun liberalization and social retreat are the response. This problem is especially acute regarding the matter of reversing course on mass incarceration, whose entire edifice was built on soothing public anxieties about real and imagined crime waves.

A core challenge for contemporary antipolicing struggles in building broader opposition is traversing this landscape of class and racial segregation, and of the fear that was produced out of the sequential processes of suburbanization and central city revanchism. Old prejudices and cultural paranoia die hard. Popular protests against police violence mobilized thousands of citizens across the country, but legitimacy for the current carceral regime was restored with relative ease. In recent years, artists have attempted to traverse these metropolitan social-spatial divisions and spark a more progressive political consciousness of the problems that afflict urban life. During the aughts, the Rochester-based artist and professor Heather Layton staged a performance piece titled "(Sub)urban Homicide."[37] Layton undertook her project when Rochester held the unfortunate title of "murder capital" in the state of New York because its per capita homicide rate surpassed those of the New York City boroughs. Although Rochester was facing a wave of gun violence, Layton was disturbed by how little attention and concern there was in the suburbs where she and her husband lived and worked. Layton took a map of gun fatalities in the city of Rochester and used tracing paper to mark the site of each homicide. She then turned the tracing paper over like the page of a book, transposing the homicide map onto Rochester's southeast suburbs, including Brighton and Pittsford. She identified proximate addresses for each site on this suburban map, and created memorials for each of the victims, who were mostly black men, including flowers, personal cards, photos, and descriptions of how they died.[38] Layton brought something akin to the familiar curbside memorials of stuffed animals, votive candles, photographs and mementos that are too familiar in urban quarters out into the relative peace of suburbia. Her memorials appeared on private lawns, a college campus and a grocery store parking lot. Through the simple displays, Layton attempted to prick the conscience of suburbanites, and make gun violence more palpable, less abstract.

In a similar vein, Englewood native Tonika Johnson launched the Folded Map project in Chicago.[39] She imagined the project as a visual investigation of Chicago's segregated landscape, using a map of the city's massive grid of cardinally directed streets. By folding the map in half, Johnson overlaid corresponding blocks on the North and South sides of the city, e.g., 6720 North Ashland in Rogers Park and 6720 South Ashland in Englewood, in the hope of comparing the physical, economic and social differences of these locations. She created resident pairs, or "map twins," through this process and began interviewing Chicagoans from diametrical addresses on the same street, ultimately bringing these disparate residents together to create new connections and friendships and renewed public conversations about the city's history of segregation and continuing problems of inequality.

Both artists provide the inspiration for an activist political practice of disrupting social and spatial segregation, pressing citizen engagement and imagining urban life beyond the neoliberal city. Layton and Johnson's respective public art installations might inspire a different approach to building the just city, one where we fold the map, alter entrenched mental and social boundaries, make contact, gather new alliances against the failings of the neoliberal project and establish new battlefronts.

Don Mitchell explores how we might reverse the course of social agoraphobia and its role in reproducing the neoliberal city of security and profit-making. Mitchell draws on Lefebvre's discussion of "La Fête," or the festival, those moments of Dionysian revelry when "everyday life is turned on its head (even as the festival was part of everyday life)."[40] Such moments of protest disrupt the normal ideological and political script of urban life, and reclaim public spaces, the street, parks and plazas for the purposes of collective use value and pleasure. "In other words, la Fête—and thus the city as oeuvre, and thus the right to the city —is dangerous," Mitchell writes; "it is indeed, against safety, and against security, at least as it is conceived in the contemporary city defined by fear of public space."[41]

Public Works and the Class Relation

The creation of universal public works, inspired by the highly successful CCC and WPA programs of the New Deal but tailored to contemporary conditions, could undermine the very basis of modern policing by addressing the problem of surplus population and reorganizing labor around use values, thereby ending basic need and the alienation of the broader urban laboring classes. This proposal is inspired, in part, by Fredric Jameson's arguments in favor of compulsory national service, conceived as a means of dual power where national conscription enables the construction of a new post-capitalist order while hastening the withering away of the old.[42] The focus on public works here, however, is a matter of immediacy and pragmatic strategy—of how progressive forces might instigate the remaking of urban life given actually existing conditions. Like Jameson's proposal, government-funded and popular-democratic public works might establish a new socio-economic structure, where labor time is reorganized outside the market context and redirected towards socially beneficial activities, goods and services. Universal public works, administered at the municipal, state-wide or federal level, could have the combined effect of transforming urban society by reorienting labor towards the production of use values. Rather than the current state of affairs, where elites in cities like Baltimore and Chicago are deeply committed to a post-Fordist accumulation model centered around real estate and tourism-entertainment, a different, more egalitarian and socially just city might rise instead. Imagine a city where popular will and deliberation, instead of capitalist profit-making, determine the direction of metropolitan planning, land use, municipal budgets and how social labor will be organized and deployed.

Black Lives Matter activists have provoked critical public debate in this direction, by demanding the scaling back of police department budgets and the re-routing of recuperated public funds towards investments in youth. Antipolicing activists have proposed various detailed plans for divestment in police and the reallocation of public monies for education, jobs, job training and social programs.[43] *Freedom to Thrive: Reimagining Public Safety and Security in Our Communities* is one of the most progressive statements produced by antipolicing forces. This report was co-authored and prepared by Kumar Rao and Kate Hamaji of the Center for Popular Democracy, Mabre Stahly-Butts of Law for Black Lives, and Janaé Bonsu, Roselyn Berry, Denzel McCampbell and Charlene Carruthers of Black Youth Project 100, in conjunction with twenty-seven local organizations. The document opens with direct criticism of the core contradictions of the neoliberal project—"governments have dramatically increased their spending on criminalization, policing and mass incarceration while drastically cutting investments in basic infrastructure and slowing investment in social safety net programs"—and closes with a call for participatory budgeting and more popular democratic control over the determination of public spending priorities.[44] Against the present carceral apparatus built on racist fear, social agoraphobia and the regulation of the poor, the report sketches a different social democratic approach that ensures public safety through the guarantee of broad economic security. "The choice to resource punitive systems instead of stabilizing and nourishing ones does not make communities safer," the authors contend; rather, "a living wage, access to holistic health services and treatment, educational opportunity, and stable housing are far more successful in reducing crime."[45] The report goes on to offer more in-depth examinations of twelve urban jurisdictions, including Chicago.

The report's section on Chicago makes a persuasive case for divestment in policing and security and a more redistributive social policy. The authors detail the broader racial disparities in Chicago policing as well as the lopsided priorities of the Emanuel administration's city budget. Black working-class Chicagoans bear the overwhelming brunt of police violence in the city. Of those shot by police between 2008 and 2015, the report details, 74 percent were African American and 14 percent Latino.[46] The same is true for police harassment. Of the more than a quarter of a million stops in the summer of 2014 that did not lead to an arrest, 72 percent of those stopped were black and 17 percent Latino. These are especially stark figures given that white (non-Latino), black and Latino populations each make up roughly one-third of Chicago's total population. The report also makes clear just how much the city has invested in a carceral approach to poverty, rather than progressive social programs or even the most basic support services. In 2017, Chicago spent $1.5 billion of its $8.2 billion operating budget on policing.[47] By comparison, for every dollar allocated to the police department, the city spent two cents on public health, a nickel on family and support services, and twelve cents on the Department of Planning Development, which oversees affordable housing development in the city. In light of these social disparities and spending priorities, the authors call for "a participatory city budget in which the public has the power to defund the Chicago Police Department and reinvest those resources in Black futures by setting a living wage and by fully funding health care, social services, public schools and sustainable economic development projects."[48] Perhaps the most immediate impact of such vision and agenda-setting is reorienting public discussion around municipal spending priorities, and preempting the "how will we pay for it" question that opponents and fiscal conservatives always raise whenever progressive social spending is proposed. This and other reports published by local and national formations have set out in compelling ways where city funding goes, and have made clear the hypocrisy, immorality and wrong-headed sociology that guides the carceral dimension of the neoliberal project.

The "Counter-CAPs Report: The Community Engagement Arm of the Police State," published by the organization We Charge Genocide, offers consonant proposals. With sociologist and activist Brendan McQuade serving as lead author, this report provided blistering criticism of community policing as a solution to the problems of abuse and violence against civilians. Far from engendering more democracy, in practice community policing is most often a process where only a "self-selecting group of empowered community members, who are frequently gentrifiers, work with police to deflect criticism and build local support for policing."[49] The report's conclusions were based on months of data collection undertaken by We Charge Genocide's Real Community Accountability for People's Safety working group, which studied the Chicago Alternative Policing Strategy (CAPS) program implementation. They found that CAPS meetings mostly mobilized whiter and more affluent Chicagoans, and that participation was generally low. Moreover, CAPS engaged in "deputized surveillance" of participants, actively promoting peer surveillance and suspicion of neighbors, encouraging residents to report nuisance crimes like loitering and public drinking. CAPS representatives also encouraged identifying and monitoring "bad tenants" and supplying information to authorities that might lead to evictions. As extensions of zero-tolerance and stress policing, only now carried out by residents themselves, most of these strategies were pitched in coded language, where "bad tenants" and "suspicious persons" avoided overt references to black and brown Chicagoans, who would likely be viewed as out of place in the neighborhoods where CAPS found eager supporters. In response to the clear limits of the CAPS program and community policing as a solution, We Charge Genocide called for divestment in the CPD and reinvestment in social services, education and health care. "Every helicopter that is flown, every bullet that is shot and every baton that is swung is not just an injury to those targeted by police," the report concluded, "it is also a theft from the city's struggling schools, health clinics, libraries and community centers."[50]

Such proposals constitute the most promising policy agendas established by Black Lives Matter organizing. Its defunding demands, however, may not be ambitious enough, and in most incarnations this redistributive strategy remains rather limited by an older and defeated horizon of welfare statism. In other words, while the calls to "Fund Black Futures" or target black youth resonate with Black Lives Matter devotees, without broad popular support they are likely to replicate the older machinations of ethnic patronage politics, only with more militant, gender-egalitarian, queer-affirming political commitments interwoven. In a city like Chicago, "black," "poor," "unemployed" and "overpoliced" are largely synonymous. This is, however, an effect of both the flight of more upwardly mobile African Americans as better housing options became available elsewhere, and of Chicago's unique distinction among the largest US cities in having retained large white middle and affluent classes throughout the period of urban crisis and industrial contraction. The result of these historical processes was the sharpening of racial and class inequality —the median family income for African Americans in Chicago in 2010 was $29,371, while that for white households was $58,752 (and even higher for non-Latino white households at $64,692).[51] Still, there are other non-black citizens who would benefit from such redistributive policy, and perhaps more importantly, the focus on youth excludes a sizable adult portion of the black population who have been criminalized and condemned to a life of low-wage, non-unionized and often precarious work. A more fulsome policy vision is warranted, one that is not targeted by age or ethnicity, but universal, focused on eliminating unemployment and poverty in the short run, but ultimately aimed at abolishing the capitalist wage relation altogether.

Not only have such universal public works programs worked in the past, but more favorable political conditions—including the growth of support for socialism in the wake of Bernie Sanders's 2016 presidential bid, the broad cultural valorization of volunteering and community service under neoliberalization, and popular desire for an end to urban violence and crime—have softened the ground for even more grandiose and impactful re-imaginings of socialized labor to take root. None of this will be achieved, however, by appealing to the same old ethnic patronage politics for which Chicago is infamous. Rather, such advances will require building coalitions among those urban dwellers who are most deeply impacted by crime and policing; commuters, gentrifiers, tourists and other middle-class citizens who desire access to the city but are wary of the repressive means underlying their mobility; and other constituencies such as housing and anti-eviction activists, advocates for the homeless, and teachers, social workers, unionists and politicians who want to create a more just urban life and more sane means of producing public safety in large metropolitan contexts—again, *folding the map*, altering entrenched mental and social boundaries, gathering new alliances and establishing new beach heads against urban neoliberalization.

In the context of Chicago, universal public works would be open to all adult residents who desire employment. It would make more sense if implemented at the federal level, but in a city like Chicago, which operates like a city-state, a localized program of this kind might go a long way towards rebuilding the city, demonstrating the virtues of a more expansive national program, reducing wealth and income inequality, and providing numerous essential goods and services for city dwellers, natives, newcomers and visitors alike, in a decommodified manner.

Such a program would have manifold benefits for the city. In economic terms, public works would provide jobs for those who cannot obtain market-based employment. In paying employees above the prevailing wage, the program could apply progressive pressure to low-wage labor markets in the region. By providing previously unemployed, underemployed and poor residents with more income, public works would have an immediate multiplier effect in working-class neighborhoods, raising demand at the existing neighborhood-level businesses that provide basic goods and services—e.g., grocers, convenience stores, restaurants, dry cleaners, laundromats, clothiers, etc.—and sparking new investment given the rising consumer capacity. Although this might be overstated, the option of safe, legal employment might also help to deter survival crimes and forms of unregulated and criminalized work.

Whereas Depression-era public works programs were intended to address immediate hardship, and were largely determined by federal and local administrators, a metropolitan public works project could do much more. Rather than the "three hots and a cot" and basic remuneration provided by the Civilian Conservation Corps, a municipal public works program in a city the size of Chicago could pay a more fulsome living wage. Rather than supplying labor for the construction of bridges and buildings that have been prioritized and designed by elites, a municipal public works project could be driven by its workforce, in conjunction with neighborhood-level assemblies, activist organizations, design professionals, engineers and urban planners. In other words, such labor could be organized on a popular basis in response to the actual needs and desires of specific neighborhoods, and in accordance with the broad, democratically determined priorities of city residents.

A core assumption guiding this defense of public works is that the abolition of the class relation, which produces surplus value through exploitation, will not end the social necessity of labor. Even in a post-capitalist context, *labor*, the reproduction of the species in both the sexual and metabolic senses, and *work*, the realization of our individual and collective creative capacities (i.e., the meaning implied in expressions like one's "life work" or "work of art"), would remain necessary because these are defining features of the species. Recurring left premonitions of the coming end of work—rather than the defeat of compulsory wage labor as a figment of capitalism—have resurfaced periodically among leftists and assorted technocrats since the sixties, with each and every leap forward in computer technology, robotics, cellular communications and biotechnological engineering. In his survey of the latest wave of left writings of the "fully-automated, luxury communist" sort, Anton Jäger offers numerous critical insights, the foremost target of which is the post-workerist tendency to conflate capitalist employment with work.

Work, Jäger reminds us, is not the same as wage labor. "Although not a historically generalizable notion—societies have hugely divergent ways of interacting with their environment, whether natural or social—humanity's interaction with nature (and, therefore, 'his reproduction of nature as a whole') can take myriad forms," Jäger writes. "Some of these can be highly exploitative, as in slave societies, while others are more spontaneous and free (think of the shared games of hunter-gatherers)."[52] Rather than some anarchist dream, where societal needs might be met through some combination of automation and spontaneous activity carried out by smaller collectives, Jäger proposes a socialist alternative where work is organized through democratic planning and according to societal needs. Jäger is right to criticize such utopic tendencies, which are ill-suited to meeting our needs in complex, highly urbanized societies. Even in a post-capitalist world, he writes, "key tasks will still be subject to societal demands. Many of those tasks will have to be *socially* decreed. And whether we like it or not, even a post-capitalist society would have to find a mechanism to impose tasks on the population to carry out 'socially necessary' labor (childrearing, education, sanitation). In doing so, it would inevitably inject a degree of heteronomy into some forms of labor."[53] Rather than the notions of spontaneity and free association that underlie anarchist post-capitalism, as well as the Universal Basic Income (UBI) idea increasingly popular among Silicon Valley technorati, Jäger warns that "some form of coercion would be required for this task; a coercion that is definitely *abstract*—not based on personal power based in specific individuals—but also not arbitrary, with workers' organizations' actions predicated on the fact that they exist through consistent processes of deliberation."[54] Some level of coercion, planning backed by territorial democratic forms of power, and conscientious thinking would all be necessary in order to avoid reproducing capitalist society's individualistic and consumerist understandings of need. "It should, then, be the task of a socialist society," Jäger concludes, "to recognize these relations of inter-dependence and attempt to create a world in which the structures that help us to facilitate the needs of others are open to accountability and contestation."[55]

We might extend Jäger's criticism of the anarchistic focus on spontaneity, which also conflates capitalist institutions and laws with social organization and authority more generally. We should reject private property, while envisioning forms of social organization and authority that are not limited to capitalist class relations. We should and must build more just, democratic forms of territorial authority. Again, how might a city as geographically vast and populous as Chicago—and others much larger like Los Angeles or Tokyo—be governed effectively without territorial power and social organization, albeit democratic or popular in form? Moreover, laws can and should be the highest expression of civic and socially just values. So, while volunteering to help disaster victims, or committing to a worker-owned firm or cooperative housing arrangement are all expressions of altruism and mutuality, so are antidiscrimination laws, which establish enforceable social norms and provide real recourse for those who are treated unfairly, and punishment for those who discriminate against blacks, women, people with disabilities, and so forth. Moreover, the basic premise of the public works project outlined here—that no one should be without a means of subsistence and that care work, transportation, health care and other needs should not be commodified—is a statement of values that, if institutionalized, could diminish the power of the capitalist values of private property and exploitation presently enshrined in law.

In terms of citizen-neighborhood impact, large-scale urban public works could transform the physical, aesthetic and social value of the city. Workers could be engaged in all manner of material and creative labor that remains undone in certain parts of the city. Publicly funded and democratically administered labor, organized around use values rather than market exchange, could radically transform neighborhoods long shuttered and abandoned because of capitalist planning and for-profit land speculation. We are all too familiar with the kind of urbanism that capital produces, a social and physical landscape defined by uneven development. The kind of public works project outlined here would not be panacea by any means, but non-capitalist planning could go a long way towards repairing some of the inequalities that have been produced by deep disparities in wealth and power across different urban populations and neighborhoods. Like the New Deal project decades ago, which shouldered the costs of social reproduction, contemporary public works programs might go further, not only taking essential goods and services needed by all out of the market exchange system, but also bringing an unprecedented level of public deliberation and insight into planning the urban form.

For the purpose of this provisional exercise, some areas where we might see public works flourish in a city like Chicago are transportation, care work and green technologies. Central to the neoliberal model is the transferal of the costs of social reproduction, the shift of basic needs from public goods and services to market commodities. This process has been especially acute in Chicago, which was a New Deal Democratic stronghold and later a bristling laboratory of neoliberal experimentation. Most of the changes wrought by privatization are widely felt by Chicago residents and often codified in terms of racial disparity, but other aspects of the new order and the daily injustices it produces are less perceptible.[56]

In regard to transportation, public works might not only enhance the existing system of transportation, but also, in the spirit of taking back the streets, create greater mobility by transforming the postwar city made for automobiles. In the city of Chicago in particular, the L, or elevated mass transit rail system, is highly uneven, underutilized and unsafe. The North side lines are the most heavily patronized because of population density, whereas some lines on the West and South sides are less used outside of commuter rush hours. In many cases, vast tracts of the city are completely beyond the reach of the rail service. Expansion of the rail system would then be one major physical improvement to the city's infrastructure.

Beyond that, the provision of simple but much-needed services could enhance the system, potentially increase ridership, but most of all make the system more valuable for residents and visitors alike. Public works could be used to create safety-oriented foot patrols of the transit system to enhance security, especially during off-peak hours and when the emptiness of some stations and the isolation of riders heightens crime risks. At present the city deploys police during major events to monitor select stops, but their work is geared towards terrorism-deterrence and the public performance of security for tourists and visitors. All trains in recent years have been outfitted with multiple cameras, but these have done precious little to enhance safety, even if they provide some grist for detective work after muggings and fights have occurred. Electronic surveillance offers little comfort to the greying nurse pulling a late shift, now standing on the CTA Blue Line's Illinois Medical District platform alone, waiting for a westbound train at midnight. Between 2015 and 2019, criminal reports on Chicago's mass transit system rose from 4,116 to 6,321 incidents per year.[57] And since the start of the Covid-19 pandemic, as ridership has sagged, violent crime on CTA trains and buses has increased yet again.[58] Such security foot patrols might also be deployed beyond the CTA system, on public pedestrian and bicyclist thoroughfares like the city's Lakefront path and the 606/Bloomingdale Trail, a three-mile linear park built on an old elevated railbed.

Alongside foot patrols, other basic services like de-icing train platforms (the current winter practice is to cake outdoor platforms with sand) and the installation of heat lamps (which are in short supply on most platforms) or radiate floor systems could also improve the experience and safety of the CTA system. Increased provision of bus aides, interpreters and platform guides could be achieved through a city-wide public works project. These are all forms of labor that might be deployed seasonally and would only require short, intensive training programs.

In addition to physical and service improvements to the city's transportation system, there is also a tremendous societal need for care work; here, public works could improve an industry that has been traditionally devalued, exploitative, low-wage or unwaged. A municipal public works project could be used to raise the floor in traditionally devalued care services, which have long been defined historically as compulsory women's work or the low-paid servant work of nannies, house cleaners and nurses. While some feminist theorists have argued for the emancipation of women from such culturally conscripted biological and social reproductive labor, others have demanded "wages for housework."[59] And of course, during the Cold War consumer expansion, some, including the then vice-president Richard Nixon in his exchange with Soviet leader Nikita Khrushchev, imagined a world where technological relief would emancipate housewives from the most drudgerous of chores. Technological and commercial remedies have indeed lessened the burden of reproductive labor for those who can afford to pay for these commodities and services, but care work—household cleaning, child rearing, care of aging or disabled family members, food preparation and so forth—remains devalued and structurally dependent on wage earners, with the most vulnerable shouldering this kind of labor, e.g., late arriving and undocumented immigrants, unmarried women, minorities, those with little occupational choice and power. Public works have been used in the past to provide non-commodified services to the greatest number, and, likewise, many states have adopted universal pre-kindergarten programs to lessen the household cost burden on working-class parents and guarantee a modicum of preschool education for all children.

Might contemporary public works be reimagined and designed in such a way as to abolish compulsory women's work, establish a living wage for traditionally domestic care work, and make such labor more collective and egalitarian? Why should the care of the most vulnerable citizens, the very young, the very old and those with disabilities or illness, be the most devalued labor? Non-commodified and publicly organized care might also have broader health benefits and address the problems of social isolation that define urban living for too many. We know that the high morbidity rates among older and poorer residents during the 1995 Chicago heatwave disaster were due to their social isolation. Over the course of five days that July, temperatures soared as high as 106 degrees Fahrenheit, and some 739 Chicagoans succumbed to heat-related illnesses. Many of these people lived on blocks where they were isolated from their neighbors and remained inside due to fear of crime. As the heat increased, some simply had no nearby friends or relatives to do regular check-ins, and were discovered after they had succumbed to heatstroke, cardiac arrest or other ailments.[60] We might imagine more creative deployments of care work in ways that effectively break such alienation. This might take the form of mobile care units attending to physical and mental health as well as social and emotional needs, modeled along the lines of the traditional house calls made by doctors in the United States historically, and in more rural and underdeveloped parts of the world.

Public works might also provide employment for educated, skilled and creative but out-of-work residents, in the mold of

the New Deal WPA, by creating literacy programs, adult education programs, writer's workshops and fix-it/DIY schools. Such
programs would be of use to those adults who want to pursue
education, but who may not have the desire, means or time to
pursue conventional community college or university degree
programs. Additionally, Saturday DIY schools could greatly
enhance the quality of life for hundreds of residents, and possibly spare older consumer products from the landfills. Many
states have already passed "right to repair" legislation, which
breaks the copyright monopolies and control over repairs that
corporations have over certain consumer goods like automobiles
and electronics.[61] Such legislation makes it easier for consumers
to repair older goods and seeks to arrest the entrenched process
of planned obsolescence. If this kind of legislation was enacted
at the federal level it would surely drive up the need for more
Saturday DIY/repair schools and publicly managed workshops
of the sort described here. Such attempts to reverse obsolescence
are but one way that municipal public works might connect to
the making of a broader green economy.[62]

Citizens serving within this hypothetical public works program
in Chicago could also be deployed to install various green technologies in households, public right of ways and buildings.
Installations of carbon monoxide and smoke detectors, remediation of lead paint and leaded water systems, as well as litter
clean-up, wetlands restoration and prairie grass planting are
all basic, relatively low-skill activities that would create greater
safety and security for the population, and beautify and improve
the health of the locally built environment and ecology. Larger-
scale projects might include installation of water-permeable
surfaces as a means of run-off and flood prevention, as well as
solar photovoltaic panels and wind turbines. The latter renew-
able energy sources could be installed on public properties, streets
and highways to improve efficiency, but equally important, these
same types of technologies might be installed in low-income
homes, public housing and apartment buildings to reduce the
energy costs shouldered by the most vulnerable residents.

There are limitations to municipal-level public works, which can only meet the needs of a discrete population and may not be adopted widely because of the relative balance of class and popular forces in different cities. Nevertheless, throughout US history, local and state politics have served as laboratories for policy experimentation, often contributing to national policy shifts in substantial ways. As already noted, the urban context constitutes the most favorable arena for progressive and radical left forces to contest capital's power over life, labor and resources. Of course, there are likely to be two immediate objections to this public works strategy from the contemporary left. One objection might be that this is a "lion in sheep's clothing," a proposal that aims at ushering in the abolition of wage labor but is in reality just another jobs program, one that raises worker spending capacity and stabilizes capital accumulation against working-class rebellion and social instability, very much in the mold of the New Deal vision of creating the consumer society. In other words, despite the best intentions, when operationalized, public works will only aid in the reproduction of the current order, enlarging the public sector and shrinking the ranks of the poor, but ultimately allowing a more humane version of urban capital accumulation and consumer culture to persist. This is a risk of any policy proposal, but how progressive or revolutionary such a public works project might be is dependent on the expanse and quality of the progressive forces that can be brought to bear in real historical time and space.

A second line of criticism might be voiced by those who fear a universal public works program will divert resources from those who need it most, or, in accordance with the popular antiracist criticism of the New Deal, that such a policy will only reproduce racial and gender inequities. These claims are at best paranoid, resting on a flawed, ahistorical understanding of the New Deal and, in particular, of the benefits of previous public works programs for blacks and women. The momentary integration that defined Depression-era public works and the wartime defense industry set the stage for the birth of the civil rights and feminist movements after World War II. In any case, why should contemporary redistributive policy be destined to repeat the alleged mistakes of legislation enacted nearly a century prior? Those who trade in this argument lack the courage and willingness to do the work that would be necessary to bring a different world into being. If funded and structured with democratic, egalitarian and anticapitalist values in mind, public works would be capable of having the most powerful impact on the most dispossessed.

In addition to these objections, pushing for such a program in Chicago would face the challenges of negotiating the city's legendarily conservative aldermanic system of patron–clientelistic relations, outright cronyism and deference to investor class interests.[63] The political strategies and victorious campaigns of local teachers against privatization might serve as a guide here. The internationally recognized organizing successes of the Chicago Teacher's Union during the 2012 strike led by the late Karen Lewis and the 2019 strike led by her successor Jesse Sharkey provide a model for pursuing progressive reform in the city, although their demands confronted the public school district administration and mayor, rather than the aldermanic city council and mayor directly. The 2012 strike was an impressive display of solidarity that united public school teachers and staffers, students, families, neighborhoods and community organizations within and beyond the city limits.[64] Although the teachers won a new contract, the Emanuel administration responded with a wave of school closures, many of which were in the city's most distressed neighborhoods. Subsequently, activists waged a hunger strike to save the Walter Dyett High School, which sits on the northernmost edge of Washington Park. The 2012 strike rattled the Emanuel administration, and it seemed that Lewis, before she was diagnosed with cancer, might mount a serious challenge to the sitting mayor. The strike reverberated throughout the country and was clearly the inspiration for a subsequent wave of red-state strikes, labor actions in Republican-dominant and often antiunion "right to work" states such as West Virginia, Arizona and Oklahoma, as well as massive strikes in more progressive territories like Los Angeles.[65]

The 2019 CTU strike provides an equally powerful model for how progressive left forces can reorient public budget priorities and achieve meaningful reforms that guarantee greater inequality. True to form, local corporate news coverage focused on how parents would be inconvenienced by the strike, how high school sports teams might miss their opportunity for post-season play because of Illinois state rules, and how generous first-term mayor Lori Lightfoot and the Chicago Public School (CPS) administrators were being in terms of compensation. Such coverage downplayed, or missed altogether, the progressive character of the strike, which went beyond traditional demands for better teacher pay and benefits. Under the leadership of CTU president Sharkey and vice-president Stacy Davis Gates, the union used the contract negotiation process to reverse the negative effects of austerity over the last few decades and to push for greater equity and social justice across the large, sprawling school district. At the heart of the deliberations was the CTU's demand for increased funding to hire librarians, school social workers, aides and other support staff, especially at schools that served the poorest neighborhoods. The union was able to create a different narrative than the one usually promoted by corporate news media, city officials and foundation-funded think tanks, i.e., that strikes are orchestrated by greedy, overpaid and undeserving teachers. Instead, the CTU successfully advanced a vision for education beyond austerity, where improved working conditions for teachers and school staff, better and more support for student learning, the more just distribution of education resources, and the success of the CPS as a district are all one and the same. Their vision prevailed over that of the investor class. Although a public works program would have to be achieved through council legislation rather than collective bargaining, the CTU strikes demonstrated that broad interracial publics in the city of Chicago were supportive of redistributive policy and were compelled by a more progressive ethos of building a more just city.

Conclusion

Since the end of Emanuel's reign, popular and neighborhood-based organizations and campaigns throughout Chicago continued to achieve significant victories, most notably the summer 2021 passage of an ordinance creating a democratically elected civilian oversight board to govern the CPD. The ordinance produced a rare debate in the city council chambers that reflected sharp political fault lines across aldermanic wards and the power of reform forces that had been gathering strength since the Laquan McDonald protests. Some alderpersons were especially energetic and adamant in their calls for reform in the wake of the 2021 killings of thirteen-year-old Adam Toledo and twenty-two-year-old Anthony Alvarez within days of each other, both on the city's southwest side, in majority-Mexican enclaves. The ordinance was touted in the press as the most progressive police reform legislation to have come in the wake of George Floyd, but the truth of that assertion will be tested in its implementation. Will Chicago's new civilian oversight board fall prey to the same rough-and-tumble, pay-to-play politics that have defined so much of the city's political lore and reality? Will it serve as a means of redistributing power and reducing police–civilian violence, or of deflecting popular demands to roll back stress policing and carceral infrastructure? Chicago has a long history of ostensibly democratic institutional reforms—from previous police oversight mechanisms to the creation of local school councils rather than a democratically elected school board—that did not result in operational democracy or progressive outcomes for citizens.

The civilian oversight board is one significant post–George Floyd victory, but on other fronts reform has proven more difficult. Chicagoans were less successful in achieving a defund and dismantle agenda in the year after George Floyd's murder. Private institutions in the city and surrounding suburbs rode the wave of international protests. Some colleges and universities reduced police budgets and, in some cases, cut ties with police altogether. Some suburban public schools ended the use of school resource officers. But the CPS did not see system-wide changes enacted.[66] Efforts to remove police from the city's public schools were less successful, with only a minority removing officers from their campuses. Although Lightfoot made a crucial shift from opponent to supporter of the civilian oversight board ordinance, she has proven to be just as dedicated a defender of neoliberalism and policing as her predecessor.

When Lightfoot was elected in 2019 to succeed Emanuel, some on the left cheered. Her historic victory as the first black woman and first openly gay mayor of the city, they argued, reflected both the power of popular forces to contest the Emanuel regime and the growing influence of women of color and queer activists within and beyond the city.[67] Keeping in mind that many of these same activists organized against Lightfoot as a functionary of the Emanuel administration and as a mayoral candidate, I want to cast doubt on the most triumphal accounts, which seem to lose sight of the sources of her victory and the character of her politics. Lightfoot was installed by a coalition that was largely based in the northern and more affluent parts of the city, and while her support was broader in the run-off, it was the whitest reaches of the city that pushed her forward in the head-to-head contest with Cook County Board president Toni Preckwinkle. The triumphal accounts from some on the left perhaps unintentionally echo longstanding notions of Chicago machine politics, which often attributed an electoral victory to this or that favored precinct, ethnic group, cabal or group of constituencies. How helpful is such thinking now? Such mischaracterizations of Lightfoot's victory and her political views wrongly suggest that BLM forces will be the power behind the throne. Aside from a hot microphone gaffe where she dismissed a police union rep as a "FOP clown," Lightfoot's actions have toed a very familiar line of commitment to tourism-entertainment and real estate development, and to the carceral apparatus that makes that growth regime possible.

There was also much confusion regarding Lightfoot's role in police reform during the most embattled years of the Emanuel administration. She rose to public notoriety as an intermediary on matters of police–civilian conflict, serving as leader of both the Chicago Police Board and the Chicago Police Accountability Task Force. While the former was a longstanding institution, created in 1960 and charged with nominating the superintendent, adopting rules and regulations for the department and adjudicating disciplinary cases, the latter was formed in the wake of the Laquan McDonald video-release controversy to review the CPD's system of accountability. Such positions may have given Lightfoot's devotees the impression that she would be an agent of change, but the experience of local antipolicing forces told another story. At one public hearing, Lightfoot seemed especially testy, tamping down on public comment in a manner that silenced the family of Rekia Boyd and drew fire from BYP100 activists in the room who demanded that Dante Servin, the off-duty cop who shot and killed Rekia Boyd and injured another man, be fired at once. More telling, since her election, Lightfoot has not only expressed support for Emanuel's plan for a new police training academy, another proposal that local antipolicing forces have vehemently opposed, but in her first year called for a more expansive cop academy. Her plan surpassed the existing $95 million price tag and would transform shuttered neighborhood schools into police training facilities.[68] After the resignation of police superintendent Eddie Johnson in fall 2019, Lightfoot quickly appointed former Los Angeles top cop and second-generation officer Charlie Beck to serve as interim, against loud disapproval from BLM activists in both cities. Only a year before, Sheila Hines-Brim, the aunt of Wakiesha Wilson, who died in LAPD custody, had confronted Beck at a police commission meeting and slung her niece's ashes at him in protest. Beck's appointment by Lightfoot also prompted BLM Los Angeles activists to publish an open letter warning Chicago residents of the new interim's résumé as the head of the "most murderous police department in the nation," citing the LAPD's "45 officer-involved-shootings and in-custody deaths in 2019."[69]

Those who read Lightfoot's race, gender and sexuality as signs of her progressivism should focus instead on her actual stances on matters of policing, economic development, collective bargaining rights and concrete forms of racial equality. On all of these fronts, she has proven in no uncertain terms that her politics are at least in step with her predecessor, if not to Emanuel's right on some issues. Celebrations of Lightfoot's victory miss the continuity across administrations, and the nature of power and governance in a metropolis like Chicago. The mayor and city council are important figures in terms of decision-making, but they alone are not the governing regime, which is comprised of powerful interests beyond city hall, and even beyond the city limits.

None of the celebrations of Lightfoot's alleged connection to progressive social struggles mention the policy stances on economic development she took in the first months of taking office, which were firmly committed to a neoliberal, downtown growth agenda. Far from being a progressive warrior, Lightfoot moved quickly in endorsing various megaprojects during her transition. She embraced "the 78" and the Lincoln Yards project, two of the city's most highly publicized, planned megadevelopments. Both projects rely on millions of dollars of public and private investment to create entirely new neighborhoods from whole cloth. The 78, named so because it will add to the existing seventy-seven Chicago neighborhoods, is to be built on a 62-acre vacant site, just south of Roosevelt Road and along the south branch of the Chicago River. The $7 billion project will connect the South Loop to Chinatown, and include a new $300 million CTA Red Line station, 13 million square feet of new building space, 10,000 residential units, parkland and a water taxi stop. The project's boosters claim that once completed the 78 will harbor a workforce of some 24,000 Chicagoans. Originally one of multiple sites proposed by the city during the Amazon headquarters competition, Lincoln Yards will redevelop 55 acres of brownfield on both sides of the Chicago River's North Branch into 6,000 new housing units, 21 acres of park space, a new Metra commuter station, an extension of the Bloomingdale Trail, a new sports stadium, and office and commercial retail space.[70] Public financing for both projects was approved during Emanuel's last meeting with the city council, which committed a combined $1.6 billion to the projects—$800 million for Lincoln Yards and $700 for the 78.[71] Whether under the leadership of Daley, Emanuel or Lightfoot, the consistent thread over the last three decades is the power of global capital to impress its will on Chicago and the working lives, neighborhoods and collectively produced wealth of its residents.

As an expansion of the redistributive demands made by BLM forces, the creation of metropolitan public works might serve as one practical and achievable means of abolishing the economic conditions of unemployment and dispossession that contemporary policing and mass incarceration were designed to manage. By ending unemployment and raising wage floors, Chicago and other cities might in the short run reduce the prevalence of property crime and violence connected to criminalized and informal sectors. Instead of increased funding for surveillance, police and incarceration—the repressive neoliberal strategies for addressing inequality and crime—we might achieve public safety through the guarantee of greater economic security. Going a step further, the creation of a popularly controlled public works program might also revolutionize urban life by decommodifying various elements of social reproduction such as transportation, care and energy. What has been outlined here is provisional and suggestive, intended to spark debate and kindle solutions that can only be achieved through active political struggles. If a public works program of the sort described were ever to be implemented at the scale of a city like Chicago, out of necessity it would take on a popular character that we cannot fully anticipate. What would Chicago look like in terms of transportation, care economies, energy use, ecology, leisure, recreation and everyday life, if democratic popular will, and not the profit motive, shaped these determinations of urban existence? Popular protests against police violence have opened up new vistas, but a tremendous amount of political work remains to be done. Moreover, the path to realizing greater police reforms or, better yet, achieving a different order predicated on economic security rather than repression, will require majority alliances in Chicago and elsewhere that do not yet exist. And by definition, such alliances must be hewn from the hard rock of the society as it exists, with all its relations of domination, social divisions, bad faith, misinformation, fears, prejudices and reaction. There is simply no other way forward but through politics.

6

The Labor of Occupation

Neil Blomkamp's 2004 short film *Tetra Vaal* is a critical parable of policing as labor. At little more than a minute in length, the film captures the core social role of policing: the regulation of those social forces that threaten private property and profit-making. Likewise, Blomkamp's work reminds us that policing, like all other living labor under capitalism, is labor subject to being replaced by automated technological solutions. In *Tetra Vaal*, Blomkamp workshopped the unique visual style that would become his signature, an ultra-realistic aesthetic that employs CGI to create a likely dystopia, integrating existing weaponry as well as experimental prototypes, futuristic technology and megacity slum conditions. The film was a forerunner of Blomkamp's third feature film, *Chappie*, which featured the same robot from *Tetra Vaal*, but this time in a science-fiction action-comedy. That big box office flick, however, loses some of the critical left politics of its predecessor. Despite their sometimes bold class analysis, Blomkamp's big budget, feature-length films seem to slide back into a liberal politics of individual heroism and self-actualization. His formative short, however, is chilling and prophetic.[1]

Tetra Vaal is a faux corporate advertisement for the eponymous corporation marketing robotic scouts to regulate South African townships. Here we glimpse a slender robotic guard, wearing a South African Police badge, striding through the streets with an assault rifle slung over its back while township dwellers go about their daily lives. They appear either already acclimated to or dominated by its presence. We even momentarily view the distressed urban landscape of traffic-choked streets, a tattered Panasonic billboard, smoldering barrel stoves, goat herds, children playing and busy market stalls, all viewed from the robot's perspective, before witnessing it engage in an intense firefight with an unseen combatant. The repressive application of this technology is made clear immediately. "What if," the opening caption reads, "we could build a system to help police developing nations?" We never see any whites in the film. They only appear as disembodied voices of security expertise and corporate marketing. Only the mechanized "mzungu" remains, settler class power as the ghost in the shell.

In *Tetra Vaal*, Blomkamp depicts the living labor of policing as potentially replaceable, a set of tasks that can be Taylorized, programmed, automated and made more efficient through experimentation and artificial intelligence. When a bullet fells the robotic scout, the film cuts to the industrial workshop where it is being repaired. Next, we see the rehabbed scout running at a steady clip on a treadmill before being placed back on patrol. Unnamed narrators, perhaps the robots' designers, satisfied clients, or maybe corporate pitchmen, reassure us that, unlike a highly skilled human sniper or beat cop who may be negatively affected by stress, cold, fatigue, and other variable conditions, this robotic alternative is "unbeatable."

The dystopian worlds conjured up by Blomkamp, where autonomous policing is used to secure society against deep inequality, have already been surpassed by our times. In the United States, the technology transfers between military and domestic policing legitimated through Executive Order 1033, the porous institutional boundaries and circular career tracks connecting active military service, policing and private security, and the broader siege mentality that has come to define American popular thinking after decades of urban crisis, drug wars, mass shootings, military adventurism and terrorism have combined to produce and legitimate architectural fortressing and militarized policing.[2]

In 2016, Dallas police ended a standoff with sniper Micah Xavier Johnson, who had killed five police officers and injured nine others, in what was the first documented use of a weaponized robot to kill a suspect in the United States. After two hours of bloodshed and negotiation, Dallas police loaded a pound of C4 explosives onto an Andros-series F5 robotic unit, produced by the Northup Grumman subsidiary Remotec.[3] Typically used for bomb disposal, the robot was maneuvered to its target by remote control, minimizing the risk to officers, to deliver the blast that killed Johnson. Amid the largest gathering of Native American tribes in decades to protest the ongoing construction of the Dakota Access Pipeline, which would desecrate ancestral burial grounds and jeopardize fresh water sources, the North Dakota legislature approved the non-lethal weaponization of drones.[4] Connecticut legislators debated the passage of similar legislation in 2017. In January 2020, Alameda County Sheriffs employed a camera-equipped robot, a Bearcat armored vehicle and a SWAT team to end a months-long struggle to evict a group of homeless parents, Moms 4 Housing, who had occupied a vacant home in protest of rent intensification.[5] In 2019, Boston Dynamics, a firm at the forefront of developing robots for industrial and military usage, revealed it had completed a three-month pilot project with the Massachusetts State Police to employ a "Spot," a robotic dog used for bomb detection.[6] Drones and robots are, of course, only one frontier of high-tech policing. Other technologies are already in various stages of development, experimentation, piloting and roll out in the United States and police departments globally, such as data mining and predictive policing, networked surveillance and fusion centers, shot locators, facial recognition software and new forensic techniques, as well as fully autonomous police cars and retrofitted automated units that enable police to issue traffic tickets without leaving the safety of their squad cars.[7]

This chapter sketches a left-critical view of police as a peculiar category of alienated workers and contemplates the social contradictions and latent political possibilities therein. Loyalty to the "enemies of workers" orthodoxy has prevented too many on the left from developing a keen historical-materialist analysis of the day-to-day working lives and roles of actual law enforcement officers, the ways different classes experience policing, the unique social conditions of late capitalism, and the roiling social contradictions that define working-class life in the United States. There are nearly 1.5 million law enforcement officers in the United States, serving in a vast mosaic of some 18,000 municipal, county, state and federal units, as well as a comparably sized workforce of private police. Police are not one-dimensional cogs, even if they are geared towards a particular social function. Police are not socially or politically monolithic. What is needed is a more dialectical view of police as labor, one that maintains the ethical condemnation of the primary function of police while appreciating their actually existing role as public workers within the neoliberal landscape of consumer capitalism and real estate–centered urban economic development. There are compelling political reasons for undertaking such an analysis because it is unlikely left progressive forces will achieve substantial reform without winning the war of position, securing popular consent for a different approach to public safety.

Police exist to protect private property and capitalist class interests; however, as argued here, the function of policing has evolved along with the substantial transformations of US society during the Cold War, including the suburbanization of American cities, which segregated urban space more intensively along class and racial lines; the elevation of middle-class consumerism as aspirational identity; and the erosion of working-class institutions and political power. The "enemies of the working class" argument remains true but is less compelling in relation to a society where so many working people do not possess a class hatred of capital, and where hundreds of millions of Americans view police power as legitimate and necessary for their own security and happiness. This is a longer standing political problem for the American left, and an acute problem facing contemporary Black Lives Matter protests and criminal justice reformers.

Unlike other parts of the public sector that have experienced violent contraction and defunding under neoliberalization, the experience of police departments nationally has been quite different. Growing economic insecurity among the masses, and fears of both real and imagined crime, have provided a ready pretext for the expansion of police departments and police budgets even as other elements of the public sector wither under advancing privatization. This expansion of police budgets, however, has not necessarily translated into hiring more officers; many departments face manpower shortages, often resorting to overtime pay and subcontracting to meet labor needs.[8] Despite being somewhat recession-proof, police departments have felt public pressure not just in the recent decades of street protests, but from constant waves of public outrage and demands for reform and more accountability over many years. Lawsuits by the families of those victimized or killed by police have rightly led to massive payouts in different cities. Watchdog organizations, FOIA requests, viral videos and political activism have forced the egregious actions of individual officers and the malfeasance of many departments into plain sight. In this context, capital-intensive policing has emerged as a viable means of addressing labor shortages and circumventing the problems highlighted by Black Lives Matter.

There are numerous reasons why we should reject this technological fix to the current problems of policing. Various forms of labor-saving technologies have the capacity to make conflicts less hazardous for officers, but in removing human decision-making, physical risks to officers and the personal responsibility that might be legally adjudicated or disciplined, such technologies may well make lethal policing more politically insulated. Moreover, as numerous critics have pointed out, once well-established strategies of stress policing and racial profiling are cloaked in scientific reason and managerial efficiency, departments may become impervious to the lines of criticism made popular through BLM demonstrations. Police should be just as concerned about the advance of intelligence-led and autonomous policing as civil libertarians, BLM activists and other critics are, because such technological change will have the same effect as it has had on other workers historically. Policing will likely undergo the same process of labor-force contraction, deskilling and reskilling that have defined deindustrialization and technological transformation in other industrial sectors. Some police may well find themselves in the reserve army they were once charged with regulating, with their labor increasingly undertaken by a small workforce of engineers and data managers.

Police as Alienated Workers

The most radical voices of contemporary antipolicing argue that the problem before us is not merely one of a few bad apples, or poorly trained cops, but rather of the institutions of policing and prisons themselves. This interpretative current is of long standing on the left, and not just in the United States; it is perhaps best summarized in the old skinhead and punk slogan, "All cops are bastards!" Often abbreviated as ACAB when scrawled in aerosol paint, this phrase captures the experience of police repression among the proletarian youth subcultures of Great Britain during the sixties and seventies and continues to resonate with similarly situated urban working-class populations around the world, wherever their autonomous activity and opposition runs counter to powerful interests.

In what follows, however, we will attempt an even more critical historical interpretation of policing, one that retains the powerful condemnation of police and their function in reproducing capitalist social order, while at the same time examining the labor relations that constitute policing as an institution and facet of the public sector. Perhaps unintentionally, the ACAB slogan captures this contradiction. If we revisit the origins of the term "bastard," both as an epithet for a child who is born out of wedlock and as the Christian moral judgment against such an unlawful act of procreation, then other interpretations of the slogan come into view. Cops are bastards, illegitimate offspring, in the deeper sense that they are born out of an unholy union between the capitalist class and the workers they exploit. Police are those segments of the working class who are enticed to do the labor of protecting capitalist interests, often in a context of declining options for stable working-class employment, and yet these same segments are armed and sicced against the collective organization and power of the workers themselves. Like the child born out of wedlock and destined to be a social outcast, police are alienated from the working class and shoulder society's moral and social contradictions.

A fundamental dimension of the Marxist notion of alienation is the estrangement of workers from the value they produce. Police are workers in the broadest possible sense of those who must sell their labor power in order to survive. Like other public workers, police do not produce surplus value; rather, their labor is reproductive, securing the conditions for perpetual accumulation. They are therefore fundamental to the maintenance of the capitalist social order. Marx, of course, did not limit his discussion of alienation to exploited workers, but saw individual capitalists as socially alienated as well. "The worker's propertylessness," he wrote, "and the ownership of living labour by objectified labour, or the appropriation of alien labour by capital—both merely expressions of the same relation from opposite poles—are fundamental conditions of the bourgeois mode of production, in no way accidents irrelevant to it."[9] Even as capitalists have exercised tremendous collective social power over workers, colonial subjects, societal institutions and the earth's resources, individual capitalists remain disempowered in many ways, compelled to transform their respective enterprises, adopt machinery and reorganize the labor process to stay competitive. Within the process of capital accumulation, the individual values or ideological dispositions of capitalists are subordinated to the coercive laws of competition.[10]

Of course, the quality of alienation that police experience is different, even from that of other public sector workers like postal employees or teachers. Police secure the essential private property rights and social conditions that make profit-making possible, ensuring a functioning system of property rights, courts and, perhaps most important of all, the control and readying of a subordinate labor force in compliance with the historically discrete requirements of capitalist production and distribution. Police regulation and prisons exist for those who might upset the capitalist social order by breaking its rules, whether in terms of basic disobedience of traffic laws or violation of property rights through so-called survival crimes, or in terms of intentional collective defiance of the status quo through organized work stoppages, slowdowns, factory occupations and street demonstrations. Of course, this repressive dimension of policing, its essential role, remains largely hidden from view by those who abide the norms and expectations of the capitalist social order. For these social strata, policing's role of serving and protecting their interests as condo owners, middle-class consumers, vacationers, or investors looking to, say, redevelop a shuttered warehouse into artist lofts, police fulfill a valuable role as guardian. Abolitionist and left criticism too often brushes aside this avuncular face of policing, even though this cultural consent to police authority is fundamental to perpetuating the current order. While police killings have dominated activist understandings of the institution, so much of the work that police do, such as procedural work and public relations, is mundane and largely valued by majority publics.

Even as millions of Americans have rejected police abuse and killing of civilians, most continue to see police as protectors of the public good, a view that forgets the fundamental role of police. Police have occupied a supersized role within American culture for decades, with their social beneficence valorized in popular entertainment, especially television and film. The crime-solving heroics of beat cops, cerebral crime-scene technicians, renegade officers, hard-boiled detectives, charismatic chiefs and amiable family men have provided material for multiple entertainment genres and subgenres, including noir pulp fiction, buddy cop action-comedies, procedural crime television dramas, documentary films and reality shows.[11] Such pop cultural renditions of policing are not uniform, nor are they all flattering, but taken in total they constitute a complex portrait of the social role of policing, public attitudes towards law enforcement, and the complicated demands of this branch of the bureaucracy bestowed with the legitimate use of force. Public perceptions of police, which were already favorable, have remained consistently strong over the last few years despite the moral force of Black Lives Matter protests.

Against such popular sentiments, Micol Seigel describes police as *violence workers*, reminding us that the legitimate use of state violence is the essence of police power. "The violence meted out by police is sometimes hard to see, and many people understand it as exceptional," Seigel writes. "They think police use violence only in extreme cases or when cops go bad, as in the wrongful use of force."[12] Police are the "human-scale expression of the state," she adds.[13] Seigel's conceptualization is useful, especially within an American context where police are imagined as protectors of benign public order. In this regard, Seigel's arguments are clarifying and cut through contemporary popular interpretations of the policing problem as rooted in some combination of corruption, racist fear, poor training, rogue officers or "bad apples," or the lack of civilian oversight. At the same time, to refer to police as violence workers carries two immediate burdens. At the level of theory, the characterization seems to suggest that we can govern without coercion. Saying that police are the human-scale expression of the state is not necessarily pejorative in certain contexts where law enforcement actually does secure the public good (arrest and prosecution of rapists, investigations of militias, responding to mass shootings, etc.). And, flowing from this first point, even if we acknowledge that the legitimate use of force is the basis of police power and state sovereignty, police routinely undertake a tremendous range and volume of tasks that have very little to do with the threat or execution of force. This is why terms like "police brutality" and even "police violence" came into common usage, precisely because the vast majority of Americans rarely experience the strong arm of law enforcement revealed in viral videos. When she characterizes police as violence workers, Seigel rightly reminds us of the essential source of police power, but she too notes that the vast majority of daily activities undertaken by officers are service-oriented and nonviolent.[14]

Police work encompasses affective labor: speaking to school children, engaging in public relations work, serving as emergency/ first responders in traffic collisions, house fires and other accidents, consoling victims of trauma, working with families and communities to solve crimes, collecting and interpreting crime-scene evidence, among other tasks. Too much contemporary left criticism of policing remains at the level of protest, a condemnation of the institution, stopping short of a critical-dialectical analysis of the institution, of the internal contradictions of those who carry out its work and the diverse American publics who support them.

Although he has been fashioned into a plaster saint of the antiracist left, James Baldwin's commentaries on ghetto policing provide us with some inspiration in crafting a more dialectical view of police as alienated workers. In his 1960 essay "Fifth Avenue, Uptown," Baldwin describes the Harlem ghetto where police move "like an occupying soldier in a bitterly hostile country," but he takes care to note the damage this daily work of managing the ghetto, *the labor of occupation*, does to police themselves. Baldwin led his *Esquire* magazine readers down tenement blocks and street corners they likely had never seen with their own eyes. Far from the glorious shopping corridor of Midtown Manhattan, Baldwin describes another side of Fifth Avenue, a netherworld where "so many, for so long," have been "struggling in the fishhooks, the barbed wire of this avenue."[15] This is the "wide, filthy, hostile Fifth Avenue," where tower block housing "hangs over the avenue like a monument to the folly, and the cowardice, of good intentions." And it is here that the most vulnerable are "victimized, economically, in a thousand ways—rent for example, or car insurance," Baldwin writes. "Go shopping one day in Harlem—for anything—and compare Harlem prices and quality with those downtown."[16] For Baldwin, the deep inequality reflected in the geography of Fifth Avenue, combining both opulence and destitution on the same street, yet worlds apart, and the pursuit of affluence and possessions, is the source of America's cultural ruin. The "American equation of success with the big time reveals an awful disrespect for human life and human achievement. This equation has placed our cities among the most dangerous in the world and has placed our youth among the most empty and most bewildered."[17] And yet this unjust order has to be maintained, an order where blacks are relegated to inferior housing, overcrowding, high prices for low quality goods, menial jobs or no jobs at all, and "the dark, the ominous schoolhouses from which the child may emerge maimed, blinded, hooked, or enraged for life."[18] Police must maintain the boundary dividing the different worlds of Fifth Avenue, of Manhattan, and throughout the country.

In a feat that is rare in today's social media debates and cancel culture, Baldwin demands that black humanity be recognized without losing sight of the dehumanizing effects on those charged with maintaining America's unjust racial order by force of arms.[19] The individual policeman is motivated by noble intentions, but all pretenses are shattered as he becomes fully aware of the social contradictions of his charge and the toll it takes on his spirit day in and out. And here Baldwin is clear about the cross purposes in play, about how faithful service to America does not include Harlem's denizens, but rather entails their daily harassment and perhaps death. "It is hard," Baldwin asserts, "to blame the policeman, blank, good-natured, thoughtless and insuperably innocent for being such a perfect representative of the people he serves." Baldwin says of the white officer assigned to patrol the ghetto: "He, too, believes in good intentions, and is astounded and offended when they are not taken for the deed. He has never, himself, done anything for which to be hated—which of us has?—and yet he is facing, daily and nightly, people who would gladly see him dead, and he knows it. There is no way for him not to know it: there are few things under heaven more unnerving than the silent, accumulating contempt and hatred of a people." The white officer stands on the dividing line between white affluence and black depravation. "The white policeman, standing on a Harlem street corner, finds himself at the very center of the revolution now occurring in the world," Baldwin writes. "He is not prepared for it—naturally, nobody is—and what is possibly much more to the point, he is exposed as few white people are to the anguish of the black people around him."[20]

How does the white patrolman live with himself? How does he reconcile his expressed purpose, to serve and protect, with his daily work, the violent containment of the black ghetto? Baldwin's insight regarding how the white officer resolves this moral dissonance is telling: "Even if he is gifted with the merest mustard grain of imagination, something must seep in. He cannot avoid observing that some of the children, in spite of their color, remind him of children he has known and loved, perhaps even of his own children. He knows that he certainly does not want *his* children living this way."[21] How does he manage the injustice of his occupation with the sense of humanity reinforced in him through daily interactions with black subjects? "He can retreat from his uneasiness in only one direction: into a callousness which very shortly becomes second nature," Baldwin concludes. "He becomes more callous, the population becomes more hostile, the situation grows more tense, and the police force is increased."[22] Instead of yielding to his conscience, his sense of right and wrong outside of the dictates of the job, the white patrolman retreats into racist ideology. He justifies his tasks as being necessary because of some cultural inferiority of ghettoized blacks, a move that will only deepen his resolve to uphold the law, however unjust. Baldwin foretells the conflagrations to come, the inevitability of rebellion against exploitation, predation and police brutality. "One day, to everyone's astonishment, someone drops a match in the powder keg and everything blows up," Baldwin writes. "Before the dust has settled or the blood congealed, editorials, speeches, and civil-rights commissions are loud in the land, demanding to know what happened. What happened is that Negroes want to be treated like men."[23]

Baldwin's 1966 essay "A Report from the Occupied Territory" deepens these insights. His premonitions having played out as Harlem, Rochester and Watts exploded into rioting, he is wiser and more critical regarding how he and other well-positioned blacks were cast in a brokerage role when black protests surged during the Johnson years. Baldwin describes the deplorable conditions and police violence that Harlem's residents endured amid the 1964 rebellion, especially the savage police beating of a young black door-to-door salesman, who was left partially blind. He also reflects critically on the machinations of Washington elites, and on his recruitment as a black spokesman along with others "no longer as totally at the mercy of the cops and landlords as once we were." He is unwilling to continue playing the role of "a good little soldier" who the Washington elites could consult about the Negro problem, and call on to disperse the black mob. These elites are less concerned with doing what is necessary to abolish the conditions that have produced mass rebellion than with suffocating any uprising that threatens their hold on formal power. Baldwin translates the elite's anxieties and veiled questions during their Washington luncheons into more explicit questions, getting to the source of their worries and the cure they desire: "Do you think that any of those unemployed, unemployable Negroes who are going to be on the streets all summer will cause us any trouble? What do you think we should do about it?" "But later on," Baldwin continues, "I concluded that I had got the second part of the question wrong, they really mean, what was I going to do about it?"[24] He is unwilling to play along, especially since they have little sincere interest in attacking the root causes of black mass discontent.

Once again, Baldwin grasped the economic and political forces that produced ghettoization. In harmony with James Boggs, Bayard Rustin and many others at the time, Baldwin made clear the immediate impacts of technological change on black labor. "The jobs that Negroes have always held, the lowest jobs, the most menial jobs, are being destroyed by automation," he notes. "No remote provision has yet been made to absorb this labor surplus."[25] Baldwin is clear about the abuses and transgressions of police, but again and again he returns to the broader structural conditions that need to be permanently changed, castigating the sheepishness of Washington liberals on these matters at every turn. He recalls his frustration in these occasional luncheons, and the failure of his hosts to understand the source of the "deep and dangerous estrangement" experienced by millions of Negroes. He wonders how they could not see the vulgar contradiction at work: "The principle on which one had to operate was that the government which can force me to pay my taxes and force me to fight in its defense anywhere in the world," Baldwin insists, "*does not have the authority* to say that it cannot protect my right to vote or my right to earn a living or my right to live anywhere I choose." He questions their reluctance to confront corporate powers, "the real estate lobby in Albany ... which is able to rebuild all of New York, downtown," but which is also responsible for unlivable conditions in Harlem. "Why is it not possible to attack the power of this lobby?" Baldwin asks. "Are their profits more important than the health of our children?"[26]

Baldwin pinpoints the limits of Great Society liberalism, which, despite its advances, stopped short of imposing limitations on capital in real estate markets through rent controls, housing cooperatives and sustainable public housing, all strategies that had helped previous generations of working-class white ethnics, but that were now abandoned under the capital-dominant growth policies of the postwar urban transformation. Instead of public goods, more policing would be on order in the decades after Baldwin's searing analyses of Harlem's ghettoization. The police are "simply the hired enemies of this population," Baldwin reminds us. "They are present to keep the Negro in his place and to protect white business interests, and they have no other function ... they know that they are hated, they are always afraid." Within this context, calls for blacks to "respect the law" are obscene, according to Baldwin: "Law is meant to be my servant and not my master, still less my torturer and my murderer." "To respect the law," he concludes, "in the context in which the American Negro finds himself, is simply to surrender his self-respect."[27]

Baldwin employs the notion of *occupied territory* as a metaphor for the discrete conditions of ghetto life and repressive policing, which most Americans were unfamiliar with amid the prosperity and optimism of the fifties and sixties, the days of space exploration and Camelot. In our own times, the forms of surveillance, repression and control that Baldwin experienced and witnessed in Harlem are no longer relegated strictly to the most dispossessed segments of society, but have become more general. Baldwin understood that these contradictions were unstable, socially untenable and morally unjust, bound to explode beyond the state-prescribed zones of containment. He attempted to prick the conscience of the nation, eventually shunning the role he was assigned by politicians more interested in controlling black rebellion than building a more just order. Baldwin understood police as workers, simultaneously heroic, villainous and tragic depending on the contexts and the relative class position of different publics.

The writer and filmmaker Pier Paolo Pasolini offered a similar take on police as tragic figures of the working class, but workers nonetheless. Remarking on the 1968 Battle of Valle Giulia, when Italian student militants clashed with police in Rome, Pasolini enraged the protestors and gave comfort to their critics when he valorized the cops as workers. Of course, Pasolini's views on police were more complicated than the critics conceded. His films were marked by bold protests against police violence—recall the ending of his 1962 film *Mamma Roma*, where young Ettore dies in a jail cell, bound and half-naked, screaming out for his mother. More importantly, the police never sided with Pasolini.[28] The police were, however, the "sons of poor people," Pasolini wrote. "They come from the outskirts, whether rural or urban." The protesting students, on the other hand, possessed "spoiled rich young men's faces." They were, according to Pasolini, "fearful, uncertain, desperate," "bullies, blackmailers and cocksure." "And then look how they're dressed up: like clowns," wrote Pasolini, "with that coarse fabric stinking of mess rations and the common people." "At Valle Giulia, yesterday," Pasolini went on, "there was indeed a fragment of class struggle: and you, friends (though on the right side) were the rich, while the cops (who were on the wrong side) were the poor."[29] Pasolini spoke as well of the acute alienation experienced by police, compounded by their paltry wages, "barely forty thousand lire a month." "Worse than everything, of course, is the psychological state they're reduced to, with no longer a smile, no longer in friendship with the world, separated, excluded," an exclusion Pasolini claimed "has no equal." Like Baldwin, he saw the brutish attitude of police as the inevitable consequence of this alienation, "humiliated by the loss of their quality as human beings or that of the cops (to be hated leads to hate)."

Italian autonomist Marxist Franco Berardi decries Pasolini's statement on police as "old populist rhetoric" and "Paccottiglia," which translates roughly as junk.[30] Pasolini was, according to Berardi, "a bad poet and an old-fashioned ideologue whose knowledge of Marxist philosophy was quite poor," but he was "a man of extraordinary vision." "Pasolini was totally wrong in his appraisal of the student movement because he missed the crucial point"; namely, that "the social origin of the students was not the important thing as much as the new role that cognitive work was destined to play in the transformation of capitalist production and in the political composition of the working class." The upheavals of 1968 in Italy and across the industrialized world "marked the initial emergence of cognitive work, which in the following decades became the main engine of production," Berardi writes. "The alliance between students and industrial workers was not a rhetorical exhibition of solidarity, but a sign of the increasing productivity and interdependence of industrial labor, the application of new technologies, and the prospect of liberating social time from the slavery of labor."[31] Against

Pasolini's characterization, Berardi also reminds us that many of the students hailed from the working class, even if others were the children of professionals and the petit-bourgeoisie. These are all important correctives to Pasolini's criticisms, but they may well miss the kernel of truth in Pasolini's initial intervention, which was less about the sociological origins of the police or the students, and more a reminder that left revolutionary politics should be anchored in the broad interests of the workers against those of capital—that it requires organizing the working class more broadly, in an historical process that necessarily includes engaging and winning over some reactionary elements, including military, police and would-be police.

The growing economic centrality of cognitive work after 1968, and the shifting sense of class consciousness that transformation precipitated, have made it more difficult to think and act in politically class-conscious terms in places like the United States. The social conditions of the mass worker, which dominated the economies of North America and Europe throughout the first half of the twentieth century, were marked by large-scale migration, Fordist urbanism, shop-floor unionism and point-of-production conflicts over wages, work rules and safety conditions. In the era of the mass worker, the role of police was unequivocal: to defend the interests of capital and crush working-class threats. As argued throughout this book, the economic-spatial transformations that accelerated after World War II did not simply transform Americans' understandings of their working lives, aspirations and political allegiances. Not only did millions come to see their immediate material interests as synonymous with those of corporations and the Cold War US state, they also saw police protection as benevolent and necessary for the advancement of those commonly held interests. These concomitant processes of large-scale suburbanization, middle-class expansion, the growing centrality of cognitive work, the invention of new forms of leisure consumption and entertainment, the powerful role of mass communication and the decimation of the old basis of worker organization and power, all served to shift the social fault lines of class conflict, even as the general tendencies of capitalism remained constant. Pasolini's statement on the police, like Baldwin's careful exposition of how officers reconciled their job assignment with degrading the humanity of blacks they encountered, were attempts to understand this new landscape produced out of the postwar economic and social transformation. We should follow their lead, however imperfect their assessments may be, because each points the way towards a more comprehensive analysis of societal contradictions and illuminates the path towards building a broad counterpower capable of winning a different order. Contemporary policing maintains its central function of protecting private property and capitalist interests above all others, but the institution of policing, and the hundreds of thousands who carry out its day-to-day functioning, are not reducible to this historical role. As with all other groups of workers, and all other large and complex institutions, there are internal social divides, different political interests at play, and unpredictable actors. Moreover, the work of occupation carries its own severe burdens and estrangement, both of which can become too much to bear for those charged with maintaining social order through violence and coercion.

The Hazards of Occupation

In February 2021, Clyde Kerr III, a forty-three-year-old black father, sheriff's deputy and army veteran who had served in Iraq and Afghanistan, looked directly into the camera and offered a searing criticism of policing in the United States. Kerr was the son of famed New Orleans jazz trumpeter and educator, Clyde Kerr, Jr. He was also a skilled cook who dreamed of opening a food truck. In a series of videos posted to Facebook, the longtime deputy conveyed a deep sense of turmoil over his profession, and condemned the criminal justice system as demonic. "I've had enough of all of this nonsense, serving a system that does not give a damn about me or people like me," Kerr said, speaking directly to recent protests over the killings of George Floyd. "You have no idea how hard it is to put a uniform on in this day and age with everything that's going on."[32] Kerr also evoked the names of Botham Jean, who was shot to death in 2019 inside his Dallas apartment by an off-duty police officer, and Breonna Taylor, who was killed in 2020 inside her Louisville home by police serving a no-knock warrant. The three videos Kerr posted were an extended suicide note. At one point he explained that his decision to take his life was an act of protest, and this was the time for "dramatic and bold" action.[33] On February 2, 2021, Kerr sat in his patrol car and took his life outside the Lafayette Parish Sheriff's Office.

Across the country, cities like Chicago have been grappling with the problem of police suicides for some time. In September 2017, CPD officer Regine Perpignan shot and killed herself on the parking lot of the Calumet District police station on Chicago's far South side. The twenty-six-year veteran officer had two daughters and a granddaughter. Perpignan had been battling depression, and relatives said she sought help through the department and was momentarily relieved of duty. "They put her back on duty too fast," her brother Roland Perpignan told reporters. "Someone who's been having mental issues and you know is not well should not be going back to duty ... and given a gun."[34]

On Sunday night, July 9, 2018, thirty-six-year-old officer Brandon Krueger shot himself while sitting his in car outside the same Calumet District station. Krueger was a Marine Corps veteran who had served a tour in Iraq. He worked for the department's Bureau of Organized Crime, which oversees narcotics and gang investigations. For a time, Krueger was assigned to the Englewood neighborhood, which has endured some of the highest homicide rates in Chicago. Less than a year before he took his own life, Krueger was involved in a deadly shooting while off-duty. He travelled to south suburban Hazel Crest to purchase a computer from Aaron and Dakvarie Brandon, black teenaged brothers. Krueger claimed that when the teens attempted to rob him, he opened fire, killing Aaron and injuring

Dakvarie. No charges were ever brought against Krueger, but after his death, the mother of the Brandon brothers filed a wrongful death suit against Krueger's estate and another suit against the Village of Hazel Crest for covering up the incident.[35] According to Krueger's mother, Diane Milani, he struggled with depression after his tour in Iraq, and the shooting incident worsened his condition. She recalls him sobbing after reading an obituary for the teen he had killed. Krueger's troubles were further compounded by divorce. He was receiving counseling at the Veterans Affairs hospital prior to his death. Less than two months before Krueger shot himself, his ex-wife made an emergency call to police after he started a video chat with her where he appeared to be attempting suicide.

Only two days after Krueger's death, forty-seven-year-old Vinita Williams collapsed at the Calumet District station. Although the ten-year veteran's death was not by suicide—it was later determined that she died of a heart attack—the third on-duty death of an officer in the same far South side district sent shockwaves through the department and served as another reminder of the real costs of police workplace stress. Five Chicago police died by suicide in 2018. Eight more CPD officers died by their own hand in 2019. Ten New York City police died by suicide the same year.

Nationally, more police officers die from suicide than from arrest-related shootings and traffic accidents combined. The Justice Department reported that between 2013 and 2015 the suicide rate among CPD officers was 60 percent higher than the national law enforcement average. This conclusion was based on CPD's official reporting of a suicide rate of 22.7 per 100,000. The Fraternal Order of Police provided figures that suggested an even higher rate of 29.4 per 100,000 department members.[36] While police who are killed by armed assailants in the line of duty are afforded a hero's funeral, with rows of officers in full dress uniform, spontaneous motorcycle rallies, roadside crowds viewing the procession, and social media outpourings of gratitude, police who die by suicide have for too long been made invisible.

First responder suicides are underreported in mainstream news media. The federal government does not officially track police suicides. Police officers are 69 percent more likely to die from suicide than are other workers, and detectives who work day in and day out on violent crime cases are 89 percent more likely. The data we have on police suicides is incomplete, having been gathered by independent researchers and nonprofit foundations. For the years where we have data, we know that there were 141 police suicides in 2008, 143 in 2009, 126 in 2012, 108 in 2016 and 140 in 2017.[37] The actual rate of police suicide is likely greater still, since some deaths are intentionally misclassified either to protect the reputation of the deceased or because reporting a death as suicide would jeopardize the survivor benefits for the families they leave behind.

Like other first responders, police develop an intimacy with death, and a familiarity with the worst aspects of the human condition. They experience the immediate aftermath of homicides, brawls, suicides, mass shootings, traffic accidents, industrial and environmental catastrophes, so we, the broader public, do not have to, shouldering the responsibility and trauma of such life-altering events. Some have argued that the culture of policing, and of first responders more generally, which requires the appearance of mental toughness and unflappability, may dissuade some from pursuing effective and sustained mental health support. Depression, anxiety, post-traumatic stress disorder and suicidal ideation do not likely stem from a single incident, but rather from compounding experiences of the trauma and job stress of first responder service, along with the broader family stressors and personal and social crises we all experience in varying ways. Speaking directly to the context of Chicago, clinical psychologist and former CPD officer Carrie Steiner holds that the high suicide rate stems from the uniquely high level of trauma experienced by Chicago first responders over the last decade. Between 2014 and 2019, Chicago police investigated nearly 3,000 homicides resulting in what Stein calls "cumulative trauma." "When you're seeing all of that trauma, you start to change your total core belief system," she points out, "and you're going to have more pessimistic officers, more officers that just don't believe that what they do has a purpose."[38]

Despite the dismal trend in police suicide, many departments have not allocated adequate investment and personnel to address the problem, and the CPD's mental health services for officers were woefully understaffed for years. As reported in the 2017 Justice Department investigation, Chicago only provided three in-house clinicians for a workforce of 12,500, compared to Los Angeles, which has twelve clinicians for 10,000 employees, and the Miami-Dade police department, which provides six counselors for 2,900 officers and 1,700 staff.[39] Those three Chicago clinicians were saddled with staffing some 7,498 mental health consultations/appointments in 2015. The consent decree issued by the Obama administration's Justice Department recommended that the CPD hire a minimum of ten clinicians and provide non-emergency counseling to officers within two weeks of a request, as well as round-the-clock emergency counseling. The CPD was slow to follow through on these recommendations despite pressure from those within law enforcement for police departments to take more aggressive measures to address mental health concerns.

The voices of current and retired officers, as well as health care professionals, have since grown louder, breaking the silence that once shrouded this issue, with many placing the blame squarely on management for failing to recognize the problem and talk openly about it with staff. "I found myself suicidal as the result of post-traumatic stress disorder and depression," writes Andy O'Hara, "and, as a police officer, felt the need to hide my mental health challenges due to the stigma that exists within the culture of law enforcement."[40] A twenty-four-year veteran of the California Highway Patrol, O'Hara set up Badge of Life, a nonprofit organization that collects data on police suicides and provides training and resources for police mental health and suicide prevention. "There is a code of secrecy around mental illness in police agencies across the nation," O'Hara continues, "a code that is difficult to break though." "Rather than advising officers to get help when they 'need it,'" O'Hara insists, "it should be strongly encouraged that officers attend regular therapy sessions with a licensed counselor, whether it is through an employee counseling service or on the 'outside' to assure confidentiality."[41] This crisis of police suicides, the real risks and stressors facing officers, popular protests against police violence, the actions of legislative budget hawks looking to reduce spending, and the well-established circuits of industrial technology transfers between the national military and domestic policing have combined to accelerate the turn to capital-intensive policing. Many have come to embrace *dead labor*—the increased use of automated technologies and logistics—as a more politically and fiscally viable alternative to the problem of *dead officers*, felled by criminal assailants or by their own hands.

The Nightmare and Dream of Autonomous Policing

Sgt. Henry Lawson is a twenty-three-year veteran of the Wardenville Police Department. He keeps his tie loosened. Drinks coffee continuously. Still takes a smoke whenever he can, and curses e-cigarettes as the devil's making. He's chief detective on staff, it is a little after 5 a.m. and he's just begun a homicide investigation. A shot locator picked up the sound of a single discharge around 4:45 a.m., and a responding officer discovered the deceased after talking to neighbors.

Lawson pulls onto the curb. Not much to see at the crime scene. A single gunshot wound to the chest, likely a small caliber handgun. No signs of struggle. The victim is seated in a peeling vinyl Barcalounger. His television and gaming system are still paused. Half a pepperoni pizza, a translucent green ganja pipe and spent cans of cheap beer sit on the coffee table. The victim is a twenty-three-year-old white male, Chris Lincoln, known to his friends as "Chopper." He split his time between working the afternoon shift at a local Tim Horton's, selling prescription meds and occasionally uploading unboxing videos of collectible action figures.

From his car, Detective Lawson uses software that aggregates data from numerous social media sites, records of restricted drug purchases from pharmacies throughout the state, missing persons and open search warrants, the census and other databases. Within a few minutes, he is able to map a network of Lincoln's friends, illustrated in a web of encircled photos with colored border-shading ranging from green to yellow to red to reflect the intensity of interactions and plausibility of suspects. Lawson also integrates this emerging social map with metropolitan and regional gang databases, as well as arrest and conviction records from the local police department and state and federal agencies. What emerges is not only a visual display of Lincoln's social world, spanning nearly a thousand or so social contacts, but how and through whom that world is connected to the region's narcotics economy. His aunt Viola Lincoln shows up as an intense connection, but she has no prior convictions, only unpaid tickets. Lawson momentarily opens a web search of her name, finding mostly articles in the local weekly about Viola's volunteer work, a Pinterest trove of mid-century modern furniture and décor ideas, and her stray online photos. Some of Lincoln's more intense social connections are less savory. Lawson focuses on the prime suspects generated by the software's algorithm—individuals with close ties, prior offenses, especially for violent crimes, and geographic proximity. Three high matches emerge, their photos encircled almost completely in red—Raymont Sandifer, Julia West and Antonio Mathias. Sandifer is immediately ruled out. He has been in the county jail for the last week waiting to post bail. West and Mathias were in town based on voluntary social media location info. West is brought in for questioning and released, but Mathias can't be located.

Lawson requests a networked surveillance camera search for Mathias's late model Ford Mustang, pearl white with a black fender panel waiting to be painted. Within minutes Lawson is able to pull up the route of Mathias's movements over the last twenty-four hours, using public and private surveillance as well as traffic cameras. Two pertinent details emerge. His car was near Chris Lincoln's house the night of the murder, and its most recent location is 1372 West Lowell Street. Lawson searches the location and the previous suspect mapping—the house is the residence of Mathias's girlfriend Tangela Neil, though legally belonging to her father according to public records. Mathias's fingerprints also match those found on beer cans at Lincoln's place. Lawson contacts the department's Autonomous Tactical Unit (ATU) specialist, and they consult with the department chief. The three decide to proceed with an arrest at midnight based on the determinations of the prime suspect software, the print matches and the location of Mathias's car the night of the murder. Closed-circuit security video also recorded Mathias and Lincoln entering a nearby convenience store around 6 p.m. the night before. A warrant is issued before Lawson refills his coffee and fishes out his next cigarette.

The ATU specialist, Crystal Kinsey, is a recent university graduate who is interned with a nationally recognized robotics company. Technically, she's still subcontracted through that company, lending her expertise in drones and industrial robotics to the local police department. Kinsey and Lawson park their tactical van at the end of the 1300 block of West Lowell Street. Kinsey releases two small aerial drones that circle the perimeter of Tangela Neil's property. Hypersensitive audio recording equipment as well as thermal cameras detect at least three persons inside the house, one apparently a young child. Lawson gives the ok signal for the arrest process to begin. Three robotic dogs fitted with body armor and non-lethal weapons are dispatched. All three are equipped with multi-directional cameras. Two proceed to the rear of the house, where the residents are located, and one bot approaches the front door. Their movements are smooth and virtually silent against the whir of nearby highway traffic and the occasional burst of laughter and muffled music flowing from the wood-frame houses lining the block. The dogs give an audible warning of the arrest and simultaneously force open the front and back doors—each dog's "head and neck" is actually a reticulated claw. They release non-toxic smoke grenades into the house to disorient the occupants and reduce visibility. The lead bot locates the child, presents her with a stuffed animal and plays the theme music from the highest-rated children's show in that market. Softly grasping her hand, the police dog leads her through the haze and out the front entrance. Kinsey wraps her in a Mylar blanket and takes her to the rear of the police van, out of sight. Neil is caught first in the living room. Disoriented, she submits, is cuffed and led outside. Mathias barricades the bedroom door in the chaos and escapes through a window. He sprints towards a nearby patch of pinewoods, but the third bot fires a bolo-like device that wraps his lower legs, causing him to crash shoulder first into a firewood rack in the neighbor's backyard. Lawson secures his hands with flexible cuffs.

Kinsey and Lawson load the suspects into the van, reading them their Miranda rights. Inside the van's detention compartment, mounted retinal scans of Mathias and Neil record the arrest and upload the time, address and other pertinent information to the state's criminal offense cloud archive. A relative of Neil, who lives two blocks over, is already on hand to take the daughter for the night. Lawson savors some menthol while Kinsey inspects the drones and dogs as she stores them for recharging and records any damage.

An arrest that may have taken days if not weeks of legwork, interviews and interrogation, and required a small phalanx of SWAT officers, was executed in less than twenty-four hours, before the coroner could deliver a full autopsy report on Lincoln's body, and with few warm-blooded workers involved. Wardenville's police department had shrunk from nearly ninety beat cops and office staff down to forty in less than a decade. After years of budget shortfalls and population loss, city officials had to find other ways to maintain public safety in this rusting midwestern city of 35,000.

Of course, Wardenville is fictional, but all the technology brought to bear here already exists and could easily be implemented to meet the needs of cash-strapped jurisdictions, depopulated regions and cities where police brutality and the public relations and legal morass such incidents created have prompted reductions in waged employees. Scientists, military and law enforcement personnel have debated the ethics of using robotics and artificial intelligence in the field for some time now, but except for fleeting protests over the use of weaponized drones, much of the US public still sees unmanned weaponry as the realm of science fiction. What we witnessed in Dallas in 2016 in the case of Micah Xavier Johnson troubled civil libertarians, anti–police brutality protesters and some law enforcement officials alike, but the use of robotics provided the remedy some are looking for.[42] Given the many existing uses of big-data policing, the ongoing legislation to weaponize drones in select states, and the incredibly agile and dexterous robotic police dogs developed and piloted by Boston Dynamics, the world of autonomous policing sketched here is already at hand.

These tools do not stand outside the nexus of capitalist class relations, institutional power and bourgeois ideology; rather, such technologies emerge from that cradle, bearing the interests of their creators. Against hegemonic notions of impartial scientific truth, Andrew Feenberg reminds us that technological development is socially constituted and deeply ideological. In every technology—that is, in every solution to a problem, whether a toaster, automated car wash or dating app—we find the condensation of those historically discrete interests, social values and biases that precipitated and shaped their invention. "The technical ideas combined in the technology are relatively neutral," Feenberg notes, but in every manifestation we can trace "the impress of a mesh of social determinations that preconstruct a domain of social activity in accordance with certain interests and values."[43] "Capitalism is unique in that its hegemony is largely based on reproducing its own operational autonomy through technical decisions." Moreover, he concludes, "Capitalist social and technical requirements are condensed in a 'technological rationality' or a 'regime of truth' that brings the construction and interpretation of technical systems into conformity with the requirements of a system of domination."[44]

Technology-intensive policing is not merely a matter of using smarter tools, as politicians, police superintendents and engineering wunderkinds might have us believe, no more than the adoption of robotic spot welders on automotive assembly lines or shipping containers in industrial ports were simply a matter of efficiency. The latter technologies were born in response to barriers to capital accumulation, namely the organized power of autoworkers and longshoremen, respectively. New technology-intensive forms of policing have been precipitated by different historical forces, including the pressures of various publics, victims' families, civil libertarians, prisoners' rights advocates and, more recently, Black Lives Matter demonstrations, who have demanded peace, safety, more racial justice and greater transparency from police departments. Intelligence-led policing and automated technologies provide a means of circumventing the kind of genuine reforms demanded by antipolicing forces, reforms that would require social redistribution and substantial changes to the current order. The use of drones either with remote operation, artificial intelligence or some combination of these, replaces human judgment and responsibility with algorithmic decision-making and bureaucratic detachment, potentially evading the legal morass that might stem from shootings committed by flesh-and-blood officers. Such technologies are born out of established modes of policing, inheriting their biases and values, without altering the broader class relations policing exists to manage, and yet producing new problems. Protests that focus on the extremes of police violence without fully contesting the social hegemony of policing, how and why policing retains the consent of vast portions of the public, will only further the adoption of these technologies, especially when robotics engineers and other scientists have also gained the trust of publics and popularized the efficacy and humanity of their design solutions.

The robotic police dogs described in the Wardenville hypothetical are inspired by the actual designs of Boston Dynamics, a firm that has captivated public imagination over the past two decades with viral videos depicting highly mobile, nimble, humorous and multifunctional robots. The rise of Boston Dynamics also reveals the ideological and technical linkages between the American military and domestic policing. With an infusion of DARPA (Defense Advanced Research Projects Agency) funding, the company was called upon to develop a pack robot, the Big Dog, capable of carrying heavy equipment alongside troops into the battlefield.[45] The software and engineering developed in that original Big Dog design have since spawned a few generations of quadruped and biped robots, with numerous potential military and industrial applications. Each generation of Boston Dynamics robots has developed greater traction, improved capacity to navigate uneven terrain, and greater speed and functionality. The Cheetah, for instance, set the land speed record for a quadruped robot, clocking a higher peak speed than 100 meter world-record holder Usain Bolt.[46] Videos of the two-wheeled Handle robot, whose silhouette resembles a person riding a Segway, feature it nimbly stacking boxes in a warehouse, moving them from shelf to pallet with ease.[47] And despite its stature, standing at 6 feet 5 inches tall, it is incredibly agile. Videos of the Handle show it navigating stairs and executing a move like a skateboarder's "ollie," where it achieves a rolling four-foot vertical leap.

Boston Dynamics' Spot robot is much lighter and more compact than its predecessors and is poised for immediate usage by law enforcement. Like the rest of the company's products, the Spot appeals to the sci-fi geek and technophile in many of us. It reflects the broad societal valorization of scientific progress, which, though threatened in today's wave of conspiracy theory and anti-intellectualism, reigned throughout the Cold War era, is celebrated by the ruling class as necessary to maintain US imperialism, and remains cherished by Americans in general as the material incarnation of the good life, evidence that high-tech capitalism might solve all problems. The development of military technology has long been intimately connected to domestic prosperity, with defense spending serving as a dominant driver of local economic development and job creation since World War II. Likewise, the surplus uses of military technologies, such as aerosol cans, food preservation, automotive engineering, jet propulsion, etc., secured domestic faith in the virtuousness of military invention, providing tangible applications that were seen as improvements to daily life.

Within this cultural context, the Spot robot may be welcomed by publics who are impressed by gadgetry, others who see it as a social necessity to keep law enforcement out of harm's way, and still others who may see the device as a more humane alternative to the exploitation of German Shepherds and Rottweilers for police work. Boston Dynamics' campaign to capture the public imagination and make the Spot a familiar sight on construction sites, transportation terminals and city streets is well under way. One viral video published by the firm shows a team of Spot robots pulling a truck uphill, another features a unit dancing to Marc Ronson and Bruno Mars' "Uptown Funk" without missing a beat, and one of the most popular videos shows the robot opening a door as a person repeatedly attempts to stop it.[48]

The introduction of the Spot robot and other similar technologies will likely be seen as a boon to law enforcement. The Spot requires routine maintenance but not a living wage, medical leave or recreation time. Like all consumer goods, the Spot will have a life span, either because of attrition or planned obsolescence, but it will not require a retirement banquet, commemorative plaque or set of golf clubs, nor, to the delight of fiscal conservatives, will it need a pension. While the videos of the Spot are charming, once such technology is integrated into the entrenched modes of policing it will become no different from a taser, Monadnock PR-24, Dodge Enforcer, Glock 9mm, body camera, Mossberg riot shotgun or any other technology used by police to enforce state power.

From Policing the Feral City to Policing the Smart City

There is no way to separate out the martial origins of this technology from its domestic application, especially when law enforcement proceeds now with many of the same ideological assumptions about the "enemy" and the same strategic and tactical approaches developed in international combat. The origins of the ongoing robotics and logistics revolution in policing lie in American military research and development, and in particular the long-gestating ideas about reducing US troop casualties and achieving total battlefield supremacy that gained renewed financial and political support in response to the strategic challenges of the Iraq War. Richard J. Norton's 2003 essay "Feral Cities" offers precious little about the actual social character, quotidian experiences and economic life of mega-city slums, but it does provide us with a journey into the new imperial heart of darkness and the paranoia and preoccupations of an investor class now facing down the ruin, volatility and uncertainty it has unleashed on the planet. Norton defines a "feral city" as "a metropolis with a population of more than a million people in a state of government which has lost the ability to maintain the rule of law within the city's boundaries yet remains a functioning actor in the greater international system." "In a feral city," he continues, "social services are all but nonexistent, and the vast majority of the city's occupants have no access to even the most basic health or security assistance. There is no social safety net." Such cities, Norton anticipates, will be defined by "massive levels of disease" and "enough pollution to qualify as an international environmental disaster zone." Blomkamp's Johannesburg makes an appearance in Norton's advisory as well, as a cautionary tale of sorts. Norton sees Johannesburg as being on the brink of going feral, becoming a place where police are "waging a desperate war for control of their city, and it is not clear they will win."[49] Never does Norton attribute such worsening social and environmental conditions, poverty and political instability to either the longer historical project of imperialism, or to contemporary predation by extractive industries and powerful northern-based corporations. It is this very system that he hopes to preserve, despite its pernicious consequences for billions of people globally.

This relation between the "feral city" and the "greater international system" is a crucial linchpin of Norton's claims, and the source of his concern. His essay is descended from the anxious post-Cold War discourse established in Robert Kaplan's 1994 essay, "The Coming Anarchy," where he warned of the advent of a "rundown, crowded planet of skinhead Cossacks and juju warriors."[50] Like Kaplan in that earlier essay, Norton is equally concerned about those conditions that might threaten international trade and capital flows. The connective thread between Kaplan's and Norton's essays is their commitment to the neoliberal capitalist order. This is the source of their worry—not necessarily pandemics, roving gangs, dangerous tribalism, powerful cartels, criminal syndicates and ecological ruin as such, or even what these destructive forces might mean for local populations, but how these developments may undermine the hegemony of northern capital and perpetual accumulation. Both made the case for military intervention and security as a means of preserving the international capitalist economy.

So-called feral cities "would exert an almost magnetic influence on terrorist organizations," Norton claims, and pose unique challenges to military intervention and the maintenance of order. "Such metropolises will provide exceptionally safe havens for armed resistance groups," he warns, "especially those having cultural affinity with at least one sizable segment of the city's population." The city's vast size, Norton cautions, "with its buildings, other structures, and subterranean spaces, would offer nearly perfect protection from overhead sensors, whether satellites or unmanned aerial vehicles." "Collecting human intelligence against them in this environment," he concludes, "is likely to be a daunting task."[51] Norton's concerns are old, of course. The powerful have always obsessed over how to maintain their power. In his defense of military forces as the only legitimate option, we can hear echoes of the "Mad Mullah" and "Mau Mau" discourses that gripped British administrators and settlers and justified their brutality against native peoples, and, closer to home, of the myth of the urban sniper that dominated public understandings and media coverage of urban rebellions in the sixties and provided the pretext for national guard mobilizations.

More direct democracy, greater distribution of global wealth, reparations and improved infrastructure and health care for the "wretched of the earth" are not Norton's concern. His ideological commitment to the current capitalist world system prevents him from considering the virtues of armed resistance and the anarchy he fears for the millions of people who have been history's losers from the age of imperial conquest through post-colonial independence, proxy wars and neoliberalization. "Some elements, be they criminals, armed resistance groups, clans, tribes, or neighborhood associations," he writes, "exert various degrees of control over portions of the city."[52] He rules out whatever political aspirations these groups embody as illegitimate; they are merely impediments to capital flows and profit-making. The only prescription Norton can provide is more sophisticated military technologies that might surmount the logistical and tactical problems created by mega-city slums. His fears of the ungovernable city have their domestic American correlates as well, and so much of US law enforcement philosophy—beginning with the urban crisis of the sixties and local responses to black rebellion—have assumed force is the only effective state response to deepening inequality, a governing ideology that has become more entrenched under neoliberalization.

These perceptions of urban danger, assumptions about black and brown criminality, and class hatred of the poor will continue to inform how new technologies are implemented within departments. While the prospect of police robots continues to provide nightmare fuel for the populace and grist for science-fiction writers, data-driven policing, also referred to as "intelligence-led policing" and predictive policing, is already in motion, and a growing chorus of lawyers, community activists and academics have raised the alarm about its potential dangers, even as broader publics remain oblivious to these developments. The fictional scenario sketched out here, where an officer utilizes his squad car's lap top to sift through enormous data archives, networked surveillance cameras, social media profiles and commodified data to quickly develop a likely suspects list, reflects technologies and strategies that are already in use.[53] Far from being made from whole cloth, these developments in policing trail earlier logistics revolutions in industrial production and transnational shipping, where data on consumer preferences, waste and other aspects of commodity production and distribution is collected, catalogued and marshalled to generate greater efficiency. Intelligence gathering has long been a central activity of modern policing, from the cliché of the trench-coated detective going door-to-door collecting clues with notepad in hand, to the more chilling methods of secret police wiretapping, undercover cops infiltrating and undermining revolutionary organizations and criminal syndicates alike, and ubiquitous video surveillance. The rapid circulation of information, the broad public consent to data mining through social media and retail activity, the corporate sale of such data, and advances in artificial intelligence have combined to create new modes of intelligence gathering for the purpose of social regulation. In China, surveillance cameras and facial recognition technology have been used to regulate jaywalking. Mounted cameras at some crosswalks photograph offenders, use facial recognition to identify and fine those who break street-crossing rules, and instantaneously display their names and photographs on digital displays, publicly shaming them for their infraction.[54] Westerners have criticized this practice and the prospects of a more expansive social credit system in China, but the same modes of policing through data are already in use here in the United States, with little opposition beyond the most active layers of antipolicing activists, academics and civil libertarians.

Elizabeth Joh's critical work on new technologies and autonomous policing considers the dangers of the smart city, one pervaded by visual and data surveillance and real-time feedback loops. "In a smart city, controls might arise from the urban infrastructure itself," Joh writes. "Those identified as probably shoplifters or credit card thieves might be banned from entering certain places."[55] Hence, we can already see how the hardscapes that defined the initial wave of urban revanchism—a world of Jersey barriers, mounted police, checkpoints, private security and perimeter fencing—can be supplanted with less physically imposing but no less secure systems of regulation that restrict the movement of those deemed criminal and undesirable through social credit ranking, retinal scanners, facial recognition, public shaming and electronic detention. "An all-purpose public autonomous robot might identify you as a threat and automatically deploy an electric stun gun," Joh anticipates. "Your own autonomous car—in conjunction with road sensors—might make it impossible to speed, change lanes illegally or run red lights. Some forms of law breaking might be rendered impossible and others discouraged through denials of entry and provision of incentives."[56]

Some of these technologies of autoregulation are already in use in the United States in forms that are often touted as virtuous responses that improve public safety. In some states, those who have been found guilty of drunk driving can have a mandatory breathalyzer installed in their automobiles, which will prevent the motorist from starting the ignition if she fails the sobriety test. Electronic detention has been advanced by some who see it as a more humane and social alternative to warehousing in brick-and-mortar prisons. Electronic monitoring via ankle bracelets has been in use for years now in various jurisdictions throughout the United States and is increasingly touted to reduce jail overcrowding and the public costs of housing nonviolent offenders and those awaiting trial. Others see such technologies, sometimes referred to as e-carceration or electronic incarceration, as a better alternative to the social isolation of prison, since house arrest allows the accused and convicted to maintain some semblance of connection to family and community. A growing number of critics, however, have challenged the turn to e-carceration, seeing it not as a more socially just alternative to the current system of mass incarceration, but as a more nefarious refinement of that system, one based on risk assessments hewn from the same racist and class assumptions that currently guide stress policing and targeting practices. "Challenging these biased algorithms may be more difficult than challenging discrimination by the police, prosecutors and judges," writes celebrated legal scholar Michelle Alexander. "Many algorithms are fiercely guarded corporate secrets. Those that are transparent—you can actually read the code—lack a public audit so it's impossible to know how much more often they fail for people of color."[57]

There are other critics of e-carceration and policing through big data, who share Alexander's sense that these technologies will perpetuate Jim Crow–like inequalities, but there is reason to believe that the turn towards technology-intensive policing will have the opposite effect, analogous to previous revolutions like the extensive use of DNA evidence in crime investigations.[58] The cultural certitude of scientific evidence and mathematical reason, though not devoid of human biases and fallibility, can have the longer-term effect of intensifying the precariousness of the most submerged segments of the working class regardless of ethnicity, and, simultaneously, making the forms of policing and social regulation impervious to charges of racism and demands for racial redress. In his study of intelligence fusion centers, Brendan McQuade offers a more compelling accounting of these developments. "Decarceration does not challenge the punitive approach to mass incarceration," he writes. "Instead, it realigns the criminal legal system around mass supervision, an administrative strategy that emphasizes policing and surveillance over imprisonment to manage class struggle and continually (re)produce capitalist social relations."[59] Given the ways that particular forms of liberal antiracism have been embraced throughout the era of neoliberalization and mass imprisonment, the processes of decarceration and more efficient policing are already unfolding in a manner that is propelled by certain antiracist commitments even as it retrenches capitalist class relations.

One illustrative case of how police reform and corporate antiracism work together is the CPD's collaboration with Clarity Partners on predictive policing. This Chicago-based company came to the public's attention in 2016, after it was tapped to help in creating a "strategic subject list" for the CPD. The list could be used to build social network profiles of shooting victims instantaneously using banked data, and law enforcement would employ that information in investigations and efforts to prevent retaliatory shootings. In September 2016, *Crain's Chicago Business* published an article celebrating the innovativeness of Clarity Partners and the potential impact the firm might have on crime reduction strategies. That story inadvertently exposed the pilot project and drew a round of public scrutiny and protests against the already embattled Rahm Emanuel mayoral administration. The article described how the strategic subject list would work, giving a glimpse of the new intricacies of surveillance: "Now, for example, the software's user interface can pull a photo of a shooting victim, with a spider web radiating to known associates and yet more ties extending to their associates, mapping an entire social network in one glance."[60] Although the principal investigators supervising the pilot project waved off claims of the project's predictive capacity, this was clearly a next logical step. Most immediately, such strategies create a greater likelihood of civil rights violations and risks to privacy, and, worse, this mode of policing through data management, like the advancement of DNA testing and crime forensics, will intensify current inequalities, lending an air of scientific infallibility to a system that is fundamentally unjust and predicated on the maintenance of class hierarchy.

What was especially galling about this public-private collaboration was the way racial justice was incorporated in an opportunistic manner. Clarity Partner co-founder David Namkung is Korean and qualifies for minority contracting setasides under federal and municipal ordinances. Perhaps the perfect cover story for an administration under pressure from Black Lives Matter activists. Yet at the same time, Clarity Partners defended the data set, claiming that it does not track by race and neighborhood. This latter claim seems highly implausible, unless somehow a criminal suspect's legal residence is excluded and not pertinent to police work. It also seems rather disingenuous given Chicago's well-known history of racial segregation. While the city is not as segregated as it once was, it still possesses the largest contiguous black urban settlement in the country, and race, class and residence are more synonymous in Chicago than in most American large cities.

Although it has been a flashpoint for organizing against mass incarceration, the notion of the prison-industrial complex may well overstate the centrality of the profit motive in the carceral expansion.[61] There was certainly money to be made in policing and prisons, but as Loïc Wacquant has argued, statecraft was more decisive in the carceral expansion as politicians sought to address and assuage public fears over crime and social unrest.[62] What the Clarity Partners case makes clear, however, is the cozy relationship between the repressive state apparatus, corporations and the university. In 2009, Miles Wernick, an engineering professor at Illinois Institute of Technology, developed the algorithm that Clarity used to construct its crime-prevention database. According to their projections, Clarity expected to rake in $21 million in revenue in 2016, largely due to public sector contracts. Their revenue has grown by 623 percent since 2008. The company has been named by Inc. 5000 as one of the fastest growing firms for seven consecutive years. Not surprisingly, Clarity Partner's relationship with the CPD is not limited to their development of the strategic subjects list; the company has also been a continuing sponsor of the Chicago Police Memorial Foundation, which hosts an annual ceremony and other events to recognize officer bravery and honor those lost in the line of duty. In contrast with the military-industrial complex, which former general Dwight Eisenhower decried during his farewell address as president in 1961, the prison-industrial complex does not have the same broad economic impact or the promise of job creation for millions, but one can easily see how community anxieties about crime, constituent pressure, short-term self-interest, the promise of academic recognition or professional accolades, adoration of peers, marquee contracts and grants, coveted pork-barreling for politicians and the profit motive of corporations all converge to propel these projects forward. And yet, these same disparate actions and self-interests at play also inhibit sustained critical reflection by all the individual parties involved on the potentially negative social consequences of these new experiments in more efficient policing.

Police and Left Political Organizing

Attempts by popular and worker struggles to influence police have been difficult historically, because of the recalcitrance and conservatism of policing as an institution, and the popular left antipathy towards police already described here. As historian Sidney Harring notes: "Although some working-class political actions achieved success ... even when they were successful, they usually managed only to restrict the scope of anti-working-class police activity, never to redirect the police against the bourgeoisie."[63] This is generally true, but there are important and instructive exceptions, such as the role of police in repressing white supremacist insurrection at the Battle of Liberty Place in Reconstruction New Orleans, and the emergence of splinter formations like the Afro-American Patrolman's League and other groups and solitary actors who confronted police brutality from within departments. Such real historical events reveal that police are not socially monolithic, and contradict the common arguments, already prevalent before the murder of George Floyd, that the power of police unions and the protections insured through union contracts permit misconduct to flourish unpunished and make it difficult to press for substantive reforms. A small chorus of progressive-to-radical left union voices have pointed out the empirical and political limitations of this argument, instead defending collective bargaining for all public workers and pointing to the possibility of organizing progressive elements of police for effective reforms.

Many BLM activists, criminal justice reformers and citizens believe that police unions protect bad cops and enable bad behavior, but as Gordon Lafer makes clear, this activist canard is not supported empirically.[64] Police unions may advocate for terrible legislation and oppose reforms like mandatory body cameras and civilian oversight, but, Lafer notes, "it's a mistake to believe that these things come from police unions, against the wishes of kinder-hearted mayors and governors, or that getting rid of police unions would eliminate a lot of the problems of police brutality." When we look at the picture nationally, as opposed to anecdotal evidence, it becomes clear that taking away the collective bargaining rights of police would have little impact on violence against civilians. For example, five southern states where police unions are illegal—Virginia, North Carolina, South Carolina, Tennessee and Georgia—do not have lower rates of arrest-related deaths and police brutality incidents than unionized jurisdictions. In fact, some states like Tennessee have higher levels of police violence than states where police unions are the norm. Between 2013 and 2019, police in Tennessee killed civilians at a per capita rate of four persons per 100,000 among the total population and 5.5 per 100,000 for African Americans.[65] Comparatively, states with collective bargaining agreements had lower per capita rates of police killings. New York had 1.1 per 100,000 for the general population and 3.3 for African Americans, while Michigan recorded 1.7 per 100,000 for the general population and 4.4 for African Americans.[66] There is no correlation or causality between the presence of police unions and increased violence against civilians.

If these numbers are not enough to challenge BLM and left activist fealty to anti–police unionism, the vocal support of the American Legislative Exchange Council (ALEC) for abolishing police unions should give pause. Why would ALEC, an organization that has opposed the minimum wage, Medicaid expansion, public transportation and antidiscrimination laws, and other progressive public policies be opposed to police unions? Simply put, because the issue of police unions could possibly provide a bulwark for waging the continued assault on public sector unionism ALEC has supported for years.[67] All of this, as many dedicated unionists have begun to make clear, is an attack on collective bargaining and a distraction from the motive force of lethal police–civilian conflicts. "Police brutality exists," as Lafer reminds us, "primarily because it is functional for the dominant economic and political class."[68]

Left unionists like Carl Rosen, president of the United Electrical, Radio and Machine Workers of America (UE), may provide us with one way out of the morass. In a talk that was part of a November 2015 panel on Labor Unions and Police Accountability organized by the Chicago Labor Speakers Club, Rosen makes a compelling case for the role that social justice unionism might play in achieving greater police accountability. "Since the lack of police accountability has its greatest impact on working-class communities," Rosen begins, "this is an issue that the labor movement cannot afford to avoid."[69] Furthermore, he contends that because of the disproportionate impacts on communities of color "unions have an additional need to tackle this issue head on." Rosen reminds his audience of the longer history of police repression of labor organizing, before noting that in most contemporary union actions, the police are working *with* not against organized labor, a reflection of the non-militancy of the contemporary labor movement more than the progressive disposition of police. Rosen makes a compelling case for more dialogue between the labor movement and police unions, on the basis of the shared working-class origins of members across sectors, and public sector union solidarity in the context of austerity. Rosen notes that in places like Ohio, police unions were decisive in winning the fight against Right to Work legislation. To underscore this last point, he mentions the shared good will and solidarity between police and the Chicago Teachers Union during the 2012 strike, where police seemed to be allowing teachers to shut down streets in the Loop at will. Rosen contends that if the conversation is less about police personnel and more about a system that has been structured to enable and condone bad behavior and cover-ups, then there is a better chance to get labor on board. Rosen's approach to police unions is critical, but also strategic and grounded in the fact that most central labor councils across the country view police unions as kindred, even if they disagree with police practices. It is also worth noting that police and law enforcement officers are represented by other unions besides the Fraternal Order of Police. AFSCME (American Federation of State, County and Municipal Employees) also represents over 100,000 public safety workers alongside other public sector workers, and the Teamsters organize police, corrections and probation officers across the country. Moreover, as Rosen and others on the panel noted, police are connected to other public sector workers, union members and the broader working class through family and kinship, marriage and social connections. Rosen suggests that there may be a way for the labor movement to create greater police accountability, and, however delicately, leverage police unions to define more clearly the line between the proper defense of a member who has been accused of wrongdoing, and the defense of overzealous and unacceptable behavior. In other words, while unions are legally obligated to defend their members' interests, no union mounts a defense for every grievance or defends members in all situations. The same practical logic should apply to police unions as well. Perhaps the biggest takeaway from Rosen's comments is the view that police unions are wrong on the matter of police violence, but through protracted work they might be moved to a more just position—a position that is unthinkable within some antipolicing activist circles.

Rosen's arguments emerge from a set of intellectual and political assumptions different from those held by critics of Danny Fetonte's 2017 election to the leadership of the Democratic Socialists of America (DSA). Although founded in the early eighties, the DSA emerged from the 2016 election as a reborn organization, reinvigorated by the power of Vermont senator

Bernie Sanders' unsuccessful attempt to secure the Democratic Party's presidential nomination. As the New Democratic core of the party fought to secure Hillary Clinton's nomination, Sanders's populist left message and longtime commitments to socialism inspired millions of Americans, sparking renewed conversations about public works, free higher education, single-payer health care, postal banking and other policies that were once beyond the pale of acceptable political debate. The DSA's membership grew exponentially in the wake of the Sanders challenge and the election of Donald Trump, growing from roughly 6,000 to some 25,000 members by late 2017, and surpassing 50,000 members in early 2019.

Fetonte was successfully elected to the DSA's National Political Committee, but was later accused of failing to acknowledge his previous work for CLEAT (Combined Law Enforcement Associations of Texas), a union organizing police and corrections officers, leading many members to denounce him as a "cop" and a "narc," and fueling calls for his resignation. The core objection to Fetonte focused on his alleged non-disclosure of his full record of associations, but equally the debate surrounding his candidacy became a means for various individuals and tendencies within DSA to voice commitment to Black Lives Matter sentiments. Some argued that having someone with previous ties to a police union would undermine DSA's capacity to build coalitions with racial and ethnic minorities, a position some DSA members rightly criticized as patronizing. This line of criticism wrongly assumed police abuse was a priority issue within those communities, and that working-class black and brown populations possessed a unified, antipolicing position, which they do not. Santa Fe DSA member Emmet Penney, like many others, argued that had he known about Fetonte's connection to CLEAT, he would not have supported his candidacy for the NPC. Penney reiterated the left orthodoxy regarding the police but with an added Black Lives Matter flourish: "To me, cops aren't members of the working class. They're the bulldogs of the rich. They're white supremacy's first line of domestic defense."[70] Penney also charged that Fetonte had created a "sectarian, antidemocratic culture" in the Austin chapter. Of course, online debate is where intellectual life goes to die, and this was true of the Fetonte affair. Insinuation, guilt-by-association, outright falsehoods and ad hominem attacks quickly filled the ether as calls for Fetonte's removal swelled. For example, Penney runs down a list of CLEAT's reactionary policy stances, including their opposition to the Sandra Bland Act in Texas and their defense of a police officer charged with raping a handcuffed black woman in his patrol car, among other injustices. At no point, however, does he demonstrate what Fetonte's actual stances were in any of these incidents or on CLEAT's official positions.

The virtues of Fetonte's actual record of activism and his demonstrated political commitments were sadly drowned out in the torrent of online jeers. Fetonte's involvement with CLEAT was defined by progressive stances, support for public sector unionization alongside opposition to the known problems of the criminal justice system, and opposition to his work from more conservative elements in the organization. His time with CLEAT included working with prison staff fighting the neo-Nazi practice of tattooing and shunning inmates diagnosed with HIV/ AIDs. Real and legitimate opposition to police unions by some DSA members spurred the opposition to Fetonte, but paranoia and antiracist virtue signaling defined the chorus against him. In his candidate statement, Fetonte said he was running "to build a broad-based activist organization that works in the streets and at the ballot box to support folks who are standing up for their rights. I am running to bring a deeper understanding to the NPC about the labor movement … to bring an understanding of the challenges we face in the South … to help understand how working in electoral politics like Bernie Sanders can strengthen our organization."[71] Fetonte possessed decades worth of union experience, which by all accounts was in line with the antiracist, pro-feminist, pro-LGBTQ politics professed by many DSA faithful. Moreover, he was a proven leader, having guided numerous successful labor organizing and antiausterity campaigns. The battle against privatization during the late 1980s waged by the Communications Workers of America (CWA) and the Texas State Employees Union (TSEU) was one such case, where Fetonte and other organizers were able to galvanize broad, multiracial opposition to plans to de-unionize and subcontract food service jobs at Stephen F. Austin University.

The debates over Fetonte were fueled by the posturing and virtue signaling common to online culture, with opposition to Fetonte serving as a symbolic proxy for opposition to police violence and a commitment to racial justice. The DSA's standing rules and electoral processes were upended when they conflicted with the subcultural norms of contemporary social media politics, which are not about building the sustained relationships and deep social bonds that enable work towards long-term goals, but about the short-run expression of one's political and aesthetic commitments. Rosen's remarks to the Chicago Labor Speakers Club were guided by an entirely different set of considerations that prioritized social bonds and longer-term strategic thinking. Rather than scoring points for the sake of self-aggrandizement and social acceptance by whatever cliques matter to you, the work of union organizing, while not perfect, is generally more purposive, focused on winning tangible gains for workers through collective bargaining, grievance processes and legislation. It is conscious of jeopardizing social bonds and solidarity built up over time, which are necessary for achieving those tangible gains, and ultimately focused on building collective power for workers.

A false conclusion bound up in the "enemies of workers" adage is that those who work as police are intrinsically and permanently reactionary. There is good evidence to support this conclusion, and one need look no further than the actions of police unions, which often protect those accused of misconduct. Likewise with the "blue wall of silence," the closing of ranks, the refusal to cooperate with investigations into police conduct and, as we have seen in high-profile cases such as the killing of Laquan McDonald, the outright falsification of reports, destruction of evidence and obstruction of justice carried out by police to protect one of their own. But there is more to the story here. No sector of workers is immune from capitulation and reaction, acting in ways that go against broader class interests or the discrete interests of other segments of workers. We can find reactionary tendencies throughout the history of the laboring classes in the United States and elsewhere. Racial prejudice, nativism and narrow self-interests immediately come to mind, but there are other illustrations of the "Teamsters versus Turtles" variety where workers in big agribusiness, extractive industries, heavy manufacturing and transportation have remained committed to the perpetuation of their sectoral interests despite the disastrous consequences for the planet, contributing to polluted working-class environs, enormous waste and climatic change. Police like all other workers embody the social contradictions of capitalism, but their social function is tragic and exceptional. This tension between the need to survive in the short term versus the potential power of the working class against capital has only ever been surmounted through the historical process of social struggle, the tedious work of deliberating shared concerns, devising concrete strategies for advancing shared political interests and imposing that collective will on society.

If we take a longer view of the history of police and anticapitalist struggles, beyond our social media threads, surprising moments arise where the social function of police breaks down and different political possibilities burst forth. Industrial armies, national guards, gendarmes and police were conjured into being to protect the interests of capital and defend the rule of private property, but their appearance has always been accompanied by rag-tag bands of deserters, renegades, vigilantes, whistleblowers and dissenters, modern-day ronin who reject their prescribed social role often at great personal risk. During the Paris Commune, the ruling class lost its power over the national guard, which had over time evolved into a working-class body, one that ultimately sided with the communards. The democratic processes created by and for the bourgeois took on a new life as the national guard's demography shifted. "The election of officers was originally designed to bind and enthuse the rich in the defense of their class interests," Donny Gluckstein writes in his account of the Paris Commune. "In the hands of the working class such democracy would grow into the powerful tool of a new type of state."[72] Although very different in scale and historical impact, there are comparable examples in the United States where police as workers take on a different political role, in particular a brief period from the postwar years to the scourge of crack cocaine in the eighties when black law enforcement elements attempted to respond progressively to the lack of service and protection for black communities and to the problem of police brutality.

Throughout the postwar years, black communities throughout the country pushed for more hiring of black officers, under the rationale that blacks would provide better service in communities long neglected by police. Such segregation-era campaigns were also responding to the problem of underpolicing and neglect, which might startle contemporary assumptions about the relationship between police and black communities. As James Forman, Jr. notes, this fight for the hiring of more black officers was "an essential, if forgotten part of our nation's civil rights struggle."[73] Likewise, advocates of police hiring believed that black officers would be less likely to abuse black suspects—as Afro-American columnist John Lewis said emphatically, "black policemen do not shoot black jay walkers." There was also a noteworthy class dimension to this argument for racial integration. Some blacks thought that, unlike white officers, black cops would be better able to discern respectable upstanding members of black neighborhoods and communities and so focus on the real criminals. In addition to this concern with black social policing of class, many thought that black officers would make the best crime fighters. Unlike whites they would be more committed to reducing crime in the communities they were a part of and would serve as role models capable of gaining the trust of black publics—more than just policemen they would be "representatives of the race," as civil right activists in Atlanta believed during the postwar years.

Of course, there were many limitations to this particular brand of liberal police reformism within postwar black communities. The results were mixed and complex, reflecting diverse experiences, unfulfilled promises and the limits of race-consciousness as a way of understanding black life, but also reductions in police violence and real improvements in public safety within black communities. There were some who joined the police force with a civil rights ethic in mind and a commitment to serve black communities with an unprecedented level of attention, respect and sense of duty. Future Los Angeles mayor Tom Bradley was one such case. When he served as a police lieutenant, Bradley openly opposed the practices of LAPD chief William H. Parker, famously confronting him in the aftermath of the 1965 Watts rebellion, demanding that charges of police brutality made by blacks be taken seriously and fully investigated. Bradley's reputation as a police reformer was so great that many portrayed him as anti-LAPD throughout his long tenure as mayor.[74] The civil rights liberalism that drove public demands for black hiring, however, sometimes ran counter to the immediate self-interests of those seeking police jobs. "There is nothing wrong with seeing policing as a source of stable employment or upward mobility," Forman notes, "but the fact that so many blacks joined the force for these reasons undermined the theory that integration would change police practice."[75] Moreover, the broader social context of black urban life and policing changed radically during the post-segregation years, with deepening class polarization, an expanding drug economy, a surge of violent crime that disproportionately affected black communities, and the scalar expansion of the carceral apparatus in ways that very few anticipated during the civil rights struggles of the fifties and sixties.

Black integration in public sector employment increased as blacks gained control of urban administrations. Like the broader legacy of black political integration, policing during this period is defined by identifiable improvements and dashed hopes. Black officers in New York, Los Angeles, Cleveland, Miami and Houston began forming their own organizations in the late 1930s, and this activity would intensify with the gains of civil rights movement and the expansion of the black share of the public sector workforce. Reflecting both a broad push for societal integration and the prevailing Black Power sentiments of the sixties and seventies, black police formed their own member-based organizations outside of the established police unions, groups such as the Officers for Justice (OFJ) in San Francisco, the Afro-American Patrolman's League (AAPL) in Chicago, the National Association of Black Law Enforcement Officers (NABLEO) and the National Organization of Black Law Enforcement Executives (NOBLE). AAPL was explicitly opposed to police brutality and its organizers saw their work as "Black Power policing."[76] In 1969, the Patrolman's League began a police brutality complaint and referral service for black Chicagoans. According to historian Tera Agyepong, "League members would help people to file an official report, investigate claims, take photographs of victims so they could be used as evidence against individual officers and provide information and legal referrals if the case was beyond the scope of issues handled by that office."[77] As might be expected, the CPD strongly opposed AAPL's efforts. League founder Renault Robinson was given a one-year suspension, and he along with other members were arrested in 1970 at a downtown theater and charged with disorderly conduct. That incident mobilized black community support for AAPL, but CPD repression of the organization and FBI surveillance and harassment eventually led to its demise. In its constitution, NOBLE defined its purpose as in part developing "communication techniques for sensitizing police executives, police officers, institutions and agencies in the criminal justice system to the problems of the black community."[78] The legacy of these organizations was mixed and contradictory. In a sense, their formation reflected the prevalent race-conscious politics of the time, with many pinning the causes of crime on underlying socioeconomic inequality and demanding progressive state intervention. Yet at the same time, these progressive black police organizations would largely be overtaken by the expansion of the War on Drugs and the growing demand for more punitive policies, including mandatory minimum sentencing.[79]

These civil rights and activist approaches to the problems of policing were limited and short-lived. There was a small window, captured in numerous studies of black political incorporation during the seventies and eighties, where real reductions in documented cases of police violence occurred under black-led governing regimes in cities like Gary, Oakland, Atlanta and Detroit.[80] Their momentary successes were swept away in the carceral expansion of the Reagan-Bush years and with the turn to stress policing that was part of neoliberal revanchist project. The point here is not to suggest that we simply need a return to black police organizing or hiring more black officers as solutions to police violence, but rather to illustrate that policing has been a site of struggle, albeit episodic, that the most progressive segments of police have spoken out against oppressive practices and openly clashed with conservative unions and entrenched top brass, and that policing as an institution is fraught with all the class contradictions and ideological contestation that course through society writ large. Rather than some monolith of the type imagined in ACAB sloganeering, the institution of policing is constituted by flesh-and-blood labor, often drawn from the most dispossessed segments of the working class, who carry myriad motivations for becoming officers and have a vast array of experiences of the carceral apparatus. While it is common for many on the left to cling to "enemies of the workers" condemnations as a way of signaling the depth of their political commitments, there have been other moments when left activists sought to engage those laborers who constitute the state's repressive arm. Perhaps the greatest illustration of this approach, and one that bears many lessons for today, is the GI Coffeehouse movement during the Vietnam War.

The expansion of antiwar sentiments within the ranks of the enlisted was a decisive factor in the troop withdrawal from Vietnam.[81] Active-duty soldiers, veterans and left activists who saw the importance of organizing antiwar opposition within the armed forces initiated the GI Coffeehouse movement. In 1967,

Jeff Sharlet started *Vietnam GI*, an independent newspaper, which reached a circulation of 15,000 and had a Vietnam mailing list of 3,000; it was only one of nearly 300 newspapers published and circulated among troops.[82] The opposition was organic, orchestrated primarily by enlisted troops and veterans, but students and left organizations were also instrumental in building solidarity. They approached this work with a perspective that may seem foreign to latter-day activists. As historian Jonathan Neale points out, Socialist Workers Party cadre had a policy of not refusing the draft, which was based on the experience of the Bolsheviks during World War I. "Because the Bolsheviks were part of the working class," Neale notes, "they had organized inside the army against the war, overturned the officers, and taken their country out of the war."[83] Like the attitudes towards police that dominate the time of Black Lives Matter, many on the left during the Vietnam War did not support the idea of organizing troops, and viewed soldiers with contempt. Activists like Joe Miles, who had been drafted in 1969, however, threw themselves into organizing within the ranks. They set up coffeehouses near military bases, creating a space for open conversation and kindling antiwar sentiment. The GI coffeehouse movement helped to facilitate the creation of new soldier-led antiwar organizations and newspapers across all branches of the military, and spawned a national network of coffeehouses, bookstores and storefronts. Other groups like GIs for Peace reflected the progressive spirit of the time. An organization of soldiers stationed in the El Paso/Fort Bliss area, this group sought to "promote peace, secure constitutional rights for servicemen, combat racism, improve enlisted living conditions, and provide aid to the local Chicano community."[84] The desertion rate tripled over the course of the war, and soldiers scrawled "FTA" (Fuck the Army) and peace signs on their helmets and other equipment. Incidences of fragging also exploded, marking the loss of authority on the battlefield and the beginning of the end of the war.

Like any organizing effort, the coffeehouses were not without their limitations and challenges. Matthew Rinaldi points to two central faults of the original conception. "First, the initial coffee-houses were located at major basic training bases, the idea being to struggle with the brass for the mind of the GI during his basic training," Rinaldi writes. "If the brass won, this thinking ran, they would have an effective killer in Vietnam; if the coffeehouse won, there would be refusals and disaffection." This strategy was flawed, however, as Rinaldi points out, because of the complete isolation of basic trainees. "The second error concerned the nature and style of the coffeehouses," according to Rinaldi, who notes that initially activists thought that by "creating a semi-bohemian counterculture setting, it would be possible to reach the most easily organised GIs." This strategy succeeded in attracting soldiers, but not necessarily politicizing them in the ways activists had anticipated. Luckily, as Rinaldi details, the coffeehouse format was flexible and could be transformed to address and surpass such problems, in the end becoming an effective tool for building opposition against the war. Remarking on the unique character of antiwar organizing within the military during Vietnam, Rinaldi writes, "it represented an attempt to radicalize the working class in uniform while it was subjected to particular pressures, in a period when the working class in civilian life was relatively dormant."[85]

The parallels between organizing soldiers and police are not exact. Vietnam was the last major American war fought with forces raised through legal conscription. The ethical conflict between the compulsory universal draft and the evasions of middle-class and wealthy Americans from combat service provoked working-class resentment and opposition throughout society and within the military ranks. Police departments are often drawn from former military, and others who are *conscripted-by-class*, but the voluntary nature of the service is distinct from the conditions that New Left activists confronted during Vietnam. Still, there are important lessons that might be drawn from the approaches of left unionists, the experiences of the Afro-American Patrolman's League and other progressive organizations formed by black officers, and the heroic story of the GI Coffeehouse movement. All of these historical episodes suggest that building popular support for social justice among those who carry out the work of war and occupation is not impossible, but rather it may mark the extent of the left's popular power at given historical junctures. During the course of Black Lives Matter protests, law enforcement officials across the country organized public forums and other events to lead conversations about race and policing. There is no reason to believe that such conversations, and others of the closed-door sort Carl Rosen proposed between left progressive unions and those representing police, cannot create the beginnings of a popular coalition for achieving more just forms of public safety, and a world where massive investment in the policing of immiserated surplus populations is no longer viewed as legitimate.

We have already entered a phase where public safety might be maintained with fewer flesh-and-blood police doing the work. Policing through the use of robotics and artificial intelligence may not take the fantastic forms anticipated in science fiction, especially in those jurisdictions that cannot afford expensive technological upgrades or where local citizens successfully oppose their implementation, but the use of algorithms and massive data-mining, as well as the regulation of populations through video surveillance, facial recognition, electronic monitoring and social credit ranking systems, are already in motion in the United States and other technologically advanced capitalist countries. Such developments will proceed apace, and undergo continued experimentation and refinement, especially if they provide more putatively humanistic forms of order maintenance than the kind of brutality recorded with cell phones and police dash cameras. Computer software designers, robotics engineers, military-industrial corporations, law enforcement unions, mass incarceration reformers, politicians, ex-offenders and community organizations have already rallied behind e-carceration, mandatory body cameras, non-lethal weapons and other technological fixes to the well-known excesses and abuses of police officers in the field. Public pressure from Black Lives Matter protestors has perhaps unintentionally hastened such technocratic reforms.

These technical fixes have enabled some police departments to defuse the abolitionist demands raised by the most militant BLM protestors.

Rather than pursue technical fixes or reductions in police labor, left progressive forces galvanized through Black Lives Matter should push for the abolition of the very class inequalities modern policing has been designed to manage and contain. Public safety and security must be reimagined alongside the decommodification of basic human needs and, ultimately, the abolition of the capitalist class relation. There are already unarmed police patrolling many large metropolitan areas around the globe. Instead of militarized police, we might envision genuine public servants dedicated to the nonviolent de-escalation of domestic conflicts and mental health crises. This desire to serve as community servants is after all the very impulse that compels many individuals into careers as police, firefighters, emergency medical technicians, teachers, and so forth. The problem is not the impulse, often provoked by working-class experiences of misery and trauma, and, often enough, by positive interactions with public servants; rather, the problem lies in how such benevolent sentiments of service and duty are mobilized to maintain and regulate capitalist class society. If left forces do not amass the kind of popular and legislative majorities necessary to create progressive reforms—or if various campaigns create effective pressure but do not venture beyond incremental demands—then we will likely see local and state governments respond only with technical measures that reduce risks to the mental well-being and physical safety of officers and some civilians. The danger, however, is that such measures may reduce the public relations morass that accompanies every viral video of police wilding, thereby deflecting public pressure, while leaving the underlying class relations intact under a patina of efficiency, impartiality and technological fetishism. This is not a brave new world, but rather the craven old world we already know too well, one where the most dispossessed and precarious segments of the working class are regulated and repressed.

Conclusion

Abolish the Conditions

On January 6, 2021, thousands of Trump supporters stormed the US Capitol building, eventually breaching the House of Representatives chamber and forcing the evacuation of congresspersons who had gathered for a joint session to certify the electoral college vote and the election of Joe Biden to the presidency. Only hours earlier, the defeated Trump had stirred up the crowd at his "Save America" rally on the White House Ellipse, repeating the false claims about election irregularities and Democrat tampering he had voiced consistently throughout the 2020 campaign year. He had come to power promising to end "American carnage." He used the phrase in reference to everything from Chicago's murder rate, which he blamed on weak-on-crime Democrats, to the loss of US manufacturing jobs to other nations. Yet from start to finish, Trump's presidency was defined by domestic levels of violence unseen in recent years, in what at times seemed to many to be the opening skirmishes of a new civil war. His presidency began with the August 2017 white supremacist rally in Charlottesville, Virginia, which saw the death of thirty-two-year-old paralegal, activist and waitress Heather Heyer, who was killed by James Alex Fields, Jr., an Ohio neo-Nazi who plowed his car into a crowd of antiracist protestors. Even in the wake of Heyer's death and dozens of other injuries, Trump never repudiated the white supremacists, instead saying that there were "good people on both sides" of the conflict in Charlottesville. And now, as he reluctantly prepared to leave the White House without conceding the election, Trump played his hand, stoking a deadly attack on the US Capitol building on a scale that had not been seen since the nineteenth century. In the days and weeks after, the mass majority of Americans condemned the attacks and Trump's refusal to support a peaceful transfer of power to the Biden administration.

The insurrectionists were a motley of ultra-right forces who had moved from the fringes of American public life to momentarily occupying the halls of the national Congress. They were the antithesis of the America reflected in so many cities, a civic culture broadly supportive of religious tolerance, antiracism, cosmopolitanism, pro-reproductive rights, pro-LGBTQ rights, antimisogyny and pro-consent, and favoring redistribution and egalitarian social policies. As Adolph Reed, Jr. made explicit in a pointed 2021 essay, "The Whole Country is a Reichstag," this iteration of reactionary conservatism has been a long time in the making, and the reactionary and racist dimensions did not begin with Trump but date back to the Cold War, McCarthyite anticommunism, the John Birch Society, the Ku Klux Klan, the America Firsters and the pioneering presidential campaigns of Barry Goldwater and George Wallace. Trumpism has merely stripped away the veneer from what has always been a doggedly pro-capitalist, antidemocratic and anti-working-class politics lying at the core of the New Right. And in a startlingly short period of time, as Reed notes, Trumpism has crowded the Republican Party with an alliance of "committed reactionaries, opportunist political operatives, anti-vaxxers, survivalists and other more or less dangerous antigovernment hobbyists, internet conspiracists, unhinged psychopaths, militant anticommunists, zealous anti-abortionists and other Christian fanatics, would-be libertarians, gun nuts, unambiguous fascists and ethnonationalists, actual (i.e., not simply people who say or do things that affront liberal anti-racists) white supremacists, xenophobes, sexists and anti-LGBTQ militants, desperate people seeking answers and solutions to the material and emotional insecurities that overwhelm their lives, and, of course, the grifters who follow alongside the herd looking to pick off the weak and vulnerable."[1] While each of these discrete if oft-overlapping groups and tendencies might appear relatively small in their numbers, their growing alliance, coordination and funding portend a decidedly more threatening moment of violent, antidemocratic reaction.

Some protestors even called for the vice-president's execution because of his unwillingness to support Trump's claims of a stolen election and decision to preside over the electoral college certification and peaceful transition of power. Shouting "Hang Mike Pence," the insurrectionists stormed through the fencing and other ill-prepared barricades ringing the Capitol building. In the end, six people died in the fracas. Some 138 police were injured. Two rioters pepper-sprayed Capitol officer Brian Sicknick, a forty-two-year-old New Jersey native and military veteran. He died the following day after suffering two strokes. Millions were horrified and dismayed by the video footage of the insurrection and the violence meted out against a grossly outnumbered and seemingly unprepared police presence. In one widely circulated video, DC Metropolitan police officer Daniel Hodges stood helpless, crushed in a doorway as insurrectionists beat him mercilessly with his own baton. In the months after the insurrection, four officers who responded that day died by suicide, once again underscoring a quiet national epidemic and the unmitigated occupational hazards of law enforcement.[2]

If there was any shred of uncertainty about his vile motives, Trump made them unequivocal in his closing act as president. Only a few months earlier he had chided Black Lives Matter protestors as "thugs" and "terrorists." Now, clinging to power, he hailed his violent supporters laying siege to the Capitol building as "great patriots who have been badly and unfairly treated for so long."[3] His desire to retain power overrode the usual sanctimonious talk of most American elites regarding democratic institutions and processes. Trump's Republican Party stripped away the pretense of liberal democracy and revealed the ugly core of their agenda: mass voter repression, unchecked oligarchic power and unfettered capitalism. Although some pundits kept up the myth that Trump's base was comprised of an alienated white working class, the stories of the insurrectionists who were identified, often through their own social media posts, and arrested in the months after the riot revealed a different reality. Most were not the backwater lumpen whites that liberals love to hate and lampoon; instead they were a *lumpen bourgeoisie*, small profit-hungry entrepreneurs, allergic to taxes, state regulation and redistributive politics, and smitten by Trump's brash and unapologetic performance of the capitalist boss. Ashli Babbitt, who was shot and killed by Capitol police when she tried to breach a barricaded door inside the building, was a military veteran and QAnon follower, and also the owner of a pool-cleaning service in the San Diego area. Thien Ly and Thu Ly, owners of Tank Noodle (a.k.a. Pho Xe Tang), a popular Vietnamese restaurant in Chicago's Edgewater neighborhood, faced a torrent of backlash from loyal customers after videos and pics of them at the Capitol riot surfaced. Most infamously, Dallas real estate broker Jenna Ryan flew on a private jet to join the protests. She was later arrested after the FBI discovered Facebook videos showing Ryan and other "Stop the Steal" supporters trespassing the Capitol building. There were many other insurrectionists just like the Ly family and Ryan. By late August 2021, 622 persons had been arrested and charged with crimes for their role in the insurrection; the accused reflected supporters who were white, middle-aged and drawn from the consumer middle class and relative business elite in their cities and communities.[4]

The Capitol insurrection not only revealed the frailty of American democratic institutions, and the capacity of proto-fascists to bring the country to the brink of crisis, it also revealed the limitations of abolitionism, the radical left wing of BLM forces who seek to dismantle police departments and prisons. One immediate criticism that circulated through the ether compared the heavy police presence and repression during the BLM protests only a few months prior to the apparent unpreparedness of police assigned to protect the Capitol grounds and the seeming wide license given to the Trump supporters.[5] At the height of the popular protests over the murder of George Floyd, Trump had deployed federal law enforcement, armed with rubber bullets and chemical weapons, to repel protestors from Lafayette Square, a public park adjacent to the White House, ahead of a photo opportunity in front of St. John's Church, and yet he refused to condemn the Capitol rioters. For all his pandering to Blue Lives Matter reactionaries during his rally speeches, Trump ultimately saw cops as being as disposable as anyone else when they got in the way of his impotent gambit for authoritarian power. He praised Babbitt as a fallen hero "who truly loved America" and condemned the police officer who shot her in an attempt to defend the Congress as a "murderer."

Even beyond Trump's malice and hypocrisy, the widely differential treatment between the two events smacked of "white privilege" for many observers. "We all know what would have happened if the Capitol protestors had been black" was a common refrain in the aftermath of the crisis. "What a joke," said BLM activist and founder of Campaign Zero, Johnetta Elzie. "I mean, they didn't even pinch the white people. It wasn't even like a family dispute. In a family dispute, you might at least hit your sister or something like that. This wasn't even that. It was almost like tear gas was not readily available."[6] On the one hand, this popular criticism merely amplified a longer and legitimate narrative about police repression of Black Lives Matter protests dating back to Ferguson, but on the other hand it also expressed a pro-policing sentiment, the sense that the insurrectionists deserved to be reined in effectively. What the images of right-wing insurrectionists scaling the Capitol walls, assaulting police officers, shouting racist epithets, stealing furniture and computers from congressional offices, and calling for the execution of legislators all made certain for the vast majority of Americans was that there was still a place for police, courts and prison cells.

In a relatively short time, less than a decade, Black Lives Matter has evolved from a hashtag slogan into a broad banner for anticarceral and antiracist forces throughout the United States and around the world. In the wake of the police murder of George Floyd, BLM demonstrations momentarily secured majority public support for their central contention regarding racist policing, and, in the year after, produced a tidal wave of local and state legislation. Ten states passed laws that created databases for officer misconduct, disciplinary actions and decertifications, with some states requiring public access. Scores of municipalities debated and revised their use-of-force policies, mandating officers to provide emergency medical aid to suspects, banning the use of chokeholds and restricting the use of deadly force against suspects fleeing on foot or in vehicles. Other cities like San Francisco launched crisis response teams to deal with mental health emergencies rather than deploy armed cops.[7] As one might have anticipated, such changes have roughly mirrored the electoral map of red and blue states, with Deep South and upper–Great Plains states largely failing to enact any substantive statewide legislation, and the most progressive policy movement occurring in the oceanic coastal states and most populous regions.[8] Overall, however, reform has not materialized in the manner that many assumed might follow such a massive outpouring of outrage as occurred over Floyd's death. Progress in defunding and dismantling police departments, a signature demand of the radical and abolitionist elements of BLM, has been largely confined to a few jurisdictions. At least twelve major cities, including Austin and Los Angeles, pledged to reduce police budgets and invest in violence prevention, job creation, housing and other programs. Still, in other places like Minneapolis, which was the epicenter of the George Floyd protests, a veto-proof city council majority in favor of dismantling the police department unraveled by the end of the summer of 2020, and ultimately voted to spend $6.4 million on officer recruitment.[9]

In the midst of international protests over the police murder of George Floyd, those of us on the left who had been consistently skeptical of Black Lives Matter and the problem of identitarianism in general faced a torrent of gloating criticism and derision. For many liberals and socialists, the George Floyd protests seemed to fly in the face of our criticisms of racial politics as a political dead-end. Some of us were called out by name and dismissed in social media threads and podcasts as irrelevant. Others faced reluctance from magazine editors to publish our work for fear of backlash. And of course, there was no act of contrition or acknowledgement of the integrity of our criticisms from the naysayers, wokelords, colleagues, publishers and even close friends, even after the owl of Minerva had spread its wings and the second wave of Black Lives Matter did not deliver the kinds of concrete changes so many had hoped for. Instead, BLM's rebirth proved to be a boon for the corporate bosses who now used blackwashing to insulate themselves from essential worker demands for protective equipment and better wages amid the pandemic. As we had argued forcefully in the early days of the protests, the real beneficiaries would be the neoliberal politicians who reinvented themselves as social justice warriors, and a few too many activists-come-celebrities who rode the wave of the "Great Awokening" into the limelight and a higher tax bracket.[10]

This book has argued that BLM is essentially the latest permutation of racial liberalism, proposing a set of bourgeois strategies and solutions for addressing the structurally determined conflict between police and the surplus population. During the 2020 George Floyd protests, the politics of Black Lives Matter seemed especially militant and stood in sharp contrast to the pro-policing, authoritarian posturing and hubris of the Trump administration. The fundamental BLM demand, that black lives equally deserve protections guaranteed under the Constitution, momentarily achieved majority-national support. Through slogans like the "New Jim Crow" and "Black Lives Matter," the problem of expansive carceral power was codified as a uniquely black predicament. Police violence, however, is not meted out against the black population en masse but is trained on the most dispossessed segments of the working class across metropolitan, small town and rural geographies.

The preceding chapters have examined the political contradictions and limits of contemporary antipolicing struggles, and explored what directions left politics might take now that BLM has pressed the matters of police power, an outsized carceral infrastructure, structural unemployment and racial inequality into public debate. At the heart of the analysis is the view that broad, popular majorities are necessary to roll back carceral power and eliminate poverty and dispossession. Indeed, when have major, progressive political changes been achieved in American life without building popular and legislative majorities? BLM protests have compelled many Americans to rethink the role of police and consider new means of achieving public safety and addressing inequality. The liberalness of the racial frame leads back towards reformist politics and ethnic brokering and, as such, undermines the most progressive-to-revolutionary aspirations of many activists and citizens who have crowded under the BLM banner and desire an end to mass incarceration and fatal police–civilian encounters. If there is an anticapitalist or even downwardly redistributivist politics expressed by different Black Lives Matter elements, it has been drowned out in the flood of black wealth creation, fetishism and nostalgia of Jim Crow black entrepreneurship, corporate diversity initiatives, disparities discourse, and a reparations demand which has served more as Potemkin housing for post-segregation, neoliberal black politics than a viable political demand with popular traction. None of these political tendencies addresses the fundamental problem underlying mass incarceration, namely the turn from welfare to warfare as the means of regulating relative surplus population. Instead, the singular focus on and imprecision of institutional racism as the framing favored by BLM protestors deprioritizes and obscures the predicament of the most submerged and dispossessed elements of the black population. Moreover, the black exceptionalist view of policing and prisons has isolated the predicament of the criminalized black poor from that of millions of other Americans who face routine surveillance, arrest and carceral regulation.[11] A dogged focus on antiblack racism cannot explain the problem before us and is counterproductive to building the kind of broad popular coalitions capable of reversing the carceral expansion, coalitions that have yet to materialize beyond the most liberal reaches of the country.

In concert with other critical works on policing and prisons, this book has illuminated the ways carceral power is deeply implicated in the reproduction of "postindustrial" capital accumulation. Far from being an extension of slavery or even Jim Crow, the punitive turn in American society and resulting carceral expansion were rooted in Cold War–era developments, namely the radical transformation of American cities after World War II through suburbanization, capital intensification in manufacturing and the retreat from New Deal social democracy. Within this emerging milieu, the black and brown inner-city poor assumed the role of the miner's canary, suffering through the violence of labor force contraction and joblessness often before, and frequently more visibly than, other populations in small factory towns and the country's industrial interior who would feel the full aftershocks. During the urban riots of the late sixties, law-and-order rhetoric demonized the inner-city poor, who were allegedly at fault for the deteriorating conditions in some American cities and whose continued dependence on state support was seen as a drag and an unfair tax burden on the rapidly expanding middle class. Antiblack and antiurban moral panic helped to drive the carceral build-up, but in many cities this political turn would not have been possible without the support of black and brown publics who were desperately seeking solutions to the rising crime, nuisance behavior and declining neighborhood life many experienced through the heroin crisis of the seventies and the crack cocaine crisis of the eighties and early nineties. The stony ground of conjuncture that produced the carceral expansion should once again underscore the importance of majoritarian coalitions for contemporary struggles, especially at the local and state levels where the carceral infrastructure was built. Likewise, it should provide a strong tonic against essentialist understandings of political constituencies that conflate corporeal identity with political interests and felt needs.

Many of the police killings that have become flashpoints for political mobilization have revealed the ways contemporary modes of stress policing are connected to local urban accumulation regimes largely predicated on the FIRE and tourism-entertainment sectors. During the late eighties and nineties, stress policing was an essential beachhead in urban revanchist politics in places like New York City and Los Angeles. Big-city governing coalitions increasingly targeted open-air drug markets, homeless encampments, gang activity and nuisance crimes like graffiti, public intoxication and permit violations to clear the ground for renewed economic development and real estate valuation, boost the tarnished reputation of urban living and lure the middle class and wealthy back to the city as visitors and residents. The popularity of "broken windows" policing as a legitimate strategy took off at the same time national politicians began to dismantle what was already a paltry social safety net by global civilized standards. The black and brown poor faced ever expansive violence, both the very visible and militarized violence of municipal and state police, but also the less acknowledged violence in the form of deaths from lack of health insurance and access to quality care, poverty and hunger, disproportionate exposure to environmental hazards, systemic denial of education and legitimate employment opportunities, predation by pay-day loan centers, price gouging by appliance rentals and convenience stores, and regular disrespect from authority figures and dishonor within national political discourse.

At various turns, this book has criticized the underclass mythology that has animated so much antiwelfare and pro-policing policymaking from the sixties through the Obama and Trump years. The underclass myth is pernicious and promiscuous; at one time associated primarily with the black inner-city poor, this characterization of the poor as self-sabotaging and unassimilable has been deployed more broadly to blame the unemployed and unemployable throughout the country for their plight. Black Lives Matter forces have been steadfast in challenging the demonization of victims of police violence, but at times this strategy has repressed acknowledgment of the kinds of survival crimes so many have turned to amid mass obsolescence and declining real wages. What is still needed after years of popular mobilizations against policing is effective political organizing that might slowly rid American popular consciousness of the falsehood that criminalized forms of work—prostitution, theft, carjacking, fencing, drug dealing, etc.—are somehow more ominous and deserving of punishment than tax evasion, insider-trading, embezzlement, money laundering and other white-collar crimes which create much greater social harm. Millions of Americans abhor the idea that any citizen might be racially targeted and subjected to abuse by police, but these same legions are not as unnerved and ready to take to the streets over the reality that so many citizens in central cities, but also in suburbs, small towns and rural areas, are locked out of traditional paths to gainful income, education and social mobility. Any measure that will reduce the levels of police violence against civilians, and reverse the decades of damage and suffering wrought by mass incarceration, should be supported. Dismissing such policy changes as reformist may confer an air of militancy on those hoping to build their brand in academe or the online echo chambers of the left, but such posturing is noxious, selfish and tone-deaf to the real suffering experienced by millions of Americans still caught in the carceral dragnet.

The abolitionist belief that we might achieve public safety through spontaneous, decentralized forms of society flourished during the summer of 2020. We caught a glimpse of this anarcho-liberal utopia at the local scale—and it was disastrous. In Seattle, activists took over six square blocks in the Capitol Hill neighborhood east of downtown, which encompassed the East Precinct police headquarters and Cal Anderson Park. Originally called the Capitol Hill Autonomous Zone, the area was subsequently renamed the Capitol Hill Occupied Protest (CHOP) and deemed a police-free zone. Throughout June 2020, CHOP served as a center of radical democratic experimentation, with live music, popular art and creativity, cooperative economics and mutual aid, and BLM teach-ins and protests. CHOP rehearsed the familiar social ideals and aesthetics of the antiglobalization and Occupy Wall Street demonstrations, but, like those events, it also reflected the limitations of New Left countercultural politics.

At best, like its predecessors, CHOP served as a demonstration city of sorts, a momentary space where participants were able to dream and think together, and find rapture in speaking truth to power. The utopic view of the zone as standing outside of the carceral regime, as some "no-cop co-op," was always a myth though. Despite the claims to autonomy, from its inception CHOP always existed at the discretion of constituted power, as a concession of the city elites to the protests and a liberal strategy of control through managed retreat. Likewise, the short life of the zone is a reminder that social justice, if it is to have any meaningful and universal character for citizens, needs to be legislated, not dramatized or acted out outside of political life. Finally, even as an experiment in "cop-free" social living, CHOP ultimately failed and descended into lawlessness. The zone was plagued by a spate of violent crimes, including four shootings that resulted in two deaths, and multiple reports of rape, assault and robbery. And, while some activists celebrated the banishment of police from the area, CHOP played host to equally volatile and heavily armed bands of left watchmen, right-wing militia and alt-right groups, as well as private security hired by local businesses during the occupation. Right-wing pundits used these developments to criticize Seattle's center-left political leadership and to impugn Black Lives Matter, but there was also organic opposition to the occupation from Seattle residents. As the incidents of violence increased, there was mounting public pressure, especially from tech workers and other more affluent residents in the area, for the restoration of police control. In the year after George Floyd's murder, other cities continued to be plagued by rising levels of homicide and violence.

More policing and punishment provided a cheap solution to the problem of rising crime beginning in the late sixties, but it was always an immoral and socially disastrous solution. Yet while increased policing is clearly not the answer, neither is the countercultural response, which amounts to DIY policing ill-suited to achieving public safety in a large, complex urban environment, or, worse, produces a head-in the-sand dynamic where we can pretend crime and violence are not real issues or will magically disappear when police disappear. Given that neoliberal statecraft has been the only game in town—and many activists have now even repudiated the social democracy period in twentieth-century American life as hopelessly racist and outmoded—some can only imagine state and institutional governance as mechanisms of state violence and capitalist class interests. This is an ahistorical, unsophisticated and politically fatalistic perspective. Under democratic and popular control, state power has been fundamental to working-class progress across historical time and national contexts, and it remains necessary for transitioning from mass incarceration to a more socially just order, a transition that will necessarily involve consecrating popular and working-class interests in core governing institutions. No society emerges fully formed and devoid of the vestiges of custom, folklore, ruling ideas, myths, latent social conflicts and hierarchies of class position, or forms of expertise and authority that preceded it. As the corporate response to the police murder of George Floyd clearly illustrated, the capitalist class will continue to embrace liberal antiracism and even anti-policing measures insofar as they enhance its power and secure the conditions for perpetual compound growth. Through the summer of 2020, Black Lives Matter was good for business, whether the Hollywood film industry, apparel manufacturers like Nike dependent on sweatshop labor oceans away, the manufacturers of body cams and shot locators, or e-commerce giants looking to quell worker rebellion and virtue signal their way into larger market shares. Whatever reforms are achieved will have to be defended through continued political struggle against powerful classes who rely heavily on policing to secure their interests.

Although it represents the leading edge of anticarceral politics, abolitionism is limited by anarcho-liberal assertions and, equally, by the lack of a critical perspective on the state and left political transition. The very use of the term "abolition" by anticarceral activists has generated considerable trepidation and confusion. Clearly, activists who call themselves abolitionists want to align with the most progressive currents of the nineteenth-century antislavery movement. Likewise, within the context of mass incarceration, the term "abolitionist" demarcates a more revolutionary political project than the various technocratic and liberal responses to the problems of policing and prisons. Contemporary abolitionists want us to imagine a world without pervasive violence, militarized police or warehouses for the criminalized poor, and to think creatively about how we might achieve public safety, eliminate material need and ensure greater freedom and self-determination for the greatest number. On all these matters of revolutionary left politics and radical imagination we are mostly in agreement. The choice of the term "abolition," however, in reference to policing, has served as a badge of courage and radical commitment in activist circles, but clearly does not resonate among the broader population in the same ways. Equally concerning, the criticisms of state violence and policing proffered by some abolitionists drift towards unhelpful utopic thinking and seem to assume that we can somehow separate force from politics.

Force is an inseparable part of modern political life. Just forms of social order require coercion and force, understood here as the capacity to uphold and execute the law, the ability to arbitrate disputes within the citizenry and ultimately to defend the just order from saboteurs, opponents and those who might seek to overturn it. Antislavery abolitionists did not seek to abolish the state but to abolish the institution of slavery, and to secure that good state force was essential. The ultimate abolition of African chattel slavery in the United States required the Union Army's victory over Confederate troops and an end to the plantocracy of the southern states. Likewise, during the Reconstruction period after the war, federal occupation proved the most integral thing standing between meaningful black freedom, understood as the right to property, the franchise and self-governance, and the reimposition of merchant-landlord class power.

State force and coercion were instrumental as well during the Second Reconstruction, which commenced with the Supreme Court's 1954 *Brown* decision overturning the legal precedent of Jim Crow segregation. At critical junctures during the process of desegregation, the national guard, federal marshals and the army's airborne infantry division were mobilized to secure concrete and basic citizenship rights for black southerners. The moral force of civil disobedience was essential in shifting public opinion and spurring legislative action, but it was also often part of a sequential strategy to bring the Department of Justice to town. State force, that is, was necessary to pry open both the "whites only" schoolhouse door and the polling station. This fact is lost in the contemporary left and Black Lives Matter fixation on local police and FBI repression of civil rights activists and the Panthers.

What is needed is abolition of a different sort—not the dismantling of police departments and the complete closure of prisons, but the abolition of the conditions that police have been charged with managing over the last half century of welfare-state devolution and privatization. In a widely circulated editorial during the George Floyd protests, abolitionist Mariame Kaba wrote: "Whether you want to get rid of the police or simply to make them less violent—here's an immediate demand we can all make: Cut the number of police in half and cut their budget in half."[12] "Fewer officers," for Kaba, would equal "fewer opportunities for them to brutalize and kill people." The funds recuperated from police budgets, Kaba rightly insists, should be used to increase spending on better jobs, health care and housing, all of which would provide immediate relief to many in need; likewise, she contends that restorative justice models are a progressive alternative to simply locking up offenders.

Calls to cut police budgets and implement restorative justice, however, are leftist in form but rightist in substance. Such demands follow the same arc of privatization that has defined the transformation of the public sector in other areas such as public housing, education, the postal service and infrastructure development for decades. The result is always the same—break the power of unionized public sector workers; weaken the capacity of the state to address broad social problems *and* diminish public expectations that the state should do so; and empower foundations, nonprofit organizations, entrepreneurs and for-profit corporations to provide boutique services that never meet the real demands of the public. The fact that right-wing lobby organizations like the American Legislative Exchange Council have jumped on the defund/restorative justice bandwagon should give pause to left antipolicing forces who prioritize these demands without thinking carefully about the actual relation between police unions and violence, and the implications for public sector workers more broadly.[13]

The virtue of restorative justice is that it seeks to repair all parties involved in a criminal act. The victim's psychological, medical, financial or other needs are prioritized. Yet the perpetrator is also viewed in their totality, not merely reduced to the crime they committed, and seen as deserving of support, repair and real rehabilitation as well. Although the subject warrants a much longer, dedicated treatment, restorative justice has the potential to be scaled up as a normalized facet of the US criminal justice system, and some local courts have already incorporated it into sentencing processes, especially in the realm of juvenile justice. In its current foundation-friendly form, though, this approach is unproven. In fact, just as the summer 2020 protests began to lose momentum, it was revealed that a well-known Chicago activist who underwent an accountability process with Kaba after he was found guilty of rape had assaulted others even after the completion of that process.[14] Perhaps this case was a terrible outlier, but it would seem that this particular offender, a person immersed in Black Lives Matter activist subculture, would have been most likely to experience transformation and benefit from a process overseen by his peers. Even if we condemn the ineffectiveness and brutality of prison as a means of rehabilitating criminal offenders, why should we believe that restorative justice and not prison time is a more effective means of ensuring public safety? Further, if a person who commits rape violates what is a society-wide law, should he be able to opt out of the justice system, a move that would make most anticarceral activists seethe if it were afforded to wealthy criminals? Most of us would want a loved one who has been accused of a crime to be given a second chance for most offenses. Most of us would want to see the life of the victim and the offender restored in ways that are impossible in the current order. But what responsibility do we have to the broader communities and society we are part of, especially when the consequences are not limited to the victim and the offender, or other parties designated by those facilitators of a restorative remedy? This particular Chicago case involved a respected, celebrated activist and is a reminder that restorative justice is still a niche alternative not available to all offenders, and certainly not to the thousands of similarly situated sex offenders who lack his same network connections and social standing.

Perhaps inadvertently, demands to defund and right-size police departments, and to fund restorative justice and ceasefire-type conflict mediation approaches instead, will accelerate the turn to capital-intensive policing already in motion. Capital-intensive policing will not solve the fundamental problem that contemporary policing was engineered to address, the management of relative surplus population. Without eliminating the very impetus of modern policing, which is the defense of capitalist interests, we will inevitably reproduce the same order but with a more tolerable veneer, one where the open social conflicts are forced out of view, and more secure segments can once again go back to their cubicles, online shopping, social media posting and secure neighborhood life. As argued here, the demand to defund police departments and reroute public monies towards social spending, particularly for black and brown working-class youth, has revived much-needed public discussion about redistributive politics and spending priorities. This demand, however, does not go far enough, often not venturing beyond the paltry forms of social assistance and job training that activists decried as inadequate during the Great Society and after, or touting feel-good "community empowerment" initiatives like Cure Violence and others that have dubious track record of ensuring public safety. Moreover, the demand to defund police departments is a weak call for redistribution, focusing on outsized police budgets while neglecting the broader and much more lucrative urban public wealth transfers that are made under the pretense of private economic development. Police budgets in many cities are trivial when compared to the sum total of tax breaks, land grants, infrastructure improvements, public contracts and other giveaways that are doled out to corporations and developers. We need a more expansive criticism of how public resources are allocated and distributed in cities, one that approaches the process of urban accumulation in total, otherwise, with the rather distracting focus on police budgets, we are targeting only an ancillary aspect of the broader accumulation regimes that reproduce tremendous wealth and deprivation.

Abolishing the conditions that policing is charged with managing might begin with public works, which address structural unemployment while also providing more expansive public goods. As sketched here, metropolitan public works programs might mobilize the unemployed and underemployed to target and improve widely used amenities like public transportation, raise working conditions and wage floors in historically devalued sectors like care work, or advance the proliferation and use of green technologies. Together, these and other public works projects would not only eliminate unemployment and the last resort of dangerous criminal employment for many citizens, they would simultaneously create effective demand and infuse long-neglected neighborhoods with investment and economic development. Moreover, each of these proposed public works initiatives would enhance the overall quality of urban living and, if implemented under democratic popular and neighborhood control, deepen citizen investment and oversight in urban planning and reorient the sense of political possibility at the level of everyday life. The Depression-era Works Progress Administration and Civilian Conservation Corps serve as important historical precedents, projects that not only cured unemployment but were also organized around use value, producing public goods such as parks, post offices, schools and other public buildings; a literate population; public murals and travel guides; roads and bridges, etc., some of which are still cherished and enjoyed nearly a century later. Yet while these legendary public works provide inspiration, a revitalized vision might surpass them in terms of popular democratic control, and out of necessity should be tailored to new conditions and the specific challenges and place-based needs of a world overrun by privatization. The advancement of genuine public works would dramatically improve daily life for wide sectors of the public, especially those populations and spheres of activity that have been neglected and devalued because they do not serve the profit motive.

Popular democratic power is needed to end the carceral regime and build a society where police killings are rare and where neither birthright nor compulsory wage labor determine one's right to food, clothing, shelter, health and other basic needs. This has been a vexing problem for the left for decades, with many now arguing vehemently against the very premises of coalition-building, working-class-led politics and broad redistributive policies. This political defeatism has been decades in the making. The early writings of the urbanist Marshall Berman—who experienced the postwar transformation, the ensuing urban crisis and fiscal abandonment, and the retaking of his beloved New York by the investor class, and who offered searing insights with each new saga—may have provided us with a compass rose of sorts, a way of thinking about building the left that might guide us out of the current morass of neoliberalization, endless protests without effective power, and creeping popular authoritarianism. More importantly, building a powerful majority-left will move us closer to reorganizing society around the very ideals of social justice, equality, antiracism and antiviolence that have permeated the streets, parks and plazas in America's large cities and small towns.

Berman's 1972 *Partisan Review* essay "Notes Toward a New Society" was perceptive in identifying this particular weakness of the American New Left as it emerged in the context of Cold War conservatism, middle-class expansion and black political struggle. Unlike so many of his peers, Berman was not seduced by the lure of black vanguardism and Third Worldism as some fast track to building a popular left on the unique and inhospitable terrain of Cold War America. Berman opens by saying that the most "intense and most disturbing arguments on the Left in the late sixties [have] been over the possibilities of modern man creating a decent society." He notes that the New Left has posed the question as follows: "Can a socialist revolution be made *by* Western men, or *along with* them, or *apart from* them, or only *against* them? The real question is: Is there any hope for us? Radicals of the sixties have forced this question to the surface in every advanced industrial country. It has taken on a special urgency in the USA."[15] Surveying the political landscape of the Nixon years, Berman laments the loss of basic optimism regarding the power of ordinary people. He holds that "the most vital impulse of New Left activity has always been populist, driven by a characteristically American faith in everyday people, a faith that, for all the inequities in American society and the oppressive acts of the American government internationally, the American people themselves are still a source of decency and hope." "This is the faith," he continues, "that has inspired the continuing drive for participatory democracy and community control."[16]

Berman offered sharp criticism of Herbert Marcuse's *One-Dimensional Man*, a defining text of the New Left. For Berman, Marcuse's criticism of the American public was too absolute, painting the new American middle class into a corner politically, and cutting off the possibility that they might be well aware of the manipulative aspects of the culture industry, and could rebel against its alleged power over them. Moreover, some New Leftists who took up Marcuse's arguments abandoned any sense that a homegrown revolutionary politics was possible—it must come from outside the American middle and working classes. The "Marcusean sociology has been transformed into Manichean cosmology," Berman wrote. "The Weathermen take the idea of 'outside' force with a crude, grim literalism: The basic opposition is one of geography. 'America' is condemned, root and branch, as an 'oppressor nation' whose sole source of support is the life and labor of the 'peoples of the world.' The American oppressors include not only the rich, the owners of wealth and property, the bourgeoisie, but 'virtually all the white working class,' blue- and white-collar alike, who enjoy small 'privileges but very real ones, which give them an edge of vested interests and tie them to the imperialists.'"[17] Berman culls these passages from the Weathermen's famous article "You Don't Need a Weatherman to Know Which Way the Wind Blows," the title taken from Bob Dylan's "Subterranean Homesick Blues."[18] So for Marcuse (for a time at least), SDS and later the Weathermen, most white Americans were a lost cause. Opposition would come from outside of that population, from blacks, colonized peoples, etc.

Berman hints at the pathology of "Weatherpeople" who reject their own class: "The Weatherpeople take great pains to disaffiliate themselves from us. When they learned 'to reject the ideal career of the professional,' it did not occur to them to try to create their own career models, or to connect themselves with radical traditions within their own country, their own culture, their own class ... In other words, we can serve as a sort of Fifth Column for the Third World, but not for ourselves—since we're not worth saving. Our role, our historic mission, is to be overcome someday." "So much of the paraphernalia of the sixties—from beads and psychedelic drugs to sentimental idealizations of the 'Third World,'" Berman concludes, "expresses an archetypical modern impulse: a desperate longing for any world, any culture, any life but our own."[19]

In the decades since the sixties, the problematic thinking about race and left politics that so troubled Berman has become the received wisdom throughout much of the society, from academic cultural studies to the antiracist liberalism of the New Democrats, who have imagined and cultivated a coalition of people of color, LGBTQ communities and segments of enlightened whites, including those of the donor class from Wall Street to Silicon Valley, even as they have laid waste to the kind of progressive-left interventionism many of those same constituencies once advanced and symbolized. The Trump administration's incompetent and antiscientific response to the Covid-19 pandemic, and the disproportionate impacts felt by people of color during the early months of the crisis, helped to catalyze Black Lives Matter's second coming. In turn, the rising chorus of protestors throughout the summer of 2020 lifted the Biden-Harris ticket to victory, but neither the protests nor the return of New Democrats to the White House addressed the fundamental contradiction underlying the policing crisis, or for that matter, the pandemic crisis.

There are important lessons the late Berman might provide to contemporary struggles, especially as Black Lives Matter demonstrations have repopularized the same problematic dynamics of black vanguardism and white deference ("allyship" in contemporary parlance). Such New Left notions originated out of the segregated landscape of the affluent society, confused the very basis of political work—which is always shared interests rather than moralism or corporeal identity as such—and continue to distract from the difficult task of building a counterpower capable of producing a different, more egalitarian order, one no longer predicated on exploitation, mass obsolescence, alienation and pervasive violence. Some activists and intellectuals balk at this perspective, but any left movement that hopes to change our current state of affairs and effectively contest capitalist class power must be obsessively concerned with how to build *majoritarian* opposition, how to win over those segments of the citizenry who are apathetic or even antagonistic to the prospect of revolutionary change. Such questions of political organizing necessarily entail engaging citizens beyond the emotionally powerful and episodic context of mass demonstrations, the anti-intellectualism of social media, and the subcultures of die-hard activists. Rather, this protracted work involves confronting legitimate fears of crime, racism and underclass mythology, and the material interests and false needs that are fulfilled through capitalism. These are the concrete social realities and contradictions that have produced the policing crisis and carceral build-up that Black Lives Matter demonstrations have confronted. It is only through facing those contradictions head on that we might even begin to transform these injustices and produce a society where racism has lost its power, poverty is unthinkable and police killings are only the subject of museum exhibits.

Acknowledgments

Thank you to Asher Dupuy-Spencer for leading this project through production. Thanks as well to Mark Martin and Tim Clark for their editorial labor. I am grateful for the many friends, colleagues, fellow travelers and comrades whose knowledge, criticism, generosity and encouragement were vital to the completion of this book: Zhandarka Kurti, Rod Sias, Stephen Ward, Andy Clarno, Adolph Reed, Jr., Roberto Asphlom, Touré F. Reed, Thomas J. Adams, Ken Mitchell, Ann Marie Scheffel, Andre Dockens, Lavar Pope, Michael Leo Owens, Megan French-Marcelin, Daniel Zamora, Althea Legal-Miller, Twyla Blackmon-Larnell, Robert Brenner, Donnell Walton, Thane Gauthier, Tom Ricker, Duwarn Porter, Pascal Robert, Willie Legette, Nikol Alexander-Floyd, Justin Rose, Douglas Medina, Jason Myles, Adrienne Dixson, Jay Arena, Matt Birkhold, Jen Lemen, Gregor Baszak, Nicholas Robertson, Preston Smith, Shanti Singham, Adolphus Belk, Jr., Arden Stern, Lauren Williams, Jarrod Shanahan, Kenny Stancil, Stephen Wilberley, Colleen Lye, Jennifer Pan, Amber A'Lee Frost, Nicole Ashcoff, Vivek Chibber, Corey Robin, Bhaskar Sunkara, Connor Kilpatrick, Lucas Piniero, Aaron Benanav, John Clegg, Nicholas Brown, Michelle Boyd, Kenneth Warren, Suzanne-Juliette Mobley, Atef Said, Patricia Macias-Rojas, Johari Jabir, the late Michael Brooks,

Jane Rhodes, Walter Benn Michaels, Todd Cronan, Rene Rojas and Greg Larnell. Iron sharpens iron.

Thank you to my family, who have lifted me up in my worst moments and helped me become a better version of myself: Cabral Johnson, Zora Johnson, Kimathi Johnson, Sekile Nzinga, Cherida Gary, Ethel Johnson and my extended family of nieces, nephews, aunts, uncles and cousins. Thank you all.

Notes

Introduction

1 Alexia Elejalde-Ruiz, "Central Camera, Iconic Loop Business for 121 Years, Vows to Rebuild as Building Burns during Unrest over George Floyd's Death," *Chicago Tribune*, May 31, 2020.

2 Jarrod Shanahan and Zhandarka Kurti, "Prelude to a Hot American Summer," *Brooklyn Rail*, July–August 2020; Larry Buchanan, Quoctrung Bui and Jugai K. Patel, "Black Lives Matter May Be the Largest Movement in US History," *New York Times*, July 3, 2020; Allison Pries, "These Are All the Cities Where Protests and Riots Have Erupted over George Floyd's Death," NJ.com, June 2, 2020.

3 Fernando Alphonso III, "CNN Center in Atlanta Damaged during Protests," *CNN*, May 29, 2020.

4 Hallie Golden, "Seattle Protestors Take Over City Blocks to Create Police-Free 'Autonomous Zone,'" *Guardian*, June 11, 2020.

5 Jacqueline Serrato, "Abandoned Communities Arrange Black and Brown Truce," *South Side Weekly*, July 9, 2020.

6 Matthew Hendrickson, "Dread Head Cowboy Says He Has No Regrets about Horseback Protest," *Chicago Sun-Times*, September 30, 2020.

7 "Message from George Floyd to the Youth before His Death," *YouTube*, May 27, 2020.

8 Keeanga-Yamahtta Taylor, "The Black Plague," *The New Yorker*, April 16, 2020.

9 Les Leopold, "COVID-19's Class War," *The American Prospect*, July 28, 2020; see also Touré F. Reed, "The Dangers of Letting Racecraft Displace Class during the Pandemic," *Jacobin*, August 13, 2020; Dean E. Robinson, "Why COVID-19 Racial Disparities Make the Case for Medicare for All," *Common Dreams*, June 9, 2020.

10 Paul Krugman, "Trump Takes Us to the Brink," *New York Times*, June 1, 2020.

11 Cedric Johnson, "Trumpism, Policing and the Problem of Surplus Population," in Jasmine Kerrissey, Eve Weinbaum, Clare Hammonds, Tom Juravich and Dan Clawson, eds., *Labor in the Time of Trump* (Ithaca: Cornell University Press/ILR, 2019).

12 Richard V. Reeves, *Dream Hoarders: How the American Upper Middle Class Is Leaving Everyone Else in the Dust, Why That Is a Problem, and What to Do About It* (Washington, DC: Brookings Institution, 2017); Peter Temin, *The Vanishing Middle Class: Prejudice and Power in a Dual Economy* (Boston: MIT Press, 2017); Thomas M. Shapiro, *Toxic Inequality: How America's Wealth Gap Destroys Mobility, Deepens the Racial Divide, and Threatens Our Future* (New York: Basic Books, 2017).

13 "Partisanship Drives the Latest Shift in Race Relations Attitudes," Monmouth University Polling Institute, July 8, 2020.

14 Giovanni Russonello, "Have Americans Warmed to Calls to 'Defund the Police'?," *New York Times*, July 3, 2020; Ann North, "Defunding the Police: Americans' Shifting Attitudes, Explained by a Recent Poll," *Vox*, June 23, 2020; Scott Neumann, "Police Viewed Less Favorably, but Few Want to 'Defund' Them, Survey Says," *NPR*, July 9, 2020.

15 Eric Roper, "Poll: Cuts to Minneapolis Police Ranks Lacks Majority Support," *Star Tribune*, August 19, 2020; Brandt Williams, "Poll: Reallocate Money from MPD, but Keep the Department," *MPRNews*, August 15, 2020.

16 Just Leadership USA, "Bill of Rights for Criminalized Workers," at jlusa.org.

17 James Kilgore, "The Spread of Electronic Monitoring: No Quick Fix for Mass Incarceration," *Prison Legal News*, April 9, 2015; see also Kilgore's blog, *Challenging E-Carceration: The Voice of the Monitored*, at challengingecarceration.org; Michelle Alexander, "The Newest Jim Crow," *New York Times*, November 8, 2018.

18 Thomas Frank, *The Conquest of Cool: Business Culture, Counterculture, and the Rise of Hip Consumerism* (Chicago: University of Chicago Press, 1998).

19 Gerald Horne, *The Fire This Time: The Watts Uprising and the 1960s* (New York: Da Capo Press, 1997); Joshua Bloom and Waldo E. Martin, Jr., *Black against Empire: The History and Politics of the Black Panther Party* (Berkeley: University of California Press, 2013); Donna Jean Murch, *Living for the City: Migration, Education, and the Rise of the Black Panther Party in Oakland, California* (Chapel Hill: University of North Carolina Press, 2010); Chris Rhomberg, *No There There: Race, Class, and Political Community in Oakland* (Berkeley: University of California Press, 2004); Robert O. Self, *American Babylon: Race and the Struggle for Postwar Oakland* (Princeton: Princeton University Press, 2003).

20 Tom Wicker, *A Time to Die: The Attica Prison Revolt* (Chicago: Haymarket, 2011); Heather Ann Thompson, *Blood in the Water: The Attica Prison Uprising of 1971 and Its Legacy* (New York: Vintage Books, 2017).

21 Sidney L. Harring, *Policing a Class Society: The Experience of American Cities, 1865–1915* (Chicago: Haymarket Press, 2017), 4–5.

22 See John Clegg and Adaner Usmani, "The Economic Origins of Mass Incarceration," *Catalyst* 3:3 (2019), 9–53; Nathaniel Lewis, "Mass Incarceration: New Jim Crow, Class War, or Both?," *People's Policy Project*, January 30, 2018; Lester Spence, "Policing Class," *Jacobin*, August 16, 2016; Adolph Reed, Jr., "How Racial Disparity Does Not Help Make Sense of Patterns of Police Violence," *Nonsite*, September 16, 2016.

23 Adam Rothman and Barbara J. Fields, "The Death of Hannah Fizer," *Dissent*, July 24, 2020.

24 Justin M. Feldman, Sofia Gruskin, Brent A. Coull and Nancy Krieger, "Police-Related Deaths and Neighborhood Economic and Racial/ Ethnic Polarization, United States, 2015–2016," *American Journal of Public Health* 109:3 (2019), 458–64; Christian Parenti, "The Surprising Geography of Police Killings: Back-of-the-Napkin Calculations on Race, Region and Violence," *Nonsite*, July 9, 2020; Zaid Jilani, "95% of Police Killings in 2015 Occurred in Neighborhoods with Incomes under $100,000," alternet.org, July 8, 2015.

25 Charles Bethea, "'The Plight of the Fight': A View from Atlanta after the Killing of Rayshard Brooks," *The New Yorker*, June 17, 2020.

26 "Rayshard Brooks Vows to 'Keep Going Until I Make It' in Interview before His Death," *NBC News NOW*, June 18, 2020.

27 Terra Duvall, Kala Kachmar and Davy Costello, "'Rogue' Unit or Targeted Initiative? Why Police's New Place-Based Squad is Causing a Stir," *Louisville Courier-Journal*, June 4, 2020.

28 Astead W. Herndon, "How a Pledge to Dismantle the Minneapolis Police Collapsed," *New York Times*, September 26, 2020.

29 Siddhartha Mitter, "The Revolutionary Mayor of Jackson, Mississippi," *Al Jazeera America*, October 1, 2013; Jamiles Lartey, "A Revolutionary, Not a Liberal: Can a Radical Black Mayor Bring Change to Mississippi?," *Guardian*, September 11, 2017; John Nichols "How to Be a Radical Mayor," *Nation*, October 7, 2019; Katie Gilbert, "The Socialist Experiment," *Oxford American*, September 5, 2019.

30 Farah Stockman, "The Truth about Today's Anarchists," *New York Times*, September 30, 2020; Jay Caspian Kang, "Can We Please Talk about Black Lives Matter for One Second?," *New York Times*, July 2, 2020.

31 Jaeger Blaec, "The Complicated Rise and Swift Fall of Portland's Wall of Moms Protest Group," *Portland Monthly*, August 3, 2020; Rose Minutaglio, "Portland's Polarizing 'Naked Athena' On Why She Stripped Down," *Elle*, July 29, 2020.

32 Aaron Blake, "A Slip in Support for Black Lives Matter?," *Washington Post*, August 29, 2020.

33 Cedric Johnson, "The Wages of Roediger: Why Three Decades of Whiteness Studies Has Not Produced the Left We Need," *Nonsite*, September 9, 2019.

34 For nuanced treatments of black politics and the expansion of the carceral state, see Michael Javen Fortner, *Black Silent Majority: The Rockefeller Drug Laws and the Politics of Punishment* (Cambridge, MA: Harvard University Press, 2015); Donna Murch, "Crack in Los Angeles: Crisis, Militarization and Black Response to the Late Twentieth-Century War on Drugs," *Journal of American History* 102:1 (2015), 162–73; James Forman, Jr., *Locking Up Our Own: Crime and Punishment in Black America* (Farrar, Straus & Giroux, 2017).

35 Rothman and Fields, "The Death of Hannah Fizer."

36 Mariame Kaba, "Yes, We Mean Literally Abolish the Police," *New York Times*, June 12, 2020; Cindi Ross Scoppe, "Scary Demands to 'Defund Police' Won't Fix Anything. These Reforms Will," *Post and Courier*, June 13, 2020; Eric Levitz, "Defunding the Police is Not Nearly Enough," *New York Magazine*, June 12, 2020; Michelle Brown, "Transformative Justice and New Abolition in the United States," in Pat Carlen and Leandro Ayres

França, eds., *Justice Alternatives* (New York: Routledge, 2020); Alex Vitale, *The End of Policing* (London: Verso, 2017); Angela Davis, *Are Prisons Obsolete?* (New York: Seven Stories Press, 2003); Dan Berger, Mariame Kaba and Dave Stein, "What Abolitionists Do," *Jacobin*, August 24, 2017; Roger Lancaster, "How to End Mass Incarceration," *Jacobin*, August 8, 2017.

37 Katie Brenner, "Justice Dept to Investigate Louisville Police, Garland Says," *New York Times*, April 26, 2021.

38 Jamiles Lartey and Abbie Van Sickle, "That Could Have Been Me: The People Derek Chauvin Choked before George Floyd," *MPRNews*, February 5, 2021; Shaila Dewan and Serge F. Kovelski, "Thousands of Complaints Do Little to Change Police Ways," *New York Times*, June 8, 2020.

39 Leila Fadel, "A Former Minneapolis Police Officer's Case Shows an Example of Selective Justice," *NPR*, June 14, 2020.

1. Policing Capitalist Society

1 Adolph Reed, Jr., "The Myth of Class Reductionism," *New Republic*, September 25, 2019.

2 Barbara Fields, "Ideology and Race in American History," in J. Morgan Kousser and James M. McPherson, eds., *Region, Race and Reconstruction: Essays in Honor of C. Vann Woodward* (Oxford: Oxford University Press, 1982), 151; see also Karen E. Fields and Barbara J. Fields, *Racecraft: The Soul of Inequality in American Life* (London: Verso, 2014).

3 Fields, "Ideology and Race," 151.

4 Ibid., 146.

5 Ibid., 151.

6 Ibid., 150.

7 Ibid., 150–1.

8 Michelle Alexander, *The New Jim Crow* (New York: New Press, 2010), 2.

9 King had this to say about Woodward's work and what it revealed about the false premise of racial segregation: "Racial segregation as a way of life did not come about as a natural result of hatred between the races immediately after the Civil War. There were no laws segregating the races then. And as the noted historian, C. Vann Woodward, in his book, *The Strange Career of Jim Crow*, clearly points out, the segregation of the races was really a political stratagem employed by the emerging Bourbon interests in the

South to keep the southern masses divided and southern labor the cheapest in the land. You see, it was a simple thing to keep the poor white masses working for near-starvation wages in the years that followed the Civil War. Why, if the poor white plantation or mill worker became dissatisfied with his low wages, the plantation or mill owner would merely threaten to fire him and hire former Negro slaves and pay him even less. Thus, the southern wage level was kept almost unbearably low." Martin Luther King, Jr., "Address at the Conclusion of the Selma to Montgomery March," in Clayborne Carson and Kris Shepard, eds., *A Call to Conscience: The Landmark Speeches of Martin Luther King, Jr.* (New York: Hachette Book Group, 2001), 122–3.

10 C. Vann Woodward, *The Strange Career of Jim Crow* (Oxford: Oxford University Press, 1966), 29.

11 Ibid., 65.

12 Marie Gottschalk, *Caught: The Prison State and the Lockdown of American Politics* (Princeton: Princeton University Press, 2016, revised ed.), 241–57; Jeff Manza and Christopher Uggen, *Locked Out: Felon Disenfranchisement and American Democracy* (Oxford: Oxford University Press, 2008); Elizabeth A. Hull, *The Disenfranchisement of Ex-Felons* (Philadelphia: Temple University Press, 2006); Jonathan Simon, *Governing through Crime: How the War on Crime Transformed American Democracy and Created a Culture of Fear* (Oxford: Oxford University Press, 2007); Mary Patillo, David Weiman and Bruce Western, eds., *Imprisoning America: The Social Effects of Mass Incarceration* (New York: Russell Sage Foundation, 2004).

13 Jeff Manza and Christopher Uggen, "Punishment and Democracy: Disenfranchisement of Nonincarcerated Felons in the United States," *Perspectives on Politics* 2:3 (2004), 491–505; Brian C. Kalt, "The Exclusion of Felons from Jury Service," *American University Law Review* 53:1 (2003), 65–189; Alec Ewald, "Criminal Disenfranchisement and the Challenge of American Federalism," *Publius* 39 (2009), 527–56; Margaret Love and David Schlussel, *The Reintegration Agenda during Pandemic: Criminal Record Reforms in 2020*, Collateral Consequences Resource Center, January 2021; Jean Chung, *Voting Rights in the Era of Mass Incarceration: A Primer*, The Sentencing Project, July 27, 2021; Michael Leo Owens, "Ex-felons' Organization-based Political Work for Carceral Reforms," *The ANNALS* 1 (2014), 256–65; Michael Leo Owens and Adrienne R. Smith, " 'Deviants' and Democracy: Punitive Policy Designs and the

Social Rights of Felons as Citizens," *American Politics Research* 40:3 (2011), 531–67.

14 Loïc Wacquant, "From Slavery to Mass Incarceration: Rethinking the 'Race Question' in the US," *New Left Review* 13 (January/February 2002).

15 Vanessa Barker, *The Politics of Imprisonment: How Democratic Process Shapes the Way America Punishes Offenders* (Oxford: Oxford University Press, 2009); Mark Jay and Phil Conklin, *A People's History of Detroit* (Durham, NC: Duke University Press, 2020); Fortner, *Black Silent Majority*.

16 Cited in James Forman, Jr., "Racial Critiques of Mass Incarceration: Beyond the New Jim Crow," *New York University Law Review* 87 (2012), 125.

17 Cited in ibid., 126.

18 Gottschalk, *Caught*, 128.

19 Alexander, *New Jim Crow*, 12.

20 Isabel Wilkerson, *Caste: The Origins of Our Discontents* (New York: Random House, 2020).

21 Alexander, *New Jim Crow*, 13. Of course, making sure our laws are applied equally as per the 14th Amendment is a perfectly legitimate goal, but it is a goal of realizing a more perfect liberalism.

22 Nick Slater, "The Nice Cop," *Current Affairs*, January 22, 2018.

23 Sharon LaFraniere and Mitch Smith, "Philando Castile Was Pulled Over 49 Times in 13 Years Often for Minor Infractions," *New York Times*, July 16, 2016.

24 Nicole Santa Cruz, Ruben Vives and Marisa Gerber, "Why the Deaths of Latinos at the Hands of the Police Haven't Drawn Much Attention," *Los Angeles Times*, July 18, 2015.

25 Ta-Nehisi Coates, *Between the World and Me* (New York: Spiegel & Grau, 2015); Imani Perry, *Breathe: A Letter to My Sons* (Boston: Beacon, 2019).

26 Christine Hauser, "Black Princeton Professor Says She Was Handcuffed to Table over Parking Ticket," *New York Times*, January 9, 2016.

27 See Kenneth W. Warren, *What Was African American Literature?* (Cambridge, MA: Harvard University Press, 2011), 9.

28 Angie Schmitt, *Right of Way: Race, Class, and the Silent Epidemic of Pedestrian Fatalities in America* (Washington, DC: Island Press, 2020).

29 The 2019 death of cloud rapper Juice WRLD (a.k.a. Jarad Anthony Higgins) from an accidental drug overdose was provoked by a similar incident of white vigilantism. In this case,

a charter jet pilot transporting Juice WRLD and his entourage from Los Angeles to Chicago called police to report that his passengers, who were all black men, were in possession of drugs and guns. Police met the plane at Chicago's Midway airport, and out of fear of arrest Juice WRLD swallowed a bag of Percocet pills, which caused a fatal seizure. His death was senseless and avoidable. No one was charged with any crime, even though marijuana was seized in the incident (marijuana was to become legal throughout Illinois within a few weeks), and his bodyguards were carrying guns with legal permits.

30 "Barriers to Work: People with Criminal Records," National Conference of State Legislators, July 17, 2018; Matthew Friedman, "Just Facts: As Many Americans Have Criminal Records as College Diplomas," *Brennan Center*, November 17, 2015.

31 Loïc Wacquant, "Class, Race and Hyperincarceration in Revanchist America," *Daedalus* (Summer 2010), 74–90; Loïc Wacquant, *Punishing the Poor: The Neoliberal Government of Social Insecurity* (Durham, NC: Duke University Press, 2009).

32 Brett Story, "The Prison in the City: Tracking the Neoliberal Life of the 'Million Dollar Block,'" *Theoretical Criminology* 20:6 (2016), 257–76; see also Brett Story, *Prison Land: Mapping Carceral Power Across Neoliberal America* (Minneapolis: University of Minnesota Press, 2019); Todd Clear, *Imprisoning Communities: How Mass Incarceration Makes Disadvantaged Neighborhoods Worse* (Oxford: Oxford University Press, 2009).

33 Minority discourses of underclass ideology do not always originate from the same hubristic place as the New Right. Neither do those minority articulations of the myth advance the same immediate antiwelfare policy interests. But they have the same effect, providing legitimacy to notions that might otherwise be contested within black and brown spaces. In black nationalist rhetoric, on the neo–Chitlin' Circuit comedy stage, in the black Protestant pulpit, in B-movies marketed to "urban" audiences, and in urban legends and folklore, the same accounting of the inner-city poor as the source of their own ruin is reproduced by and for black audiences. A key difference, of course, is that black audiences often participate in underclass myth-making in ways that are ironic and most often grounded in a more diverse, experiential understanding of what constitutes black life.

Still, we should be wary of all attempts to view the underclass mythology as simply an "antiblack" notion. The jokes of Jewish comedians in the heyday of Catskills resorts, the comedy

offered by Cajun joke-tellers in Southwest Louisiana, the Blue
Collar Comedy tour led by Jeff Foxworthy, and the sub-genre
of Mexican comedy pioneered by Richard "Cheech" Marin and
Paul Rodriguez and made sublime by George Lopez, all converged around the same punch lines even if they were delivered
in slightly different idioms. All trade in the view that the working
class are incapable of assimilation and lampoon their ill-fated
attempts at middle-class aspiration. Preindustrial habits, agricultural ways, large and unruly families, criminality, laziness and
daily survival—whether phrased in terms of the "artful dodger,"
"immigrant ingenuity" or "hustling"—unite what are only super-
ficially distinct working-class narratives.

Perhaps one of the easiest places to witness the non-racial character of contemporary underclass ideology is in the afternoon
paternity-test shows that blanket most local television stations
on weekdays. The hosts are household names for millions—Jerry
Springer, Sally Jesse Raphael, Maury Povich, Laura Pozzo, Steve
Wilkos, among others. It is worth noting that for a time this same
time slot was once the province of talk shows pioneered by Phil
Donahue and Oprah Winfrey in the eighties. Where Donahue
carved out a space for public debate of various social and political issues, Oprah began in the same mold before reinventing
the afternoon talk show as an amalgam of feminist-lite public
therapy, product placement and celebrity worship. Both versions
of afternoon talk have been supplanted by programs that showcase the personal travails, infidelities and often heartbreak of
ordinary working people. The format is uniform across networks
—some poor pleb suspects that her husband or boyfriend has
been unfaithful, perhaps with a coworker, best friend or relative. Often a baby is involved, and someone charges that the
progeny is not theirs. Accusations fly, tears are shed, and then the
show's host, feigning sincere concern for the guests' wellbeing,
tries to resolve the conflict with a paternity or lie-detector test.
As if scripted, when the big reveal is made, the guests respond
in a few stock ways, either in celebration and reconciliation, or
with the heartbroken guest shrieking and sprinting off stage in
embarrassment at the news of infidelity, or in some cases with the
vindicated now shouting down their discredited accusers. These
television shows feature all the underclass stereotypes and moralizing we have come to associate with the black urban poor, but
their guests are diverse and often interracial. All are lower-income
workers, a fact not lost on the show's producers, who lure guests

with roundtrip airfares, hotel costs and a free vacation to New York or Chicago, with the bonus of appearing on national television. Such shows are the reality-television answer to daytime soap operas, which have always traded in the intimate, sexual and traitorous drama of domestic life. A key difference is the shift in subjects, from peering in through the curtains on the seemingly perfect lives of the well-heeled and the beautiful, to taking a front seat view on the depths of depravity, coarseness, incestuous desires and irresponsibility that many believe are standard for the lower reaches of the working class.

Another illustration of how the underclass notion is not an exclusively anti-black trope can be found in the Showtime network's successful drama series *Shameless*, which was adapted from a British television show of the same name. *Shameless* is set in Chicago's Bridgeport neighborhood, incidentally the ancestral home of the Daley political dynasty. The show follows the adventures of the Gallaghers, a hard-living and dysfunctional white working-class family headed by the father Frank Gallagher whenever he is not on a drug bender, though in most seasons they are held together by the oldest of the brood, Fiona. *Shameless* is a masterpiece of pop schadenfreude. At times engaging, the show's dense and rollicking plotlines often provide some playful criticism of contemporary urban class relations. The Gallaghers and their fellow working-class Chicagoans dwell in an environment defined by aggressive policing, government corruption, gentrification pressures, budget cuts, racism, the weight of middle-class pretensions, and everyday violence. And yet, the underclass myth is always present.

From one season to another, the Gallaghers are always done in by their poor choices. Each season introduces new hopes— acceptance to college; access to a private school; a stable, well-paying job; a potential, upwardly mobile spouse; sobriety; a successful business opportunity, etc.—but the Gallaghers, from the oldest to the youngest, always find a way to ruin it all. They seem to have leapt from some forgotten pages of Moynihan's study. Their own behavior and self-sabotage are always to blame, not the structural forces in their midst. The culture of poverty dissolves any sense of political possibility for the show's working-class protagonists, beyond existential protests, hustling, nihilism and momentary carnal pleasure. Interestingly enough, the modest worker cottage house the Gallaghers call home is not located in Bridgeport at all, but on Chicago's majority-black

West Side, and was owned by a black woman, Vivian Bell, who
had lived in the North Lawndale community

34 Paul J. Hirschfield, "Lethal Policing: Making Sense of American
Exceptionalism," *Sociological Forum* 30:4 (2015), 1112.

35 Ibid., 1112–13.

36 Ibid., 1113.

37 Alysia Santo and R.G. Dunlop, "Where Police Killings Often
Meet with Silence: Rural America," *New York Times*, August 13,
2021.

38 Ibid.

39 Jacob Kang-Brown and Ram Subramanian, *Out of Sight: The
Growth of Jails in Rural America*, Vera Institute of Justice,
June 2017; Bill Rankin, "Number of African Americans Sent
to Georgia Prisons Hits Historic Lows," *Atlanta Journal-
Constitution*, January 25, 2018.

40 Marie Gottschalk, "Caught in the Countryside: Race, Class and
Punishment in Rural America," *Political Power and Social Theory*
37 (2020), 25–52.

41 Ibid., 30; Bruce Wester and Becky Pettit, "Incarceration and
Social Inequality," *Daedalus* (Summer 2010), 8–19.

42 Eli Hager, "A Mass Incarceration Mystery: Why Are Black
Imprisonment Rates Going Down? Four Theories," *The Marshall
Project*, December 15, 2017.

43 Mark Neocleous, *The Fabrication of Order: A Critical Theory of
Police Power* (London: Pluto Press, 2000), xii, original emphasis.

44 Harring, *Policing a Class Society*, 19.

45 Karl Marx, *Capital, Volume I* (London: Penguin, 1976), 876.

46 David Harvey, *The New Imperialism* (Oxford: Oxford University Press, 2005), 145.

47 Marx, *Capital, Volume I*, 905.

48 Among others, Chicago rapper Common has amplified this bad
historical interpretation in his song "A Letter to the Free," where
he says: "Slavery's still alive. Check Amendment 13. Not whips
and chains, all subliminal. Instead of 'nigga' they use the word
'criminal.'"

49 Nikhil Pal Singh, "The Whiteness of Police," *American Quarterly*
66:4 (2014), 1092.

50 Christian Parenti, *The Soft Cage: Surveillance in America from
Slave Passes to the War on Terror* (New York: Basic Books, 2003),
13–23; Sally Hadden, *Slave Patrols: Law and Violence in Virginia
and the Carolinas* (Cambridge, MA: Harvard University Press,
2003).

51 Parenti, *Soft Cage*, 35–7.

52 Ibid.; see also Christopher Waldrep, *Roots of Disorder: Race and Criminal Justice in the American South, 1817–1880* (Urbana: University of Illinois, 1998); David Grimstead, *American Mobbing, 1828–1861: Toward Civil War* (Oxford: Oxford University Press, 1998); Paul A. Gilje, *Rioting in America* (Bloomington: Indiana University Press, 1996).

53 Dennis C. Rousey, *Policing the Southern City: New Orleans, 1805–1889* (Baton Rouge: Louisiana State University Press, 1997).

54 Thomas Reppetto and James Lardner, *NYPD: A City and Its Police* (New York: Henry Holt, 2000).

55 Harring, *Policing a Class Society*, 10.

56 Ibid., 15.

57 Ibid., 11.

58 Friedrich Engels, *The Condition of the Working Class in England* (New York: Penguin, 1987 [1845]), 37.

59 Harring, *Policing a Class Society*, 101–48; Jeremy Brecher, *Strike!* (Boston: South End Press, 1972); Herbert Gutman, "Class, Status and Community Power in Nineteenth-Century Industrial Cities— Paterson, New Jersey, A Case Study," in Frederick Cople Jaher, ed., *The Age of Industrialism in America* (New York: Free Press, 1968); Herbert Gutman, *Work, Culture, and Society in Industrializing America* (New York: Vintage, 1977); David Montgomery, "Labor, Radicalism and the State in Late Nineteenth-Century America," *Journal of Social History* 3 (1980), 219–47; David Montgomery, "Strikes in Nineteenth-Century America," *Social Science History* 4:1 (1980), 81–104; James Green, *Death in the Haymarket: A Story of Chicago, the First Labor Movement and the Bombing that Divided Gilded Age America* (New York: Anchor Books, 2006).

60 Khalil Gibran Muhammad, *The Condemnation of Blackness: Race, Crime, and the Making of Modern Urban America* (Cambridge, MA: Harvard University Press, 2010), 1.

61 Vera Dika, "The Representation of Ethnicity in *The Godfather*," in Nick Browne, ed., *Francis Ford Coppola's "The Godfather" Trilogy*" (New York: Cambridge, 2000), 76–108; Peter Bondanella, *Hollywood Italians* (New York: Continuum, 2004); Richard Gambino, "The Crisis of Italian American Identity," in A. Kenneth Ciongoli and Jay Parini, eds., *Beyond "The Godfather"* (Hanover: University Press of New England, 1997), 269–88; Carlos E. Cortes, "Italian Americans in Film: From Immigrants to Icons," *MELUS* 14:3–4 (1987), 107–26.

62 Patrick A. Langan, *Race of Prisoners Admitted to Federal and State Prisons, 1926–1986* (Washington, DC: Bureau of Justice Statistics/US Department of Justice, 1991), 5.

63 Muhammad, *The Condemnation of Blackness*, 272–3.

64 Ibid., 273.

65 John Clegg and Adaner Usmani take up this matter of explaining racial disparity while acknowledging the very real impact of crime on black populations: "We know from court records and witness reports, for instance, that the vast majority (roughly 90 percent) of homicides are intra-racial. Arrest records of suspects can thus be reasonably checked against racial disparities (in victimization) derived from coroner's reports. In 1970, for instance, coroners indicate that African Americans were nine times more likely to be murdered as whites, while they were eleven times more likely to be arrested for murder in the same year. By 1980 the ratio had fallen to 5.7 for victimization and 5.9 for arrests ... any explanation of racial disparities in violence must account for their twentieth-century provenance, which is but one reason that biological or other racist explanations of these disparities are a non-starter. So where do these disparities come from? ... Behind racial disparities in offending lies long-standing inequality in life circumstances. African Americans are overrepresented in crime because they are more likely to live in America's worst neighborhoods, at the bottom of its stretched class structure, with few opportunities to escape, and few public resources available for their self-development or safety." See Clegg and Usmani, "The Economic Origins of Mass Incarceration."

66 Stuart Hall, Chas Critcher, Tony Jefferson, John Clarke and Brian Roberts, *Policing the Crisis: Mugging, the State and Law and Order* (Basingstoke: Palgrave Macmillan, 2013 [1978]); Ruth Wilson Gilmore, *Golden Gulag: Prisons, Surplus, Crisis, and Opposition in Globalizing California* (Berkeley: University of California Press, 2007); Ruth Wilson Gilmore, "Globalisation and US Prison Growth: From Military Keynesianism to Post-Keynesian Militarism," *Race and Class* 40:2/3 (1998/99), 171–88; Theodore G. Chiricos and Miriam A. Delone, "Labor Surplus and Punishment: A Review and Assessment of Theory and Evidence," *Social Problems* 39:4 (1992), 421–46; Todd Gordon, "The Political Economy of Law-and-Order Policies: Policing, Class Struggle, and Neoliberal Restructuring," *Studies in Political Economy* 75 (2005), 53–77.

67 See Nathaniel Lewis, "Mass Incarceration: New Jim Crow, Class

War or Both?," *People's Policy Project*, January 30, 2018; Nathaniel Lewis, "Locking Up the Lower Class," *Jacobin*, January 30, 2018.

68 Marx, *Capital, Volume I*, 794–7.

69 Ibid., 799.

70 Rhonda F. Levine, *Class Struggle and the New Deal: Industrial Labor, Industrial Capital, and the State* (Lawrence: University Press of Kansas, 1988), 17.

71 Nelson Lichtenstein, *State of the Union: A Century of American Labor* (Princeton: Princeton University Press, 2002).

72 Naomi Murakawa, *The First Civil Right: How Liberals Built Prison America* (Oxford: Oxford University Press, 2014); Elizabeth Hinton, *From the War on Poverty to the War on Crime: The Making of Mass Incarceration in America* (Cambridge, MA: Harvard University Press, 2016); Heather Ann Thompson, "Why Mass Incarceration Matters: Rethinking Crisis, Decline and the Transformation in Postwar American History," *Journal of American History* (December 2010), 703–34; Heather Ann Thompson, *Blood in the Water: The Attica Prison Uprising of 1971 and Its Legacy* (New York: Vintage, 2017); Robert Chase, "Civil Rights on the Cell Block: Race, Reform and Violence in Texas Prisons and the Nation, 1945–1990," PhD Thesis, University of Maryland-College Park, 2009; Heather McCarty, "From Con-Boss to Gang Lord: The Transformation of Social Relations in California Prisons, 1943–1983," PhD Thesis, University of California-Berkeley, 2004; Vesla Weaver, "Frontlash: Race and the Development of Punitive Crime Policy," *Studies in American Political Development* 21 (2007), 230–65; Mary Louise Frampton, Ian Haney Lòpez and Jonathan Simon, eds., *After the War on Crime: Race, Democracy, and a New Reconstruction* (New York: NYU Press, 2008); David Garland, *The Culture of Control: Crime and Social Order in Contemporary Society* (Chicago: University of Chicago Press, 2001); Jordan T. Camp, *Incarcerating the Crisis: Freedom Struggles and the Rise of the Neoliberal State* (Berkeley: University of California Press, 2016).

73 Stuart Hall, Raphael Samuel and Charles Taylor, "Then and Now: A Revaluation of the New Left," in Oxford University Socialist Discussion Group, eds., *Out of Apathy: Voices of the New Left Thirty Years On* (London: Verso, 1989).

74 Camp, *Incarcerating the Crisis*; see also Jordan T. Camp and Christina Heatherton, eds., *Policing the Planet: Why the Policing Crisis Led to Black Lives Matter* (London: Verso, 2016).

75 See Eldridge Cleaver, "On the Ideology of the Black Panther Party," in Kathleen Cleaver, ed., *Target Zero: A Life in Writing* (New York: Palgrave Macmillan, 2006), 177.

76 Stuart Hall, "The Great Moving Right Show," *Marxism Today*, January 1979, 15.

77 Hall et al., *Policing the Crisis*, 344.

78 Ibid., 386.

79 Ibid.

80 Ibid., 386–7.

81 Ibid., 379.

2. Making Consumers and Criminals

1 Terry Teachout, *Pops: The Life of Louis Armstrong* (New York: Houghton Mifflin, 2009), 310–11.

2 A. Ricardo López with Barbara Weinstein, "We Shall Be All: Towards a Transnational History of the Middle Class," in A. Ricardo López and Barbara Weinstein, eds., *The Making of the Middle Class: Towards a Transnational History* (Durham, NC: Duke University Press, 2012), 1–25.

3 Paul Passavant, "The Strong Neo-liberal State: Crime, Consumption, Governance," *Theory and Event* 8:3 (2005), 1–48; see also Pat O'Malley, "Containing Our Excitement: Commodity Culture and the Crisis of Discipline," *Studies in Law, Politics and Society* 13 (1993), 159–86.

4 Clegg and Usmani, "The Economic Origins of Mass Incarceration"; Catherine Cubbin, Linda Williams Pickle and Lois Fingerhut, "Social Context and Geographic Patterns of Homicide Among US Black and White Males," *American Journal of Public Health* 90:4 (2000), 579–87.

5 Clegg and Usmani, "Economic Origins," 11–12; Forman, "Racial Critiques of Mass Incarceration: Beyond the New Jim Crow."

6 See Jordan Camp, *Incarcerating the Crisis: Freedom Struggles and the Rise of the Neoliberal State* (Berkeley: University of California Press, 2017); Naomi Murakawa, *The First Civil Right: How Liberals Built Prison America* (Oxford: Oxford University Press, 2014); Elizabeth Hinton, *From the War on Poverty to the War on Crime: The Making of Mass Incarceration in America* (Cambridge, MA: Harvard University Press, 2016).

7 See Forman, *Locking Up Our Own*; Michael Fortner, *Black Silent Majority*.

8   See Michael Zweig, *The Working-Class Majority* (Ithaca: Cornell University Press, 2000).

9   Ibid.; Juliet Schor, *The Overworked American: The Unexpected Decline of Leisure* (New York: Basic Books, 1992).

10 Jefferson Cowie and Nick Salvatore, "The Long Exception: Rethinking the Place of the New Deal in American History," *International Labor and Working-Class History* 74 (2008), 5.

11 Ira Katznelson, *When Affirmative Action Was White: An Untold History of Racial Inequality in Twentieth-Century America* (New York: W.W. Norton, 2005); Ta-Nehisi Coates, "The Case for Reparations," *The Atlantic*, June 2014; Richard Rothstein, *The Color of Law: A Forgotten History of How Government Segregated America* (New York: Liveright Books, 2017); Keeanga-Yahmatta Taylor, *Race for Profit: How Banks and the Real Estate Industry Undermined Black Homeownership* (Chapel Hill: University of North Carolina Press, 2019).

12 Touré F. Reed, *Toward Freedom: The Case Against Race-Reductionism* (London: Verso, 2020); see also Larry Dewitt, "The Decision to Exclude Agricultural and Domestic Workers from the 1935 Social Security Act," *Social Security Bulletin* 70:4 (2010), 3–4.

13 Neil M. Maher, *Nature's New Deal: The Civilian Conservation Corps and the Roots of the American Environmental Movement* (Oxford: Oxford University Press, 2008); Nick Taylor, *American-Made: The Enduring Legacy of the WPA: When FDR Put the Nation to Work* (New York: Bantam, 2009).

14 Nick Taylor, *American Made: The Enduring Legacy of the WPA: When FDR Put the Nation to Work* (New York: Bantam Books, 2009), 108.

15 Like many blacks who joined the CCC camps, Luther Wandall's experiences ran up against Jim Crow strictures, but contrary to contemporary voices who condemn the New Deal as irredeemably racist, his recollections are more complex, critical but also filled with a sense of gratitude for the program. Wandall's description of his arrival at Camp Dix is exemplary: "We reached Camp Dix about 7:30 that evening ... And here it was that Mr. James Crow first definitely put in his appearance. When my record was taken at Pier I, a 'C' was placed on it. When the busloads were made up at Whitehall Street an officer reported as follows: '35, 8 colored.' But until now there had been no distinction made. But before we left the bus the officer shouted emphatically: 'Colored boys fall out in the rear.' The colored from several buses were

herded together and stood in line until after the white boys had been registered and taken to their tents. This seemed to be the established order of procedure at Camp Dix. This separation of the colored from the whites was completely and rigidly maintained at this camp." Of course, his experiences did not end there, and on the whole Wandall characterized his as following: "Of course, it reflects, to some extent, all the prejudices of the US Army. But as a job and an experience, for a man who has no work, I can heartily recommend it." See Luther Wandall, "A Negro in the CCC," Crisis 42 (1935), 244, 253–4.

16 Suzanne Mettler, "'The Only Good Thing Was the G.I. Bill': Effects of the Education and Training Provisions on African American Veterans' Political Participation," *Studies in American Political Development* 19 (2005), 31–52; see also Michael J. Bennett, *When Dreams Came True: The GI Bill and the Making of Modern America* (Washington: Brassey's, 1996).

17 Lizabeth Cohen, *Making a New Deal: Industrial Workers in Chicago, 1919–1939* (Cambridge: Cambridge University Press, 1990); Ahmed White, *The Last Great Strike: Little Steel, the CIO and the Struggle for Labor Rights in New Deal America* (Berkeley: University of California Press, 2016); Charles D. Chamberlain, *Victory at Home: Manpower and Race in the American South during World War II* (Athens: University of Georgia Press, 2003).

18 Will P. Jones, *The March on Washington: Jobs, Freedom, and the Forgotten History of Civil Rights* (New York: W.W. Norton, 2014).

19 See Rhonda F. Levine, *Class Struggle and the New Deal: Industrial Labor, Industrial Capital and the State* (Lawrence: University of Kansas, 1988); Meg Jacobs, "'Democracy's Third Estate': New Deal Politics and the Construction of a 'Consuming Public,'" *International Labor and Working-Class History* 55 (1999), 27–51.

20 Thomas Jessen Adams, "The Theater of Inequality," *Nonsite*, August 12, 2014.

21 Ibid.

22 Franklin D. Roosevelt, "Presidential Statement on National Industrial Recovery Act," June 16, 1933, The Social Welfare History Project, socialwelfare.library.vcu.edu.

23 Kenneth T. Jackson, *Crabgrass Frontier: The Suburbanization of the United States* (Oxford: Oxford University Press, 1985), 193; Robert A. Beauregard, *When American Became Suburban* (Minneapolis: University of Minnesota Press, 2006).

24 David Harvey, "The Right to the City," *New Left Review* 53 (September–October 2008), 27.

25 Lizabeth Cohen, *A Consumer Republic: The Politics of Mass Consumption in Postwar America* (New York: Vintage Books, 2004), 195.

26 Jackson, *Crabgrass Frontier*, 207.

27 Price, Fishback, Jesseica LaVoice, Allison Shertzer and Randall Walsh, "The HOLC Maps: How Race and Poverty Influenced Real Estate Professionals' Evaluation of Lending Risk in the 1930s," National Bureau of Economic Research Working Paper Series, October 2021.

28 Reed, *Toward Freedom*; Preston H. Smith II, *Racial Democracy and the Black Metropolis: Housing Policy in Postwar Chicago* (Minneapolis: University of Minnesota, 2012); Beryl Satter, *Family Properties: Race, Real Estate, and the Exploitation of Urban Black America* (New York: Picador, 2021); Arnold R. Hirsch, *Making the Second Ghetto: Race and Housing in Chicago, 1940–1960* (Chicago: University of Chicago Press, 2021 [1983]).

29 David Goldberg and Trevor Griffey, eds., *Black Power at Work: Community Control, Affirmative Action, and the Construction Industry* (Ithaca: Cornell University Press, 2010).

30 Daniel Horowitz, ed., *American Social Classes in the 1950s: Selections from Vance Packard's* The Status Seekers (Boston and New York: Bedford Books of St. Martin's Press, 1995), 69.

31 Herbert Marcuse, *One-Dimensional Man: Studies in the Ideology of Advanced Industrial Society* (Boston: Beacon, 1964), 9.

32 Ibid., 226.

33 John Hannigan, *Fantasy City: Pleasure and Profit in the Postmodern Metropolis* (New York: Routledge, 1998), 33.

34 Ibid., 41.

35 Ibid., 33.

36 The renewed attention to the old expression "I'm free, white and twenty-one" provides some insight into how whiteness studies and activist discourse of white privilege encourage ahistorical and reductionist views of the making of the middle class, and the fact of class diversity among whites. Amid the feverish race talk of the 2016 presidential election primaries, *Jezebel* magazine published an article and brief video about the history of the phrase. The article and social media conversations took up the phrase "I'm free, white and twenty-one" as evidence of the durability of white privilege in American social life and politics. The *Jezebel* article also featured an accompanying video montage

of the phrase's appearance in various motion pictures. Like so much of the popular writing that circulates online, the article managed to get history wrong, even as it referenced the archival material, by excluding useful context and stopping short of full exposition of the subject matter. This renewed media interest in the phrase shed little light on its historical significance and the reasons for its disappearance from popular culture but was more of an exercise in legitimating contemporary beliefs that American culture is endemically racist, and advancing the styles of liberal antiracism, e.g., Black Lives Matter, Afropessimism, that were amplified during the Obama years and amid surging antipolicing protests.

First, this phrase, "free, white and twenty-one," attained popularity during the Depression, a moment when the material circumstances and political allegiances of millions of blacks and whites converged, and amid a gathering storm of interwar New Negro political militancy. Its appearance during that moment is not evidence of an unchanged set of social conditions as proponents of "white privilege" often assume, but quite the contrary. The very fact that we need a refresher on the phrase's origins today underscores that it was truly historical, the creation of a vanished set of Jim Crow conjunctures—i.e., racially codified segregation with "whites only" signage, separate and unequal public schools, the Redshirts, literacy tests, a white-dominated culture industry (there were no Oprahs, Cathy Hughes, Jordan Peeles, Black Twitter, etc.), ascendant notions of freedom as consumer choice, and so forth. Like so much contemporary race talk, "white privilege" is a flexible category that can apply to everything and all contexts. As such, it functions as a sophisticated epithet rather than genuine social insight.

It is worth noting too that this declaration needed to be made publicly and repeatedly by whites at the time, and its social truth was neither self-evident nor inalienable. Rather whites had to declare this claim to freedom and citizenship during the middle twentieth century. Few contemporary interlocutors consider the social contradictions and historical contingency underlying this fact. Why did whites have to make this claim, if as so many contemporary observers hold, their whiteness and white privilege were already a bygone cultural conclusion supported extensively by the social structure and institutions? The origin of this phrase has as much to do with the fact of pervasive white poverty, the ongoing processes of twentieth-century European ethnic immigration and the uncertainty of assimilation during the interwar period than most contemporary, pedestrian discussions of white privilege concede. It is not surprising that the birth of the postwar middle class and the political advances of the civil rights movement would banish the phrase from popular usage.

The pioneering 1959 science fiction film *The World, the Flesh and the Devil* provides a powerful coda to the phrase, marking the end of its common usage. The film appeared amid the tumult of desegregation protests, such as Wichita lunch counter sit-ins, which would serve as the spark of student-led actions against segregated public accommodations. Harry Belafonte, a civil rights activist and confidante of Martin Luther King, Jr., starred as the lead character, Ralph Burton, a black mine inspector who survives an apocalyptic event only to emerge from the shaft to realize that he may well be the last person left on earth. He makes his way to New York City in search of survivors, only to find the metropolis destroyed and deserted. Abandoned vehicles clog the bridges and thoroughfares. He broadcasts daily from an abandoned radio station in search of other survivors and eventually makes contact with Sarah Crandall, a white woman. The two begin a guarded friendship, with Sarah developing a deep attraction to Ralph. When she evokes the phrase "I'm free, white and twenty-one" to defend her prerogative to live wherever she chooses, Ralph fires back, condemning her banal racism. In that moment, when she clings to an ideology of implicit superiority and natural entitlement even when the entire social edifice that secured her position has been decimated, the irrationality of Jim Crow racism is brought fully out into the open. Their heated exchange and the depiction of interracial romance and intimacy, at that historical moment when such subject matter was still taboo, cements the film's place as a powerful parable of mid-twentieth century American society, and creative statement of antiracist liberalism. Far from the kind of Afro-futurist imaginings during the time of Black Lives Matter, where black advancement is somehow disconnected and unrelated to that of whites, this film ends with racial comity. Although Ralph clashes with Benson Thacker, a white man who vies for Sarah's attention, he ultimately lays down his gun and makes peace with Benson. The film closes with this interracial threesome walking hand in hand into the future. See Andrew Heisel, "The Rise and Fall of an All-American Catchphrase: 'Free, White and 21,'" *Jezebel*, September 10, 2015.

37 Johnson, "The Wages of Roediger."

38 Hirsch, *Making the Second Ghetto*.

39 Jackson, *Crabgrass Frontier*, 219.

40 Vern Baxter and Maria Casati, "Building Black Suburbs in New Orleans," in Thomas J. Adams and Matt Sakakeeny, eds., *Remaking New Orleans: Beyond Exceptionalism and Authenticity* (Durham, NC: Duke University Press), 199–218.

41 See Carole Goodwin, *The Oak Park Strategy: Community Control of Racial Change* (Chicago: University of Chicago Press, 1979).

42 Rothstein, *The Color of Law*.

43 Hirsch, *Making the Second Ghetto*.

44 Smith, *Racial Democracy and the Black Metropolis*, xvi.

45 Albert Murray, *South to a Very Old Place*, in Henry Louis Gates, Jr. and Paul Devlin, eds., *Albert Murray: Collected Essays and Memoirs* (New York: The Library of America, 2016), 317.

46 Usmani reviews Naomi Murakawa's *The First Civil Right* and Elizabeth Hinton's *From the War on Poverty to the War on Crime* in "Did Liberals Give Us Mass Incarceration?," *Catalyst* 1:3 (2017).

47 Ronald J. Schmidt, Jr., *This is the City: Making Model Citizens in Los Angeles* (Minneapolis: University of Minnesota Press, 2005), 72; see also Alisa Sarah Kramer, "William H. Parker and the Thin Blue Line: Politics, Public Relations and Policing in Postwar Los Angeles," PhD Thesis, American University, 2007; Robert Bevan, "Screening the L.A.P.D.: Cinematic Representations of Policing and Discourses of Law Enforcement in Los Angeles, 1948–2003," PhD Thesis, University College London, 2011.

48 Quoted in Schmidt, *This is the City*, 72.

49 Ibid., 78.

50 Raphael J. Sonenshein, *Politics in Black and White: Race and Power in Los Angeles* (Princeton: Princeton University Press, 1993), 59–60.

51 Quoted in Schmidt, *This is the City*, 85.

52 Director Carvin Eison's documentary film *July '64* (produced by ImageWordSound) chronicles the often neglected Rochester riots. Set off by police brutality, Rochester's three-day-long rebellion was among the first of the decade. The aftermath of that event brought Malcolm X to the city, where he would deliver his last public address at Corn Hill Methodist Church and inspire the formation of FIGHT (Freedom-Integration-God-Honor-Today), an organization that would pressure Eastman

Kodak, the city's largest employer, to provide more job training, investment and hiring for black Rochesterians. One of the more poignant moments in the film retells how the Mangione convenience store in the city's near north section was spared by looters. The store was owned by the father of Chuck and Gap Mangione who would go on to become prolific jazz musicians. Rochester residents, like All-American footballer and 1965 Olympian Trent Jackson, recalled the way the elder Mangione treated his black customers with generosity and respect, often extending credit to those who could not pay for needed groceries.

53 Cohen, *A Consumers' Republic*, 371–3.

54 See Frank Kusch, *Battleground Chicago: The Police and the 1968 Democratic National Convention* (Chicago: University of Chicago Press, 2008).

55 Anthony Flint, *Wrestling with Moses: How Jane Jacobs Took On New York's Master Builder and Transformed an American City* (New York: Random House, 2009); Robert Kanigel, *Eyes on the Street: The Life of Jane Jacobs* (New York: Alfred A. Knopf, 2016); Robert A. Caro, *The Power Broker: Robert Moses and the Fall of New York* (New York: Vintage Books, 1975); Robert Fishman, "Revolt of the Urbs: Robert Moses and His Critics," in Hillary Ballon and Kenneth T. Jackson, eds., *Robert Moses and the Modern City: The Transformation of New York* (New York: W.W. Norton, 2008), 122–9.

56 Marshall Berman, "It Happens Every Day," in Joan Ockman, ed., *The Pragmatist Imagination* (New York: Princeton Architecture Press, 2001), 215.

57 Jane Jacobs, *The Death and Life of Great American Cities* (New York: Random House, 1961), 36.

58 Ibid., 36.

59 Ibid., 37.

60 Ibid., 42.

61 Stuart Schrader re-reads Jacobs in light of contemporary anti-policing protests. See his "Reading Jane Jacobs in the Era of #BlackLivesMatter," *Harvard Design Magazine* 42 (2017).

62 Neil Smith, *The New Urban Frontier: Gentrification and the Revanchist City* (London: Routledge, 1996); John Arena, *Driven from New Orleans: How Nonprofits Betray Public Housing and Promote Privatization* (Minneapolis: University of Minnesota, 2012); Sylvie Tissot, *Good Neighbors: Gentrifying Diversity in Boston's South End* (London: Verso, 2015).

63 Jacobs, *Death and Life*, 34.

64   Ibid., 31.

65   See Touré F. Reed, "Why Moynihan Was Not So Misunderstood at the Time: The Mythological Prescience of the Moynihan Report and the Problem of Institutional Structuralism," *Nonsite*, September 4, 2015; Daniel Geary, *Beyond Civil Rights: The Moynihan Report and its Legacy* (Philadelphia: University of Pennsylvania, 2015); James T. Patterson, *Freedom is Not Enough: The Moynihan Report and America's Struggle Over Black Life from LBJ to Obama* (New York: Basic Books, 2010); Lee Rainwater and William A. Yancey, eds., *The Moynihan Report and the Politics of Controversy* (Cambridge, MA: MIT Press, 1967).

66   Lyndon B. Johnson, "Commencement Address at Howard University: 'To Fulfill These Rights,'" June 4, 1965, at lbjlib.utexas. edu.

67   Daniel P. Moynihan, "The President and the Negro: The Moment Lost," *Commentary*, February 1967.

68   Ibid.

69   Alice O'Connor, *Poverty Knowledge: Social Science, Social Policy, and the Poor in Twentieth-Century U.S. History* (Princeton: Princeton University Press, 2001); see also Kenneth Clark, *Dark Ghetto: Dilemmas of Social Power* (New York: Harper and Row, 1965); Oscar Lewis, *Children of Sanchez: Autobiography of a Mexican Family* (New York: Vintage Books, 1961); Oscar Lewis, *La Vida: A Puerto Rican Family in the Culture of Poverty—San Juan and New York* (New York: Vintage Books, 1966); Oscar Lewis, "The Culture of Poverty," in Daniel Patrick Moynihan, ed., *Understanding Poverty* (New York: Basic Books, 1969).

70   Reed, "Why Moynihan Was Not So Misunderstood at the Time."

71   Josh Levin, *The Queen: The Forgotten Life Behind an American Myth* (New York: Little Brown and Company, 2019).

3. The Roots of Black Lives Matter

1   Phil A. Neel, *Hinterland: America's New Landscape of Class and Conflict* (London: Reaktion Books, 2018); Reeves, *Dream Hoarders*; Temin, *The Vanishing Middle Class*; Shapiro, *Toxic Inequality*.

2   Marx, *Capital, Volume I*, 792.

3   Chris Lebron, *The Making of Black Lives Matter: A Brief History of an Idea* (Oxford: Oxford University Press, 2017), xiii.

4   Ibid., xxi, original emphasis.

5   Adolph Reed, Jr., "Why Is There No Black Political Movement," in *Class Notes: Posing as Politics and Other Thoughts on the American Scene* (New York: New Press, 2000), 5.

6   Touré F. Reed, *Towards Equality: The Case Against Race Reductionism* (London: Verso, 2020).

7   Jones, *The March on Washington.*

8   James Boggs, *The American Revolution: Pages from a Negro Worker's Notebook* (New York: Monthly Review Press, 1963), 37.

9   Thomas Sugrue, *The Origins of the Urban Crisis: Race and Inequality in Postwar Detroit* (Princeton: Princeton University Press, 1996), 147.

10 Boggs, *American Revolution*, 30–1.

11 Ibid., 52.

12 Ibid.

13 Ibid., 39.

14 Ibid., 46.

15 Ibid., 47.

16 Ibid., 41.

17 Ibid., 37.

18 George Jackson, *Blood in My Eye* (Baltimore: Black Classics Press, 1996).

19 Amy Sonnie and James Tracy, *Hillbilly Nationalists, Urban Race Rebels, and Black Power: Community Organizing in Radical Times* (Brooklyn: Melville House, 2011), 67; see also Jakobi Williams, *From the Bullet to the Ballot: The Illinois Chapter of the Black Panther Party and the Racial Coalition Politics of Chicago* (Chapel Hill: University of North Carolina Press, 2013).

20 The slender, bespectacled Lee cuts a memorable presence in the closing segments of the 1969 documentary film *American Revolution II*, a film that illuminates the difficulty and rewards of political organizing. In some of the film's most memorable scenes, we find Lee wading through rows of white working-class residents, gently coaxing them through Socratic dialogue, and winning them over to the Panthers' revolutionary politics. The film is shot in an immersive verité style and opens with footage of mass demonstrations at the 1968 Democratic National Convention along Michigan Avenue and Grant Park. We witness comedian Dick Gregory improvising a march to McCormick Place Convention Center, recasting the hundreds of marchers as merely a group of friends walking to his house to evade the strict stipulations laid down by the Richard J. Daley administration and the Illinois National Guard. The film turns from the chaos

of the DNC to the equally frenetic scene of a black pool hall, where one Panther attempts to interview and persuade patrons, rather unsuccessfully, of the importance of anti–police brutality organizing. Their lively and humorous banter and the closing segments about the Panthers' attempts to organize the Young Patriots all convey the challenges of organizing, presenting us with a more sober view of the sixties, one that combines both mass protests and mass complicity—rebellion and capitalist hegemony. At various turns, the organizers run smack up against the wall of ideological hegemony among various segments of the working class. This film is not sentimental, and for that reason should be studied carefully and discussed by contemporary activists and citizens eager to end the policing crisis. In one of the final sequences, we witness a community police meeting, moderated by Lee, where residents have a chance to express their grievances directly to a police administrator. Like the opening sequences of disorderly, helmeted and billy club–carrying CPD, this police liaison's clumsy answers, disingenuous posture, and outright blame-labeling of residents in the face of their police brutality testimonies all seem rather innocent, if not laughable, when compared to today's policing apparatus. *American Revolution II*'s black-and-white imagery is very much a time capsule, one that captures the embryonic stages of the carceral state, before elaborate public relations machinery and military-grade weaponry became central dimensions.

This Rainbow Coalition set about organizing in a manner that paralleled and extended the Panther model to other ethnic groups. The Young Lords and Young Patriots in Chicago created their own programs for "survival pending revolution," e.g., health clinics staffed by dissident doctors, free breakfast programs for schoolchildren, legal services, etc. Amy Sonnie and James Tracy contend that these programs treated the poor with greater dignity and respect for their self-determination than the bureaucratic services extended through the War on Poverty. Peggy Terry, who served as a mentor for the Patriots' survival programs, recalled that Uptown's poorest residents were "treated with all the courtesy and dignity of a society matron going to the highest priced doctor you could find anywhere."

These programs had the effect of building a popular constituency, legitimizing these organizations as real and effective in the eyes of the poor, one bowl and one immunization at a time. This dimension of the Panther's survival programs is often misread by latter-day activists and even some academics, who recite FBI director J. Edgar Hoover's infamous condemnation of the free-breakfast programs in a selective manner that forgets the full context of his statement and thereby conclude wrongly that Hoover was against black self-help. I have heard this misreading recited over and again, most famously as a disembodied epigraph in the film *The Black Power Mixtape*. These interpretations neglect Hoover's anticommunism and fail to see how authorities viewed the programs of the Panthers, and for that matter the Lords and Patriots, as a means of deepening communist sympathy in the heart of America's cities. Hoover opposed the free-breakfast programs because they promoted "at least tacit support for the BPP among naïve individuals" and "impressionable youths" building legitimacy and support among the ghetto poor for socialist revolution. See also Amy Sonnie and James Tracy, *Hillbilly Nationalists, Urban Race Rebels, and Black Power: Community Organizing in Radical Times* (Brooklyn: Melville House, 2011); Ray Santisteban, The *First Rainbow Coalition*, directed by Ray Santisteban, Independent Lens, 2019.

21 Williams, *From the Bullet to the Ballot*, 167–90; Simon Balto, *Occupied Territory: Policing Black Chicago from Red Summer to Black Power* (Chapel Hill: University of North Carolina, 2019); Daniel S. Chard, *Nixon's War at Home: The FBI, Leftist Guerillas, and the Origins of Counterterrorism* (Chapel Hill: University of North Carolina, 2021).

22 Heather Ann Thompson, "Why Mass Incarceration Matters: Rethinking Crisis, Decline, and Transformation in Postwar American History," *Journal of American History* (December 2010), 703–34.

23 Adolph Reed, Jr., *Stirrings in the Jug: Black Politics in the Post-segregation Era* (Minneapolis: University of Minnesota, 1999).

24 John Clegg and Adaner Usmani discuss these trends, drawing on FBI Uniform Crime Reports and Bureau of Justice statistics. See Clegg and Usmani, "The Economic Origins of Mass Incarceration."

25 Khalil Gibran Muhammad, "'Black Silent Majority' by Michael Javen Fortner," *New York Times*, September 21, 2015; Kim Moody, "The Roots of Racist Policing," *Spectre*, July 27, 2020.

26 Quoted in Jay and Conklin, *A People's History of Detroit*, 200.

27 Ibid., 201.

28 Nelson Algren, *Chicago: City on the Make* (Chicago: University of Chicago Press, 2001).

29 Andrew Diamond, *Chicago on the Make: Power and Inequality in a Modern City* (Berkeley: University of California Press, 2017), 8–11.

30 John Arena, *Driven from New Orleans: How Nonprofits Betray Public Housing and Promote Privatization* (Minneapolis and London: University of Minnesota, 2012).

31 Elizabeth Wilson, *The Sphinx in the City: Urban Life, the Control of Disorder, and Women* (Berkeley: University of California Press, 1991), 9.

32 Rhonda M. Williams, "Accumulation as Evisceration: Urban Rebellion and the New Growth Dynamics," in Robert Gooding-Williams, ed., *Reading Rodney King, Reading Urban Uprising* (New York: Routledge, 1993), 83–7; Ruth Wilson Gilmore, *Golden Gulag: Prisons, Surplus, Crisis and Opposition in Globalizing California* (Berkeley: University of California Press, 2007), 30–86.

33 "Coast Police Chief Accused of Racism," *New York Times*, May 13, 1982; see also Murch, "Crack in Los Angeles."

34 Mike Davis, "LA: The Fire This Time," *Covert Action Information Bulletin* 41 (Summer 1992), 12.

35 Murray Forman, *The Hood Comes First: Race, Space, and Place in Rap and Hip Hop* (Middletown, CT: Wesleyan University Press, 2002), 106–45; Tricia Rose, *Black Noise: Rap Music and Black Culture in Contemporary America* (Hanover: Wesleyan University Press, 1994).

36 See Nikol Alexander-Floyd, *Gender, Race, and Nationalism in Contemporary Black Politics* (New York: Palgrave MacMillan, 2007); Willie Legette, "The Crisis of the Black Male: A New Ideology in Black Politics," in Adolph Reed, Jr., ed., *Without Justice for All: The New Liberalism and Our Retreat from Racial Equality* (Boulder, CO: Westview, 1999), 291–324.

37 Jay-Z, Molly Crabapple, Jim Batt, Kim Boekbinder and Dream Hampton, "The War on Drugs is an Epic Fail," *New York Times*, September 15, 2016.

38 Demian Bulwa, Charles Burress, Matthew B. Stannard and Matthai Kuruvilaurl, "Protests over BART Shooting Turn Violent," *San Francisco Chronicle*, January 8, 2009; Farai Chideya, "Hundreds Protest in Oakland over BART Shooting," *National Public Radio*, January 8, 2009.

39 The anticapitalist politics of the Oscar Grant protests, Occupy Oakland and the various social struggles who forged those historical events are reflected in a pathbreaking trilogy of films

that emerged from the Bay Area in the space of a year. *Sorry to Bother You* (2018), directed by rapper Boots Riley, *Blind-spotting* (2018), which starred Daveed Diggs of the celebrated musical *Hamilton*, and the subtle and unexpected artistry of *The Last Black Man in San Francisco* (2019) each provided critical takes on the revanchist remaking of the Bay Area, and in ways that are accessible, humorous, nuanced, imaginative, impactful, surreal and welcome. Each film broke radically from the usual fare of Hollywood films about black working-class life and made explicit connections between black suffering and capitalist political economy. *The Last Black Man in San Francisco* belongs in the same category of other recent films like *Creed, Hunter-Gatherer* and *Moonlight*, which molted off crack cocaine–era urban tropes of redemptive black patriarchy and offered more complicated and diverse portrayals of black masculinity.

40 George Ciccariello-Maher, "From Oscar Grant to Occupy: The Long Arc of Rebellion in Oakland," in Kate Khatib, Margaret Killjoy and Mike McGuire, eds., *We Are Many: Reflections on Movement Strategy from Occupation to Liberation* (Oakland: AK Press, 2012), 41.

41 Ibid.

42 See Cedric Johnson, *The Panthers Can't Save Us Now* (London: Verso, 2022); Adam Szetela, "Black Lives Matter at Five: Limits and Possibilities," *Ethnic and Racial Studies* 43:8 (2020), 1358–83.

43 Alicia Garza, "Herstory," at blacklivesmatter.com; see also Alicia Garza, *The Purpose of Power: How to Build Movements for the 21st Century* (London: Doubleday, 2020), 95–122.

44 Krissah Thompson and Scott Wilson, "Obama on Trayvon Martin: 'If I had a son, he'd look like Trayvon,'" *Washington Post*, March 23, 2012.

45 Frank James, "Trayvon Martin Tragedy Edges onto Presidential Trail," *NPR*, March 23, 2012.

46 Kenneth Warren, "The Poetics and Politics of Black Lives Matter," *Nonsite*, September 10, 2020.

47 The problems of social media noted here in relation to civic life have also encroached on the integrity of intellectual work. Academia has never been devoid of hierarchies, exclusions, abuses of power and unethical practices, but the porosity of social media life and scholarly pursuits have made it more difficult to engage in honest, informed criticism in a world where any argument that is out of step with a widely accepted line can provoke an online

feeding frenzy. The right-wing has seized upon the problem of "cancel culture" as a way of shielding their reactionary commitments to religion over science, patriarchy over women's rights, whiteness over diversity and private property rights over labor from any criticism. Yet cancellation is still a bigger problem, even beyond the right-wing's cynical mobilizations of the term.

One case in point is the furor over graduate student Adam Szetela's 2019 article "Black Lives Matter at Five," which criticized the limits of the identity politics spawned by recent antipolicing protests. The online "debate" over Szetela's article was unfounded, unfair and telling, a familiar sign of the times. It was yet another example of how social media has not helped enhance public debate and, maybe more disturbing, it provided troubling evidence of viral anti-intellectualism infecting academe.

The first line of Shantel Gabrieal Buggs's Twitter posts, which sparked the outrage, sets the tone. She wanted to start a discussion about "how white folks who don't actually understand the movement shouldn't be writing about it," and hers was precisely the kind of faulty premise that Szetela went to great lengths to criticize, the specious notion that corporeal identity is synonymous with analytic insight and political interests. Buggs and her Twitter mob were upset because Szetela was white but offered little of substance about where his arguments were actually wrong. Despite their claims about the lack of evidence, in their rush to grab their pitchforks and favored academic tracts, the critics also diminished the scholarship that Szetela engaged with, much of it authored by people of color. The fact that there were black academics who agree with some of his claims about identitarianism, and the limits of black ethnic politics was inconvenient for those who wanted to argue that Szetela was an illegitimate interlocutor on this subject solely because he was white. This was a ruse, however, because if Szetela had begun his article in the usual manner of white confessional and self-loathing that so many liberal academics adore, and proceeded to write an article praising the pioneering, critical spirit of BLM activism, none of these people would have taken to social media to claim his work was illegitimate. His identity provided an easy, soft target for those who objected to the ideological content of his work. This reaction to Szetela's article was about policing the kind of Marxist class analysis he offered. If he had toed the familiar identitarian line, he might have been celebrated as a good "ally" by the same crowd.

Not long after Buggs's initial post, a petition was started calling for the retraction of Szetela's article. This did not happen, but like similar calls against Rebecca Tuvel's 2017 *Hypatia* article about transracialism, it reveals a new terrain where some academics are now willing to censor articles they do not agree with, and worse to oppose articles that are written by persons with bodies and social locations they deem not authorized to speak on the subject matter. See Adam Szetela, "Black Lives Matter at Five: Limits and Possibilities"; Emma Pettit, "'You Have to Provide Evidence': A Journal Article on Black Lives Matter Draws Scholarly Fire," *Chronicle of Higher Education*, July 30, 2019; see also Rebecca Tuvel, "In Defense of Transracialism,"; Rogers Brubaker, "Uproar over 'Transracialism,' " *New York Times*, May 18, 2017; Lindsay McKenzie, "Journal's Board Disavows Apology for 'Transracialism' Article, Making Retraction Unlikely," *Chronicle of Higher Education*, May 18, 2017.

48 Working in different art forms, both the 2017 documentary film *Whose Streets?* directed by Sabaah Folayan and Damon Davis, and Kristiana Rae Colón's play *Florissant and Canfield* provide helpful explorations of the internal contradictions of the Ferguson protests. Both works combine the immersive experiences of their creators and bring voice to the perspective of working-class black Ferguson. *Whose Streets?* is essentially war reporting, dispatches from the frontlines as told by residents and activists in the face of heavily armored police units, while *Florissant and Canfield* succeeds in capturing the internal dialogues and aspirations of the protestors.

Folayan and Davis's film offered a necessary alternative to the forty-eight-hour corporate news cycle, which sent its cameras to Ferguson in the moments of flare up, fixated on property damage and looting, but failed to provide a sustained look at how the lives of black working-class locals were transformed in myriad ways as the investigation, trial, skirmishes, recurrent mobilization, and cycles of hope and despair unfolded over months after the killing of Michael Brown. The opening scene literally places black working-class St. Louis residents in the driver's seat, as the audience is treated to a rear passenger perspective, riding down a rainy street, while the driver waxes eloquent on systemic inequalities. *Whose Streets?* excels in placing its audience at the heart of the protests, foregrounding the perspective of eyewitnesses and residents, and exposing the militaristic tactics of police. In one dramatic scene, black Ferguson residents stand within the fencing of their own property, and almost immediately after declaring their compliance with police orders, a phalanx of police fires a canister in the direction of the residents and camera crew. In another especially powerful scene, Dhoruba, a Ferguson resident sits calmly on his couch with his infant daughter and partner nearby, and displays evidence of police tactics, a collection of rubber bullets, spent shotgun shells, chemical weapons and assorted, exploded CS gas cannisters used against the protestors.

Colón is a poet, playwright and cofounder of the Chicago-based #LetUsBreatheCollective, which staged a sustained protest encampment outside the Homan Square black site on Chicago's West Side, where police engaged in off-the-books detention and interrogation of thousands of mostly black suspects. Colón marshals her activist experiences during the Ferguson protests and keen ear for dialogue to immerse her audience in a movement culture coming into being and the lively debates between locals, newcomers, lovers and comrades. The play was workshopped at the University of Illinois at Chicago in 2018 and featured a large and diverse cast. Reflecting the core sentiments and zeitgeist of Black Lives Matter more effectively than any programmatic statement or editorial, Colón's script is pure poetry, filled with vernacular humor and coursing with the romance and hopes of the antipolicing struggles that took shape in Ferguson. She captures the tension between black Ferguson residents and white activists, mostly anarchists, who descended on the town to express their opposition to police, but who would move on leaving the locals to pick up the pieces of their riot-torn neighborhoods and communities. See Spencer Ackerman, "Homan Square Revealed: How Chicago Police Disappeared 7,000 people," *Guardian*, October 19, 2015.

49 Warren, "The Poetics and Politics of Black Lives Matter."

50 Drew Franklin, "DeRay McKesson's Baltimore Mayoral Run Has a Teach for American Problem," *In These Times*, February 22, 2016.

51 "ALL FACTS NO CAP: The Truth about Tamika Mallory's Cadillac Commercial," *YouTube*, March 30, 2021.

52 Troy L. Smith, "Samaria Rice Rebukes Tamika Mallory, Others 'Benefitting Off the Blood' of Police Brutality Victims," cleveland. com, March 16, 2021.

53 Adrienne Maree Brown, "Disrupting the Pattern: A Call for Love and Solidarity," adriennemareebrown.net, April 17, 2021.

54 Ibid.

55 David Harvey, "Response to Alex Dubilet," *Syndicate*, April 1, 2015; see also David Roediger, *Class, Race, and Marxism* (London: Verso, 2017), 1–4; Joe R. Feagin, "Beyond the Class-Race Binary," *Monthly Review*, September 1, 2018.

56 Harvey, "Response to Alex Dubilet."

57 Alexi Dubilet, "Dispossession, Uselessness, and the Limits of Humanism," *Syndicate*, April 1, 2015.

58 Joshua Clover, *Riot. Strike. Riot: The New Era of Uprisings* (London: Verso, 2019).

59 See Szetela, "Black Lives Matter at Five."

60 @TefPoe, December 14, 2017, twitter.com.

4. The World of Freddie Gray

1 Stokely Carmichael and Charles V. Hamilton, *Black Power: The Politics of Liberation in America* (New York: Vintage Books, 1967), 161.

2 Kerner Commission (US Riot Commission), *Report of the National Advisory Commission on Civil Disorders* (New York: Bantam, 1968), 1.

3 Carmichael and Hamilton, *Black Power*, 161.

4 Ibid.

5 Carmichael and Hamilton, *Black Power*, 42–5.

6 Stokely Carmichael, "Berkeley Speech," in *Stokely Speaks: From Black Power to Pan-Africanism* (New York: Vintage, 1971), 47.

7 Keeanga-Yamahtta Taylor, "Black Faces in High Places," *Jacobin*, May 4, 2015.

8 Reed, "Why Moynihan Was Not So Misunderstood at the Time"; Smith, *Racial Democracy and the Black Metropolis*; Jones, *The March on Washington*.

9 Kent Germany, *New Orleans After the Promises: Poverty, Citizenship, and the Search for the Great Society* (Atlanta: University of Georgia Pres, 2007); Reed, *Stirrings in the Jug*, 88–9.

10 David Harvey, *A Brief History of Neoliberalism* (Oxford: Oxford University Press, 2005), 4; Jason Hackworth, *The Neoliberal City: Governance, Ideology and Development in American Urbanism* (Ithaca: Cornell University Press, 2007); Jaime Peck, Nik Theodore and Neil Brenner, "Neoliberal Urbanism: Models, Moments, and Mutations," *SAIS Review* 29:1 (2009), 49–66; Jaime Peck, *Constructions of Neoliberal Reason* (Oxford: Oxford University Press, 2010).

11　Peter Levy, "Dream Deferred: The Assassination of Martin Luther King, Jr. and the Holy Week Uprising of 1968," in Jessica Elfenbein, Thomas L. Hollowack and Elizabeth M. Nix, eds., *Baltimore '68: Riots and Rebirth in an American City* (Philadelphia: Temple University Press, 2011), 8.

12　Ibid., 4–7.

13　Peter Hermann and John Woodrow Cox, "A Freddie Gray Primer: Who Was He, How Did He Die, and Why Is There So Much Anger?," *Washington Post*, April 28, 2015; Faith Karimi, Kim Berryman and Dana Ford, "Who Was Freddie Gray, Whose Death Has Reignited Protests Against Police?," *CNN*, May 2, 2015; Jana Kasperkevic, "In Freddie Gray's Neighborhood, More than a Third of Households Are in Poverty," *Guardian*, April 28, 2015.

14　David Harvey, *Spaces of Hope* (Berkeley: University of California Press, 2000), 133; David Harvey, "A View from Federal Hill," in Elizabeth Fee, Linda Shopes and Linda Zeidman, eds., *The Baltimore Book: New Views of Local History* (Philadelphia: Temple University Press, 1992).

15　Rhonda Levine, *Class Struggle and the New Deal: Industrial Labor, Industrial Capital, and the State* (Lawrence: University Press of Kansas, 1988); Nelson Lichtenstein, *State of the Union: A Century of American Labor* (Princeton: Princeton University Press, 2002); Cohen, *A Consumers' Republic*; Sugrue, *The Origins of the Urban Crisis*; Barry Bluestone and Bennett Harrison, *Deindustrialization of America: Plant Closings, Community Abandonment, and the Dismantling of Basic Industry* (New York: Basic Books, 1982); Judith Stein, *The Pivotal Decade: How the United States Traded Factories for Finance in the Seventies* (New Haven: Yale University Press, 2010); Jefferson Cowie and Joseph Heathcott, *Beyond the Ruins: The Meanings of Deindustrialization* (New York: Cornell University Press, 2003).

16　Harvey, *Spaces of Hope*, 148.

17　Edna Bonacich and Khaleelah Hardie, "Wal-Mart and the Logistics Revolution," in Nelson Lichtenstein, ed., *Wal-Mart: The Face of Twenty-First Century Capitalism* (New York: The New Press, 2006), 163–87.

18　Jane Berger, "'There is Tragedy on Both Sides of the Layoffs': Privatization and the Urban Crisis in Baltimore," *International Labor and Working-Class History* 71 (2007), 29–49; Williams, "Accumulation as Evisceration."

19　Harvey, "A View from Federal Hill," 141–2.

20 Alec MacGillis, "The Tragedy of Baltimore," *New York Times Magazine*, March 12, 2019.

21 Wacquant, "Class, Race and Hyperincarceration in Revanchist America."

22 Kasperkevic, "In Freddie Gray's Neighborhood."

23 Lester Spence, "Corporate Welfare is Draining Baltimore," *Boston Review*, May 14, 2015.

24 Touré F. Reed, "Why Liberals Separate Race from Class," *Jacobin*, August 22, 2015.

25 "Transcript: Illinois Senate Candidate Barack Obama," *Washington Post*, July 27, 2004.

26 Bill Cosby, "Address to the NAACP on the 50th Anniversary of *Brown v. Board of Education*," May 17, 2004.

27 "The O Interview: Oprah Talks to Barack Obama," *O, The Oprah Magazine*, November 2004, 248–51, 288–92.

28 Paul Street, *The Empire's New Clothes: Barack Obama and the Real World of* Power (New York: Paradigm Publishers, 2010), 140–2.

29 "Transcript of Obama's Remarks at Chicago Academy," *The Root*, February 15, 2013.

30 "Remarks by President Obama and Prime Minster Abe of Japan in Joint Press Conference," White House, Office of the Press Secretary, April 28, 2015.

31 Steven Thrasher, "My Brother's Keeper Initiative to Ensure 'You Matter,' Obama Explains in Bronx," *Guardian*, May 4, 2015.

32 "Remarks by the President at Launch of the My Brother's Keeper Alliance," White House, Office of the Press Secretary, May 4, 2015.

33 Ron Cassie, "Big Brothers Big Sisters Sees 3000 Percent Jump in Mentor Inquires," *Baltimore*, May 7, 2015.

34 Megan Sherman, "'One Baltimore' Rally Unites Groups Against Privatization," *The Real News*, October 30, 2014; Yvonne Wenger, "Baltimore Officials Say There's No Plan to Privatize Water System," *Baltimore Sun*, October 24, 2014.

35 Luke Broadwater, "Rawlings-Blake Announces 'One Baltimore' Campaign," *Baltimore Sun*, May 7, 2015.

36 Adrienne Dixson, "Whose Choice? A Critical Race Perspective on Charter Schools," in Cedric Johnson, ed., *The Neoliberal Deluge: Hurricane Katrina, Late Capitalism, and the Remaking of New Orleans* (Minneapolis: University of Minnesota, 2011); Vincanne Adams, *Markets of Sorrow, Labors of Faith: New Orleans in the Wake of Katrina* (Durham, NC: Duke University Press,

2013); John Arena, *Driven From New Orleans: How Nonprofits Betray Public Housing and Promote Privatization* (Minneapolis: University of Minnesota Press, 2012); Kristen Buras, *Charter Schools, Race, and Urban Space: Where the Market Meets Grassroots Resistance* (New York: Routledge, 2015).

37   Arena, *Driven From New Orleans*, 145–86.

38   Megan French-Marcelin, "Gentrification's Ground Zero," *Jacobin*, August 28, 2015.

39   Cedric Johnson, "What's Left for New Orleans? The Peoples Reconstruction and the Limits of Anarcho-liberalism," in Thomas Jessen Adams and Matt Sakakeeny, eds., *Remaking New Orleans: Beyond Authenticity and Exceptionalism* (Durham, NC: Duke University Press, 2019), 261–87.

40   MacGillis, "The Tragedy of Baltimore."

41   "Jamal Bryant G Checked by PFK Boom and Shy Lady Heroin," *YouTube*, May 25, 2016.

42   David Madden and Peter Marcuse, *In Defense of Housing* (London: Verso, 2016), 47.

43   Ibid.

44   David Harvey, "A Tale of Three Cities," *Tribune*, January 10, 2019.

45   Glyn Robbins, "Knives, Lives and Homes," *Housing Matters* blog, April 8, 2018.

46   Luke Broadwater and Talia Richman, "Gilmor Homes Demolition Planned—132 Units to Come Down, 120 families to be Relocated under Mayor's Proposal," *Baltimore Sun*, January 11, 2018; see also Yvonne Wenger, "Residents to Begin Moving Out of a Section of Baltimore's Gilmor Homes to Clear Way for Demolition," *Baltimore Sun*, April 11, 2019; Michael Anft, "Three Years After His Death, Freddie Gray's Neighborhood Faces a New Loss," *City Lab*, April 19, 2018.

47   Patrick Sisson, "In Baltimore, Under Armour's Owner Invests in $5.5 Billion Bet on His City," *Curbed*, April 11, 2017; Adam Marton, Natalie Sherman and Caroline Pate, "The Port Covington Redevelopment Examined," *Baltimore Sun*, September 2016.

48   Harvey, *Spaces of Hope*, 141.

49   Melody Simmons, "City Council Passes $660 Million TIF Package for Port Covington," *Baltimore Business Journal*, September 19, 2016.

50   Jeff Ernsthausen and Justin Elliot, "One Trump Tax Cut Was Meant to Help the Poor. A Billioniare Ended Up Winning Big," *ProPublica*, June 19, 2019.

5. Whose Streets?

1 Mark Brown, "Sessions Ruffles Rahm's, Lisa's Feathers with 'Lame Duck' Consent Decree Crack," *Chicago Sun-Times*, October 19, 2018.

2 Dan Hinkel, "Praise, Criticism at Hearing for Consent Decree That Would Reform Chicago Police Department," *Chicago Tribune*, October 24, 2018.

3 Larry Bennett, Robert Gardner and Euan Hague, eds., *Neoliberal Chicago* (Urbana: University of Illinois Press, 2017); Diamond, *Chicago on the Make*; Kari Lydersen, *Mayor 1%: Rahm Emanuel and the Rise of Chicago's 99%* (Chicago: Haymarket Books, 2013); Larry Bennett, *The Third City: Chicago and American Urbanism* (Chicago: University of Chicago Press, 2010).

4 Heather Cherone, "City Council Approves Elected Board to Oversee Chicago Police in 36–13 Vote," *WTTW*, July 21, 2021; John Byrne, "Chicago Police Oversight Compromise Announced; Civilian Panel Wouldn't Have Power to Remove Superintendent," *Chicago Tribune*, July 19, 2021; Mark Guarino, "Oversight of Chicago Police Handed to New Civilian Commission after Years of Public Pressure," *Washington Post*, July 21, 2021; Chicago Civilian Oversight Ordinance, July 17, 2021, at news.wttw.com.

5 Fran Spielman, "Civilian Police Review Will Finally Pass City Council in February or March, Alderman Says," *Chicago Sun-Times*, January 23, 2020; Gregory Pratt, "Several Incoming Aldermen Say They'll Back Stalled Chicago Police Civilian Oversight Plan," *Chicago Tribune*, May 14, 2019; April Lane, "Know Your Movements: The #EraseTheDatabase Campaign," *South Side Weekly*, October 16, 2018; Mike Dumke, "Cook County Takes Steps to Erase Its Regional Gang Database," *ProPublica Illinois*, February 20, 2019; Editorial Board, "Wipe Chicago's Disastrous Gang Database and Start from Scratch," *Chicago Tribune*, April 11, 2019.

6 Lydersen also captures the way that Emanuel's top-down approach to governance, and generous concessions to the investor class helped to breed broad discontent with this administration: "From that viewpoint, the messy attributes of democracy—sit-ins, protests, rallies, people demanding meetings and information and input—simply slow down and encumber the streamlined, bottom-line-driven process Emanuel knows is best. But many regular Chicagoans see injustice, callousness, and even cruelty in this trickle-down, authoritarian approach to city governance.

They see the mayor bringing thousands of new corporate jobs subsidized with taxpayer dollars while laying off middle-class public sector workers like librarians, call center staffers, crossing guards, and mental health therapists. They see him closing neighborhood schools, throwing parents' and students' lives into turmoil. They see him (like Daley) passing ordinances at will through a rubber-stamp City Council, leaving citizens with few meaningful avenues to express their opposition to policies changing the face of their city." Lydersen, *Mayor 1%*, 6.

7   Rahm Emanuel, "Public Safety Remarks as Prepared," Mayor's Press Office, September 22, 2016, chicago.gov.

8   Gottschalk, *Caught*, 258.

9   Kim Janssen, "Michigan Avenue Black Friday Protests Cost Stores 25–50 Percent of Sales," *Chicago Tribune*, November 30, 2015; Mary Wisniewsk and Nick Carey, "'Black Friday' Protest of Police Shooting Shuts Main Chicago Shopping Street," *Reuters*, November 27, 2015.

10   Christy Gutowski and Jeremy Gorner, "The Complicated, Short Life of Laquan McDonald," *Chicago Tribune*, December 11, 2015; Christy Gutowski, "'This Kid Had an Impact on People': The Trouble Life and Fleeting Potential of Laquan McDonald," *Chicago Tribune*, September 14, 2018.

11   *16 Shots: The Shooting of Laquan McDonald*, WBEZ Chicago and Chicago Tribune, wbez.org.

12   Spencer Ackerman, "Homan Square Revealed: How Chicago Police 'Disappeared' 7,000 People," *Guardian*, October 19, 2015.

13   Jamie Peck and Nik Theodore, "Carceral Chicago: Making the Ex-Offender Employability Crisis," *International Journal of Urban and Regional Research* 32:2 (2008), 251–81.

14   John Byrne, "Rahm Emanuel Tells Spike Lee He's Not Happy about Chiraq Title," *Chicago Tribune*, April 15, 2015.

15   Bryan Smith, "The Ballad of Ed 'Bad Boy' Brown," *Chicago Magazine*, March 13, 2017.

16   Clegg and Usmani, "The Economic Origins of Mass Incarceration"; Forman, "Racial Critiques of Mass Incarceration"; Forman, *Locking Up Our Own*; Gottschalk, *Caught*.

17   Editorial Board, "What Are We to Make of a Big Crowd of Unruly Teenagers?," *Chicago Sun-Times*, April 18, 2019.

18   "French Tourists Warned to Stay Away from South, West Sides," *CBS Chicago*, November 19, 2013.

19   D. Bradford Hunt, *Blueprint for Disaster: The Unraveling of Chicago Public Housing* (Chicago: University of Chicago Press,

2009); Costas Spirou and Larry Bennett, "Metropolitan Chicago's Geography of Inequality," in Bennett et al., eds., *Neoliberal Chicago*, 47–71; Larry Bennett, Janet Smith and Patricia Wright, eds., *Where Are Poor People to Live? Transforming Public Housing Communities* (Armonk, NY: M.E. Sharpe, 2006); Edward Goetz, *New Deal Ruins: Race, Economic Justice, and Public Housing Policy* (Ithaca: Cornell University Press, 2013).

20 Robert R. Aspholm, *Views from the Streets: The Transformation of Gangs and Violence on Chicago's South Side* (New York: Columbia University Press, 2020), 156.

21 Ibid.

22 Lydersen, *Mayor 1%*, 193–212.

23 Smith, *The New Urban Frontier*, 3–29; Clayton Patterson, ed., *Resistance: A Radical Social and Political History of the Lower East Side* (New York: Seven Stories Press, 2007).

24 Daniel Singer, *Prelude to Revolution: France in May 1968* (Chicago: Haymarket Books, 2013); Andrew Feenberg, *When Poetry Ruled the Streets: The French May Events of 1968* (Albany: State University of New York Press, 2001); Henri Lefebvre, *The Explosion: Marxism and the French Upheaval* (New York: Monthly Review Press, 1969).

25 Henri Lefebvre, "The Right to the City," in Eleonore Kofman and Elizabeth Lebas, eds., *Writings on Cities* (Oxford: Blackwell, 1996), 158.

26 David Harvey, "The Right to the City," in *Rebel Cities: From the Right to the City to the Urban Revolution* (London and New York, Verso, 2012), 4.

27 Lefebvre defines urban society as "the society that results from industrialization, which is a process of domination that absorbs agricultural production. This urban society cannot take shape conceptually until the end of a process during which the old urban forms, the end result of a series of discontinuous transformations, burst apart." Henri Lefebvre, *The Urban Revolution* (Minneapolis: University of Minnesota, 2003), 2.

28 Andrew Merrifield, *The New Urban Question* (London: Pluto, 2012), 5.

29 Ibid., 79. Merrifield says this translation of Rousseau's original French text is "woefully inadequate" and that this "standard translation hints of a certain bourgeois re-appropriation and makes Rousseau's radical text sound a lot less radical than it might still be." Rousseau's original French text reads: "la plupart prennent une ville pour une cité, et un bourgeois pour un citoyen,

ils ne savent pas que les maisons font la ville, mais que les cit-oyens font la cité." Merrifield writes that the word "town" is a "much too archaic term, and a much too limited (and redun-dant) political jurisdiction to have meaning for a contemporary reader" and "city" is a "problematic basis for a 'modern' concept of citizenship." Merrifield retranslates Rousseau's original state-ment with these linguistic limitations in mind.

30 Ibid., 80–1.

31 Ibid., 82–3.

32 Ibid., 86.

33 Don Mitchell, "Against Safety, Against Security: Reinvigorat-ing Urban Life," in Michael J. Thompson, ed., *Fleeing the City: Studies in the Culture and Politics of Antiurbanism* (New York: Palgrave Macmillan, 2009), 232–3.

34 Ibid.

35 The challenges we face in reversing course and building the kind of popular consent for a socially just city may be even more daunting still, especially in contexts where the public sphere, those spaces where public spiritedness might take shape between citizens, has been degraded and diminished. In her 1998 ethno-graphic study *Avoiding Politics*, Nina Eliasoph concluded that in ordinary everyday contexts, like volunteer settings, social clubs and recreational activities, Americans' political talk was defined by "strenuous disengagement." Surprisingly, Eliasoph found that this practice of political avoidance was even prevalent among activists, who were more than willing to share their political views in private, but would often shrink from providing full, overt political justification for their stances in public settings like press conferences. For instance, Eliasoph witnessed some seasoned environmentalists who, when facing the public, would couch their opposition in more innocuous terms of "speaking for them-selves," rather than speaking for any fully formed constituency or marshalling their copious knowledge of scientific evidence and the documented harm of a planned incinerator project looking to secure public approval. These activists were making adjustments to the political terrain of the moment, one of capitalist triumphal-ism and left-political abeyance. Eliasoph's study was conducted during the nineties in part, in the immediate aftermath of the Cold War, and was published before antiglobalization protests emerged as a popular force throughout North America.

Some might argue that the popularity of social media and the expansion of struggles like Occupy Wall Street and Black Lives

Matter have rendered Eliasoph's conclusions timebound, and we are witnessing the expansion of open political talk in ways that were missing among her research subjects. Our own times, they might argue, are defined by continuous political engagement rather than avoidance. Such conclusions about the impact of social media, however, would be overstated. Eliasoph was concerned with the development of public spiritedness, the sense of a life in common with other citizens, and how that life might be enriched and advanced through coordinated political action. This may hold true for the activist elements in society, and certainly social media has provided space for thinking collectively, debating social issues and discovering common ground, but these same spaces have also played host to all manner of antisocial, anti-intellectual, conspiratorial and certainly antipublic rhetoric. Eliasoph discusses the public sphere as those spaces between us where political talk happens and where public spiritedness can take shape. Twitter, Facebook, Instagram and Snapchat are hardly the public square. Such platforms may augment public discussions and organizing, but they are primarily for-profit media, which are engaged in willful disinformation, data mining (again, for profit) and commercialization more than promoting the quality of progressive political communication that preoccupied Eliasoph's formative work.

These ethereal spaces may, more than anything, help to nurture the kind of personality she described as *cynical chic*, whose extensive knowledge of the problems facing us does not become the source of political engagement, but the cause of paralysis and retreat. Eliasoph describes the way cynical solidarity often took shape in discussions, and how extensive understanding of current affairs could paradoxically also further the process of "political evaporation" and alienation. "Cynics were incredibly knowledgeable about politics," Eliasoph writes. "Cynical solidarity relied on first invoking the world's problems to show that I recognize the problems and, along with you, am not a 'bubba.' The second step was to say why the problems do not affect me. Usually, the answer is that I have rendered myself impervious, through laughter. So, the image of powerlessness peeps in, but the door quickly slams on it. Knowledge of one's own powerlessness was a taken-for-granted prerequisite of conversation but when it became an explicit topic, participants quickly showed that they were not so powerless after all: they were impervious and somehow exempted themselves." In the end, this über

well-informed person never leaves the safety of her own beliefs
and knowledge of how the world works to engage with other
citizens in the unpredictable moil of real politics. Social media
provides the perfect platform for this mode of disengagement,
a place to display one's knowledge, demonstrate superiority to
those less knowledgeable, trash the views of those who disagree
with you, and register your politics in the form of securing "likes,"
tracking shares, signing petitions and trolling, all of which are
proto-political and do not involve the risk-taking, compromise,
learning and bonds of trust that are necessary to build solidarity
and achieve concrete forms of social good. See Nina Eliasoph,
*Avoiding Politics: How Americans Produce Apathy in Everyday
Life* (Cambridge and New York: Cambridge University Press,
1998), 161–2.

36 Mitchell, "Against Safety, Against Security," 231–3.

37 Tim Louis Macaluso, "Mapping the Murders," *City*, July 14,
2006.

38 I lived in Rochester during the violent crime wave that provoked
Layton's intervention. Of course, Chicagoans and residents of
larger cities may scoff at the comparatively small raw numbers
of homicides in a city like Rochester during the 2000s, but
Americans in large metropolitan areas should not accept high
levels of violence as some inevitable state of affairs. My reports
on Rochester's homicide rates always made my Toronto friends
shudder whenever I traveled there for a talk or weekend getaway.
Such numbers, although tame by American urban expectations,
were unthinkable in a city like Toronto, which was fifteen times
larger than Rochester. It is worth noting too that in smaller and
mid-sized cities, the experience of crime and violence, like other
things, is more intimate. All of the social buffers, degrees of personal separation, and physical distance that you might have as a
resident in a sprawling metropolis are stripped away. During my
last five years or so in Rochester, multiple shootings happened
within a block of my house. The first was a midnight incident
where someone fired multiple shotgun blasts into the window of
a neighbor's home. Apparently, the same offender returned weeks
later to set that house on fire. A second gun incident was actually
a pair of drive-by shootings on the same day, in front of a convenience store where my oldest child and dozens of middle-schoolers
waited for the city bus every day. The curbside memorials of votive
candles and balloons you can find in working-class black and
brown urban neighborhoods across the country were common

in the southwest part of the city where I lived. Part protest, part public grieving, these small monuments remained on side streets and major thoroughfares until their deflated Mylar, melted wax and tattered stuffed animals were swept up by sanitation workers or buried in the region's endless snowfall.

What was especially clear during my Rochester years, however, was the informalization of death in contexts where murder had taken on such a degree of intergenerational regularity and frequency. Having grown up in a majority-black, southern Louisiana world that was heavily impacted by the crack cocaine crisis and the carceral build-up during the eighties, I had lost friends and classmates to gun violence as victims and perpetrators. My sister's boyfriend was killed when he attempted to intervene in a dispute between his father and a young drug dealer. He bled out waiting for an ambulance to arrive and died less than a mile from the nearest hospital. At the wake, my cousin and I could not stand over his body for long, which looked nothing like the affable and athletic kid we knew. We both managed to wish awkward condolences to the family, before finding the nearest exit. We stood on the steps of the funeral home, enveloped in the warm gusts and crystalline sky that did not seem to match the occasion, both remarking on the father's bewildered face and the terrible finality of it all. In Louisiana during the late eighties, you were still expected to wear your "Sunday best" to a funeral. Catholics were more relaxed about this, and there were different generational expectations as well, but jeans and sneakers were a show of disrespect in a world that was still populated by generations who had spent their lives as domestics, sharecroppers and hired hands. Some of the elders in my childhood church were present when the cornerstone was laid in the 1920s, and old men wore the same suits tailored by country seamstresses when they were young men and kept over the decades for every wedding, funeral and Sunday mass. In the context of the Jim Crow segregation they had survived, a suit of gabardine was a suit of armor, commanding respect in the world within the veil despite whatever laws the planter class concocted to control their labor and degrade their spirits.

During the aughts in Rochester, my southern experience contrasted sharply with the crowds outside Regency Funeral Chapel on Genesee Street, or Latimer and Sons on Plymouth, mostly wearing bright T-shirts with the silkscreened image of the deceased and Bible scriptures, a favorite saying or nickname emblazoned in bold lettering. Death had lost its formality. The crack cocaine years and successive waves of homicide in American cities has transformed black mourning, retaining the jubilation of protestant burial practices but incorporating new rituals that reflected different economic conditions and the grim routinization of urban violence.

39 Ashlee Rezin, "Activist's Art Project Analyzes Chicago's Segregation in 'Folded Map' Project," *Chicago Sun-Times*, November 15, 2018.

40 Mitchell, "Against Safety, Against Security," 242–3.

41 Ibid., 242.

42 Building critically on comments of then general Dwight Eisenhower, Jameson proposes the universal army, national conscription as a means of establishing a new socioeconomic structure. Jameson writes: "Indeed, in order to see this new army—the universal army—in the proper light, it is necessary to understand that it is not a new form of government but rather a new social structure, or better still, a new socioeconomic structure, as we shall see. In the transitional phase—that of dual power —the coexistence of the old state and the new one will indeed seem to be a rivalry of governmental powers; little by little, however, it will be understood that it is the old state which is in reality the 'government,' and destined as such to 'wither away,' and the new structure, which is in fact the society at large or, if you prefer, the completion of that 'civil society' which Hegel in his own time took to be simply the sphere of private life and of business and commerce. There are suggestive analogies to this process in antiquity: for example, when Augustus founded the Roman Empire as such, he was careful to leave the institutions of the Republic in place. The Senate continued to exist, to meet and deliberate, to give lengthy speeches on the order of those pre-power tribal chieftains of whom we have already spoken, and with the same effects." Fredric Jameson, *American Utopia: Dual Power and the Universal Army* (London: Verso, 2016).

43 The Movement for Black Lives, "Invest-Divest," at policy.m4bl. org; The Center for Popular Democracy, Law for Black Lives, and the BYP100, *Freedom to Thrive: Reimagining Public Safety and Security in Our Communities*, July 2017, at popular democracy.org.

44 Ibid., 1–2.

45 Ibid., 1.

46 Ibid., 20–1.

47 Ibid., 22–3.

48 Ibid., 20.

49 "Counter-CAPS Report: The Community Engagement Arm of the Police State," *We Charge Genocide*, October 2015; see also Brendan McQuade, "Against Community Policing," *Jacobin*, November 18, 2015.

50 "Counter-CAPS Report," 15.

51 Roberta Gardner, Black Hawk Hancock and Kenneth Fidel, "Class and Race-Ethnicity in a Changing City: A Historical Perspective on Inequalities," in Bennett et al., eds., *Neoliberal Chicago*, 19–20.

52 Anton Jäger, "Why 'Post-Work' Doesn't Work," *Jacobin*, November 19, 2018; see also Anton Jäger, "Back to Work: Review of David Graeber's Bullshit Jobs," *Nonsite*, September 9, 2019.

53 Ibid.

54 Ibid. For an extended critical treatment of the UBI proposal, as presented by 2020 Democratic presidential hopeful Andrew Yang, see Amber A'Lee Frost, "Andrew Yang and the Failson Mystique," *Jacobin*, September 18, 2019.

55 Jäger, "Why Post-Work Doesn't Work."

56 Not long after I arrived in Chicago, I made a passing remark in the classroom about the CTA's fare structure being fundamentally unjust to urban dwellers and especially the working class. Most of the students in that class were black, and all grew up on the city's South and West sides, or inner-ring suburbs. They bristled at my comment, and some quickly said that everyone pays the same rate, so how could that be unfair? We then got into a discussion that set the tone for the course in ways that I could not have anticipated. Having lived in the Washington, DC metro area as a graduate student, I was familiar with a point-to-point fare system, where you paid only for the duration of your trip. The comparative illustration struck home with the students, even among those who were not the most engaged or animated in those early class discussions. Immediately they could see the basic unfairness, that it cost the same for a suburban commuter to take the Skokie yellow spur in the Northern suburbs, making multiple connections to reach their job in the Loop as it would for an unemployed person from Lawndale to reach the Harold Washington Library for a job fair. Needless to say, students saw their city with different eyes, they were on guard, and brought into subsequent class discussions a rich trove of anecdotes and life stories that made the class especially lively and relevant, and

deepened my love for my new adopted home. Since that formative classroom discussion, transit fares have increased, new stations have been built and others renovated, CTA has piloted rapid bus services within the Loop, and city elites for a time courted billionaire Tesla founder Elon Musk about creating a high-speed transit service from O'Hare International airport to the Loop, all while vast portions of the South and southwest sides of the city remain underserved, and for some neighborhoods, beyond the reaches of the CTA rail system. We spent much of that course ferreting out the ways neoliberalization had shaped the spatial politics of Chicago, patterns of development and underdevelopment, the costs of social reproduction, the quality and wage-levels of jobs available throughout the city, and most of all, the ways that public investments subsidized FIRE sector growth to the detriment of working-class neighborhoods.

57 "No Bail for Man Charged in 2 Blue Line Robberies," *Chicago Sun-Times*, February 26, 2020.

58 Tom Schuba, Manny Ramos and Jesse Howe, "More CTA Riders Getting Attacked, with Violence at a Level Not Seen in a Decade," *Chicago Sun-Times*, August 5, 2022.

59 Mariarosa Dalla Costa and Selma James, *The Power of Women and the Subversion of the Community* (London: Butler and Tanner Limited, 1972); see also Selma James, *Sex, Race and Class: The Perspective of Winning: A Selection of Writings, 1952–2011* (Oakland: PM Press/ Common Notions, 2012).

60 Eric Klinenberg, *Heat Wave: A Social Autopsy of Disaster in Chicago* (Chicago: University of Chicago Press, 2015).

61 Kate Aronoff, Alyssa Battistoni, Daniel Aldana Cohen and Thea Riofrancos, *A Planet to Win: Why We Need a Green New Deal* (London: Verso, 2019).

62 Kyle Wiens, "You Gotta Fight for Your Right to Repair Your Car," *Atlantic*, February 13, 2014; Mark Sullivan, "'Right to Repair' Legislation Has Now Been Introduced in 17 States," *Fast Company*, January 18, 2018; David Grossman, "'Right to Repair' Is About a Whole Lot More Than iPhones," *Popular Mechanics*, February 16, 2017.

63 Diamond, *Chicago on the Make*.

64 Micah Uetricht, *Strike for America: Chicago Teachers against Austerity* (London: Verso, 2014); Elizabeth Todd-Breland, *A Political Education: Black Politics and Education Reform in Chicago since the 1960s* (Chapel Hill: University of North Carolina Press, 2018).

65 See Eric Blanc, *Red State Revolt: The Teacher's Strike Wave and Working-Class Politics* (London: Verso, 2019).

66 Tracy Swartz, "Some CPS Schools Could Start Year with 2 Officers Despite Votes to Reduce Police Presence. Decision on CPD Contract Delayed," *Chicago Tribune*, August 24, 2021.

67 Salamishah Tillet, "Black Women in Chicago, Getting Things Done," *New York Times*, May 18, 2019; Barbara Ransby, "The Rising Black Left Movement Behind Chicago's Historic Election," *Nation*, April 1, 2019.

68 Curtis Black, "Lightfoot's Cop Academy Bombshell Raises Questions about Leadership Style," *Chicago Reporter*, June 28, 2019; Maira Khwaja, "Lori Lightfoot's Dark Promises," *South Side Weekly*, March 19, 2019.

69 "An Open Letter to Chicago Residents about Charlie Beck," *Black Lives Matter Los Angeles*, November 7, 2019.

70 Crain's Editorial Board, "Lightfoot Made the Call She Had to Make," *Crain's Chicago Business*, April 12, 2019.

71 Fran Spielman, "City Council Oks $1.6 Billion in Subsidies for Lincoln Yards, the 78," *Chicago Sun-Times*, April 10, 2019.

6. The Labor of Occupation

1 In many respects, *Chappie* is the ideological polar opposite of *Tetra Vaal*. The short film invites us to contemplate the dystopia-to-come with autonomous policing, beckoning our curiosity with "What if ..." captions, and piques our latent suspicion of the corporate pitch. It is clear that the robotic scout and the engineers, executives and politicians who champion its virtues should be brought under closer scrutiny, not the market vendors and workers going about their daily lives. *Chappie*, on the other hand, reaches for an old right-wing canard of what happens when powerful weapons fall in the "wrong hands," in this case a gang of outlaws, whose leaders and Chappie's adopted parents are played by Yolanda Visser and Ninja of the real life zef rap group Die Antwoord. The film has its moments, and ultimately, attempts to humanize those who are often portrayed as villains in political debates and corporate media, lumpen droogs who resort to crime for survival. Who needs this liberal narrative of underclass redemption, especially when so much of Blomkamp's previous work was more adroit in capturing the perils of unfettered capitalist development and expansive carceral power already in our

midst? In addition to *Tetra Vaal*, Blomkamp's 2009 film *District 9* turned the anti-communist alien invasion trope of the Cold War into an allegory of racism and class inequality, and *Elysium* imagined a future where the wealthy have absconded from the earth altogether taking their life saving medicine and high technology into the heavens, leaving behind the poor in Los Angeles to a brutish and short slum existence.

2 Micol Seigel, *Violence Work: State Power and the Limits of Police* (Durham, NC: Duke University Press, 2018); Radley Balko, *Rise of the Warrior Cop: The Militarization of America's Police Forces* (New York: Public Affairs, 2014); Stephen Graham, *Cities under Siege: The New Military Urbanism* (London: Verso, 2010).

3 Kevin Sullivan, Tom Jackman and Brian Fung, "Dallas Police Used a Robot to Kill. What Does That Mean for the Future of Police Robots?," *Washington Post*, July 21, 2016.

4 Jeff Ward-Bailey, "North Dakota Becomes First State to Legalize Weaponized Police Drones," *Christian Science Monitor*, August 27, 2015.

5 Katie Shepherd, "Riot Police in Armored Vehicle Roust Homeless Mothers from Illegally Occupied Oakland House," *Washington Post*, January 15, 2020.

6 Ally Jarmanning, "Mass. State Police Tested Out Boston Dynamics' Spot the Dog. Civil Liberties Advocates Want to Know More," *WBUR*, November 25, 2019.

7 Ian G.R. Shaw, *Predator Empire: Drone Warfare and Full Spectrum Dominance* (Minneapolis: University of Minnesota, 2016); Andrew Guthrie Ferguson, *The Rise of Big Data Policing: Surveillance, Race and the Future of Law Enforcement* (New York: New York University Press, 2017); Brendan McQuade, *Pacifying the Homeland: Intelligence Fusion and Mass Supervision* (Berkeley: University of California Press, 2019); Virginia Eubanks, *Automating Inequality: How High-Tech Tools Profile, Police, and Punish the Poor* (New York: St. Martin's Press, 2017).

8 Martin Kaste, "America's Growing Cop Shortage," *National Public Radio*, December 12, 2018; "Inside the Decline of Rural America's Police Force and Its Pipeline of New Recruits," *NBC News*, November 8, 2019; Tom Jackman, "Who Wants to Be a Police Officer? Job Applicants Plummet at Most Departments," *Washington Post*, December 4, 2018.

9 Karl Marx, *Grundrisse* (New York: Penguin, 1993), 832.

10 Most of us have experienced this estrangement of values in our working lives, even with regard to management. Recall those

situations where the well-liked, affable boss is forced to make tough decisions (firing employees, cutting hours, docking pay for transgressions, etc.) that contradict his expressed feelings, adoration, tender moments, and "friendships" with employees. These are instances when the impersonal character of the capitalist mode of production is revealed. As well, in many ways, Marx's discussions of the coercive laws of competition in the *Grundrisse* and *Capital* anticipate the limitations of contemporary notions of corporate responsibility, green capitalism, participatory-management and even the solidarity economy, ideas that assume individual firms can adopt progressive ecological practices or democratic labor arrangements despite the overwhelming pressure to stay competitive, reduce costs, improve efficiency, and expand profitability. See Marx, *Grundrisse*, 832.

11 Sean McCann, *Gumshoe America: Hard-Boiled Crime Fiction and the Rise and Fall of New Deal Liberalism* (Durham, NC: Duke University Press, 2000).

12 Seigel, *Violence Work*, 7.

13 Ibid., 9.

14 Ibid., 9

15 James Baldwin, "Fifth Avenue, Uptown," *Esquire*, July 1960, 72.

16 Ibid., 72.

17 Ibid., 73.

18 Ibid., 73.

19 It is worth noting here that Frantz Fanon's *Wretched of the Earth* climaxes with a discussion of the damage that colonial occupation does to the colonizer as well as the colonized. This section stands in sharp contrast from the intoxicating prose of the opening chapters on revolution, but it is equally powerful albeit more foreboding. We are invited to peruse the clinician's journal and all the horrors he has documented in a war zone. In the last substantive chapter of the book, "Colonial War and Mental Disorders," Fanon provides an inventory of the trauma endured by French settlers and natives, police and FLN fighters, children and adults because of the violence that is inflicted to maintain colonial rule. In case no. 5, he retells the story of a French police inspector haunted by the torture he is charged with carrying out, and who in turn torments his wife and children. His harrowing account of this inspector's deterioration is worth quoting in full: "R- -, thirty years old, referred himself to us of his own free will. He is a police inspector who for some weeks realized that 'something was wrong.' Married with three children.

Smokes a lot: three packs a day. He has lost his appetite and his sleep is disturbed by nightmares. These nightmares have no particular distinguishing features. What bothers him most is what he calls his 'fits of madness.' First of all, he does not like to be contradicted: 'Doctor, tell me why as soon as someone confronts me, I feel like hitting him. Even outside work I feel like punching the guy who gets in my way. For nothing at all. Take for example when I go to buy the paper. There's a line. So you have to wait. I hold out my hand to take the paper (the guy who runs the newsstand is an old friend of mine) and someone in the line calls out aggressively: 'Wait your turn.' Well, I feel like beating him up and I tell myself: 'if I could get you, pal, for a few hours, you wouldn't mess with me.'

"He can't put up with noise. At home he has a constant desire to give everyone a beating. And he violently assaults his children, even his twenty-month-old baby.

"But what frightened him was one evening when his wife had bitterly protested he was being too hard on the children (she had even said to him: 'For goodness sake, you're crazy ...') he turned on her, beat her, and tied her to a chair shouting: 'I'm going to teach you once and for all who's the boss around here.'

"Fortunately, his children began to cry and scream. He then realized the full gravity of his behavior, untied his wife, and the next morning decided to consult a 'nerve specialist.' He had never been like that, he says; he seldom punished his children and never quarreled with his wife. The present problem had occurred since 'the troubles.' 'The fact is,' he said, 'we're now being used as foot soldiers. Last week, for example, we operated as if we were in the army. Those guys in the government say there's no war in Algeria and the police force must restore law and order, but there is a war in Algeria, and when they realize it, it'll be too late. The thing that gets me the most is the torture. Does that mean anything to you? ... Sometimes I torture for ten hours straight." See Frantz Fanon, *The Wretched of the Earth* (New York: Grove Press, 1963), 196–7.

20 Baldwin, "Fifth Avenue, Uptown," 76.
21 Ibid.
22 Ibid.
23 Ibid.
24 James Baldwin, "A Report from the Occupied Territory," *Nation*, July 11, 1966.
25 Baldwin, "A Report from Occupied Territory."

26 Ibid.

27 Ibid. Baldwin recalls the words of seventeen-year-old Daniel Hamm, who conveys the deep alienation and cynicism of black urban dwellers at the time, but a precocious sense of how policing the black ghetto is connected to advancing downtown interests: "They don't want us here. They don't want us—period! All they want us to do is work on these penny-ante jobs for them—and that's *it*. And beat our heads in whenever they feel like it. They don't want us on the street 'cause the World's Fair is coming. And they figure that all black people are hoodlums anyway, or bums, with no character of our own. So, they put us off the streets, so their friends from Europe, Paris or Vietnam—where they come from—can come and see this supposed-to-be great city." See Baldwin, "A Report from the Occupied Territory."

The 1963 film *Take this Hammer*, recorded during spring 1963, captures comparable sentiments of blacks living in San Francisco's Hunters Point neighborhood. Baldwin is at his best conversing with black locals, flashing a wide toothy grin, occasionally taking a drag from his cigarette, and always probing and questioning, trying to get a sense of their experiences and aspirations. Like the testimony of Daniel Hamm, who is painfully aware of his low place within the priorities of New York's most powerful citizens, the blacks Baldwin encounters in San Francisco are equally aware and critical of the forces at play, as each retells of their encounters with police, difficulties in finding adequate housing, and frustrations with liberalism. The film, like of much of Baldwin's essays during the first half of the sixties, reflects black power sensibility, before black power would emerge as a popular slogan.

28 Wu Ming, translation by Ayan Meer, "The Police vs. Pasolini, Pasolini vs. The Police," *Wu Ming Foundation Blog*, October 2015.

29 Pier Paolo Pasolini, "The PCI to Young People!," in Jack Hirschman, ed., *In Danger: A Pasolini Anthology* (San Francisco: City Lights Books, 2010), 84–91.

30 Franco Berardi Bifo, "Pasolini in Tottenham," *e-flux* 43 (2013).

31 Ibid.

32 Kate Gagliano, "Deputy Who Died by Suicide Left Haunting Videos on Racist Policing Division: 'I've Had Enough,'" *Acadiana Advocate*, February 3, 2021; Ashley White, "In Videos Posted before His Death, Lafayette Sherriff's Deputy Called for Police Reform," *Daily Advertiser*, n.d.

33 Gagliano, "Deputy Who Died by Suicide."

34 Patrick Smith, "5 Chicago Police Officers Died by Suicide since July. Is the Department Doing Enough?," WBEZ Chicago/ *National Public Radio*, February 26, 2019.

35 Sam Charles and Tom Schuba, "CPD Officer Shot and Killed Teen, Later Killed Self. Lawsuit Alleges Cover Up," *Chicago Sun-Times*, September 3, 2018.

36 "Investigation of the Chicago Police Department," United States Justice Department, Civil Rights Division and United States Attorney's Office Northern District of Illinois, January 12, 2017, 123.

37 Miriam Heyman, Jeff Dill and Robert Douglas, "The Ruderman White Paper on Mental Health and Suicide of First Responders," *Ruderman Family Foundation*, April 2018.

38 Smith, "5 Chicago Police Officers Died by Suicide."

39 US Department of Justice, *Federal Reports on Police Killings* (Brooklyn: Melville House, 2017), 531–2.

40 Andy O'Hara, "It's Time We Talk about Police Suicide," *The Marshall Project*, October 3, 2017.

41 Ibid.

42 W.J. Hennigan and Brian Bennett, "Dallas Police Used a Robot to Kill a Gunman, a New Tactic That Raises Ethical Questions," *Los Angeles Times*, July 8, 2016.

43 Andrew Feenberg, *Transforming Technology: A Critical Theory Revisited* (Oxford: Oxford University Press, 2002), 77.

44 Ibid., 76.

45 On the longer history of battlefield robots, automated warfare and DARPA's role in the evolution of military and domestic policing technology, see Stephen Graham, "Robowar Dreams," in *Cities under Siege: The New Military Urbanism* (London: Verso, 2010), 153–82: Christian Parenti, "Planet America: The Revolution in Military Affairs as Fantasy and Fetish," in Ashley Dawson and Malini Johar Schueller, eds., *Exceptional State: Contemporary US Culture and the New Imperialism* (Durham, NC: Duke University Press, 2007); Boston Dynamics, "Big Dog Overview (March 2010)," *YouTube*, April 22, 2010.

46 Boston Dynamics, "Cheetah Robot Runs 28.3 mph; a Bit Faster than Usain Bolt," *YouTube*, September 5, 2012.

47 Boston Dynamics, "Handle Robot Reimagined for Logistics," *YouTube*, March 28, 2019.

48 Boston Dynamics, "Mush, Spot, Mush!," *YouTube*, April 16, 2019; Boston Dynamics, "Testing Robustness," *YouTube*,

February 20, 2018; Boston Dynamics, "UpTown Spot," *YouTube*, October 16, 2018.

49 Richard J. Norton, "Feral Cities," *Naval War College Review* 56:4 (2003), 8.

50 Robert Kaplan, "The Coming Anarchy," *Atlantic*, February 1994.

51 Norton, "Feral Cities," 2.

52 Ibid.

53 McQuade, *Pacifying the Homeland*; Jonathan Finn, *Capturing the Criminal Image: From Mug Shot to Surveillance Society* (Minneapolis: University of Minnesota Press, 2009); Brian Jefferson, *Digitize and Punish: Racial Criminalization in the Digital Age* (Minneapolis: University of Minnesota Press, 2020).

54 Paul Mozur, "Inside China's Dystopian Dreams: A.I. Shame and Lots of Cameras," *New York Times*, July 8, 2018.

55 Elizabeth E. Joh, "Policing the Smart City," *International Journal of Law in Context* 15 (2019), 179.

56 Ibid., 179.

57 Michelle Alexander, "The Newest Jim Crow," *New York Times*, November 8, 2018.

58 Ferguson, *The Rise of Big Data Policing*.

59 McQuade, *Pacifying the Homeland*, 167.

60 Claire Bushey, "What They Want to Do with the CPD's 'Strategic Subjects List,'" *Crain's Chicago Business*, September 17, 2016.

61 According to Dan Berger, the term "judicial-prison-parole-industrial complex" was used as early as 1974 by the North Carolina Prisoners Labor Union but the popularization of a more succinct phrasing is usually traced to the respective essays of Mike Davis and Eric Schlosser. See Mike Davis, "Hell Factories in the Field: A Prison-Industrial Complex," *Nation*, February 20, 1995; Eric Schlosser, "The Prison-Industrial Complex," *Atlantic*, December 1998.

62 Loïc Wacquant, *Prisons of Poverty* (London and Minneapolis: 2009), 84–7.

63 Harring, *Policing a Class Society*, 19.

64 Gordon Lafer, "Are Unions the Prime Determinants of Police Behavior?," *Nonsite*, July 9, 2020.

65 Ibid.; see also mappingpoliceviolence.org.

66 Ibid.

67 Bill Fletcher, Jr., "The Central Issue Is Police Repression, Not Police Unions," *In These Times*, June 12, 2020.

68 Lafer, "Are Unions the Primary Determinants of Police Behavior?"

69 Ibid.

70 Emmet Penney, "How the DSA Screwed Up with Danny Fetonte," *Paste*, September 1, 2017.

71 "Danny Fetonte, 2017 NPC Candidate, Local Chapter: Austin," dsaconvention.org.

72 See Donny Gluckstein, *The Paris Commune: A Revolution in Democracy* (Chicago: Haymarket Books, 2006), 101. Gluckstein gives us some sense of the guard's class composition that partly explains why this happened: "the National Guard was changing," he writes. "Firstly, the social balance within it shifted dramatically now membership had been widened form the middle class to all male citizens between the ages of twenty-five and thirty-five. The 340,000 men in the ranks constituted around three quarters of the eligible male population of Paris ... Widespread unemployment and the lure of a salary, though minimal encouraged workers to join in disproportionate numbers." Gluckstein, *The Paris Commune*, 100.

73 Forman, *Locking Up Our Own*, 79.

74 Ted Vollmer, "Bradley Struggles to Overcome His Anti-LAPD Image," *Los Angeles Times*, October 14, 1986.

75 Forman, *Locking Up Our Own*, 111.

76 Tera Agyepong, "In the Belly of the Beast: Black Policemen Combat Police Brutality in Chicago, 1968–1983," *Journal of African American History* 98:2 (2013), 253–76; see also Simon Balto, *Occupied Territory: Policing Black Chicago from the Red Summer to Black Power* (Chapel Hill: University of North Carolina, 2019), 240–51; W. Marvin Dulaney, *Black Police in America* (Bloomington and Indianapolis: Indiana University Press, 1996), 65–80.

77 Agyepong, "In the Belly of the Beast," 261.

78 Constitution and Bylaws of the National Organization of Black Law Enforcement, September 1976, amended 1 August 2018, noblenational.org.

79 Forman, *Locking Up Our Own*, 114.

80 Jay and Conklin, *A People's History of Detroit*; Bette Woody, *Managing Urban Crises: The New Black Leadership and the Politics of Resource Allocation* (Westport, CT: Greenwood, 1982); Peter Eisinger, *The Politics of Displacement: Racial and Ethnic Transition in Three American Cities* (New York: Academic Press, 1980), 85–90; Edward Greer, *Big Steel: Black Politics and Corporate Power in Gary, Indiana* (New York: Monthly Review Press, 1979); Adolph Reed, Jr., "The Black Urban Regime: Structural

Origins and Constraints," in *Stirrings in the Jug*; Herb Boyd, "Blacks and the Police State: A Case Study of Detroit," *Black Scholar* 12 (January–February 1981), 58–61; Dorothy H. Guyot, "Newark: Crime and Politics in a Declining City," in Anne Heinz, Herbert Jacob and Robert Lineberry, eds., *Crime in City Politics* (New York: Longman, 1983).

81 David L. Parsons, *Dangerous Grounds: Antiwar Coffeehouses and Military Dissent in the Vietnam Era* (Chapel Hill: University of North Carolina, 2017); David Cortright, *Soldiers in Revolt* (Chicago: Haymarket Books, 2005); Matthew Rinaldi, "The Olive-Drab Rebels: Military Organizing during the Vietnam Era," *Radical America* 8:3 (1974); Christian Appy, *Working-Class War: American Combat Soldiers and Vietnam* (Chapel Hill: University of North Carolina, 1993); Scovill Wannamaker Currin, Jr., "An Army of the Willing: Fayette'Nam, Soldier Dissent and the Untold Story of the All-Volunteer Force," PhD Thesis, Duke University, 2015.

82 Jonathan Neale, *A People's History of the Vietnam War* (New York: New Press, 2003), 155.

83 Ibid., 155–6.

84 Quoted in ibid., 158.

85 Rinaldi, "The Olive Drab Rebels."

Conclusion

1 Adolph Reed, Jr., "The Whole Country is a Reichstag," *Nonsite*, August 23, 2021.

2 Hugo Lowell, "Fourth Officer Who Responded to US Capitol Attack Dies by Suicide," *Guardian*, August 3, 2021; Petula Dvorak, "Deaths by Suicide among Police Is a Quiet Epidemic. It Needs to Be Acknowledged," *Washington Post*, August 9, 2021.

3 Julie Watson, "Comparison between Capitol Siege, BLM protests is denounced," *AP*, January 14, 2021.

4 Robert A. Pape and Keven Ruby, "The Capitol Rioters Aren't Like Other Extremists," *Atlantic*, February 2, 2021; Alina Kim, "CPOST Research Finds New Right-Wing Extremist Demographic Trend in Capitol Insurrection," *Chicago Maroon*, June 8, 2021.

5 Rachel Chason and Samantha Schmidt, "Lafayette Square, Capitol Rallies Met Starkly Different Policing Response,"

Washington Post, January 14, 2021; Leila Fadel, "'Now the World Gets to See the Difference': BLM Protestors on the Capitol Attack," *NPR*, January 29, 2021.

6 Quoted in John Eligon, "Racial Double Standard of Capitol Siege Draws Outcry," *New York Times*, January 7, 2021.

7 Ram Subramanian and Leily Arzy, "State Policing Reforms Since George Floyd's Murder," *Brennan Center for Justice*, May 21, 2021; Nicholas Turner, "What Has Changed since George Floyd's Death?," *Vera Institute of Justice*, May 24, 2021.

8 Subramian and Arzy, "State Policing Reforms."

9 Ibid.; Benjamin Wallace-Wells, "Can Minneapolis Dismantle Its Police Department?," *The New Yorker*, August 8, 2020; Astead W. Herndon, "How a Pledge to Dismantle the Minneapolis Police Collapsed," *New York Times*, September 26, 2020.

10 Cedric Johnson, "We Can't Let Corporations 'Blackwash' Capitalism," *Tribune*, June 26, 2020; Adolph Reed, Jr., "Beyond the Great Awakening," *New Republic*, December 8, 2020.

11 Gottschalk, "Caught in the Countryside"; Eli Hager, "A Mass Incarceration Mystery: Why Are Black Imprisonment Rates Going Down? Four Theories," *The Marshall Project*, December 15, 2017.

12 Kaba, "Yes, We Mean Literally Abolish the Police"; see also Mariame Kaba, *We Do This 'Til We Free Us: Abolitionist Organizing and Transforming Justice* (Chicago: Haymarket Books, 2021); Roger Lancaster, "How to End Mass Incarceration," *Jacobin*, August 18, 2017; Dan Berger, Mariame Kaba and David Stein, "What Abolitionist Do," *Jacobin*, August 24, 2017; Roger Lancaster, "Response: A Word on Words," *Jacobin*, October 2, 2017; Geo Maher, *A World Without Police: How Strong Communities Make Cops Obsolete* (London: Verso, 2021); Alex Vitale, *The End of Policing* (London: Verso, 2018).

13 Bill Mieirling, "Speaking Up on Restorative Justice," American Legislative Exchange Council, June 12, 2020.

14 Mariame Kaba, "Statement by Mariame," *Transforming Harm*, August 19, 2020.

15 Marshall Berman, "Notes Towards a New Society," in *Modernism in the Streets: A Life and Times in Essays* (London: Verso, 2017), 39.

16 Ibid.

17 Ibid., 41.

18 Weather Underground, "You Don't Need a Weatherman to

Know Which Way the Wind Blows," *New Left Notes*, February 28, 1969.

19   Berman, "Notes Toward a New Society," 43.